THE USES OF LITERACY
IN EARLY MEDIAEVAL EUROPE

(THE USES OF LITERACY IN EARLY MEDIAEVAL EUROPE ,

EDITED BY

ROSAMOND McKITTERICK

*Lecturer in History in the University of Cambridge
and Fellow of Newnham College*

The right of the
University of Cambridge
to print and sell
all manner of books
was granted by
Henry VIII in 1534.
The University has printed
and published continuously
since 1584.

CAMBRIDGE UNIVERSITY PRESS

Cambridge
New York   Port Chester
Melbourne   Sydney

Published by the Press Syndicate of the University of Cambridge
The Pitt Building, Trumpington Street, Cambridge CB2 1RP
40 West 20th Street, New York, NY 10011, USA
10 Stamford Road, Oakleigh, Melbourne 3166, Australia

© Cambridge University Press 1990

First published 1990

Printed in Great Britain
at the University Press, Cambridge

British Library cataloguing in publication data

The uses of literacy in early mediaeval Europe.
1. Europe. Literacy, history
I. McKitterick, Rosamond
302.2′094

Library of Congress cataloguing in publication data

The uses of literacy in early mediaeval Europe / edited by Rosamond
McKitterick.
p.   cm.
Includes index.
ISBN 0 521 34409 3
1. Literacy–Europe–History. 2. Social history–Mediaeval.
500–1500.   I. McKitterick, Rosamond.
LC156.A2U74   1990
302.2′244–dc20   89-34283   CIP

4ISBN 0 521 34409 3

Contents

Illustrations

Contributors

Roger Collins: The Mount School, Bath

Susan Kelly: British Academy Research Fellow, St Catherine's College, Oxford

Simon Keynes: University Lecturer in Anglo-Saxon History and Fellow of Trinity College, Cambridge

Rosamond McKitterick: University Lecturer in History and Fellow of Newnham College, Cambridge

John Mitchell: Lecturer in the History of Art, University of East Anglia

Margaret Mullett: Lecturer in Greek and Byzantine Studies, The Queen's University, Belfast

Janet L. Nelson: Reader in History, King's College, University of London

Thomas F. X. Noble: Associate Professor in History, University of Virginia

Stefan C. Reif: Director of Genizah Research, Head of Oriental Department and Senior Under Librarian, Cambridge University Library

Jane Stevenson: Lecturer in History, University of Sheffield

Ian Wood: Lecturer in History, University of Leeds

Preface

This book was conceived from the start as a collaborative venture. Each author was asked to address the central theme from the perspective of her or his specialized knowledge: we met to discuss the different aspects of the topic in July 1987, and subsequently circulated drafts of our papers among ourselves. Nevertheless, each author maintained the individuality of her or his particular area, for we were anxious to stress the enormous divergences, as well as the similarities, in the uses and emphases of literacy in different parts of Europe in the early mediaeval period. We offer the book in the hope that it will stimulate further research and thought on the uses and consequences of literacy in the early middle ages. We are all too well aware of the number of avenues left unexplored, quite apart from regions of Europe and particular periods ignored, but this in itself is an indication of the richness of the field.

The Editor wishes to thank, most warmly, all her contributors for their labours, their patience and for the enthusiasm so manifest in their contributions. She and all the authors, moreover, are indebted to the staff of Cambridge University Press, and especially to William Davies, for the interest and assistance rendered in seeing the book through the press. Acknowledgements for information and help received are recorded in the individual contributions, but the Editor wishes to record here her particular debt to Elizabeth Meyer of the University of Virginia for her timely and stimulating criticism and comments.

Abbreviations

AB	*Analecta Bollandiana*
AHR	*American Historical Review*
Annales ESC	*Annales: Economies, Sociétés, Civilisations*
ASE	*Anglo-Saxon England*
BAR	British Archaeological Reports
BBTT	Belfast Byzantine Texts and Translations
BCH	*Bulletin de Correspondance Hellénique*
BCL	Michael Lapidge and Richard Sharpe, *A Bibliography of Celtic–Latin Literature, 400–1200* (Dublin, 1985)
BL	London, British Library
BMF	E.A. Bond, *Facsimiles of Ancient Charters in the British Museum*, 4 vols. (London, 1873–8)
BMGS	*Byzantine and Modern Greek Studies*
BNJ	*Byzantinische-neugriechische Jahrbücher*
BN lat.	Paris, Bibliothèque Nationale manuscrit latin
BN n.a.lat.	Paris, Bibliothèque Nationale manuscrit, nouvelles acquisitions latines
BS	*Byzantinoslavica*
CAG	Commentaria in Aristotelem Graeca
CCCC	Cambridge, Corpus Christi College
CCSL	Corpus Christianorum Series Latina
CFHB	Corpus Fontium Historiae Byzantinae=DOT
ChLA	Albert Bruckner and Robert Marichal, *Chartae Latinae Antiquiores: Facsimile*

Edition of the Latin Charters prior to the
Ninth Century, I– (Olten and Lausanne,
1954–)

Chron. Vult.   *Chronicon Vulturnense del Monaco
Giovanni*, ed. V. Federici, 3 vols. (Rome,
1925–38)

CLA   Elias Avery Lowe, *Codices Latini
Antiquiores: A Palaeographical Guide to
Latin Manuscripts prior to the Ninth
Century*, I–XI plus Supplement (Oxford,
1935–71)

Clm   Munich, Bayerische Staatsbibliothek,
Codices latini monacenses

CMCS   *Cambridge Mediaeval Celtic Studies*

CQ   *Classical Quarterly*

CSEL   Corpus Scriptorum Ecclesiasticorum
Latinorum

CSHB   Corpus Scriptorum Historiae Byzantinae

DA   *Deutsches Archiv für die Erforschung des
Mittelalters*

DOP   *Dumbarton Oaks Papers*

DOS   Dumbarton Oaks Studies

DOT   Dumbarton Oaks Texts=CFHB

EEBS   *Epeteris Hetaireias Byzantinon Spoudon*

EHD   *English Historical Documents*, I: *c. 500–
1042*, ed. Dorothy Whitelock (2nd edn,
London, 1979)

EHR   *English Historical Review*

EJ   *Encyclopaedia Judaica*, 16 vols. (Jerusalem,
1962)

GRBS   *Greek, Roman and Byzantine Studies*

IHS   *Irish Historical Studies*

JOB   *Jahrbuch der Oesterreichischen*
                             Byzantinistik

JRS   *Journal of Roman Studies*

JTS   *Journal of Theological Studies*

LD   *Liber Diurnus Romanorum Pontificum*, ed.
                             Hans Foerster (Berne, 1958)

LP   *Le Liber Pontificalis, texte, introduction*, ed.
                             L. Duchesne, 3 vols. (Paris, 1886–1957)

McKitterick,
  Carolingians   R. McKitterick, *The Carolingians and the
                             Written Word* (Cambridge, 1989)

MGH   *Monumenta Germaniae Historica*

  AA   *Auctores Antiquissimi*, 15 vols. (Berlin,
                             1877–1919)

  Cap.   *Capitularia. Leges Sectio* II, *Capitularia
                             regum francorum*, ed. A. Boretius and V.
                             Krause, 2 vols. (Hanover, 1883–97)

  Conc.   *Concilia. Leges Sectio* III, *Concilia*, 2
                             vols. in 3, ed. W. Wattenbach (Hanover,
                             1893–1908), and III, ed. W. Hartmann, *Die
                             Konzilien der Karolingischen Teilreiche 843–
                             859* (Hanover, 1984)

  Diplomata
    Karolinorum   *Diplomata Karolinorum*, ed. E.
                             Mühlbacher and T. Schieffer, 2 vols. (I and
                             III; vol. II, *Die Urkunden Ludwigs des
                             Frommen*, ed. P. Johanek, is in preparation)
                             (Hanover, 1906 and 1966)

  Epp.   *Epistolae* I and II, Gregoriae papae
                             registrum epistelae, ed. P. Ewald and
                             W. Hartmann (Hanover, 1887–91)

  Epp. merov. et karol.   *Epistolae merovingici et karolini aevi*
                             (=*MGH Epp*. III–VIII) (Hanover, 1892–
                             1939)

  Epp. sel.   *Epistolae selectae*, 5 vols. (Hanover,
                             1916–52)

Fontes	*Fontes iuris Germanici antiqui in usum scholarum ex Monumentis Germaniae Historicis separatim editi*, 13 vols. (Hanover, 1909–86)
Formulae	*Leges Sectio* V, *Formulae Merovingici et Karolini aevi*, ed. K. Zeumer (Hanover, 1886)
Leges nat. germ.	*Leges nationum germanicarum*, ed. K. Zeumer (*Lex Visigothorum*); L.R. de Salis (*Leges Burgundionum*); F. Beyerle and R. Buchner (*Lex Ribuaria*); K.A. Eckhardt (*Pactus legis Salicae* and *Lex Salica*); E. von Schwind (*Lex Baiwariorum*) 6 vols. in 11 parts (Hanover 1892–1969)
Poet.	*Poetae aevi karolini*, ed. E. Dummler, L. Traube, P. von Winterfeld and K. Strecker, 4 vols. (Hanover, 1881–99)
SS	*Scriptores in folio*, 30 vols (Hanover, 1824–1924)
SS i.u.s.	*Scriptores rerum germanicarum in usum scholarum separatim editi*, 63 vols. (Hanover, 1871–1987)
SS rerum Langobardicarum	*Scriptores rerum Langobardicarum et Italicarum saec. VI–IX*, ed. G. Waitz (Hanover, 1878)
SS rer. merov.	*Scriptores rerum merovingicarum*, ed. B. Krusch and W. Levison, 7 vols. (Hanover, 1885–1920)
OCA	*Orientalia Christiana Analecta*
OSF	*Facsimiles of Anglo-Saxon Manuscripts*, ed. W.B. Sanders, 3 vols., Ordnance Survey (Southampton, 1878–84)
PG	*Patrologia cursus completus series graeca*, ed. J.P. Migne, 167 vols. (Paris, 1857–76)
PL	*Patrologia cursus completus series latina*, ed. J.P. Migne, 234 vols. (Paris, 1844–55)

PMLA	*Publication of the Modern Languages Association of America*
PRIA	*Proceedings of the Royal Irish Academy*
PT	*The Patrician Texts in the Book of Armagh*, ed. and trans. Ludwig Bieler (Dublin, 1979)
REB	*Revue des Etudes Byzantines*
Sawyer	Peter H. Sawyer, *Anglo-Saxon Charters: An Annotated List and Bibliography*, Royal Historical Society Guides and Handbooks 8 (London, 1968)
Settimane	*Settimane di Studio del centro Italiano di Studi sull'alto Medioevo* 1– (Spoleto, 1955–)
Settlement of Disputes	*The Settlement of Disputes in Early Mediaeval Europe*, ed. Wendy Davies and Paul Fouracre (Cambridge, 1986)
TRHS	*Transactions of the Royal Historical Society*
Vat. reg. lat.	Biblioteca Apostolica Vaticana, codices reginenses latini
Vat. pal. lat.	Biblioteca Apostolica Vaticana, codices palatini latini

Introduction

Rosamond McKitterick

This book aims to investigate the respects in which literacy and orality were important in early mediaeval Europe. It examines the context of literacy, its uses, levels, and distribution, in a number of the societies of early mediaeval Europe, that is, the area from Ireland to Byzantium and the eastern Mediterranean between *c.* 400 and *c.* 1000. None of the contributors has attempted a comprehensive survey, nor is it intended that any chapter should be regarded as an attempt to be definitive. Rather, we hope to open up a topic in relation to the early middle ages that has already been treated extensively for earlier and later periods and in modern societies. We aim to indicate some of the areas for debate and argument and make new research available to scholars and students.

In many ways the book represents, therefore, an introduction to the subject of literacy in the early middle ages. Its basic premise is that literacy is a subject with which early mediaevalists should be concerned. Our studies set out to provide the factual basis from which assessments of the significance of literacy in the early mediaeval world can be made, and to offer some suggestions about what that significance might be. In other words, the significance of literacy and why it is important to observe its uses and implications in the early middle ages have to be established on the basis of the evidence available; they cannot be assumed before we start. It is, after all, only from a firm knowledge of the evidence, its implications and its limitations as far as degrees of literacy are concerned in any one region or society at a particular time that one may build further and explore the significance of literacy, its implications and its consequences for the societies in which we observe it.

Concentration on the uses and functions of literacy, and thus primarily on literacy as a tool, in a great variety of contexts has the advantage of providing knowledge about the ways in which uses of literacy might change over time and place and thus more about the societies that changed them. It matters where literacy was applied simply because, as will be clear from the essays in this book, it was applied in different ways from a whole range of

1

different assumptions and convictions about the written word. Establishing when and where literacy is used, for what purposes and in what contexts, and what kind of literacy it is, may actually tell us about the ways in which literacy was regarded as important in early mediaeval society, and why.

It is with these considerations in mind that we embarked on our work. We were also prompted to focus on the early middle ages, however, from a sense that assumptions were being made too readily about the levels, ranges and significance of literacy in the early middle ages by those who concentrate on the eleventh and twelfth centuries and later periods. Stock's work, for example, is a subtle and illuminating exposition of the implications of literacy in the eleventh and twelfth centuries.[1] But that is one of its major drawbacks; it begins too late and is too categorical about the irrelevance of the earlier period. In his survey of literacy in Europe, Cipolla offers a theory of the close association of mercantile development and urban life and the consequent increase in literacy from the eleventh century onwards. In doing so he dismisses northern Europe in the period before the eleventh century with the words: 'from the fifth to the tenth century all evidence of literary culture based on the written word comes from the area south of the Loire'.[2] In a large survey of the kind attempted by Cipolla, detail is difficult, but such a statement is at odds with the evidence. Other surveys have fallen back with evident relief on the concepts of 'restricted literacy' or 'craft literacy' confined to clerics in early mediaeval Europe as a whole.[3] Even if these concepts were valid for the early middle ages, to invoke them in this way is merely to identify a context in which literate skills were exercised. It tells us nothing about the role of literacy and its importance for the people who used literate modes.

A further problem to tackle is the definition of literacy itself. Does literacy need to be variously defined according to circumstances? Does it invariably mean the ability to read and write, or just the ability to read, and what levels of accomplishment are conceded as indicating literacy as opposed to illiteracy? Does it not cover to some degree both the content of the written tradition and the levels of individual achievement in it? We take

---

[1] Brian Stock, *The Implications of Literacy: Written Language and Models of Interpretation in the Eleventh and Twelfth Centuries* (Princeton, 1983).

[2] Carlo Cipolla, *Literacy and Development in the West* (Harmondsworth, 1969), p. 41. For a further example of blinkered vision see J.W. Thompson, *The Literacy of the Laity in the Middle Ages* (New York and London, 1939 and 1960). An idea of the range of approaches to literacy can be gauged from the bibliography provided by Harvey J. Graff, *Literacy in History: An Interdisciplinary Research Bibliography* (New York and London, 1981).

[3] The terms are defined by Jack Goody, 'Introduction', in *Literacy in Traditional Societies*, ed. Jack Goody (Cambridge, 1968), pp. 11–20. A welcome exception to this kind of approach was provided by Patrick Wormald, 'The uses of literacy in Anglo-Saxon England and its neighbours', *TRHS* 5th series 27 (1977), 95–114.

the view that it is impossibly narrow to define literacy strictly in terms of the ability to read and write. For one thing, in terms of mediaeval terminology, *litteratus* referred to one who was learned in Latin, not someone able to read.[4] Consequently, an *illitteratus* was someone not learned in Latin. *Illitteratus*, in other words, is a term which says very little about the rank, education, ability and importance of the person concerned in any sphere of activity in the early middle ages other than Latin literature.[5] As Susan Kelly points out, indeed, in many cases one is obliged also to register the complication of the existence, in Anglo-Saxon England, for example, of a separate literary language (Latin) entirely different from the vernacular.[6] In England, the use of the vernacular for documentation and literary purposes was already common in the ninth century, a very early date in the European context, but Latin continued to have priority in literature and formal communications. In the east and south of Europe, Greek or Arabic rather than Latin fulfilled this function.

It is necessary, moreover, to allow for many levels of competence in both reading and writing. It should be remembered that one can learn to read without being able to write. Reading ability can range from the recognition of a limited number of simple words to the comprehension and enjoyment of a complex philosophical treatise. A scribe might be trained to copy out an existing text, or to take dictation, while being totally incapable of composing a text himself or herself. Reading aloud and memorization, in any case, were far more important adjuncts to education in the early middle ages than they are today.

Writing is a skill far more difficult to acquire than reading.[7] It comprises several levels of competence, ranging from the ability to copy an existing text to a capacity for literary composition in both the vernacular and in the

---

[4] The terminology was exhaustively examined by Herbert Grundmann, '*Litteratus-illitteratus*: der Wandel einer Bildungsnorm vom Altertum zum Mittelalter', *Archiv für Kulturgeschichte* 40 (1958), 1–66, and compare his earlier 'Die Frauen und die Literatur im Mittelalter', *Archiv für Kulturgeschichte* 26 (1936), 129–61. Further nuances are provided by Franz Bäuml, 'Varieties and consequences of medieval literacy and illiteracy', *Speculum* 55 (1980), 237–65.

[5] A point emphasized by Karl-Ferdinand Werner, 'Bedeutende Adelsfamilien im Reich Karls des Grossen', in *Karl der Grosse, Lebenswerk und Nachleben*, ed. Wolfgang Braunfels, 4 vols. (Düsseldorf, 1965), I, pp. 83–142, at p. 129, and English translation in *The Medieval Nobility*, ed. Timothy Reuter (Amsterdam, 1978), pp. 137–202, at p. 182.

[6] A point stressed by Kelly, below, pp. 51–61.

[7] Petrucci tackles the fundamental problem of how one learnt to write. He insists that writing and literacy were not confined to those who could write books in a technical or professional way: Armando Petrucci, 'Alfabetismo ed educazione grafica degli scribi altomedievali (secc. VII–X)', in *The Role of the Book in Medieval Culture*, ed. Peter Ganz, 2 vols., Bibliologia, Elementa ad librorum studia pertinentia 3 and 4 (Brepols, 1986), 3, pp. 109–32.

common language of Christianity in the west and east, Latin and Greek. In Umayyad Al-Andalus and in the Jewish communities of the Mediterranean, bilingualism and trilingualism in Latin/Romance and in Hebrew, Aramaic and Arabic, respectively, are assumed. Writing in the early middle ages was probably practised by only a small proportion of those able to read. One must also note the special function and status of the scribe and secretary in relation to the social status of those whom he served. The strong element of professionalism in the skills of literacy made it unnecessary for the higher groups in society to practise them on their own behalf. That a man or woman used a secretary may tell us nothing about their own ability either to write or read but it does tell us that they were accustomed to use literate modes, even if indirectly, to conduct certain of their affairs. A king or nobleman or royal official could call upon the services of a secretary to take dictation or read out documents or books. The secretary might be a cleric or a specially trained servant or even a slave. When King Alfred, for example, ordered all his judges to immerse themselves in study, he conceded that those who were too old or too knuckle-headed to learn could order someone else to read aloud to them, and implied that they might already have made provision for this.[8]

The problem of literacy is thus partly one of technical skill and the popular acquaintance with what can be done with an alphabet. It is also one of education and social custom and includes a commitment of traditions to writing. More importantly, for mediaeval studies, Stock has proposed a further sophistication in his notion of textuality. He argues that a text does not have to be written; it can be spoken aloud as a structure and coherent discourse, and within a 'textual community' such texts can influence the illiterate and quasi-literate as well as those who can read and write.[9] For Stock, the primary importance of literacy is not as a personal skill so much as a mode of communication. Thus there is a distinction to be made between the reception of texts (which need not demand literacy) and the creation of texts and their dissemination beyond the range of the human voice.

Literacy therefore clearly has different connotations according to the context in which it is considered, whether political, social, anthropological or historical. Clanchy's exposition of the shift 'from memory to written record' in post-Conquest England, firmly embedded in its historical and

---

[8] *Asser's Life of King Alfred*, ed. W.H. Stevenson (Oxford, 1904), c. 106, p. 95, translated in Simon Keynes and Michael Lapidge, *Alfred the Great: Asser's 'Life of King Alfred' and Other Contemporary Sources* (Harmondsworth, 1983), p. 110. The requirements of pragmatic as opposed to learned literacy are made clear by Malcolm Parkes, 'The literacy of the laity', in *Literature and Western Civilization: The Medieval World*, ed. David Daiches and A. K. Thorlby (London, 1973), pp. 555–77, especially p. 555.

[9] Stock, *Implications of Literacy*, p. 7.

social context, is exemplary in its demonstration of this.[10] It is also the work, above all others, which is regarded as free from the technological determinism that Goody in his anthropological–ethnographical study of literacy in 'traditional societies' allegedly encouraged with his concept of literacy as a 'technology of the intellect'.[11] Clanchy does not treat social and intellectual changes in mediaeval England as consequences of literacy, due to the inherent qualities of writing, so much as he exposes changing literate practices in a particular society which imply particular attitudes towards the written word and its use. In part, Clanchy is reacting against Goody and his followers. So, too, Street is persuasive in his characterization of the logical flaws in Goody's 'autonomous model'. Street prefers to define literacy as a 'shorthand for the social practices and conceptions of reading and writing' and proceeds according to what he labels the 'ideological model'.[12] This is preferable to Havelock's insistence that it is a 'social condition that can be defined only in terms of readership' or Pattison's unhelpful 'potent form of consciousness'.[13] Yet without Goody's identification of literacy and its uses as a vital key to the understanding of any society, much subsequent work would have been the poorer. Goody's notion of the 'consequences' or, at least, 'implications' of literacy in the process of historical change is also much more useful than some of his critics have been prepared to acknowledge.

For all their different emphases, studies of literacy in a wide variety of historical contexts reveal a common theme. It is that literacy in any society is not just a matter of who could read and write, but one of how their skills function, and of the adjustments – mental, emotional, intellectual, physical and technological – necessary to accommodate it. It is this understanding of literacy that underlies the various studies in this book.

The functions of literacy need, furthermore, to be established in relation to a particular society's needs. As those needs change, so do the particular contexts in which literate modes are required. In the essays which follow, we explore the extent to which literate modes were established in the centuries between late antiquity and the millennium. How much survived, not only of Roman patterns of literacy but also of the motivation for

[10] Michael Clanchy, *From Memory to Written Record: England 1066–1307* (London, 1979).

[11] *Literacy in Traditional Societies*, ed. Goody, p. 1. On technological determinism, see Brian V. Street, *Literacy in Theory and Practice*, Cambridge Studies in Oral and Literate Culture 9 (Cambridge, 1984), pp. 19–66. Apart from the work of the social anthropologists, Street is also implicitly criticizing the theoretical basis for such works as Walter J. Ong, *Orality and Literacy: The Technologizing of the Word* (London and New York, 1982).

[12] Street, *Literacy*, p. 1.

[13] Eric A. Havelock, *Origins of Western Literacy* (Toronto, 1976), p. 19, and R. Pattison, *On Literacy: The Politics of the Word from Homer to the Age of Rock* (Oxford, 1982), p. x.

choosing literate modes of cultural expression and legal business? What was the role of the church and the Christian faith? What, indeed, was the role of religions dependent on written revelation, such as Christianity, Judaism and Islam, in relation to literacy? How important are questions about the number of people who could read and write? Is it not more important to establish who was literate, what role in society they performed and what the likely repercussions of that role may have been? What is the relationship between writing and other means of communication such as oral discourse and pictures in the early middle ages?

Although these are the principal general questions with which we have each been concerned, inevitably consideration of particular contexts has thrown up special problems, the discussion of which in turn opens up more general issues. The contexts in which literacy is considered in this book in any case are only a few among many feasible. It did not prove possible, for example, to discuss fully the uses of literacy in late antiquity in this book. The work in preparation by Meyer, however, promises a trenchant examination of the subject, particularly in relation to law in the late Roman world. Meyer examines the initiatives which create documentary practice in the Roman world, the voluntary use of documents, and the extent to which this leads to the growing prestige of a literate system of legal practice.[14] The degree to which Egypt, from which the most papyri evidence survives, is representative of the late Roman Empire as far as the uses of literacy is concerned is also receiving attention,[15] as are the changing character of writing, the cultural context within which writing was produced, and the complex interrelationship between writing and other elements of social and cultural practice in the late Roman world.[16]

The legacy of Rome and the problems of continuity nevertheless are a constant preoccupation in many of the essays which follow. In Gaul, for example, discussed by Ian Wood, what was the status and nature of the Latin language in the centuries of Merovingian rule? Is there any truth in the traditional picture, from the classical viewpoint, of literary degeneracy approaching widespread illiteracy among the Frankish and formerly Gallo-

---

[14] Elizabeth A. Meyer, 'Literacy in late antiquity', PhD dissertation, Yale University, 1988, now in preparation for publication.

[15] Keith Hopkins, *Roman Egypt* (forthcoming), and see also the studies by Tonnes Kleburg, *Buchhandel und Verlagswesen in der Antike* (Darmstadt, 1969); G. Cavallo, *Libri, editori e pubblico nel Mondo antico* (Rome, 1975); and Roger A. Pack, *The Greek and Latin Literary Texts from Greco-Roman Egypt* (Michigan, 1952; 2nd edn 1965). See the new dimension to studies of literacy in antiquity provided by the Vindolanda tablets, studied by Alan Bowman and J. David Thomas, *Vindolanda: The Latin Writing Tablets* (Gloucester, 1984).

[16] Some of this has already been published by Mary Beard, 'Writing and ritual: a study of diversity and expansion in the Arval Acta', *Papers of the British School at Rome* 53 (1985), 114–62. There are also comments of relevance in C.H. Roberts and T.C. Skeat, *The Birth of the Codex* (London and Oxford, 1983).

Roman populations? Does the evidence available reveal literary continuity and an underlying social and cultural continuity? What differences can one detect in the literary style of the seventh century as opposed to that of the fifth? What happened also to late antique educational traditions? As in Meyer's identification of the importance of the law in late antiquity, is it primarily in the spheres of legal transactions and administration that a continuity in practice and assumptions about the usefulness of literate modes is to be observed? Further, in the consideration of literacy in Merovingian Gaul is there any substance to the customary divide between levels of culture north and south of the Loire? In what sense, above all, can the society of Merovingian Gaul be described as literate?[17]

The papacy can also be considered as an heir to Rome in terms at least of its administrative structure, for it was based in important ways on the use of the written word. How was literacy assured and transmitted within the Lateran administration? To focus on the papacy does not preclude wider consideration of the roles played by literacy in the history of the early Christian church, but, as Thomas Noble suggests, the examination of the enormous range of the kinds of records the papal administration produced and conserved can provide us with the necessary exactitude to assess how literacy was exploited by the Christian church generally.[18]

If the papacy can be regarded as the conservator of both the Roman and the Christian traditions to perhaps a far greater degree than can the barbarian successor states, the combined impact of the Roman world and the Christian church is nevertheless a preoccupation of all but one of the papers in this book. The exception, included precisely because its parallels and contrasts are both salutary and illuminating, is Stefan Reif's study of early mediaeval Jewish literacy.[19] His paper seeks to complement the other essays not only by providing an external yardstick against which to measure the significance of developments in literacy in Christian Europe, but also to draw attention to certain similar developments. The accurate evaluation of these will become possible only once the beginnings of Jewish settlement in Christian Europe have been more fully investigated.

Ireland, on the other hand, potentially presents contrast of another kind, for it appears to have supported extensive and sophisticated learned activity by its native learned classes without the use of writing at all. The Irish were aware of writing, as the ogam inscriptions attest, but they did not at first have much use for it. On this culture is imposed Christianity, requiring not only literacy but latinity. This at least is the traditional picture whose validity is tested by Jane Stevenson in the context of the Patrician documents relating to Armagh and the way literacy may have served the uses of

---

[17] Wood, below, pp. 63–81. [18] Noble, below, pp. 82–108.

[19] Reif, below, pp. 134–55.

illiteracy, expressing the values, needs and interests of the native culture, virtually untouched by Roman traditions, as well as those of the new religion.[20]

Contact with a non-Roman and non-Christian culture and problems of continuity of a different kind are provided by Roger Collins' study of literacy and the laity in early mediaeval Spain, for the principal question at issue is whether the evident literacy of Arab Spain was influenced by the survival of an educated laity from the Visigothic period.[21] What role did literacy, written records, book buying and book reading play in the society of late Umayyad Al-Andalus? What are the consequences of the lack in Islamic society of a separate priestly caste? How does the degree of literacy in Umayyad Spain compare with that evident in the Visigothic period?

The Roman and Christian heritage as it was filtered into early Anglo-Saxon England, on the other hand, has to be considered within the framework of a vigorous vernacular and oral culture to which the written word is introduced by the Christian missionaries. Susan Kelly explores the conditions attendant upon the introduction of the written word into a pre-literate society.[22] She assesses the success of literacy in England by considering the extent to which the use of the written word superseded, or was accommodated within, the established oral procedures of early Anglo-Saxon government and society and takes as her starting point the significance of the use of charters, the attitude towards written titles to property and whether the symbolic function of the diploma is more important than its value as a written record. But the relation of the vernacular to Latin literacy has to be considered. What does the appearance of vernacular documents tell us about literacy in Anglo-Saxon England? What was the extent of lay literacy? How high was the quality of ecclesiastical literacy, and what were the methods of instruction? These questions are pursued also in later Anglo-Saxon England by Simon Keynes but the focus is on the role of literate modes in government and the evidence for pragmatic literacy.[23] What evidence is there that there is a routine resort to bureaucratic methods and use of writing in the government and administration of Anglo-Saxon England before the Conquest? Keynes explores the relationship between the monarch and literacy and in particular the effects Alfred's initiatives had on tenth-century royal government. Why were the laws produced in written form and what relation does this have to their publication and implementation? Could royal officials in later Anglo-Saxon England read, and were they required to read the law in written form? What role did literacy play in the administration of the realm and communication with the royal officials?

---

[20] Stevenson, below, pp. 11–35.

[21] Collins, below, pp. 109–33.

[22] Kelly, below, pp. 36–62.

[23] Keynes, below, pp. 226–57.

The use of the written word in government and administration also provides the focus for Janet Nelson's discussion of the Carolingians, and constitutes a useful means of comparing practices and assumptions on either side of the Channel.[24] How much evidence of the practical use of writing, as a means of communication and record, is there? But she also asks who produced the documents and what role laymen played in this. Was lay literacy, active as well as passive, even in Latin, far more widespread than has often been assumed? What can be said about the symbolic uses of literacy and to what degree do they qualify the ostensibly practical ones? The function of literacy in the Frankish kingdoms under the Carolingians has to be considered within a cultural context in which the use of writing associated with the Christian and Roman past was a privileged mode of communication among other modes.

Further aspects of literacy to be considered in this book are the visual impact of letter forms and their relation to pictures. Margaret Mullett tackles the manifestations of writing and their significance in Byzantium in the ninth and tenth centuries, invoking a rather different and more continuous Roman past than that which we encounter in the germanic kingdoms of western Europe.[25] It has been customary hitherto to assess Byzantine literacy very positively and to stress the supreme power of the written word in Byzantine society and the ability of the Byzantines to appreciate it on the grounds that continuity in levels of literacy, literary production and education from the Roman period is clear. While acknowledging that there is some truth in it, Mullett challenges the impregnability of this view and examines afresh the use of literate modes in Byzantium. She points out that because of its prolonged period of iconoclasm, the place of art in relation to words was exhaustively discussed; visual material is thus as important in a study of Byzantine literacy as words. How should one assess the relationship between art and writing? Do words and pictures say the same thing? Or do pictures perform a function that words cannot? Similar preoccupations are relevant for western Europe and Rosamond McKitterick examines the relationship beteween image and word and the cultural and social context within which writing was produced in the Carolingian period.[26] What were the Carolingian views on the relative value of writing and pictures? What were the reasons and possible consequences of the Carolingian conviction of the superiority of writing to pictures? She considers the impact on the Franks of the gift of writing bestowed by the Christian faith and the law of God, and the degree to which the written word and the book had a symbolic as well as a practical role in Carolingian

---

[24] Nelson, below, pp. 258–96.   [25] Mullett, below, pp. 156–85.

[26] McKitterick, below, pp. 297–318.

society. Both these papers are complemented by John Mitchell's, for he looks in detail at the extravagant use of inscriptions – painted inscriptions on the walls, elaborate painted texts on scrolls held by life-sized standing figures, finely carved funerary inscriptions, the extensive use of inscribed tiles on the floors of rooms and passages, monumental gilt-bronze inscriptions with letters about a Roman foot high on the façades of the buildings of the monastic complex and the prominent display of any old Roman inscriptions the community was able to acquire – at the monastery of San Vincenzo al Volturno in central Italy in the first half of the ninth century.[27] What are the implications of this amazing richness of literacy displayed?

To our lasting regret it was not possible to include studies of either Byzantine or Lombard Italy. This is greatly to be lamented, not least because in Byzantine Italy one has a remarkable survival of Roman traditions which would perhaps enable one to assess continuity much more precisely than elsewhere as well as to work out the degrees to which literacy in Ravenna and the Roman areas of early mediaeval Italy was unique in comparison with the other areas we have studied. Such a study is in preparation by T.S. Brown. As far as Lombard Italy is concerned, it is clear that literacy and its uses deserves a wholescale study, but much has been published already by Chris Wickham; there is also work in preparation by Ross Balzoretti which has much of great value on the subject.[28] Ideally, therefore, both Byzantine and Lombard Italy should have been included in this volume. Similarly, a study of the Islamic world and its sets of contrasts and parallels would have been illuminating. Other areas of western Europe and, of course, the multitude of other aspects of the uses of literacy in the areas we have looked at, remain to be investigated.[29] Nevertheless, the questions raised in this book, and the particular contexts in which they were discussed, represent a deliberate selection rather than a random one. We felt that the areas chosen and the diverse uses of literacy we discuss in them, would serve to introduce the theme in all its complexity and variety as one of vital importance for study in relation to the early middle ages.

---

[27] Mitchell, below, pp. 186–225.

[28] C.J. Wickham, *Early Medieval Italy: Central Power and Local Society 400–1000* (London, 1981), pp. 124–7; *idem*, 'Land disputes and their social framework in Lombard–Carolingian Italy, 700–900', in *Settlement of Disputes*, pp. 105–24, especially p. 112, and see in the same volume Roger Collins' pertinent comments in his section of the Conclusion on 'The Role of writing in the resolution and recording of disputes', *ibid.*, pp. 207–14. See also Ross Balzoretti's University of London PhD thesis in preparation on 'The lands of Saint-Ambrose: the acquisition, organization and exploitation of landed property in north-west Lombardy by the monastery of Sant'Ambrogio c. 780–1000', where he establishes the widespread use of documents and preservation of legal records as well as the existence of a sophisticated notarial tradition centred on Milan.

[29] Simon Franklin, 'Literacy and documentation in mediaeval Russia', *Speculum* 60 (1985), 1–38.

I

Literacy in Ireland: the evidence of the Patrick dossier in the Book of Armagh

Jane Stevenson

Ireland was culturally, as well as geographically, peripheral to early mediaeval Europe.[1] In some ways, early mediaeval Ireland was shaped by the common western European inheritance, the twin legacy of imperial Rome and Christianity, but in others, it was completely anomalous. Although individual Irishmen contributed a great deal to the development of European culture, and, conversely, there is much in the history of early Ireland which should be seen in terms of the Empire and its aftermath, the fact that Ireland was never conquered by Rome resulted in radically different social and political developments of which literacy is both an example and a symptom. For instance, it has become something of a truism that literacy finds its natural environment in towns, and is normally much more prevalent in the urban than in the rural population.[2] Using this as a guideline, one would have to assume that a completely townless society, operating as a set of small units classically defined as 'tribal, rural, hierarchical and familiar',[3] and without any form of centralized government,[4] was peacefully illiterate.

---

[1] I should like to thank Rosamond McKitterick and the other contributors to this volume for their helpful comments on a draft of this paper, and also Richard Sharpe for his generous and perceptive advice. Whenever an edition of one of the texts discussed has an accompanying translation, I have noted this in the footnotes, but the translation of the passages quoted are usually my own.

[2] W.V. Harris, 'Literacy and epigraphy I', *Zeitschrift für Papyrologie und Epigraphik* 52 (1983), 87–111.

[3] D.A. Binchy, 'Secular institutions', in *Early Irish Society*, ed. Myles Dillon (Dublin, 1954), pp. 52–65, at p. 54.

[4] Although this is true in one sense, F.J. Byrne's qualification, *Irish Kings and High-Kings* (London, 1973), p. 40, should also be noted: '[their system of government] had a surface appearance of extreme fragmentation, but . . . was nevertheless linked into a coherent pattern. At no period for which we have sufficient information . . . do we find any one of the numerous and seemingly autonomous *tuatha* existing in splendid isolation.' The *tuath* was

In the case of Ireland, the truism leaves two major factors out of the equation, the order of poets (*filid*), and the dependence of the Christian church on literacy. Leaving Christian Latin literacy to one side for the moment, it is truly remarkable that the *filid* (who seem to have been unified and centralized in a way which was not true of the kings) were able to achieve a standard vernacular literary diction without significant dialectal variations across the whole of the country by the end of the sixth century, and also a high degree of standardization in orthography.[5] This argues for a great deal of self-confidence and practice in the use of literary skills within Irish vernacular culture. It also casts considerable doubts on the relevance to Ireland of another familiar truism, that in the early mediaeval west, literacy is by definition Latin literacy, and firmly in the control of the church. Because of the positively embarrassing riches of vernacular Irish culture, and the extreme complexity of the material, which I have discussed elsewhere,[6] I intend in this paper to confine my attention to Hiberno-Latin, and to examining one particular centre through which many of the issues relating to Irish ecclesiastical culture from the fifth to eighth centuries can be explored.

The church of Armagh is the primatial church of Ireland, and the coarbs (successors) of St Patrick, the apostle of Ireland, its senior churchmen. The evidence from which the early development of this primacy can be traced is in the Book of Armagh, which was written for the abbot of Armagh in 807.[7] The Book of Armagh is one of the most important early Irish manuscripts. It is divisible into three separate books of the same dimensions (*c*. 195 × 145 mm), written at the same time and in the same scriptorium. The first of these is a dossier of texts relating to St Patrick, the second is the only complete copy of the New Testament to survive from any of the Insular churches (known to students of Bible-texts as D), and the third is Sulpicius Severus' life of St Martin. Another reason why it is so important is that it is one of the most accurately datable of Irish manuscripts, because the master scribe, Ferdomnach (*ob*. 846), noted that he had completed his transcription of the Gospel of Matthew at the request of Torbach, who was abbot for only ten months in 807–8. While it was once thought that the

---

the basic social unit of Irish society. Eoin MacNeill estimated that there were between eighty and a hundred *tuatha* in early Christian Ireland (D.A. Binchy, *Celtic and Anglo-Saxon Kingship*, O'Donnell Lecture (Oxford, 1970), p. 5).

[5] Kim McCone, 'The Würzburg and Milan Glosses: our earliest source of Middle Irish?', *Ériu* 36 (1985), 85–106, at 103.

[6] J. Stevenson, 'The beginnings of literacy in Ireland', *PRIA* 89 C (1989), 127–65.

[7] Dublin, Trinity College 52 (*CLA* II. 270).

manuscript was the result of many years' work, this has now been disproved, and the whole volume shown to have been written in 807–8.[8]

There are several elements in the Patrick dossier. These, in order, are the *Vita S. Patricii*, by Muirchú moccu Machthéni, written *c*. 690;[9] a catalogue of churches founded by, or given to, St Patrick, written by Tírechán *c*. 670, together with subsidiary texts known as *additamenta* and *notulae*.[10] All these were written by an assistant scribe. In a slim booklet added next, Ferdomnach himself copied a text called *Liber Angeli*, datable to between 640 and 670, which purports to be a sort of contract between God and St Patrick, giving St Patrick authority over the entire ecclesiastical establishment of Ireland, and establishing the dignity of Armagh and its bishop.[11] Lastly, Ferdomnach included a version of St Patrick's own *Confessio*, the sole representative of a text tradition quite different from that of the other exemplars, and abbreviated by approximately one third.[12] The Book of Armagh enables us to look at literacy in Ireland from a variety of angles. It contains one of the two surviving prose texts known to have been written in Ireland in the fifth century, the *Confessio* of St Patrick, and this gives us a glimpse into the culture and society of Ireland at that time. It offers abundant evidence for the importance of Latin literacy to the seventh- and eighth-century Irish church, and some insight into the logistical problems it faced. It also gives us some information about the relationships between different centres of ecclesiastical culture. And finally, it provides us with information about vernacular literacy in seventh- and eighth-century Ireland, and the extent to which social practices dependent on literacy did or did not influence secular society.

The Patrick dossier compiled at Armagh contains much valuable infor-

---

[8] Richard Sharpe, 'Palaeographical considerations in the study of the Patrician documents in the Book of Armagh', *Scriptorium* 36 (1982), 3–28.

[9] *BCL* no. 303 (pp. 84–5). There is independent corroboration of Muirchú's existence, status and *floruit* in the guarantor list to *Cáin Adomnáin* (promulgated 697), where he appeared as a signatory (as *Murchu macui Mactheine*). See Maírín Ní Dhonnchadha, 'The guarantor list of *Cáin Adomnáin*, 697', *Peritia* 1 (1982), 178–215, at 180 and 196.

[10] *BCL* no. 301 (pp. 83–4).

[11] *BCL* no. 360 (p. 105). For the date, see Richard Sharpe, 'Armagh and Rome in the seventh century', in *Ireland and Europe: The Early Church*, ed. Próinséas Ní Chatháin and Michael Richter (Stuttgart, 1984), pp. 58–72.

[12] M. Esposito, 'St Patrick's "Confessio" and the "Book of Armagh"', *IHS* 9 (1954–5), 1–12; Douglas Powell, 'The textual integrity of St. Patrick's confession', *AB* 87 (1969), 387–409; *idem* 'St. Patrick's Confession and the Book of Armagh', *AB* 90 (1972), 371–85; R.P.C. Hanson, 'The omissions in the text of the Confession of St Patrick in the Book of Armagh', *Texte und Untersuchungen* 115 (=*Studia Patristica* 12) (1975), 91–5. The edition of the *Confessio* I quote is the most accessible, that in *St Patrick, his Writings and Muirchu's Life*, ed. and trans. A.B.E. Hood (Chichester, 1978).

mation, though chiefly about the seventh century rather than the fifth. It is a guide to the pretensions of Armagh rather than to those of St Patrick, and it shows us an ambitious church seeking to claw its way into a high-status position by inflating the reputation of a Romano-British bishop who may or may not have been its founder. Its claim to be Patrick's original and particular church is somewhat eroded by the fact that the saint was known to have been buried at Dún Lethglaisse (Down), an awkward fact which Muirchú does his best to explain away.[13]

The importance of St Patrick for literacy in Ireland is necessarily dependent on what he was actually doing there. It has recently been argued that Patrick was not, or not primarily, an evangelist to the Irish, let alone their one apostle. His sphere of activity lay mainly among the 'tot milia hominum' who, like himself, had been carried off from Britain by Irish pirates and enslaved. He was thus the roving bishop of the (British) Christians in Ireland, and only by extension a missionary bishop among the Irish themselves.[14] In his own words, 'ego ueneram ad Hibernas *gentes* [note the plural] euangelium praedicare'.[15] Some of these Britons, like Patrick himself, are likely to have been literate, or reasonably well versed in the tenets of the Christian faith. This may be why Patrick speaks less of preaching than he does of baptism and confirmation, and does not speak of teaching at all: his primary responsibility was not to inculcate the rudiments of the faith, but to provide priestly services and sacraments, and this, he emphasizes, he was assiduous in doing, at whatever cost to himself.

Patrick does indeed mention conversions among the Irish: 'filii Scottorum et filiae regulorum monachi et uirgines Christi esse uidentur'.[16] In the next paragraph, he singles out 'una benedicta Scotta genetiua nobilis pulcherrima adulta erat, quam ego baptizaui'.[17] In the same section, he mentions parenthetically 'et de genere nostro qui ibi nati sunt nescimus

---

[13] Richard Sharpe, 'St Patrick and the See of Armagh', *CMCS* 4 (1982), 33–59, at 40–3.

[14] E.A. Thompson, 'St Patrick and Coroticus', *JTS* NS 31 (1980), 12–27.

[15] *Confessio*, 37, ed. Hood, p. 30: 'I came to the peoples of Ireland to preach the Gospel'. On the other hand, Hiberno-Latin writers of the early middle ages, who had little or no sense of 'Ireland' as a cultural unit, habitually used *gens* to mean *tuath* ('population-group'/'tribe'). We have no comparative evidence to clarify St Patrick's use of this word: was he thinking in the same terms as the Irish, or, as a Romano-British citizen, treating *Hibernia* as a single political or ethnic unit? His other use of *gentes* in § 48 (ed. Hood, p. 32) does nothing to resolve what he meant by it.

[16] *Confessio*, § 41, ed. Hood, p. 31: 'sons and daughters of Irish kings are seen to be monks and virgins of Christ'.

[17] *Confessio*, § 42, ed. Hood, p. 31: 'there was a blessed Irish woman, of noble race, beautiful and grown up, whom I baptized'.

numerum eorum'.[18] If a contrast is intended between the *Scotti* whom he has been discussing and *genus noster*, then it follows that the clause should be interpreted as meaning 'our people [that is, Britons] who have been born there [Ireland]'. It is surely more natural to take the word *noster*, used by a Roman-Briton addressing other Roman-Britons, as signifying 'Roman-Briton', than it is to assume that the common ground is the Christian faith, and 'our people' are the children of Irish converts.

Dumville takes this whole argument a stage further, by drawing attention to the first notification that there was an Irish church in Prosper of Aquitaine's annal for 431:

in the famous annal for 431, . . . he makes it plain that Bishop Palladius was being sent to an already Christian Irish community ('ad Scottos in Christum credentes'). Who these Irish Christians were must now concern us. We cannot be sure that when Prosper said *Scottos* he necessarily meant 'racially Irish'; it seems doubtful that he would be so well informed. He must be taken as meaning what seems natural in the context, especially for a distant foreigner, namely 'people who live in Ireland', without further specification.[19]

So, 'Palladius, we must suppose, was the first bishop of this British population in involuntary exile . . . [and] . . . with the advent of Patrick, this community had effectively acquired a bishop from among its own number.'[20] Patrick on this argument appears to have been the *second* bishop of the Irish branch of the Christian church of post-Roman Britain. He sheds some kind of light on the literacy of fifth-century Ireland, but this must be seen within the context of his limited role there and not of the grandiose claims of his hagiographers.

If Patrick founded a Christian church among the Irish, rather than ministering entirely to British Christians, then like Augustine of Canterbury he would have had to found a school of Latin literacy and biblical study,[21] for if he did not, the Irish church would not be able to provide leaders from among its own people in the next generation. Though literacy in Ireland may not be dependent on Christianity, Christianity was certainly dependent on literacy.

Patrick says of his relationship with the Irish ruling class that 'interim

---

[18] 'And we do not know the number of those of our people who have been born there [Ireland].'

[19] D.N. Dumville, 'Some British aspects of the earliest Irish Christianity', in *Ireland and Europe: The Early Church*, ed. Ní Chatháin and Richter, pp. 16–24, at pp. 16–17.

[20] *Ibid.*, pp. 18–19.

[21] Cf. P.T. Jones, 'The Gregorian mission and English education', *Speculum* 3 (1928), 335–48.

praemia dabam regibus praeter quod dabam mercedem filiis ipsorum qui mecum ambulant'.[22] He would have been quite unable to move freely through Ireland unless he were recognized as equivalent to a *fili*, that is, a member of the native learned class, for only people of very high status and outlaws wandered about the country,[23] and an important way of distinguishing one from the other was that *filid* and the like travelled with a sizeable retinue indicative of their rank.[24] In an equivalent situation, the Irish missionary bishop Aidán, sent from Iona to evangelize the Northumbrians, had a group of followers around him despite his great personal humility, and Bede says: 'omnes qui cum eo incedebant siue adtonsi seu laici, meditari debuerunt, id est aut legendis scripturis aut psalmis discendis operam dare'.[25] Patrick, equally, may have used his time on the road to instruct his companions in Christian learning, or to teach them to read, but he does not mention doing so.

Patrick's own writing was, as he freely admitted, crude. In spite of this, he bears an indirect witness to the high standards of cultivated latinity normally expected of a Romano-British bishop, for he needed to defend himself to his *seniores* on this account. He explained to them that he was captured as a young lad, after his basic education was complete, but before he had embarked on the elaborate training in rhetoric and the manipulation of a complex, mandarin style which was the hallmark of upper-class Latin in the fifth century, and the index of intellectual and scholarly capability. His literary background barely stretched beyond the Bible, but his knowledge of the sacred text was detailed and thorough. There are a couple of passages in the *Confessio* which have some interesting implications for the nature of his literacy. He records many visions and supernatural experiences, and of these, two involve writing.[26]

---

[22] *Confessio*, § 52, ed. Hood, p. 33: 'from time to time I gave presents to the kings, apart from the rewards I gave to their sons who travelled with me'. The background to this is explained by Clare Stancliffe, 'Kings and conversion: some comparisons between the Roman mission to England and Patrick's to Ireland', *Frühmittelalterliche Studien* 14 (1980), 57–94, at 78–83.

[23] Stancliffe, 'Kings and conversion', 63–4.

[24] Eoin MacNeill, 'Ancient Irish Law: the law of status or franchise', *PRIA* 36 C (1921–3), 265–316, gives the appropriate retinue for each grade of *filid* from *Uraicecht Becc*, V.56.20–V.70.27, p. 275 (there is a new edition promised from the Dublin Institute of Advanced Studies, by Christopher McAll). The extreme status-consciousness of the *filid* was satirized in later mediaeval Ireland in *Tromdámh Guaire*, ed. Maud Joynt (Dublin, 1931).

[25] Bede, *Historia Ecclesiastica Gentis Anglorum* III, § 5, ed. and trans. Bertram Colgrave and R.A.B. Mynors (Oxford, 1969), pp. 226–7: 'all those who went about with him, whether tonsured or lay-people, had to study, that is, to perform the task either of reading the Bible, or learning the Psalms'.

[26] *Confessio*, § 23 and § 29, ed. Hood, pp. 27 and 28.

Et ibi scilicet uidi in uisu noctis uirum uenientem quasi de Hiberione . . . cum epistolis innumerabilibus, et dedit mihi unam ex his et legi principium epistolae continentem 'Vox Hiberionacum', et cum recitabam principium epistolae putabam ipso momento audire uocem ipsorum qui erant iuxta siluam Focluti . . . et sic exclamauerunt, quasi ex uno ore: 'Rogamus te, sancte puer, ut uenias et adhuc ambulas inter nos'.[27]

ad noctem illam uidi in uisu noctis <scriptum quod> scriptum erat contra faciem meam sine honore, et inter haec audiui responsum diuinum dicentem mihi: 'Male uidimus faciem designati nudato nomine'.[28]

In both cases, the content of the letter is experienced rather than read. The word *recitabam* in the first passage shows that he read aloud, as was the normal practice, but when he holds the document in his hand, he *hears* the voice, or voices, of the writer, rather than *seeing* the words on the page. It is a way of reading far removed from our abstract appreciation of written data. Probably when Patrick read the Bible, he perceived it as the voice of God speaking directly to him, which may help to account for his very personal usage of the text and his passionate identification with St Paul.

That is as much as can usefully be said about the historical Patrick and literacy in Ireland. But there is a rich harvest to be gleaned from the Patrick of the Armagh hagiographers. Both Tírechán and Muirchú buttress their texts by copious reference to their sources,[29] and provide, by their accounts of Patrick's actions, insight into the place of writing within the church of the seventh century.

It is important to remember that the church required a considerable amount of written material for efficient functioning, and so we should not be surprised to find this reflected in early mediaeval Ireland. First of all come the Psalter, the Gospels, the Pauline Epistles, and other books of the Bible. Among the very earliest surviving Irish manuscripts are Codex Usserianus Primus, a Vetus Latina gospel-text datable to *c*. 600,[30] the

---

[27] 'And it was there I saw in a vision by night a man coming as if from Ireland . . . with innumerable letters, and he gave me one of them, and I read the heading of the letter: "The voice of the Irish", and as I read out the beginning of the letter, I seemed at the same moment to hear the voice of those who were near the wood of Foclut . . . and they cried out thus, as if in one voice: "we ask you, holy boy, to come, and walk again among us".'

[28] 'That same night, I saw in a vision by night a writing which was written over against my face, without honour [i.e. without the title, 'episcopus'], and meanwhile, I heard a divine prophecy saying to me: "we were grieved to see the face of our appointed one with his name stripped bare".'

[29] For example, Muirchú says of Patrick's birthplace in I.1, 'quem uicum constanter indubitanter *comperimus* esse Ventre' (*PT*, pp. 66–7: 'we have discovered for certain and beyond any doubt that this township is Ventre'). This suggests that he was comparing different versions of incidents in his hero's life.

[30] Dublin, Trinity College 55 (A.4.15) (*CLA* II.271), discussed in Julian Brown, 'The oldest

Springmount tablets (discussed below), which carry a psalter-text,[31] and the *Cathach* of St Columba, a Gallican psalter.[32] Next in order of importance come tools for interpreting the biblical narrative, principally the works of the Latin fathers. Columbanus, writing on the Continent to Gregory the Great at the end of the sixth century, revealed his knowledge of the exegetical writings of Jerome and of Gregory himself.[33] The seventh-century *Vita S. Columbani* by Jonas of Bobbio records what was known to his disciples of his background and career in Ireland, and he makes particular mention of the importance of exegesis in his education in Ireland.[34] The third main category of Christian writing is canon law, and the recording of decisions on practical disciplinary problems. This is evidenced in Ireland by the so-called First and Second Synod of St Patrick, possibly written in the sixth century,[35] the *Collectio Canonum Hibernensis*, which draws on sixth- and seventh-century material from Ireland as well as on the Continental canons,[36] and in a slightly different field, the Irish penitentials which go back to Finnian (Uinniau), a contemporary and countryman of Gildas, resident in Ireland.[37] The fourth is the whole

Irish manuscripts and their late antique background', in *Ireland and Europe: The Early Church*, ed. Ní Chatháin and Richter, pp. 311–27, at p. 312. See also *BCL* no. 515 (p. 133).

[31] Dublin, National Museum of Ireland SA 1914:2 (*CLA* Supp. 1684); *BCL* no. 505 (pp. 130–1).

[32] Dublin, Royal Irish Academy s.n. (*CLA* II.266); *BCL* no. 506 (p. 131).

[33] *Sancti Columbani Opera*, ed. and trans. G.S.M. Walker (Dublin, 1957), pp. 2–13, at pp. 10–11.

[34] *Ionae Vitae Sanctorum Columbani, Vedastis, Iohannis*, ed. Bruno Krusch (Hanover, 1905), p. 158.

[35] *Synodus I S. Patricii* (also called *Synodus episcoporum*) is in *The Irish Penitentials*, ed. and trans. Ludwig Bieler (Dublin, 1963), pp. 54–8, and also in *The Bishops' Synod: A Symposium*, ed. M.J. Faris (Liverpool, 1976), pp. 1–8. See further *BCL* no. 599 (p. 153). *Synodus II S. Patricii* is also in *The Irish Penitentials*, ed. Bieler, pp. 184–96, See further *BCL* no. 600 (p. 153). The dating of these canons is still very much in dispute. D.A. Binchy, 'Patrick and his biographers, ancient and modern', *Studia Hibernica* 2 (1962), 7–173, at 46, placed them in the seventh century. On the other hand, Kathleen Hughes dated the first Synod to the second quarter of the sixth century, in her *The Church in Early Irish Society* (London, 1966), pp. 44–52, and the second to the second half of the same century, in 'Synodus II S. Patricii', in *Latin Script and Letters A.D. 400–900: Festschrift Presented to Ludwig Bieler*, ed. J.J. O'Meara and Bernd Naumann (Leiden, 1976), pp. 141–7, at p. 142.

[36] *Die Irische Kanonensammlung*, ed. F.W.H. Wasserschleben (Giessen, 1874; rev. edn, Leipzig, 1885), *BCL* nos. 612–13 (pp. 156–7). There are two recensions of the *Hibernensis*: The latest author cited in the A-text is Theodore of Canterbury (*ob.* 690), and the latest author in the B-text is Adomnán of Iona (*ob.* 704) (Henry Bradshaw, in *Die Irische Kanonensammlung*, ed. Wasserschleben, p. lxx).

[37] *The Irish Penitentials*, ed. Bieler, pp. 74–94, *BCL* no. 598 (pp. 152–3), and see Richard Sharpe, 'Gildas as a Father of the Church', in *Gildas: New Approaches*, ed. Michael Lapidge and D.N. Dumville (Woodbridge, 1984), pp. 193–205, and D.N. Dumville, 'Gildas and Uinniau', in *ibid.*, pp. 207–14.

complex area of ecclesiastical arithmetic and computus, which was well established in Ireland by 600, on the evidence of Columbanus.[38] Lastly, there is the keeping of annals, which may have developed from the need to keep Easter tables.[39] The first Hiberno-Latin annals were probably written in the middle of the sixth century.[40]

It is clear that in Ireland we have evidence ranging from reasonable to excellent for all these forms of written documentation essential to the smooth running of the church, and that these were proliferating during the sixth century, and well established by the beginning of the seventh. It can only have been a matter of four or five generations from the humble beginnings witnessed by St Patrick to a situation in which a very substantial technical and economic investment had been made in the creation (and, presumably, storage) of permanent written documents within the Christian centres of Ireland. This investment lay not only in the production of parchment, which was itself a substantial commitment of labour, capital and livestock, but in the training of scribes.

Tírechán, in particular, was clear that his hero was deeply concerned with Christian education. He built up a picture of Patrick as saintly thaumaturge and effective primate of all Ireland (a far cry from the harried and beleaguered bishop of the *Confessio*).[41] In the book of Armagh, there is a short collection of notes between the end of Muirchú's *Vita* and Tírechán's *incipit*. These closely resemble Tírechán's *Collectanea*, and may have been displaced from it. The first sentence is as follows: 'portauit Patricius per Sininn secum quinquaginta clocos, quinquaginta patinos, quinquaginta calices, altaria, libros legis, aeuangelii libros, et reliquit illos in locis nouis'.[42] What is implied here is an extensive and orderly programme of evangelization, in which Patrick scattered fifty Christian nuclei across the face of Ireland, providing each with a basic priest's kit: a bell, altar-furniture, a *liber legis*[43] and a gospel-book. This is just the kind of thing Patrick himself did *not* tell us, even though he says 'ordinauit ubique

---

[38] In *Epistola I*, *Sancti Columbani Opera*, ed. Walker, pp. 2–6. See also Dáibhí Ó Cróinín, 'Mo-Sinnu moccu Min and the computus of Bangor', *Peritia* 1 (1982), 281–95, at 282–5.

[39] Dáibhí Ó Cróinín, 'Early Irish annals from Easter tables: a case restated', *Peritia* 2 (1983), 74–86.

[40] A.P. Smyth, 'The earliest Irish annals', *PRIA* 72 C (1972), 1–48.

[41] Binchy, 'Patrick and his biographers', 58.

[42] II.1, *PT*, pp. 122–3: 'P. carried with him across the Shannon fifty bells, fifty patens, fifty chalices, altar-stones, books of the law, books of the Gospels, and left them at the new sites.'

[43] The sense of this is unclear: it might mean part of the Old Testament, or a guide to practice such as the *acta* of church councils. The existence of the *Synodus episcoporum* and *Synodus II S. Patricii* attest that the need for ecclesiastical legislation was felt at an early stage of the development of the church in Ireland, certainly before Tírechán's time, though not necessarily in St Patrick's.

Dominus clericos per modicitatem meam',[44] and no priest could effectively function without these things. It is odd that Tírechán's list does not include a psalter, indispensable for the Office, and particularly venerated in Ireland.[45] One possible explanation is that in Tírechán's day, the psalter was normally learned by heart as part of the preparation for priesthood. However, he noted a little later that Patrick wrote a psalter for an ordinand named Sachellus, which he himself had seen, and this might argue against the theory that psalters were not basic necessities. On the other hand, the ownership of a psalter may have been rather unusual, and the incident may simply reflect the chance survival of a single venerable manuscript which needed explanation.

A curious anecdote at the beginning of Tírechán's account is a witness to the use of wooden tablets as writing material in the early Irish church.[46] Patrick and his men were seen 'cum tabulis in manibus scriptis' ('with written tablets in their hands'); the people mistook the wooden tablets for some kind of sinister weapon, and the Christian party was nearly lynched. A group of six wax tablets, dating to *c.* A.D. 600, inscribed with a text of Ps. XXX–XXXII, have been recovered from Springmount bog, and are now in the National Museum. These tablets are *c.* 75×210 mm, *c.* 7 mm thick, and appear to have been lashed together as a group of six, waxed sides together. It is hard to imagine their being mistaken for anything potentially deadly, however unfamiliar they appeared;[47] so perhaps the bulky, Roman-style waxed tablet was not the only form of writing material in use, and Tírechán was envisaging something slimmer which could be mistaken for a dagger.

There are two possible lines of approach to this story. The debris of the Roman fortress at Vindolanda (*c.* A.D. 100) proved on excavation to contain quantities of discarded correspondence, written on pieces of new wood as thin as veneer, which was folded over and tied round the middle before being sent.[48] This is less expensive and technically less complex as writing material than the waxed tablet, and much more ephemeral and disposable. No such leaf-tablets (as Bowman calls them) have ever been found in

---

[44] *Confessio*, § 48, ed. Hood, p. 32: 'the Lord ordained priests everywhere through my agency'.

[45] See Martin McNamara, 'Psalter text and psalter study in the Early Irish Church (A.D. 600–1200)', *PRIA* 73 C (1973), 201–72.

[46] II.3 (1), *PT*, pp. 122–3.

[47] The seventh-century Abbot Adomnán at the beginning of his *De Locis Sanctis* also makes reference to writing notes on tablets: 'primo in tabulis describenti fideli et indubitabili narratione dictauit; quae nunc in membranis breui textus scribuntur' (ed. and trans. Denis Meehan (and Ludwig Bieler) (Dublin, 1958), p. 36).

[48] A.K. Bowman and J.D. Thomas, *Vindolanda: The Latin Writing-Tablets* (London, 1983), pp. 29–31.

Ireland, but it should be remembered that it was only with the Vindolanda excavations in 1973–5 that this form of script medium, which was almost certainly ubiquitous in the Roman world,[49] first came to the attention of classical archaeologists. Another purely visual comparison which comes to mind is the Scandinavian rune-stick.[50] The Irish ogam alphabet was particularly well adapted for writing on the edges of objects, and ogam-staves may also therefore have had this shape for purely practical reasons. But Patrick should reasonably be visualized as being equipped with Roman writing equipment, not Irish. The problem is probably insoluble: it remains a tantalizing insight.

There are two anecdotes of Tírechán's in which he asserts that something written by Patrick was still extant in his own day, the one mentioned above, 'et scripsit illi librum psalmorum, *quem uidi*' (my italics),[51] and one referring to the district of Selc: 'Castrametati sunt in cacuminibus Selcae et posuerunt ibi stratum et sedem inter lapides, in quibus scripsit manus sua literas, quas hodie conspeximus oculis nostris.'[52] Whatever the force of the attribution to Patrick, it seems that Tírechán had seen a psalter which was already clearly ancient in the seventh century, and also a Christian inscription, presumably in Roman script, which local tradition associated with the saint.

Tírechán presents Patrick as both writer and scribe. His *Confessio* and *Epistola* are not mentioned directly, but he is said to have sent letters to his priests Caeticus and Sachellus to rebuke them for ordaining in Mag Aí without his permission. There are four other references to his own writing:

> babtitzabat cotidie homines et illis litteras legebat ac abgatorias
> <scribebat>.

> inuenit Iarnascum sanctum sub ulmo . . . et scripsit illi elimenta.

> cui [the son of a new ordinand] scripsit Patricius abgitorium.

> babtitzauit Patricius filium et scripsit illi abgitorium.[53]

---

[49] *Ibid.*, pp. 37–44.

[50] See Kelly's chapter in this volume, below, pp. 37–8.

[51] II.5, *PT*, pp. 122–3.

[52] Tírechán, 30 (2), *PT*, pp. 146–7. 'They camped on the heights of Selc, and there they made their resting-place amidst stones, on which his hand wrote letters, which today we may see with our own eyes.'

[53] *Ibid.*, 6.1, pp. 126–7, 33.1, pp. 150–1, 37.3, pp. 152–3, and 47.1, pp. 160–1: 'he baptized people every day, and he read the letters to them, and wrote *abgitoria*'; 'he found the holy Iarnasc under an elm, and wrote *elementa* for him'; 'for whom P. wrote an *abgitorium*'; and 'P. baptized the son, and wrote an *abgitorium* for him'.

The context of these gifts of *abgitoria* appears ultimately to be ordination. They are twice given at the recipient's baptism, but in each of those cases, there is an implication that the recipient was later ordained. The association with ordination is also found in the other two examples. What is written is three times called *abgitorium*, once *elimenta*. *Abgitorium* is, of course, from Latin *abecedarium* 'alphabet'. But although the Hiberno-Latin word can bear this simple meaning, it is often used more in the sense of 'rudiments'.[54] It may be that Tírechán means to imply some form of elementary Christian knowledge, such as a creed, or the Paternoster, or the Ten Commandments. Whatever exactly Tírechán means by his *abgitoria*, it is clear that he assumes that, whatever the state of affairs among the laity, it is vitally necessary that priests should be literate and educated, and that they should have the elements of their faith to meditate on, or teach from. Tírechán's account of Patrick's efficient administration of the conversion of Ireland implies an active scriptorium in fifth-century Ireland, busy turning out enough copies of the Gospels for every church in Ireland. This in itself suggests that the need was keenly felt in his *own* time, and that the copying of basic texts to replace old worn-out ones was a never-ending task which absorbed much time and energy in a large church with many dependants, such as Armagh.

Muirchú and Tírechán both acknowledged substantial dependence on written sources. Muirchú shows that he knew the *Confessio* and possibly the *Epistola*: summarizing Patrick's background from the opening of the *Confessio*, he says the saint was 'fili[us], *ut ipse ait*, Potiti presbiteri' (my italics),[55] and he knew that Patrick had written a letter to Coroticus, though he did not quote the letter (which perhaps showed Patrick too powerless for Muirchú's purposes), and instead gave a wholly fabulous account of the metamorphosis of Coroticus into a fox.[56] In addition, Muirchú and Tírechán had various written and oral sources of information, some of which they held in common. This shows clearly that the second half of the seventh century did not mark the beginning of hagiography in Ireland, and that information on Patrick was collected at least a generation earlier.

Muirchú goes into some detail on his sources. He opens with a sort of *apologia*, an example of the familiar *topos* of authorial modesty, lamenting his incapacity for the task, and implying in his address to 'mi domine Aido' (Áed, bishop of Sleaty) that he had not taken on the job of his own volition. First of all he says that many people had already attempted to reconcile the stories about Patrick: 'multi conati sunt ordinare narrationem utique istam

---

[54] Brian Ó Cuív, 'Irish words for "alphabet"', *Ériu* 31 (1980), 100–10.

[55] Muirchú, I.1, *PT*, pp. 66–7: 'son, as he himself said, of the priest Potitus'.

[56] *Ibid.*, I.29 (28), *PT*, pp. 100–1.

secundum quod patres eorum . . . sermones tradiderunt illis'.[57] The conflict of opinions in the oral tradition has prevented anyone from creating a 'canonical version': 'propter difficillimum narrationis opus diuersasque opiniones et plurimorum plurimas suspiciones numquam ad unum certumque historiae tramitem peruenierunt'.[58] Several points are being made here. On the surface, he is saying that he is not the first person to write about Patrick, and that there is a large body of oral tradition relating to the saint, much of which is mutually contradictory. But Muirchú, on behalf of Armagh, is deliberately annexing a saint who on his own showing died at Saul and was buried at Down, and these churches are likely to object fiercely to his version of the story. This prologue is calculated to preempt potential opposition, since oral stories cannot be checked or substantiated, and any different versions can be dismissed as variants, which Muirchú had considered and chosen to reject.

Another important source for Muirchú and Tírechán is Ultán, bishop of Dál Conchobuir in Brega (ob. c. 655), who is specifically acknowledged by both writers. Muirchú says 'inueni quattuor nomina in libro scripta Patricii abud Uldanum episcopum Concubrensum', and does not mention him again.[59] Tírechán is more detailed in his reference, saying: 'Tirechan episcopus haec scripsit ex ore uel libro Ultani episcopi, cuius ipse alumpnus uel discipulus fuit'.[60] and adding, like Muirchú (who might possibly have taken this from Tírechán, rather than directly from Ultán), 'inueni quattuor nomina in libro scripta Patricio apud Ultanum episcopum Conchuburnensium'. He also depended on Ultán, his teacher, for oral traditions of Patrick: 'erat autem in una ex insolis . . . annis triginta mihi testante Ultano episcopo'.[61] There may have been a single book, referred to as *liber Ultani* and *liber apud Ultanum*, there may have been two, one written by Ultán, and one owned by him. A third reference to a written source in Tírechán's account is 'omnia autem quae euenierunt inuenietis in plana illius historia scripta'.[62] In context, *illius* may refer to Patrick, or,

---

[57] Ibid., prologus (1), PT, pp. 62–3: 'many have attempted to write this story coherently according to the traditions of their fathers'.

[58] Ibid., prologus (1), PT, pp. 62–3: 'the great difficulties which the telling of the story presents, and the conflicting opinions and many doubts voiced by many a person have prevented them from ever arriving at one undisputed sequence of events'.

[59] Ibid., prologus (6), PT, pp. 62–3: 'I found the four names of Patrick in a written book belonging to Ultán, bishop of Connor'.

[60] Tírechán, 1 (1), PT, pp. 124–5: 'T. the bishop wrote this from the words and from the book of Ultán the bishop, whose pupil or disciple he was'.

[61] Ibid. 1 (6), PT, pp. 124–5: 'he was in one of the islands . . . for thirty years, as bishop Ultán testified to me'.

[62] Ibid. 1 (1), PT, pp. 124–5: 'you will find everything which happened to him in his straightforward history'.

possibly, to Ultán. Is this *plana historia* a third book, or are all three the same?

Some additional written sources seem to lie beneath the surface of the texts, showing that these Irish writers of the mid-seventh century already had quite a variety of written material to draw on. Bieler pointed out that three sets of phrases near the beginning of Muirchú's account form rhymed, octosyllabic lines, and are somewhat poetic in diction.[63] They are compatible with one of the poetic styles used in seventh-century Hiberno-Latin hymnody, and it is quite possible that the wreckage of a lost hymn on the life of Patrick is their source. The extraordinary 'druidic prophecy' quoted in a Latin version by Muirchú[64] and surviving also in Irish, is so archaic in style, and so completely unChristian in tone, presenting as it does an unsympathetic outsider's view of the weird appearance and antics of Christian priests, without any acknowledgement of their true purpose, that it may be extremely ancient.[65] So if there is a single compendium, Ultán's *plana historia*, this itself must be a somewhat heterogeneous document, containing a *Vita S. Patricii*, at least one Hiberno-Latin poem on the saint, and some vernacular material. Ultán was not directly connected with Armagh, but took a specialist interest in Irish hagiography. He collected all the miracles of Brigit, according to the Irish *Liber Hymnorum*,[66] and may be implicated in the development of the concept, found in Armagh's *Liber Angeli* and in a later poem, 'Brigid bé bithmaith', that Patrick and Brigit are the 'two pillars' of Ireland: 'Inter sanctum Patricium Hibernensium Brigitamque columpnas amicitia caritatis inerat tanta, ut unum cor consiliumque haberent uisum . . . Vir ergo sanctus Christianae uirgini ait: "O mea Brigita, paruchia tua in prouincia tua apud reputabitur monarchiam tuam, in parte autem orientali et occidentali dominatu in meo erit."'[67] The legends of the two saints are intertwined for mutual support,[68] with Brigit

---

[63] *PT*, pp. 1–18.

[64] Muirchú, I.10 (9), *PT*, 76–7.

[65] The prophecy also survives in Irish, and in other slightly different Latin versions. See James Travis, 'A druidic prophecy, the first Irish satire, and a poem to raise blisters', *PMLA* 57 (1942), 909–15, and *PT*, p. 200.

[66] *The Irish Liber Hymnorum*, ed. and trans. J.A. Bernard and R. Atkinson, 2 vols. (London, 1898), I, p. 14, II, p. 8; and see Richard Sharpe, '*Vitae S. Brigitae*: the oldest texts', *Peritia*

[67] *Liber Angeli*, § 32, *PT*, pp. 190–1: 'between holy Patrick and Brigit, pillars of the Irish, there was so great a friendship of charity that they had one heart and one mind . . . the holy man said to the Christian virgin: "O my Brigit, your *paruchia* will be deemed to be in your province in your dominion, but in the eastern and western part it will be in my domination."'

[68] Tírechán twice links Patrick and Brigit. He notes in 16 (1) (*PT*, p. 136), that a church

the *regina Austri*, though under Patrick's patronage, and Patrick's power centred in the north.[69] The arrangement somewhat resembles an informal parallel to the relationship between the two archbishops of Canterbury and York, since more than one archbishop of Canterbury, notably Theodore, acted from time to time as though he had ultimate jurisdiction over the entire English church.

The evidence suggests that the two churches of Armagh and Kildare both launched a major propaganda campaign some time during the first half of the seventh century, having come to some kind of an agreement to back up rather than destroy one another's claims to dominance, thus slotting themselves in as First and Second in the pecking-order of the churches of Ireland.[70] The Armagh–Kildare relationship is further indicated by Muirchú, whose model (as he said in his preface) was 'pater meus Coguitosus', by whom we should almost certainly understand Cogitosus, author of the *Vita II* of St Brigit.

In pointing out that this all represents an extremely sophisticated use of the craft of literacy, cunningly exploiting its advantages over oral narrative and utilizing the rhetorical skills that can marshal a collection of shaky facts and downright misinformation into an apparently watertight case, it should not be overlooked that Armagh and Kildare are the two religious sites of Ireland most likely to have had their origins in the old religion. St Brigit is completely a-historical, and shows every sign of being the Celtic goddess of the same name, perfunctorily euhemerized and provided with a biography. Ard Machae and Emain Machae were the twin capitals of the Ulaid, not in the sense that either was a royal citadel, but that they were sacred sites of great importance. 'Cathedral Hill, the ancient Ard Macha, is the only Irish pagan celtic sanctuary-site which we can identify with any degree of certainty.'[71] Sharpe has therefore argued that the custodians of the sacred site came to a joint decision to go over to the new religion, and, being without a patron saint in the usual way, annexed St Patrick, and set about

---

founded by Patrick was held by Brigit's uncle, Mac Cairthin, and in 16 (3) (*ibid.*, p. 136), that the church in which Brigit received the veil from Mac Caille was also a foundation of Patrick's.

[69] Sharpe, 'St Patrick', 38–9.

[70] Sharpe, '*Vitae S. Brigitae*: the oldest texts', 102–3; and see further Kim McCone, 'Brigit in the seventh century: a saint with three lives?', *Peritia* 1 (1982), 107–45, at 115–18 and 136–44.

[71] Etienne Rynne, 'Celtic stone idols in Ireland', in *The Iron Age in the Irish Sea Province*, Council for British Archaeology Research Report 9, ed. Charles Thomas (London, 1972), pp. 79–98, p. 80. This has been recently reinforced by Brian Lambkin, in a paper he gave at the 1987 Irish Conference of Historians, Maynooth, in which he suggested that a pagan deer-cult was in existence at Armagh not only in Patrick's time, but even in Muirchú's.

empire-building and consolidating their position within the new religious framework.[72] It is not necessarily irrelevant that it was the two Irish religious sites with the most obvious pagan antecedents that were able to manipulate oral and written sources with such skill and flair that they imposed their version of reality not only on their contemporaries, but on every historian of the church of Ireland down to the twentieth century. Patrick and Brigit are two of the Three Thaumaturges of Ireland not from some kind of natural right, but because Ultán, Cogitosus, Muirchú and Tírechán, or perhaps rather the prelates whom they wrote to serve, put them in that position, and kept them there (the third, Columba, was the subject of an equally brilliant propaganda campaign, but one which is outside the scope of this discussion).[73]

The Patrician dossier in the Book of Armagh, besides illuminating the relationship between specific churches, also sheds a more general light on interactions between the Christians and the *filid*. This is obviously relevant to the question of the position of literacy in early Ireland. One of the more important testimonies to this relationship is the story of Patrick, Dubthach moccu Lugair and Fiacc.[74] One important thing about it is that it shows later writers, looking back at the beginnings of Christianity, assuming that Patrick turned to the orders of poets, who were, after all, the native intelligentsia, when he sought suitable candidates for the episcopacy.[75] Muirchú was evidently aware of this story, since he brought Dubthach, Patrick and Fiacc together, claiming that Dubthach was the first pagan to honour Patrick as a holy man.[76] Fiacc became first bishop of Sleaty (Sléibte), so it is interesting that Muirchú tells this story: Áed, the then bishop of Sleaty, was the man who commissioned Muirchú to write. It would seem that Áed, in the late seventh century, saw no cause for embarrassment in confirming that the founder of his see (who was also a member of his kin-group)[77] had had his first training as a pagan *fili*.[78]

---

[72] Sharpe, 'St Patrick', 53–6.

[73] See, for example, J.-M. Picard, 'The purpose of Adomnán's *Vita Columbae*', *Peritia* 1 (1982), 161–92.

[74] *Additamenta* 14. 1–5, *PT*, pp. 176–7.

[75] *Ibid.*: 'Patrick asked Dubthach for the material of a bishop from among his disciples of Leinster'.

[76] Muirchú, I.20, *PT*, p. 92.

[77] Ní Dhonnchadha, 'The guarantor list', 192–3. Áed and Fiacc were both Uí Bairrche.

[78] There is a hymn to Patrick in the *Irish Liber Hymnorum* attributed to Fiacc, though clearly much later, which claims to be based on 'stories' (*scélaib*, stanza 1) and 'writings' (*líni*, stanza 6), ed. Bernard and Atkinson, I, p. 97, II, p. 32. This composite hymn gives in the

The sources of the Patrick dossier, and the latent information about the attitude of seventh-century churchmen to writing which it conceals, by no means exhaust the interest of this material for the study of literacy. A considerable proportion of the text of Tírechán, and also the appended *additamenta*, consists of short descriptions of the donation of churches or property to God and St Patrick, by named individuals, which evidently bear some relationship to the concept of a charter.[79] As Doherty put it:

The work of Tírechán, writing about the same time, takes us closer to the detailed research undertaken to substantiate the claims so clearly reflected in Muirchú's life. Tírechán's journeys, allegedly following the missionary circuits of Patrick, were really field-surveys of old missionary and diocesan churches (not necessarily Patrician) which were now in decay or which were aligned to politically irrelevant communities.[80]

Tírechán's language for recording the perpetual gift of land, a community, or a family, to Patrick is formulaic and legalistic. He uses the word *immolo* ('I offer') to mark a formal gift, for example: 'et dixit Endeus: "filium meum et partem hereditatis meae ego *immolo* Deo Patricii et Patricio"' (my italics).[81] The permanence of gifts made to Patrick and his church is often stressed, with words like 'in saeculum', 'sempiternum', 'usque in diem iudicii'. Another word which seems to bear a precise legal significance in this context is *oblatio*, found, for example, in *Liber Angeli*: 'item ait [Patricius]: "Nonne ergo mihi sufficit quicquid deuote uouerint ac

---

fifteen stanzas which seem to be the earliest part the name Cothraige, Patrick's sojourn in the Tyrrhene Sea, and the information that he studied the 'canon' (the New Testament). This suggests an acquaintance with either Muirchú or his sources, and perhaps the possibility that a Patrick dossier was formed at Sleaty as well as at Armagh. Both Áed and his successor Conchad made a formal submission of Sleaty to the abbot of Armagh (*additamenta* 16.1–2, *PT*, pp. 178–9) which, as Ní Dhonnchadha says, 'was in effect the forging of a monastico-political alliance between Sleaty, one of the principal churches of the declining Uí Bairrche (to which Áed of course belonged) and the rising star of Armagh' ('The guarantor list', pp. 185–6). So Sleaty in Áed's time had come to identify Patrick and Armagh's interests with its own.

[79] Wendy Davies, 'The Latin charter tradition', in *Ireland in Early Mediaeval Europe*, ed. Dorothy Whitelock, Rosamond McKitterick and David Dumville (Cambridge, 1982), pp. 274–80, has discussed the distinctive characteristics of what seems to be a Celtic charter-tradition. She has found a *corpus* of 203 complete charters of a consistent and distinctive type, at least a hundred fragments of the same type, and four charter inscriptions on stone (pp. 259–61). The Tírechán *additamenta* are discussed on p. 273.

[80] Charles Doherty, 'Some aspects of hagiography as a source for Irish economic history', *Peritia* 1 (1982), 300–28, at 303.

[81] Tírechán, 15 (2), *PT*, pp. 134–5: 'and Énde said: "I offer my son and my share in the inheritance to the god of Patrick and to Patrick."'

uoluerint Christiani homines offere de regionibus atque oblationibus suis per arbitrium suae libertatis?"'.[82] Doherty concludes, 'as Eoin Mac Néill pointed out a long time ago, *oblationes* above [he gave two examples from the *additamenta* to Tírechán] is equivalent to *"idparta"*, the technical Irish word for grants to the church'. The verbs *immolare* and *offerre*, then, are being used in a highly technical sense. The force of *immolare* may be 'to alienate' with *offerre* meaning 'to grant'.[83]

The *additamenta* to Tírechán are even more legalistic in content, and form what is effectively a narrative cartulary. I will quote a couple of consecutive examples (in English, since the text is in Irish):

Ernéne made over to Cummén and to Alach and to Ernín Tír Gimmae and Muine Búachaile and Tamnach. These three nuns made over these lands to Patrick until doomsday.

Cummén and Brethánn purchased Óchter Achid together with its [whole] estate, in wood, plain, and meadow, with its enclosure and its herb-garden. Hence half this heritage belongs absolutely to Cummén, in house, in man, until her chattels be paid to her, that is, three ounces of silver, and a can of silver, and a necklace worth three ounces, and a circlet of gold [calculated] according to ancient measurements and ancient dimensions: the value of half an ounce in pigs and the value of half an ounce in sheep, and a garment worth half an ounce, all of these calculated according to ancient measurements [and given] on account of a marriage settlement.[84]

These are, as the examples show, very detailed records of transactions, even though they do not have the usual distinguishing features of a charter, such as a witness list. Their formal character shows that they were based on previously existing documents, and are evidence that the church of Armagh made some use of charters in the seventh and eighth centuries, although these are otherwise not attested in Ireland until the eleventh and twelfth centuries.[85] These records differ from the characteristic western European charter, in that they do not have a formal protocol, initial invocation, formal title and address, dating clause, or subscriptions or other signs of validation. But these formal deficiencies are also found in the other Celtic charters discussed by Davies, who notes that, as a group, Celtic charters are retrospective not dispositive in intention, and not claiming to be issued by

---

[82] *Liber Angeli*, § 13, *PT*, pp. 186–7: 'again he said: "is it not sufficient for me, whatever Christian men have devoutly vowed and wished to offer me from their land, offerings of their own free choice?"'.

[83] Doherty, 'Some aspects of hagiography', p. 305, quoting Eoin MacNeill, ed. John Ryan, *St Patrick* (Dublin and London, 1964), p. 200.

[84] *Additamenta*, *PT*, pp. 174–5.

[85] Richard Sharpe, 'Dispute settlement in medieval Ireland: a preliminary inquiry', in *Settlement of Disputes*, pp. 169–89, at p. 174.

the author of the grant. Instead, like late imperial *notitiae*, they are intended to be a narrative record of a transaction which has already taken place.[86]

The concept of a witness list was not unknown in seventh-century Ireland, as the *Cáin Adomnáin* demonstrates. This was a nationally accepted law for the protection of non-combatants proclaimed by Adomnán, abbot of Iona, at the Synod of Birr in 697, and witnessed by forty-one abbots and bishops, beginning with the bishop of Armagh, and fifty kings, from all over Ireland. The list of signatories, or witnesses, appears to be perfectly genuine.[87] In the Book of Armagh, the list of names associated with Trim in the *additamenta* may possibly represent the fragmented remains of a witness list, with the names given a perfunctory genealogical form.[88] This garbled account in the *additamenta* is the only occasion on which the principle of the guarantor or witness list can be shown to have been extended from ecclesiastical legislation to ecclesiastical charters. The *additamenta* show several different styles of writing. The documentation of patrician churches in Connacht appears to be a disjointed series of extracts from charters or *notulae*. By contrast, the ramified churches and churchmen associated with Trim and Sleaty are cast into the form of stories, full of circumstantial detail. This may represent a compromise between the ecclesiastical tradition of the charter, and the secular society's *senchas* (topographical, legal and genealogical traditions, including tribal history), the essentially oral form in which a class of specialists within Irish society maintained knowledge from one generation to the next.[89]

It is not easy to answer the question of why Armagh chose to record land transactions in this way in the context of normal Irish legal practice, which established the rights and wrongs of inheritance mainly by appeal to witnesses, memory and the swearing of oaths: 'extant sources suggest that written evidence of title to land never became widely accepted in Irish legal

[86] Davies, 'The Latin charter tradition', p. 262.

[87] Ní Dhonnchadha, 'The guarantor list', 178–81.

[88] *Additamenta*, 2 (1)–4 (2), *PT*, pp. 168–71. I owe this suggestion to Richard Sharpe, who also points out that the *plebilis progenies* ('lay succession') of Fedelmid on pp. 170–1 is particularly suspicious. The Irish concept of inheritance within an extended family group makes the nine clear generations of direct father–son inheritance which this text purports to show fundamentally implausible. The names may have started off as witnesses to the submission of Trim to Armagh. See Richard Sharpe, review of *PT*, *Éigse* 18 (1980–1), 329–32, at 331–2.

[89] F.J. Byrne, '"Senchas": the nature of Gaelic historical tradition', *Historical Studies* 9 (1974), 137–59, at 138.

practice'.[90] The normal procedures are recorded in the early vernacular lawtract *Berrad Airechta* (*The Shearing of the Court*), § 59: 'As the native law recites: where is proof found in Irish law? Do heirs have memories without ogam [inscriptions] on stones, without public lot-casting, without *mac*-sureties, without *ráth*-sureties? Although they have been proclaimed, how shall contracts of the [deceased] ancestors be enforced? It is witnesses who make fast proof.'[91] However, a little later, the concept of written evidence is introduced, though as only one of a list of alternatives: 'for those are the seven things which dissolve any [attempt at] dissolving [a contract]. Valid witnessing, immovable stones, *ráth*-sureties [as a guarantee] of prescriptive rights, *godly old writings*', etc.[92]

This charter tradition in early Ireland is, as the words translated 'godly old writings' (*senscríband deoda*) indicates, a Christian interpolation in the normal processes of Irish land law. The ecclesiastical context of the Celtic charter tradition as a whole is clear and explicit. It is also noticeable that some of the formulaic vocabulary commented on by Davies and Doherty can be paralleled in patristic and early ecclesiastical writing, for example, *immolare* meaning 'give', found in both Ambrose and Isidore.[93] Davies has argued that the background to this development was in late and post-imperial Britain.[94] Celtic charters (Irish, Welsh and Breton) represent the fossilized practice of the bishops of western Britain in the mid-fifth century, which in themselves reflect the bureaucracy of the Roman administration. The Irish canon collection records, in her view, an attempted introduction of land contracts 'more Romanorum' as early as the end of the sixth century.[95] Irish ecclesiastics were certainly persisting with the form in the eighth century for the *Collectio Canonum Hibernensis* records the appeal to written testimony in the case of a dispute *between* churches:[96] 'Sinodus

---

[90] Sharpe, 'Dispute settlement', p. 170. Gearóid Mac Niocaill, 'Admissible and inadmissible evidence in early Irish law', *The Irish Jurist* NS 4 (1969), 332–7, gives as the three main classes of admissible evidence: oath-helpers, casting of lots or submission to an ordeal and sworn evidence. Written evidence, apart from ancient inscriptions on ogam stones, was accepted only reluctantly.

[91] Translation from Robin Stacey, '*Berrad Airechta*', in *Lawyers and Laymen: Studies in the History of Law Presented to Professor Dafydd Jenkins on his Seventy-Fifth Birthday, Gŵyl Ddewi, 1986*, ed. T.M. Charles-Edwards, Morfydd E. Owen and D.B. Walters (Cardiff, 1986), pp. 210–33, at pp. 220–1.

[92] *Berrad Airechta*, § 62 (*ibid.*, p. 221).

[93] Davies, 'The Latin charter tradition', pp. 277–8.

[94] *Ibid.*, pp. 274–80.

[95] *Ibid.*, p. 268.

[96] *Die Irische Kanonensammlung*, ed. Wasserschleben, rev. edn, XLII, § 8, pp. 163–4 (see also XXXII, § 24, pp. 11–18). As Mac Niocaill pointed out, 'Admissible and inadmissible

Hibernensis: Ager inquiratur in scriptione duarum ecclesiarum, si in scriptione non inueniatur, requiratur a senioribus et propinquis, quantum temporis fuit cum altera, et si sub iubileo certo mansit, sine uituperatione maneat in eternum. Si vero senes non inuenti fuerint, dividant.'[97] There is another example of this ecclesiastical stress on written transactions in *Synodus II S. Patricii*, which Hughes dates to the second half of the sixth century.[98] 'Numquam uetitur licet, uirum obseruande sunt legis iubelei, hoc est quinquagissimi anni, ut non adfirmentur incerta ueterato tempore; et ideo omnes neguti<ati>o subscriptione <more> Romanorum confirmanda est.'[99]

Another issue which is relevant to the Irish church's problem with native land law is that of permanent tenure. It will be remembered that the *additamenta* record gifts of land to Patrick 'usque in diem iudicii'. Within secular Irish society, land was owned by the kin-group rather than the individual and was theoretically inalienable. This clashed directly with the need of the church to establish permanent land-holdings, and the compromise adopted was a period of legal warranty, based on the Old Testament *iubilaeum*, from which it was given the name *iubail/iubaile*. Within this variable period (often much less than the biblical fifty years), either party, if dissatisfied, could claim restitution. This was to ensure that land was not alienated without the full consent of the whole kin-group. The compilers of *Hibernensis* accepted the principle, but made some important exceptions to it,[100] stressing that the *iubaile* applied only to family land, but not in other

evidence', 333, we find in the *Hibernensis* evidence that the church accepted both forms of evidence: see particularly XXXVI, § 5 (*ibid.*, p. 129): 'accepi librum possessionis tuae signatum; accepi stipulationes [=*naidm*, 'enforcing surety'] et ratas [=*ráth*, 'paying surety'] et signa.' See Mac Niocaill, 'Admissible and inadmissible evidence', or Sharpe, 'Dispute settlement', for further explanation of these terms.

[97] 'An Irish synod: [the ownership of] a field should be inquired for in the records of the two churches. If it is not found in the records, it is sought among the elders and neighbours, for how long a time it was with the other [church], and if it remained clearly theirs throughout the period of warranty, let it remain theirs for ever, without argument. If it was not found, let it be divided.' Between churches, written record is tried first, then appeal to the memory of witnesses.

[98] Hughes, '*Synodus II S. Patricii*' (see n. 35). *The Irish Penitentials*, ed. Bieler, pp. 184–97, at p. 196.

[99] '*Concerning claims that have become obsolete*: Although these are not forbidden at any time, yet the laws of the jubilee year, that is, of every fiftieth year, are to be observed, so that claims that have become uncertain through lapse of time may not be asserted; and therefore every business transaction should be confirmed by signature in the Roman manner' (*The Irish Penitentials*, ed. Bieler, p. 197). There is a variant version of this canon in *Hibernensis* XXXVI, § 8 (*Die Irische Kanonensammlung*, ed. Wasserschleben, p. 130).

[100] *Hibernensis* XXXVI, § 10 (*Die Irische Kanonensammlung*, ed. Wasserschleben, p. 130). The whole of Book XXXVI (pp. 128–31) is devoted to the *iubaile* and problems of land-law.

circumstances, of which the most practically significant is the gift of land by a king to the church.

This use of charters in the Book of Armagh is a demonstration of the way in which the literate habit of mind did and did not impinge on early mediaeval Ireland. The Romano-British Christians who settled in Ireland appear to have brought the concept of the charter with them, and used it among themselves as the *Hibernensis* and the Armagh *additamenta*, which are evident copies of earlier notes of agreements, both show. Since Christianity is dependent on literacy and the preservation of documents in any case, there was little to be lost by adding the making of notes on property to the scriptorium's tasks. So the reason that the Armagh documents seem to be an isolated experiment must be sought elsewhere. The apparent failure of the most important church in Ireland to introduce the charter as an effective weapon suggests a great reluctance on the part of Irish secular society to accept the imposition of this alien approach to witnessing transactions. Secular Irish society clung to its own way of dealing with land rights. The church's way, as *Berrad Airechta* shows, was recognized to some extent, but not copied. The secular lawyers retained enough prestige and confidence to keep the church from gathering the right to record and arbitrate in land law into its own hands.[101] Tírechán's writing, even as early as the 670s, may represent a move *away* from the charter-like documents which underlie the *additamenta*, since the latter carried no evidential weight outside of the monastery walls, and towards the native Irish concept of appealing to the memory of witnesses. But whereas a secular *senchaid* orally recalled the details of a land transaction, appealing to the witness of common memory and physical objects such as standing stones, Tírechán, standing in a comparable position, wrote circumstantial stories. It is a compromise between an oral and a literate tradition, and it was successfully forced on the church by the secular legal tradition.

The Book of Armagh also offers another level of information about literacy in Ireland, which is to do with its orthography, specifically its spelling of Irish. The text includes an abundance of proper names, and much of the *additamenta* is in Irish prose. Although the book was put together at the beginning of the ninth century, from copies of the texts at least two removes from the originals, the scribes seem to have copied the

---

[101] This, as D.A. Binchy commented, was unusual: 'one of the most revolutionary innovations following the partial "reception" of Roman rules [among barbarian peoples] was the insistence that certain juristic acts, notably transfers of ownership in land, should be enforced in writing. In this way, an illiterate population had to rely on the services of the only persons in the community who were skilled in this novel and mysterious art, members of the clerical order' ('Irish History and Irish Law, I', *Studia Hibernica* 15 (1975), 7–36, at 28–9).

names in the *additamenta* as they found them in the sources. It may also be the case that Muirchú and Tírechán themselves reproduced the orthographic forms found in their written sources. Many names are preserved in very archaic forms, and, even more significantly, there are traces of more than one orthographic system in use.

The background of literacy in Ireland is complex. There is evidence, which is no later than the fifth century, that the Irish developed literacy for themselves, independent of the church, and in direct response to the literacy of the Roman Empire, with which they traded and negotiated. This evidence is in an unique and cumbersome script called ogam, which is a system of parallel strokes, apparently developed for carving on wood and stone, and possibly as a cypher. The surviving monuments are short inscriptions on immovably large boulders, normally saying '[the monument] of x, son of y', or 'of x, son of y, *moccu* z', the last element being a sort of tribal name. This material has been recently subjected to a searching examination by Harvey,[102] who has concluded that in spite of the limited nature of the surviving evidence, some part of the Irish population was literate both in Latin and Irish from a very early date.[103]

The Romano-British Christians who came to Ireland in the fifth century brought with them the Christian's far greater dependence on writing (as we have already seen in the context of the charters), and a characteristic orthographic scheme of their own, which was based on the pronunciation that they used both for their own language and for Latin. As Harvey has pointed out, in an early mediaeval context, the spoken language provides the phonetic fixed point (the concept of a 'reformed pronunciation' of Latin is a very modern one), and Latin provides the orthographic fixed point. Jackson brought out the implications of this in a lucid formulation: 'For example, they [the British] pronounced *medicus* as [meðigəs], and consequently regarded the Latin letters *d* and *c* as *meaning* respectively /ð/ and /g/ when standing between vowels, and so *mutatis mutandis* with the letters *p*, *t*, *b*, *g*, and *k*.'[104] The native Irish and the British orthographic systems are

---

[102] A. Harvey, 'Early literacy in Ireland: the evidence from ogam', *CMCS* 14 (Winter, 1987), 1–14.

[103] It seems historically plausible that the first Irish literates were the merchants or entrepreneurs who dealt directly with the Romans, and that the craft of writing filtered through the community to the native Irish learned class, which maintained considerable faith in the craft of memory-training and oral transmission, and allowed writing only a limited and subsidiary place.

[104] Kenneth Jackson, 'Who taught whom to write Irish and Welsh?', in 'Some questions in dispute about early Welsh literature and language', *Studia Celtica* 8–9 (1973–4), 1–32, at 18. Similarly, in this system, *Patricius* was pronounced /pa:drig(ius)/, *poc* ('kiss') as /po:g/, *popul* ('people') as /pobul/, etc. See also Harvey, 'Early Literacy in Ireland'.

not widely divergent, but are occasionally incompatible. However, the process by which the British-derived orthographic system superseded the native orthography is one of 'merger and adjustment between two only slightly varying systems'.[105] One of Harvey's most important findings is that there is a continuous development between the orthography of the early ogam inscriptions and the standard orthography of Old Irish, with some 'manuscript' spellings on ogam stones, and some 'ogam' spellings in manuscripts. This is complemented by McManus' work on the chronological development of Old Irish, which similarly shows a continuous development from the most archaic types of Latin loanword to the later types, rather than two distinct strata, a wave of archaic 'Cothriche' loans in the fifth century, and another wave of 'Pátraic' loans in the sixth or seventh.

Kelly demonstrated that the orthographic forms in the writings of Muirchú and Tírechán basically reflect the orthography of the original seventh-century authors, even though the Book of Armagh is at least two removes from the original exemplars.[106] One important feature of Muirchú's orthographic system is the doubling of unlenited consonants (*ard* or *ardd*; *ecne*, *eccne*; *mac*, *macc*; *Colgu*, *Colggu*)[107] Harvey has shown in his paper on early literacy in Ireland that in the ogam inscriptions, consonants are doubled to indicate unlenitability, except when they are in word-initial position, where the purely orthographic convention (borrowed from Latin) that words never begin with doubled consonants overrides the phonetic rule.[108] Muirchú's text seems to be showing some acquaintance with this native Irish spelling system, though he normally uses the British-derived method of differentiating lenited and unlenited consonants. Muirchú's treatment of Ultán's name also deviates from standard spelling: the *t* in the name stands for /d/, but when he refers to a book 'abud Uldanum episcopum' the *d* must, presumably, be read as /d/, not as /ð/ (or θ).[109] So the

---

[105] Damian McManus, 'A chronology of the Latin loanwords in early Irish', *Ériu* 34 (1983), 21–72, and *idem*, 'The so-called Cothrige and Pátraic strata of Latin loanwords in early Irish', in *Ireland and Europe: The Early Church*, ed. Ní Chatháin and Richter, pp. 179–96.

[106] Fergus Kelly, 'Notes on the Irish words, with particular reference to dating', *PT*, pp. 242–8.

[107] *Ibid.*, p. 244. The existence of orthographic rules which were to some extent mutually contradictory resulted in a good deal of uncertainty in the writers who attempted to use them. The treatment of post-vocalic /d/ is an obvious case in point, and the rule that unlenited, but non-initial, consonants should be doubled is another. Native users of orthographic systems do frequently misapply their own rules, either by false analogy or hypercorrection – an example of this in English is the misspelling of *weird*, *seize*, etc., which results from the rule '*i* before *e* except after *c*'.

[108] Harvey, 'Early literacy in Ireland'.

[109] The spelling of the sound /d/ post-vocalically (i.e. in the middle or at the end of a word) was

orthographic system used by an Irish bishop in the second half of the seventh century would appear to have some part of its origin in a system of writing the Irish language which was already ancient by his time, and independent of the Romano-British Christian influence on literacy in Ireland. Here, as in the other early Irish manuscript books, we find the confluence of two different orthographic traditions.

This philological research is very exciting in its historical implications, in that it points firmly to a native Irish tradition of literacy, which occupied only a limited place in the social structure. That is, there is not a simple opposition between a literate religion and an illiterate society, but a contrast between a native Irish tradition of literacy, and a writing-dependent Christian Church. The Book of Armagh is a crucial link in the chain of evidence.

The Book of Armagh illustrates the problem of literacy in early mediaeval Ireland in many ways. Directly, it shows the kinds of use that the seventh- and eighth-century church in Ireland made of literacy. Indirectly, it may also be used to shed light on the extent to which literacy impinged on the non-clerical population, and the gap between the church's aspirations and the social and political reality within which it had to operate. It shows us a seventh-century church with a very substantial commitment to Latin literacy, as a look at the surprisingly large amount of seventh-century Hiberno-Latin literature which survives well demonstrates.[110] But for all that, the church on its own, without the substructure of the imperial Roman administration to support it, was unable to bring the crucially important area of property rights and land law into a literate framework. For this reason, the case of early mediaeval Ireland calls into question commonly received notions about the power of literacy in itself to effect social change.

particularly problematic for Irish writers who worked in milieux in which the British-derived orthography had not yet completely superseded the native Irish spelling-system. In British, t lenites as /ð/ post-vocalically, in Irish, t lenites as /θ/. This naturally caused a good deal of confusion and hypercorrection.

[110] The 'Ireland' section of *BCL* lists approximately fifty-five texts of varying lengths and characters known to have been written in Ireland in or before the seventh century.

2

Anglo-Saxon lay society
and the written word

Susan Kelly

The study of literacy in Anglo-Saxon England in some ways resembles the hunt for a certain elusive type of sub-atomic particle: the direct evidence for its existence is negligible but the fact that it does exist can be inferred from its perceived effect upon its environment. When we scour the primary sources for references to reading and writing, to the literacy of individuals, to basic education and book-ownership, our haul is sparse indeed. Inferences drawn from scribal competency can be suggestive, but hardly provide a sufficient basis for general analysis of the quality and extent of Anglo-Saxon literacy. The conclusions that derive from this type of material are plainly limited; they tend to reinforce the traditional view that literacy was essentially an ecclesiastical preserve, for it is impossible to demonstrate that the occasional indication to the contrary is anything more than an exception. Fortunately, the argument can be amplified by considering the problem from a rather different perspective and studying the ways in which the Anglo-Saxons utilized the written word and the extent to which writing superseded speech and memory as the standard method of conveying and storing information. This approach leads us to a rather different conclusion, for it seems to show that by the end of the period, if not several centuries before, written documentation had an important place in secular society and was used in ways which could imply a degree of literacy among certain sections of the laity.

Before we can assess the impact which literacy had on Anglo-Saxon society, it is necessary to try to establish a starting point for the investigation. The obvious answer might seem to be the seventh century, when Christianity and its attendant Latin literary culture gained a foothold in England. But it would be a mistake to see pagan Anglo-Saxon society as entirely ignorant of writing. The Anglo-Saxon settlers brought with them from Germany the runic alphabet and there survives a small corpus of runic inscriptions on stones and on portable objects, which includes examples from the pagan period and from subsequent Christian centuries. Most of these inscriptions are very short, consisting of no more than a name or a couple of words, and some seem to be gibberish, with possible magical connotations. But there is a handful of slightly longer texts, the most significant being the inscriptions on the Auzon (Franks) Casket and the lines from *The Dream of the Rood* which were engraved on the Ruthwell Cross[1].

The limited nature of the evidence makes it difficult to evaluate the importance of runes in pagan Anglo-Saxon society and the extent of runic literacy. A point of some interest is that runic characters were originally devised for engraving on wood, which is only rarely preserved from the early middle ages. The site of the mediaeval city at Bergen in Norway has yielded approximately 550 runic inscriptions on wood dating from the fourteenth century, many of them letters and everyday messages cut into small wooden sticks or tablets which were easily transported.[2] There is some evidence for rune-stick letters in Scandinavian contexts as far back as the ninth century.[3] It is possible that the early Anglo-Saxons made extensive use of rune-sticks for practical communications, but the absence of even one surviving example makes it difficult to proceed beyond speculation. We do have some evidence for familiarity with the runic alphabet among the educated classes of society. For instance, the solution to certain Anglo-Saxon riddles depends upon knowledge of runes, and the poet Cynewulf used them to attach a cryptic 'signature' to some of his works.[4] In the later part of the eighth century two runes (þ, ρ) were adopted into the Roman alphabet for writing words in the vernacular, in order to represent sounds in English (/ɵ/, /ð/, /u̯/) for which there was no Latin equivalent; this suggests that some Anglo-Saxon clerics were literate in runes.[5] There are runic legends on a number of proto-pennies (*sceattas*) from the seventh and eighth centuries and on a few pennies of late eighth- and early ninth-century date from Mercia, Northumbria and East Anglia, which indicates at the very least that some moneyers were familiar with runic script.[6] But there are signs that by the later Anglo-Saxon period runes

---

1 The most accessible discussion of runes and runic inscriptions is by R.I. Page, *An Introduction to English Runes* (London, 1973).

2 A. Liestøl, 'Correspondence in runes', *Mediaeval Scandinavia*, 1 (1968), 17–27.

3 A. Liestøl, 'The literate Vikings', *Proceedings of the Sixth Viking Congress*, ed. P. Foote and D. Strömbäck (Uppsala, 1971), pp. 69–78.

4 Riddles: Page, *Introduction*, pp. 202–5. Cynewulf: K. Sisam, *Studies in the History of Old English Literature* (Oxford, 1953), pp. 1–28.

5 For the date, see A. Campbell, *Old English Grammar* (Oxford, 1959), pp. 12, 26–8, and K. Sisam, 'Anglo-Saxon royal genealogies', *Proceedings of the British Academy* 32 (1953), 287–346, at 310–11.

6 Page, *Introduction*, pp. 119–33; P. Grierson and M. Blackburn, *Medieval European Coinage, I: The Early Middle Ages (5th to 10th Centuries)* (Cambridge, 1986), pp, 158, 293, and nos. 668–9, 685–6, 707–15, 1121a–c, 1236, 1479, 1482.

were no longer in common use and might be regarded primarily as an exotic
script with cryptic possibilities.[7]

It appears that Latin and the Roman alphabet were first introduced into
the Anglo-Saxon areas of Britain by foreign missionaries from the later sixth
century onwards.[8] In southern England the primary influence was from
Rome and the Frankish church, but the north was effectively evangelized
by missionaries from Ireland and Iona and long retained strong cultural
links with these areas, even after the capitulation of the Northumbrian
clergy to Roman usage at the Synod of Whitby in 664.[9] It would be
interesting to consider whether the impact of literacy and the written word
on early Anglo-Saxon society was appreciably different in these two areas,
but the distribution of the surviving evidence makes such comparison very
difficult. From southern England we have numerous documents of secular
interest, mainly in the form of land-charters and law-codes. In the north
and east of the country this type of documentation disappeared, presumably
as a result of the upheavals of the Scandinavian settlements, and thus most
of the surviving material from the earlier period of Anglo-Saxon history in
these areas is concerned with purely ecclesiastical or scholarly matters.[10] It
is clear that Irish scholarship was an enormous inspiration to the Northum-

---

[7] See Page, *Introduction*, pp. 34–5, 69–70, 215; R. Derolez, *Runica Manuscripta* (Bruges, 1954), pp. 137–69.

[8] For the progress of evangelization see H. Mayr-Harting, *The Coming of Christianity to Anglo-Saxon England* (London, 1972). Augustine and his companions were preceded in southern England by Liudhard, the bishop who had accompanied the Merovingian princess Bertha to Kent on her marriage to King Æthelberht I: *Bede's Ecclesiastical History of the English People*, ed. and trans. Bertram Colgrave and R.A.B. Mynors (Oxford, 1969), pp. 72–4 (I.25). The marriage is usually dated to before 560, which implies the presence of literate Franks in Kent for almost four decades before Augustine's arrival. It has been suggested that this was of some significance for the recording of sixth-century events in the Anglo-Saxon Chronicle: K. Harrison, *The Framework of Anglo-Saxon History to A.D. 900* (Cambridge, 1976), pp. 121–3. There is, however, good reason to think that the marriage should be dated rather later, perhaps as late as 581: see I. Wood, *The Merovingian North Sea*, Occasional Papers on Mediaeval Topics 1 (Ålingsas, Sweden, 1983), pp. 15–16.

[9] This clear-cut division should perhaps be modified: see J. Campbell, 'The first century of Christianity in England', *Ampleforth Journal* 76 (1971), 12–29 (reprinted in his collected papers, *Essays in Anglo-Saxon History* (London, 1986), pp. 49–67). For continuing relations between Ireland and Northumbria, see K. Hughes, 'Evidence for contacts between the churches of the Irish and the English from the Synod of Whitby to the Viking Age', in *England before the Conquest: Studies in Primary Sources Presented to Dorothy Whitelock*, ed. P. Clemoes and K. Hughes (Cambridge, 1971), pp. 49–67.

[10] For an indication that the Northumbrian church did produce land-charters see Stephanus, *The Life of Bishop Wilfrid*, ed. and trans. B. Colgrave (Cambridge, 1927; paperback edn 1985), p. 16; and the reference to *regalia edicta* by Bede in his letter to Bishop Egbert: in *Venerabilis Baedae Opera Historica*, ed. C. Plummer (Oxford, 1896), p. 415 and trans. *EHD*, p. 805. See also P. Chaplais, 'Who introduced charters into England? The case for Augustine', in *Prisca Munimenta*, ed. F. Ranger (London, 1973), pp. 88–107, at pp. 101–2.

brian church in the seventh and eighth centuries, but is is difficult to decide whether this intellectual contact had an effect on the assimilation of the written word into Northumbrian society. A potentially important point is that the Irish ecclesiastics, like the English but unlike the Italian and Frankish missionaries, spoke a vernacular which had no basis in Latin, and were therefore accustomed to learning the literary language of the church as a foreign tongue. It is possible that this experience of bilingualism was of value to them in the training of Anglo-Saxon clerics in literary skills, and the consequence could have been that literacy had a deeper foundation in the Northumbrian church. The Irish may also have had some influence on the early development of a tradition of vernacular writing in England, although there is no clear evidence to this effect.[11] I will consider below the links between the vernacular literary tradition and lay literacy.

The primary and most accessible record of the interaction between early Anglo-Saxon society and the written word is the Latin land-charter (technically, diploma) and the associated vernacular documents which deal with land and property. We have some 1,500 such documents from the Anglo-Saxon period as a whole, and about a third of these purport to date from the ninth century or earlier.[12] Approximately 300 charters survive as 'originals', that is, written in contemporary script on separate sheets of parchment; the rest are later copies on single sheets and copies in monastic cartularies.[13] This is a significant collection of material, but it can be difficult to use. A

---

[11] The problems of the Irish missionaries and their attitude to the vernacular are considered by D.N. Dumville, '*Beowulf* and the Celtic world: the uses of evidence', *Traditio* 37 (1981), 109–60, at 110–20.

[12] For a general introduction to Anglo-Saxon charters, see F.M. Stenton, *Latin Charters of the Anglo-Saxon Period* (Oxford, 1955); *EHD*, pp. 369–84; N.P. Brooks, 'Anglo-Saxon charters: the work of the last twenty years', *Anglo-Saxon England* 3 (1974), 211–31. The surviving charters to the end of the reign of Edgar are edited by W. de G. Birch, *Cartularium Saxonicum*, 3 vols. and index (London, 1885–99); later charters are found only in the earlier edition of J.M. Kemble, *Codex Diplomaticus Aevi Saxonici*, 6 vols. (London, 1839–48), in vols. III, IV and VI. The vernacular documents are well edited by F.E. Harmer, *Select English Historical Documents of the Ninth and Tenth Centuries* (Cambridge, 1914), and *idem, Anglo-Saxon Writs* (Manchester, 1952); *Anglo-Saxon Wills*, ed. D. Whitelock (Cambridge, 1930); *Anglo-Saxon Charters*, ed. A.J. Robertson (Cambridge, 1939; 2nd edn 1956) Three important archives exist in modern editions: *Charters of Rochester*, ed. A. Campbell, Anglo-Saxon Charters 1 guide to London, 1973), *Charters of Burton Abbey*, ed. P.H. Sawyer, Anglo-Saxon Charters 2 (London, 1979) *Charters of Sherborne*, ed. M. A. O'Donovan, Anglo-Saxon Charters 3 (London, 1988). The indispensable guide to the study of this material is Sawyer's handbook. For more recent work see Brooks, 'Anglo-Saxon charters', and the articles listed in the annual bibliographies in *Anglo-Saxon England*.

[13] Originals and later copies on single sheets are reproduced in *BMF* and *OSF*. Facsimiles of Anglo-Saxon charters dating before *c.* 800 are to be found in *ChLA* III and IV. Charters omitted from these collections and recent discoveries appear in a British Academy volume: Simon Keynes, *A Handlist of Anglo-Saxon Charters: Archives and Single Sheets* (forthcoming). On the definition of an 'original' diploma, see P. Chaplais, 'Some early Anglo-

fairly high proportion of Latin charters are forgeries or have been in some
way tampered with or rewritten. It is possible that this is true for as many as
a third of the extant texts, and for the earlier period the percentage of
suspicious documents is higher. Some forgeries are blatant, but in other
cases the fabrication or alteration can be detected only by the most subtle
scholarship; sometimes it is not possible to prove one's suspicions of a
document. These difficulties of establishing authenticity should not prove a
deterrent against proper consideration of this type of source-material.
Charters provide the most important illustration of how the secular society
of Anglo-Saxon England absorbed the ecclesiastical gift of the written
word.

The earliest charters with any claim to authenticity date from the 670s
and come from Kent, Surrey and the kingdoms of the West Saxons and the
Hwicce. Shortly afterwards comes the first surviving East Saxon charter.[14]
The date of these charters has led scholars to associate the introduction of
this type of document with the arrival in England in 669/70 of Theodore of
Tarsus and Abbot Hadrian, together with a fresh influx of Italian clerics.
But there are difficulties in accepting this view and some grounds for
suggesting that the idea of the land-charter was current in England at a
rather earlier date. The distribution of the earliest extant texts over such a
wide area of southern England seems incompatible with a very recent
introduction. So does the fact, highlighted by Chaplais, that these charters
broadly conform to a basic diplomatic pattern which is unique to England,
while exhibiting a range of variations within that pattern which suggests
that the local charter-scribes were familiar enough with the basic model to
depart from it with confidence; if the diplomatic initiative truly belonged to
Theodore's time, we would expect a greater degree of uniformity.[15]
Chaplais has argued in detail that the evidence points to the evolution of the
Anglo-Saxon charter over a fairly long period before the date of the first
surviving examples, and to the earliest Roman missionaries as the agents
who introduced the concept into England. Other scholars have recently
suggested that the Anglo-Saxon charter had rather more diverse origins;
they point to possible instances of Frankish and even Celtic influence, and
propose that the idea of charter-writing was introduced into different parts
of England by different agents at different times in the late sixth and seventh
centuries.[16]

Saxon diplomas on single sheets: originals or copies?', in *Prisca Munimenta*, ed. Ranger,
pp. 63–87.

[14] Kent – Sawyer no. 8 (=*EHD* no. 56 (679)); Surrey – Sawyer no. 1165 (=*EHD* no. 54
(672×674)); Wessex – Sawyer no. 1164 (=*EHD* no. 55 (670×676)) Hwicce – Sawyer no.
51 (676); Essex – Sawyer no. 1171(=*EHD* no. 60 (685×694)).

[15] Chaplais, 'Who introduced charters into England?', pp. 100–1.

[16] A. Scharer, *Die angelsächsische Königsurkunde im 7 und 8. Jahrhundert* (Vienna, 1982),

Either contention requires us to account for the total disappearance of the hypothetical charters written before *c.* 670 and the improved rate of preservation immediately thereafter. An attractive explanation is that the earliest charters were written on papyrus, which was the normal medium for charter-writing in both Italy and Gaul in the sixth and seventh centuries. The survival rate of papyrus documents in western Europe is very poor indeed. The earliest surviving product of the papal chancery is a letter of Hadrian I dated 788; beween this date and the second half of the tenth century, when the papal chancery began to use parchment, only forty papal bulls have been preserved as originals, out of the thousands that are known to have been issued.[17] Of the Merovingian charters written on papyrus, Pirenne has memorably observed, 'La rareté des actes mérovingiens ne doit . . . pas nous faire illusion. Ils ne sont que les *rari nantes* échappés au gouffre de l'oubli.'[18] The chancery of the Merovingian kings used papyrus until the later part of the seventh century, when it was phased out in favour of parchment. The available evidence points to the 670s as the period of transition: we have five originals on papyrus in the name of Chlothar III (31 October 657–10 March 673), while the first original on parchment was issued by Theuderic III in September 677.[19] It may be more than a coincidence that the earliest surviving Anglo-Saxon original is a charter of Hlothhere of Kent, issued in May 679. The close connection between the Merovingian and Kentish dynasties has long been recognized. Two kings of Kent married Merovingian princesses, and many of their descendants were given Frankish names (for instance, Hlothhere is equivalent to Chlothar). Wood has recently put a strong case for the existence of Merovingian overlordship not only over Kent but also over much of southern England in the sixth and seventh centuries.[20] This political connection could have led to the imitation in England of some Frankish administrative practices, and could perhaps have prompted the

---

pp. 56–7; P. Wormald, *Bede and the Conversion of England: The Charter Evidence* (Jarrow Lecture, 1984), pp. 14–19.

[17] R.L. Poole, *Lectures on the History of the Papal Chancery down to the Time of Innocent III* (Cambridge, 1915), p. 37, and see Noble's comments in this volume, below, pp. 85–94.

[18] H. Pirenne, 'Le Commerce du papyrus dans la Gaule mérovingienne', *Comptes Rendus des Séances de l'Académie des Inscriptions et Belles-Lettres* (1928), 179–91, at 183.

[19] G. Tessier, *Diplomatique royale française* (Paris, 1962), p. 17. Tessier stresses that the scarcity of originals makes it impossible to be sure whether or not there was an abrupt abandonment of papyrus, but it seems certain that parchment was the normal medium for charter-writing in Gaul by the end of the seventh century. Papyrus continued to be used in Gaul until the eighth century and it seems unlikely that the changing practice of the chancery is to be explained by shortage of papyrus or interruption in the supply: see N. Lewis, *Papyrus in Antiquity* (Oxford, 1974), p. 92.

[20] Wood, *Merovingian North Sea*, pp. 12–18.

jettisoning of papyrus by Anglo-Saxon charter-scribes in favour of parchment. Unfortunately, this argument is difficult to sustain. As we shall see,
charters in early Anglo-Saxon England were almost certainly never written
in any form of royal chancery; they seem to have been drafted and written
mainly in episcopal scriptoria, at least until the early tenth century.
Moreover, it should be noted that the Frankish influence detectable in the
Anglo-Saxon charter is very slight. Direct imitation of the Merovingian
chancery therefore seems unlikely. The papyrus predecessors of the extant
diplomas must remain hypothetical.[21]

The peculiar nature of the Anglo-Saxon charter on its first appearance is
sufficient in itself to suggest a period of development prior to the 670s.
Superficially it seems to conform to normal diplomatic practice, but in its
essentials it breaches some of the most important diplomatic conventions.[22]
The most bizarre aspect is the complete absence of any outward mark of
validation. There is no sign of the autograph *signa* or subscriptions of the
donor, witnesses and notary which were normally found in the Italian
private charter, nor of the autograph valedictions and monograms which
validated papal and imperial documents. The Anglo-Saxon diploma
certainly concludes with a list of the subscriptions of ecclesiastical and lay
witnesses, but these are almost invariably written by a single scribe, usually
the scribe of the text. This is the case whether the subscriptions are in
subjective form (*Ego N consensi*) or objective form (*Signum manus N*), and
in spite of regular claims in the text that the subscription was autograph
(*manu propria*). There is not a single example in an Anglo-Saxon charter of
a true autograph subscription. This should not be regarded necessarily as a
reflection of massive illiteracy among clergy and laity. Italian diplomatic
made provision for the illiterate witness, who was allowed to make his mark
(usually the sign of the cross) alongside the note *signum manus N*. Both
subjective and objective subscriptions in Anglo-Saxon charters are
generally preceded by a cross, but not one of these can be proven to be
autograph; in surviving original charters the crosses are uniform and
presumably written by the scribe of the text.[23] Thus, in an apparently

---

[21] Note that a number of papal privileges and letters were sent to England in the seventh to
ninth centuries and that none of these has survived as originals: see W. Levison, *England
and the Continent in the Eighth Century* (Oxford, 1946), pp. 24–30, and pp. 255–7, for an
ingenious reconstruction of two corrupt papal privileges, apparently transcribed from
fragmentary papyrus originals.

[22] See the discussion by Chaplais, 'Single sheets', *passim*.

[23] Bruckner has suggested that the crosses in a small number of Anglo-Saxon charters might be
autograph, but his examples are not convincing: *ChLA* III, no. 186, pp. 29–31, no. 190, pp.
42–3; IV, no. 236, pp. 16–17. See, however, S.D. Keynes, *The Diplomas of King Æthelred
'the Unready', 978–1016* (Cambridge, 1980), p. 101 n. 54, for a diploma of 993 with
possible autograph crosses alongside some of the subscriptions.

genuine charter datable to 697 or 712 in favour of a monastery at Lyminge, King Wihtred of Kent declares that he has made the sign of the cross because he does not know how to write (*pro ignorantia litterarum signum sancte crucis expressi*); yet all the subscription-crosses in this charter are identical.[24] The witness list of the Anglo-Saxon charter seems to represent an attempt to imitate the outward form of a regular Italian charter without regard for its legal substance. It is difficult to believe that any Mediterranean ecclesiastic could be responsible for such a travesty. Rather, in its received form the Anglo-Saxon charter seems to reflect some measure of adaptation to English conditions and perhaps the dilution of the strict diplomatic conventions at the hands of English clerics trained by Augustine and his successors. The evidence suggests that the number of Roman missionaries who travelled to England was fairly limited, and most seem to have arrived within a few years of each other at the turn of the sixth century. It is possible that the Anglo-Saxon charter acquired its unique features during the central years of the seventh century, when the original missionaries were dying out and their English disciples were taking over the episcopal chairs and scriptoria.

The early Anglo-Saxon diploma is essentially an ecclesiastical document, unlike its Italian models which originated in secular society. In its typical form it records a grant of land by a king to an individual cleric as the representative of his community or to a member of the laity who wished to use the land to found or endow a monastery. The diploma was drafted by an ecclesiastic, usually the local bishop or one of his scribes, on behalf of the beneficiary rather than the donor.[25] The conventional *formulae* employed have a strong ecclesiastical flavour, the most obvious manifestation of this being the substitution of spiritual punishments for the secular penalties threatened against those who refused to abide by the provisions of the grant.[26] The Anglo-Saxon charter reflects the desire felt by the early churchmen to have some written guarantee for their property. But what legal force could such a document have in secular Anglo-Saxon society? It was all very well for the church to assert that its own records, drawn up in pseudo-legalistic form, were proof of ownership. It was also necessary for the validity of the written word to be recognized by the laity.

---

[24] Sawyer no. 19 (=*OSF* III.1).

[25] For discussion of charter-production in early Anglo-Saxon England, see N. Brooks, *The Early History of the Church of Canterbury* (Leicester, 1984), pp. 168–70, and P. Chaplais, 'The origin and authenticity of the royal Anglo-Saxon diploma', in *Prisca Munimenta*, ed. Ranger, pp. 28–42, at pp. 36–42. The case for production of charters by a royal secretariat in the tenth and eleventh centuries is argued by Keynes, *Diplomas*. See also Keynes, below, pp. 244–8.

[26] For penalty-clauses see Chaplais, 'Single sheets', pp. 71–2.

This difficulty seems to have been resolved, at least in part, by incorporating the charter into a formal ceremony marked by highly visible rituals. This kind of activity is not well represented in our sources, but there are occasional references in the early charters to the transfer of a sod of earth from the estate granted and to the placing of the sod or of the charter on an altar or gospel-book.[27] There is some evidence that charters might be stored on the altar or bound into a gospel-book; certainly by the later Anglo-Saxon period and perhaps at an earlier date charters were copied into blank spaces in gospel-books.[28] In this way the charter was visibly associated with the divine. It seems likely that the document was ceremonially handed over by the donor to the beneficiary as a symbol of the transaction, and there may have been some accompanying ritual in which the donor and perhaps the witnesses touched the parchment as a formal guarantee of their testimony.[29] Some early charters have been written in two stages, the witness list having been added at a later date.[30] This suggests that the text of the charter was written out by or on behalf of the beneficiary before the ceremony, and that the witness list was added during the ceremony or subsequent to it. We have some evidence that a note of the witnesses present might be made on a separate scrap of parchment (a *scedula*) for reference when completing the charter; two such *scedulae* survive, sewn onto the parchment of original charters of the ninth century.[31] It should be noted that in one of these two cases the text and witness list of the charter were written by a single scribe apparently at the same time, which implies that when this particular document was witnessed during the conveyance ceremony the parchment itself was blank. It seems likely that, in the eyes of the laity, the transfer of land was effected and guaranteed by the rituals which marked the transaction, and that the diploma was important as a part and symbol of these ceremonies, not on its own account as a written record of the transaction. The value of a diploma as a title-deed resided less in the information which it contained than in its function as a potent symbol of ownership.

This is an important key to understanding the subsequent history of the Latin diploma in England. The churchmen seem to have achieved their aim of inspiring lay recognition of the diploma as a title-deed and thus brought about the integration of the written word into land-ownership. So success-

---

[27] See, for instance, Sawyer nos. 1164 (=*EHD* no. 55), 1258 (=*EHD* no. 79).

[28] Chaplais, 'The royal Anglo-Saxon diploma', pp. 33–6. See also Collins, below, p. 117.

[29] Chaplais, 'Single sheets', p. 77.

[30] *Ibid.*, pp. 83–4.

[31] Sawyer nos. 163 and 293 (=*BMF* II. 9 and *OSF* III. 17). See M.P. Parsons, 'Some scribal memoranda for Anglo-Saxon charters of the eighth and ninth centuries', *Mitteilungen des österreichischen Instituts für Geschichtsforschung* 14 (1939), 13–32, at 15–19, 21–2.

ful was this manoeuvre that laymen also began to acquire written title to land. By the later eighth century we find charters in which a layman is named as the beneficiary and in which there is no clear indication that the land is subsequently to be used for ecclesiastical purposes. By the later Anglo-Saxon period the majority of surviving Anglo-Saxon charters are in favour of laymen, and it seems probable that this represents only a small proportion of the total number of such charters, since on the whole these documents have been preserved only if at some point they entered the archive of an ecclesiastical community. The attraction of acquiring a charter seems to have lain in the type of land tenure with which it was associated, which derived from special measures for the original endowment of the church. Land covered by a charter was *bocland* and could be freely disposed of by its owner, unlike *folcland* which was subject to the normal claims of heirs and kindred, as well as to a number of rents and dues. The Latin charter was a useful way of marking and guaranteeing alienable property, and it could be transferred together with the land to a new owner.[32]

It is this last aspect of the function of the Anglo-Saxon diploma that demonstrates the relative unimportance of its content. A very few of the surviving single-sheet charters bear an endorsement noting the transfer of the land and documentation from the original beneficiary to a new owner. Thus, when a *comes* of King Cenwulf of Mercia came into possession of a Kentish estate and its charter, recording Offa's grant of the land to an abbot in 767, he took care to have the change of ownership noted, confirmed and witnessed on the dorse.[33] This charter was being brought up to date to reflect the changing circumstances of ownership. But most original charters have no such endorsement, even in cases where ownership is known to have changed on more than one occasion. Some of the surviving records of dispute over land show that charters might be stolen or otherwise fraudulently obtained and yet still have the power of proving ownership: possession was all. A well-known eighth-century instance concerns King Cynewulf of the West Saxons. In a document of 798 recording the end of the dispute, we are told that King Æthelbald of Mercia granted a monastery at Cookham with all its lands to Christ Church, Canterbury, and to

---

[32] For discussion of these types of land tenure, see: H.R. Loyn, *Anglo-Saxon England and the Norman Conquest* (London, 1962), pp. 171–5; Keynes, *Diplomas*, pp. 31–3; Wormald, *Bede and the Conversion of England*, pp. 19–23; E. John, *Land-Tenure in Early England* (Leicester, 1960), pp. 51–3; *idem, Orbis Britanniae* (Leicester, 1966), pp. 64–127.

[33] Sawyer no. 106 (=*BMF* I.9). Other examples of endorsements to original charters recording changes of ownership are Sawyer nos. 287 and 332 (=*BMF* II.28, *OSF* I.10), but neither is straightforward. Cartulary copies of charters on occasion contain notes of changes of ownership which could be derived from endorsements, but a number of these seem unacceptable and may have been added by the cartularist or an archivist.

safeguard the donation sent a sod of earth and all the title-deeds to Christ Church to be placed on the altar there. After the death of the incumbent archbishop, the documents were stolen and given to King Cynewulf, who thereupon converted to his own use the monastery and all its possessions.[34] It would appear that land and charter might be transferred to new owners without any attempt being made to alter the text of the charter to bring it into line with the new situation. The charter was a title-deed insofar as it gave symbolic proof of ownership; the content was relatively immaterial. In cases of dispute resort was frequently made to the testimony of witnesses, local inhabitants or supporters who could give evidence about the previous history of the estate.[35]

In the ninth century we seem to see some change in the concept of the charter's function. One of the most important manifestations of this is the development of the boundary-clause. Previously charters had contained only an occasional and vague indication of boundaries in Latin, expressed in terms of the cardinal points of the compass. Reliance seems to have been placed on the fact that local estate-boundaries were well-known. There may have been a ceremony of 'beating the bounds' to impress them on local memories; in the earliest known original charter, datable to 679, King Hlothhere is made to assert (with a poor regard for spelling and grammar) that the land is to be held 'according to the well-known boundaries demonstrated by myself and my officers' (*iuxta notissimos terminos a me demonstratus et proacuratoribus meis*).[36] In the ninth century and later charter-scribes regularly included a detailed boundary-clause in English, which indicates that charters now functioned, at least in some respects, as true written records. It is important to note that this development involved the use of the vernacular.

From at least the beginning of the ninth century onwards, Latin diplomas came to be supplemented by an extensive range of documents in English or in a mixture of Latin and English, which included wills, leases and miscellaneous agreements. The most important of these documents were sealed royal writs, in which the king drew to the attention of the officials of the local shire court or other interested parties any new donation of land or transfer of property or privilege; this was in addition to the issue or transfer

[34] Sawyer no. 1258 (=*EHD* no. 79).

[35] See J.L. Laughlin, 'The Anglo-Saxon legal procedure', in *Essays in Anglo-Saxon Law* (Boston, 1876), pp. 183–305; A.J. Kennedy, 'Disputes about *bocland*: the forum for their adjudication', *Anglo-Saxon England* 14 (1985), 175–95. Patrick Wormald has recently reassessed the place of documentary evidence in such disputes: 'Charters, law and the settlement of disputes in Anglo-Saxon England', in *Settlement of Disputes*, pp. 149–68.

[36] Sawyer no. 8 (=*EHD* no. 56). See also the formal tracing of the boundaries of a Worcester estate to settle an eleventh-century dispute: Sawyer no. 1460 (*c.* 1010×1023).

of a Latin diploma and ensured that the beneficiary's right to the land would be recognized. There is some evidence that such writs might also have been used for routine administrative matters. The earliest trustworthy examples date from the reign of Cnut, but it is possible that similar documents were in use in the tenth century and perhaps earlier. Those writs dealing with land-ownership represent a significant development in the use of the written word in this area. They supplied the deficiencies of the formal Latin diploma as a witness of legitimate possession, and also regularized the informal oral procedures of guaranteeing ownership by recourse to local witnesses.[37]

Rather more complex transactions involving land and property were also recorded in vernacular documents. For example, fifty-eight wills survive from Anglo-Saxon England, of which fifty-three are in English.[38] The earliest example is the will of a Kentish reeve named Abba, which survives on its original parchment and is datable to between 832 and 840.[39] Abba made elaborate provisions for future eventualities, according to whether he were to have a child or whether his widow wished to remarry or enter a convent. His intention was to ensure that the land eventually reverted to his kindred, but even that was not the end of his concern; he further specified which members of his family were to receive the land in turn and what was to become of it after their respective deaths, and finally arranged that if his family should die out completely the estate was to pass to Christ Church in Canterbury. Whoever held the property was to donate a regular render of livestock and other produce to the monastery at Folkestone, and to make extensive gifts of money to the church and to individual clerics: 'and Freothomund is to have my sword'. On the dorse of the document appears an additional statement by Heregyth, Abba's wife, to the effect that future owners of an estate at Challock (probably not the land covered by Abba's provisions) were to pay a specified annual render to the Christ Church community. Abba's will was probably written by a Christ Church scribe; it was witnessed by the archbishop and members of the community and

---

37 For these documents see Harmer, *Writs*, and *Facsimiles of English Royal Writs to A.D. 1100 Presented to Vivian Hunter Galbraith*, ed. T.A.M. Bishop and P. Chaplais (Oxford, 1957). See also J. Campbell, 'Some agents and agencies of the late Anglo-Saxon state', in *Domesday Studies*, ed. J.C. Holt (Woodbridge, 1987), pp. 201–18, at pp. 214–25, and Keynes, below, pp. 244–8.

38 Sawyer nos. 1482–1539. Note that the Latin wills are all late copies and probably represent translations of English originals or fabrications. A number of wills appear in both vernacular and Latin versions, but invariably the vernacular text seems to be primary. A new study of Anglo-Saxon wills is being prepared as a Cambridge doctoral thesis by Kathryn Lowe: 'Literacy in Anglo-Saxon England: the evidence of the wills'.

39 Sawyer no. 1482. This is the earliest will on a separate piece of parchment. Sawyer no. 1500 (805×832) was added to a copy of the charter granting land to the testator.

named Christ Church as the ultimate beneficiary to the land after his family: in return for this last concession, the head of the Christ Church community was to afford his protection to Abba and his heirs and to act as their advocate. There is a definite ecclesiastical interest in Abba's arrangements, but it is not an overriding one; the main concern of the document is the complex provision for the future inheritance of the property within the kindred. It appears as if Abba himself recognized the value of recording this information.

Other laymen and women seem to have felt the same, for the majority of surviving wills relate to lay bequests. Many of them are concerned with the elaborate provisions surrounding the property of the wealthy and well connected. Thus we have the wills of two kings (Alfred and Eadred), two queens, an ætheling, five ealdormen and a number of other individuals known to have been related to the royal dynasty and the nobility. An outstanding example is the early eleventh-century will of Wulfric Spott, a member of an important Mercian family and the brother of Ealdorman Ælfhelm, which disposes of no fewer than eighty estates scattered over eleven counties in north-west Mercia and the southern Danelaw, as well as an enormous amount of treasure, not to mention a hundred wild horses and sixteen tame geldings.[40] There are also a number of wills in the name of men and women of less exalted rank, who make rather humbler bequests. For instance, in the middle of the ninth century Badanoth Beotting, who seems to have been a minor official in the court of King Æthelwulf of Wessex, bequeathed to Christ Church in Canterbury his heritable land, which amounted to only sixteen yokes of arable and meadow. Badanoth specified that the estate was not to pass to the church until after the death of his wife and children, and that they were to pay an annual rent to the community.[41] A number of other wills, as well as some agreements affecting the immediate relations of the parties, refer to a similar arrangement: the donor pledged land to the church and (sometimes) promised an annual rent or render, on condition that his or her heirs were allowed to retain the property for their lifetimes. Such an arrangement satisfied the demands of piety while ensuring provision for dependents, and could also enlist the advocacy of a powerful ecclesiastical community on the side of the donor and family.

The mirror of such pledges was the ecclesiastical lease.[42] Documents

---

[40] Sawyer no. 1536 (=*EHD* no. 125). See discussion by Sawyer, *Burton Abbey*, pp. xv–xxxviii.

[41] Sawyer no. 1510 (=*BMF* II.25).

[42] It is probably correct to see a continuum between an individual's pledge of land to the church and an ecclesiastical lease; they may represent the same transaction from different

recording tenancy arrangements survive in a number of ecclesiastical archives. The most important source is Worcester, which preserved a magnificent series of leases from the eighth century until the end of the Anglo-Saxon period, including no fewer than seventy-six in the name of Bishop Oswald (960/1–92). Oswald leased the lands of the Worcester community to his relatives, his clerics, his thegns and his followers almost invariably for a period of three lifetimes (that is, for the lifetimes of the beneficiary and two subsequent heirs). The scale of Oswald's leasing arrangements seems to have been unusual, but ecclesiastical leases were by no means a novelty in his day: the earliest surviving Anglo-Saxon lease which seems trustworthy dates from the second half of the eighth century, and the practice must have been widespread by 816 when the Synod of Chelsea attempted to limit the timespan of leases of church property to a single lifetime.[43] The larger churches could not hope to farm all their estates in demesne, and it made sound economic sense to let some of their property to free tenants in return for certain payments. The production of a written lease formalized such arrangements and gave the church some guarantee that the reversion clause would be honoured. We have records of well over a hundred Anglo-Saxon leases, probably representing only a small fraction of the total issued since these were ephemeral documents, but only a dozen survive as originals.[44] These show that, at least by the tenth century it was usual to produce such documents in the form of a chirograph. The text of the agreement was written out in duplicate or triplicate (and occasionally in quadruplicate) on one sheet of parchment and CYROGRAPHUM (or a variant) was added in large letters in the gaps between the copies. The parchment was then cut through the word CYROGRAPHUM and the separate pieces distributed to the interested parties and sometimes to disinterested churches or to the king for safekeeping and an additional guarantee. Thus both sides had a record of the agreement and if a dispute arose the copies could be compared and matched. The earliest surviving example of a chirographic lease comes from 904, but there is a possibility that a lost lease of 855 was originally drawn up in this form.[45] The chirograph may possibly

viewpoints. Such arrangements seem likely to have a connection with the Roman concept of *precarium* and its later development in Gaul: for this, see R. Latouche, *The Birth of the Western Economy* (2nd edn, London, 1967), pp. 24–7; M. Bloch, *Feudal Society* (2nd edn, London, 1962), p. 164.

[43] Sawyer no. 1254; *Councils and Ecclesiastical Documents Relating to Great Britain and Ireland*, ed. A. Haddan and W. Stubbs, 3 vols. (Oxford 1871), III, p. 582.

[44] Sawyer nos. 1270, 1281, 1288, 1326, 1347, 1385, 1393, 1394, 1399, 1405, 1417, 1487.

[45] Sawyer no. 1273. See Chaplais, 'Single sheets', p. 63 n. 3.

have had its origin in Ireland, but it reached its greatest formal development in England.[46] It proved a remarkably efficient document and was used for a range of purposes. The reason for the popularity of the chirograph (and perhaps the motive for its invention) may have been its capacity for involving illiterate laymen in the documentary process. The production of chirographs on a regular basis perhaps indicates that secular society took a strong interest in written documentation.

Leases might be written variously in Latin or English or in a mixture of the two. Eleven of Oswald's leases are in the vernacular, but a number of these have some Latin admixture. The rest are basically in Latin, but almost all contain some sections in English, generally a boundary-clause and perhaps a sanction or notes on the conditions of the lease. Approximately a quarter also contain within the text a very brief passage in the vernacular summarizing some portion of the Latin, most commonly the date and the provision that the land was to revert to Worcester after three lives, which were the essential details. The inclusion of such a summary might indicate that the lease might be read by someone who was literate in the vernacular but not in Latin. At any rate, the casual bilingualism of these documents displays something of the linguistic attitude of the scribes who drafted them. It appears that English was not thought to be out of place, even in an important ecclesiastical record.

Other aspects of land tenure and property-ownership were covered by different types of vernacular document. Regularly we find memoranda on the exchange or purchase of land. Thus, when a Kentish nobleman named Godwine bought a piece of land from his sister, Eadgifu, the transaction was noted in a tripartite chirograph.[47] So too was an agreement imposed upon the three monastic communities in Winchester by King Edgar which involved the adjustment of their respective boundaries.[48] We also have a number of documents in both Latin and English recording the manumission of slaves. This would seem to have been essentially an oral ceremony, but the details were frequently recorded, usually in a free space in a gospel-book, as a precaution against a subsequent challenge to the freedman's status. The surviving manumissions date from the tenth century and later.[49] At least by the eleventh century written documentation had come to

---

[46] For the possible Irish origin of the chirograph, see B. Bischoff, 'Zur Frühgeschichte des mittelalterliche Chirographum', in *idem*, *Mittelalterliche Studien*, 3 vols. (Stuttgart, 1966–81), I, pp. 118–22.

[47] Sawyer no. 1473 (1044×1048) (=*BMF* IV.28).

[48] Sawyer no. 1449 (964×975).

[49] See *EHD*, pp. 383–4 and nos. 140–50. No. 147 demonstrates the importance of a proof of free status.

play a part in another important social transaction: we have two vernacular marriage agreements, from Canterbury and Worcester respectively, detailing the property arrangements made between the groom and the bride's kindred.[50] Various documents describing disputes over property and the subsequent settlements have been preserved. Sometimes these appear to be formal records of agreements; an early example is a Worcester document of 825 concerning a dispute over swine-pasture.[51] Elsewhere we find more partisan accounts, designed to be of use in a continuing quarrel; such is the description of a dispute over toll-rights in the Wantsum Channel between the two Canterbury houses, Christ Church and St Augustine's, which consistently sets out the Christ Church point of view.[52] Many land-transactions, whether purchases, exchanges or formal settlements, were guaranteed by supporters who were willing to stand surety for the parties. Fortuitously, two lists of such sureties have survived, almost certainly the remnant of a much larger number of similar records; one of these is an extensive compilation detailing the guarantors for a series of Peterborough estates which must have been put together from scattered records and notes in the abbey's archive.[53] Alongside this we can set a long Bury St Edmunds memorandum about rents and renders which was compiled from miscellaneous material, probably shortly after the Norman Conquest.[54] We can deduce from such compilations and from the occasional fortunate Old English survival that, at least by the end of the Anglo-Saxon period, the great monastic houses kept detailed records of their estates, tenants, rents, stock and disbursements, which supplemented their formal title-deeds.[55] The king and many lay landowners might have followed the same practice; such secular records had no chance of direct survival, but they probably underlie many sections of Domesday Book.

The extent of vernacular literacy among the clergy and the laity and the implications of the use of the vernacular in formal and informal documents are issues of the greatest importance. In the tenth and eleventh centuries, English had a respected place as an alternative literary and documentary language. Some ecclesiastics composed extensively in the vernacular and many manuscripts written in this period contain vernacular texts, such as

[50] Sawyer nos. 1459 (1014×1016), 1461 (1016×1020) (=*EHD* nos. 128, 130).

[51] Sawyer no. 1437 (original charter lost).

[52] Sawyer no. 1467 (=*BMF* IV.20).

[53] *Charters*, ed. Robertson, nos. 47 (Sawyer no. 1452) and 40.

[54] *Ibid.*, no. 104.

[55] For instance, some early eleventh-century farm accounts from Ely survive on binding-strips: N.R. Ker, *Catalogue of Manuscripts Containing Anglo-Saxon* (Oxford, 1957), no. 88; see also nos. 6, 22, 77, 353.

sermons, poetry and translations from Latin. English was a medium of instruction in schools and was regularly used by the draftsmen of leases and agreements and by the royal administration for sealed writs and law-codes.[56] Moreover, from the later tenth century some churchmen made successful efforts to standardize the vernacular by promoting the use of the West Saxon dialect elsewhere in the country.[57] There are signs that some members of the church might be literate in English but have difficulty reading Latin. Bishop Æthelwold of Winchester was commissioned by King Edgar and his wife to translate the Rule of St Benedict into the vernacular, apparently for a community of nuns, and several later manu-scripts of the Rule are bilingual.[58]

Such toleration and encouragement of vernacular literacy as a necessary if regrettable substitute for latinity is usually traced back to the educational initiatives of King Alfred. In the much-discussed epistolary prose preface attached to his translation of Pope Gregory's *Pastoral Care*, Alfred set out his observations on the state of English literacy and outlined his plans to improve it.[59] He began by remarking on the good fortunes enjoyed by England in former times when learning was valued, and went on to complain of such a neglect of learning that hardly anyone south of the River Humber (and probably not many north of it) could understand the divine services in Latin or translate a letter from Latin into English. Indeed, Alfred professed to be unable to recollect a single person capable of these feats south of the Thames at the time when he became king. He saw the beginnings of this decline in the period before the immense devastation wrought by the Viking invaders, and speaks of churches filled with books and a great number of clerics who could not read the books because they were not written in their own language. As a remedy for the general ignorance of the clergy, Alfred decided to promote the translation of essential texts into English. Free-born young men who were otherwise unoccupied were to be taught to read such works in the vernacular, and those who were intended for holy orders could go on to study in Latin afterwards. We have the testimony of Asser that at least some part of this

---

[56] See, generally, D.A. Bullough, 'The educational tradition in England from Alfred to Ælfric: teaching *utriusque linguae*', *Settimane* 19 (Spoleto, 1972), 453–94. For manu-scripts written in the vernacular, see Ker, *Catalogue*.

[57] H. Gneuss, 'The origin of standard Old English and Æthelwold's school at Winchester', *ASE* 1 (1972), 63–83.

[58] *Ibid.*, 73–4.

[59] *King Alfred's West Saxon Version of Gregory's Pastoral Care*, ed. H. Sweet, Early English Texts Society, Original Series 45 (London, 1871), pp. 2–8. For a translation see S. Keynes and M. Lapidge, *Alfred the Great: Asser's 'Life of King Alfred' and Other Contemporary Sources* (Harmondsworth, 1983), pp. 124–6.

educational scheme was implemented; he tells how Alfred's sons and daughters were taught how to read books in Latin and how to write, in the company of the well-born children of almost the entire region and many of less distinguished birth.[60]

The validity of Alfred's remarks about the abysmal state of learning in ninth-century England has been meat for a great deal of discussion.[61] It seems likely that Alfred exaggerated to some degree in his implication that southern England was almost entirely bereft of competent latinists; the fact that he had recruited three Mercian teachers to help in his educational and literary projects implies that the tradition of Latin learning had not completely died out, at least in parts of Mercia.[62] But the available evidence suggests that the standards of Latin in the south were generally poor. Brooks has used the wealth of surviving ninth-century charters from Canterbury to suggest that, even in such an important centre, there seem to have been very few scribes able to draft a Latin charter by the middle of the century and these scribes themselves were unsure of grammar and orthography.[63] Later research has broadly confirmed this assessment and also indicated a gap in the copying of literary manuscripts in the central decades of the century.[64] Alfred seems to have been largely justified in his horror at the decline of Latin learning in ninth-century England and in his understanding that this decline preceded the large-scale Viking attacks; Canterbury charters of the 820s show signs of weakness in Latin grammar and composition.[65] Note, however, that poor spelling and grammar are not found only in ninth-century charters. A dreadful example is the earliest original charter, datable to 679, which was drafted in Kent while that excellent scholar, Theodore of Tarsus, was archbishop of Canterbury.[66] But, in general, reasonable standards seem to have been achieved and

---

[60] *Asser's Life of King Alfred*, ed. W.H. Stevenson (Oxford, 1904), pp. 58–9 (c. 75); Keynes and Lapidge, *Alfred the Great*, pp. 90–1.

[61] See P. Wormald, 'The uses of literacy in Anglo-Saxon England and its neighbours', *TRHS* 5th series 27 (1977), 95–114, and most recently J. Morrish, 'King Alfred's letter as a source on learning in the ninth century', in *Studies in Earlier Old English Prose*, ed. P.E. Szarmach (Albany, NY, 1986), pp. 87–107.

[62] *Life of Alfred*, ed. Stevenson, pp. 62–3; Keynes and Lapidge, *Alfred the Great*, pp. 92–3. The ninth-century Mercian compiler of the Old English Martyrology was also a competent latinist: see J.E. Cross, 'The latinity of the ninth-century Old English Martyrologist', in *Studies*, ed. Szarmach, pp. 275–99.

[63] Brooks, *Early History*, pp. 164–74.

[64] Papers by D.N. Dumville and M. Lapidge delivered at a symposium on 'England in the ninth century' which took place at the British Museum in January 1987.

[65] For example, Sawyer no. 1436 (=*BMF* II.18).

[66] Sawyer no. 8. See Chaplais, 'Single sheets', pp. 65–6.

maintained in the eighth century. The subsequent breakdown in the early ninth century may have been due in part to the attempts of the Canterbury charter-scribes to produce more ambitious and complex documents, and perhaps also to a sudden expansion of output as a result of the extensive land-transactions engaged in by Wulfred in his efforts to reorganize the archiepiscopal estates.[67]

Alfred's scheme to provide regular instruction for the laity in the vernacular and his sponsorship of the translation of important Latin works seem likely to have contributed to the enthusiasm with which English was used for literary and documentary purposes in the tenth and eleventh centuries. Moreover, his insistence that his officials set themselves to studying on pain of losing their position may have provided a foundation for the expansion in the tenth century of the range of administrative documentation in the vernacular.[68] But Alfred's own statement shows that vernacular literacy was already well established in England. Bede seems to have recognized the value of English as a medium of translation, for on his deathbed he was still working on a translation of Isidore's *De natura rerum* for the benefit of his pupils as well as a translation of the first six chapters of St John's Gospel for the church's use (*ad utilitatem ecclesie Dei*).[69] We have a number of eighth- and ninth-century manuscripts containing glossaries, in which Latin words are given an English equivalent; the main function of these seems to have been to facilitate the study of Latin vocabulary.[70] Even before Alfred initiated large-scale translation from Latin, literary texts in English were being copied in scriptoria, although none has survived in contemporary manuscripts; we learn from Asser that Alfred's mother gave him a volume of Saxon poems and that, as king, Alfred made a habit of reading English books aloud.[71] In addition, the use of the vernacular for certain types of legal document was already common in the first half of the ninth century. As already mentioned, the earliest surviving Anglo-Saxon will on a single sheet dates from the 830s. We have an apparently genuine English lease dated 852 from *Medeshamstede*/Peterborough and an English record of a dispute over swine-pasture dated 825

---

[67] Wulfred's land-transactions are discussed by Brooks, *Early History*, pp. 132–42.

[68] For this see *Life of Alfred*, ed. Stevenson, pp. 93–4 (c. 106); Keynes and Lapidge, *Alfred the Great*, p. 110. See Keynes, below, pp. 226–57.

[69] Cuthbert, *Epistola de obitu Baedae*, ed. and trans. Colgrave and Mynors, *Bede's Ecclesiastical History*, p. 582.

[70] W.M. Lindsay, *The Corpus, Epinal, Erfurt and Leyden Glossaries* (Oxford, 1921); M. Lapidge, 'The school of Theodore and Hadrian', *Anglo-Saxon England* 15 (1986), 45–72.

[71] *Life of Alfred*, ed. Stevenson, pp. 20, 59 (*cc.* 23, 76); Keynes and Lapidge, *Alfred the Great*, pp. 75, 91.

from Worcester.[72] Most impressive is a small group of vernacular documents from the middle of the century connected with the affairs of the Kentish nobility. This group includes two grants of annual renders of produce to Christ Church in Canterbury and two to St Augustine's Abbey in the same city.[73] We also find a complicated agreement, datable to c. 871, between an ealdorman named Alfred and Christ Church: in return for a lifetime lease on an estate at Croydon, Alfred promises to bequeath another estate to Christ Church, but also makes arrangements to safeguard the position of his daughter in respect of both estates.[74] Even more interesting is a slightly earlier agreement between a widow and her husband's kinsman about land which her husband had given her, the purpose of which was to ensure that the land was not alienated from his family; the archbishop and the Christ Church community are witnesses and the charter was probably drawn up in the archiepiscopal scriptorium, but the church in no way benefits from the agreement.[75]

The use of the vernacular for such legal documents in the ninth century has been attributed to the increasing scarcity of scribes capable of drawing up a Latin charter. Brooks' work on the archiepiscopal scriptorium at Canterbury, the source of most of these ninth-century vernacular texts, seems to illustrate this tendency. At Canterbury painful efforts were made to ensure that royal diplomas granting land were still produced in Latin. But elsewhere even this last distinction may have been ignored; the evidence is a unique vernacular charter in the name of King Berhtwulf of Mercia, datable to 844 or 845, which concerns a perpetual grant of land at Wotton Underwood in Buckinghamshire.[76] This charter, which survives as an original, is seen as demonstrating 'that at least one Mercian church had already at that time to resort to producing a royal diploma in English rather than Latin, and indeed a very strange form of English at that'.[77] This example may not be as straightforward as it at first appears. We know that in the ninth century it seems to have been the normal practice for a land-charter to be drawn up in the local episcopal scriptorium, although there were occasional exceptions to this rule.[78] The Buckinghamshire estate

[72] Sawyer nos. 1482, 1440, 1437.

[73] Christ Church – Sawyer nos. 1195, 1197. St Augustine's – Sawyer nos. 1198, 1239.

[74] Sawyer no. 1202.

[75] Sawyer no. 1200; see also nos. 1196, 1199. For the relationships between these Kentish noblemen and women see Brooks, *Early History*, pp. 147–9.

[76] Sawyer no. 204 (=*OSF* I.8).

[77] Brooks, *Early History*, p. 174.

[78] See above, p. 43 and n. 25.

granted by Berhtwulf would have lain in the contemporary diocese of Leicester, and the incumbent bishop, Ceolred, is one of the witnesses to this charter. In another charter, dated 844, Bishop Ceolred appears as the initial donor of an estate at Pangbourne in Berkshire, less than 30 miles from Wotton Underwood, which was subsequently granted by King Berhtwulf to the ealdormen of Berkshire; this charter, which was preserved in the archive of Abingdon Abbey, was drawn up in Latin and, although awkward in its phraseology and grammar, it conforms in most respects to the normal conventions of Latin diplomas.[79] The Pangbourne charter seems to show that the tradition of Latin charter-writing was by no means moribund in this part of the Middle Anglian diocese. It may be sensible to treat the vernacular charter concerning Wotton Underwood as an anomaly rather than a clear demonstration of declining standards of latinity. It is possible, although difficult to prove, that the document was a temporary record of the transaction for use in the conveyance ceremony and was intended to be written up in a more formal manner at a later date.[80]

The Wotton Underwood charter is the only example of a royal diploma drawn up entirely in the vernacular. In general, there was a clear distinction between royal diplomas, intended to function as title-deeds, which were invariably in Latin (although by the ninth century it was normal for a Latin diploma to incorporate some sections in English, such as a boundary-clause or a list of appurtenances and dues), and other types of document, such as wills, leases and grants of render, which might be in Latin but which were usually drawn up in-English in the ninth century and subsequently. Weak ecclesiastical command of Latin is thus unlikely to be a complete explanation for the development of a strong tradition of vernacular documentation in the ninth century. The use of English had several functional advantages. In some circumstances English was far more convenient and more accurate than Latin for the type of information that had to be conveyed; this was true for the extensive lists of renders found in ninth-century Kentish documents, which involved some vocabulary for which it would have been difficult to find an exact Latin equivalent, and also for detailed boundary-clauses. Another incentive for using English may have been the need to record a verbal statement of intent or agreement.[81] Above all, the value of English lay in its accessibility to a wider public. A Latin diploma was doubly

---

[79] Sawyer no. 1271 (=*EHD* no. 87).

[80] Compare Sawyer no. 163, discussed above, p. 44, where it seems that the parchment was blank when used in the conveyance ceremony.

[81] For the importance of the verbal declaration see Sawyer no. 1462 (=*EHD* no. 135). Anglo-Saxon wills may also have originated as public statements: see discussion by M.M. Sheehan, *The Will in Medieval England* (Toronto, 1963), pp. 3–106.

inaccessible to the uneducated. Not only did it have to be read out to them; it also required translation into the vernacular. Thus, when two letters of Pope Zacharias were presented to the Synod of *Clofesho* in 747, they were read out and then translated (*et manifeste recitata et in nostra lingua apertius interpretata sunt*); the translation may have been for the benefit of King Æthelbald of Mercia and the *principes* and *duces* who were attending the synod, but it was probably also appreciated by many of the clerics present, especially those in lower orders.[82] A document written in English could reflect more closely the oral procedures which it recorded and could be read out to the interested parties, their supporters and witnesses. While it lacked the dignity and arcane authority associated with the use of Latin, it was more functional in a secular context than any Latin document could be.

The reasons for the early development of the non-Latin vernacular as a vehicle for legal documentation must lie partly in the circumstances of early English history, which included the apparent disappearance of spoken Latin and of all vestiges of the late Roman bureaucracy; Latin was so remote from the secular side of society that greater use had to be made of the vernacular in all areas of administration and social regulation. This point is illustrated most forcibly by the surviving Anglo-Saxon law-codes. The earliest is that of King Æthelberht I of Kent and thus almost contemporary with the introduction of Latin literacy into England.[83] Bede tells us that, among the other benefits which he conferred on his people, King Æthelberht established a law-code according to the example of the Romans, which was written up in English (*Anglorum sermone*) and still observed by the men of Kent in Bede's own day.[84] Three other vernacular law-codes survive from the seventh century, two from Kent and one from Wessex.[85] It has been suggested that the reason for the use of the vernacular in this context was the inability of those clerics charged with drafting the laws to bridge the gaps in legal terminology between Latin and Old English.[86] This explanation is not convincing, since the three later seventh-century law-codes were produced in the years when Theodore and/or Hadrian were resident in Kent; they taught Roman law to their English pupils (among

[82] Haddan and Stubbs, *Councils*, III, p. 362.

[83] *Die Gesetze der Angelsachsen*, ed. F. Liebermann, 3 vols. (Halle, 1903–16), I, pp. 3–8; *EHD* no. 29.

[84] *Bede's Ecclesiastical History*, ed. Colgrave and Mynors, p. 150 (II.5).

[85] Kent – Laws of Hlothhere and Eadric (673–685?), Laws of Wihtred (695); Wessex – Laws of Ine (688–94). See *Gesetze*, ed. Liebermann, I, pp. 9–14, 88–123; *EHD* nos. 30–2.

[86] P. Wormald, '*Lex scripta* and *verbum regis*: legislation and Germanic kingship from Euric to Cnut', in *Early Medieval Kingship*, ed. P.H. Sawyer and I.N. Wood (Leeds, 1977), pp. 105–38, at p. 115.

them Aldhelm, a West Saxon) and were presumably capable of drafting a law-code in Latin if one were required.[87] In the case of the laws of Æthelberht, the path chosen involved the Roman missionaries in an even greater difficulty than finding Latin terms for unfamiliar concepts: namely, the creation of a new literary language from an unfamiliar tongue hitherto unwritten, except in runes. The magnitude of this step should be appreciated. It involved the transformation of sound into writing and required informed decisions on spelling and grammar.

Such an initiative was unlikely to be undertaken solely to produce a law-code. It must be seen in the wider context of the progress of the Roman mission in Kent. Augustine and his companions were already worried about linguistic difficulties before they arrived in England. In order to allay their anxieties, Pope Gregory arranged that they should be joined by Frankish priests who would act as interpreters.[88] Much ink has been spent on the question of the mutual intelligibility of Frankish and English; alternatively it is possible that mercantile and political contact between Kent and Gaul and the presence of Franks at Æthelberht's court had familiarized some Franks with English (and some Anglo-Saxons with Frankish).[89] In spite of the services offered by the Franks, the Roman missionaries had little chance of success unless they quickly came to terms with the English vernacular, which was essential for preaching and for the instruction of English youths and indeed for communication with their royal patrons. It was probably in the process of teaching themselves English that they came to write down the language for the first time, perhaps in the form of glossaries. The only vernacular documents to survive from the seventh century are the four southern law-codes, but it is probable that the new literary language was also used for other material, particularly items required for the basic instruction of clerics. We can seek a parallel in the development of a written vernacular in Germany, where the missionaries (Anglo-Saxons and others) were also faced with the instruction of a people with an unwritten language: the earliest texts in Old High German are glossaries, translations of the Lord's Prayer and Creed, and prayers.[90]

---

[87] Lapidge, 'School of Theodore and Hadrian', 52–3.

[88] *Bede's Ecclesiastical History*, ed. Colgrave and Mynors, p. 68 (I.23); *MGH Epp.* I, pp. 423–4 (=*EHD* no. 162).

[89] Bishop Agilbert, a Frank, declined an invitation to speak at the Synod of Whitby because he would have needed an interpreter and he had previously been dismissed by King Cenwealh because his speech was regarded as barbarous: *Bede's Ecclesiastical History*, ed. Colgrave and Mynors, pp. 300, 235 (III.25, 7).

[90] J.K. Bostock, *A Handbook on Old High German Literature* (2nd edn, Oxford, 1976), especially pp. 90–117; R. McKitterick, *The Frankish Church and the Carolingian Reforms, 789–895*, Royal Historical Society Studies in History 2 (London, 1977), pp. 184–205.

The early English church had to be tolerant of the vernacular if it was to have a priesthood of any size. In his letter to Bishop Egbert, Bede remarked that he had often given the Creed and Lord's Prayer translated into English to priests ignorant of Latin, and he recommended that not only laymen but also clerics and monks with no Latin should be taught these texts in the vernacular.[91] For the church's purposes, the encouragement of vernacular literacy as a prelude to (and often a substitute for) Latin literacy was perhaps inevitable. Without an organized procedure for educating clerics, there was a risk that the expansion of the church in England would leave the priesthood swamped with non-latinists; in the eighth and early ninth centuries the shortage of teachers was probably exacerbated by the departure of so many talented scholars for Germany.[92] It may well have been the dilution rather than the decay of learning which led to the situation bemoaned by Alfred, with a clergy in general incapable of profiting from the library stocks of the churches because the books were not in English.

Basic education in the vernacular may have been available to young laymen as well as to boys intended for the priesthood. We have a little evidence from the early Anglo-Saxon period that the sons of Anglo-Saxon noblemen might attend monastic schools, apparently in some cases as an extension of the practice of sending children to be fostered in another noble household. Thus Wilfrid as a youth was entrusted to the care of a nobleman who had entered the monastery of Lindisfarne and while living there seems to have received some kind of an education, although he was still untonsured (*laicus capite*), and does not seem to have been already destined for the church. When Wilfrid himself became a bishop, noblemen sent their sons to him to be taught (*ad erudiendum*), and Stephanus makes it clear that when these boys grew up they could choose whether to become warriors or priests.[93] We have no way of estimating the proportion of laymen and women who had the benefit of such instruction or the quality and extent of the education that they received. But it seems likely that, as in the case of young men intended for the priesthood, education was bilingual and any training in the skills of literacy would begin (and sometimes end) with the vernacular. This is the impression given by the only detailed description of the basic education of an Anglo-Saxon layman. Asser's account of the successive stages of Alfred's progress in literacy and learning is not as coherent as we might wish, but the outlines can be discerned. The

---

[91] *Baedae Opera Historica*, ed. Plummer, p. 115; *EHD*, p. 801.

[92] See for instance the references to learned men travelling to assist Boniface in Hesse and Thuringia: *Vita Bonifatii auctore Willibaldo*, ed. W. Levison, *MGH SS i.u.s.* LVII, p. 34, trans. C.H. Talbot, *The Anglo-Saxon Missionaries in Germany* (London, 1954), p. 47.

[93] *Life of Bishop Wilfrid*, ed. and trans. Colgrave, pp. 6, 44.

future king remained *illitteratus* until his twelfth year or even later, apparently because no suitable teachers were available. Before this, however, he was an avid listener to vernacular poetry and made a habit of memorizing it. At some point his mother promised a volume of vernacular poetry to whichever of her sons could most quickly understand and recite it; Asser's version of the episode is confused, but it would appear that Alfred took the volume to his tutor, who read it aloud so that he could memorize it. We next hear of Alfred's literary capacities after he became king at the age of twenty-two. Among his many activities he often read aloud (*recitare*) books in English (*Saxonici libri*), while continuing to learn by heart vernacular poems. But he was distressed by his ignorance of divine wisdom (*divina sapientia*) and the liberal arts. To repair this he assembled a coterie of learned men who would read aloud to him, thus allowing him to become acquainted with scholarly texts; Asser explains that he could not understand these works himself because he had not yet begun to read anything (*non . . . adhuc aliquid legere inceperat*). On the face of it this seems to contradict his earlier statement that the king spent part of his time reading aloud from English books. The explanation would seem to be that at this time the king was literate in the vernacular but not in Latin. We might also be correct to see a distinction between the general ability to read Latin and the ability to read complex Latin texts. Asser's account gives the impression that the king could understand spoken Latin, even if he could not read it; it is, however, possible that the scholars were translating and explaining the texts as they read. Asser notes that it was in the year 887 that Alfred first began to read and translate (*legere et interpretari*); here he presumably refers to works in Latin. There is no evidence that Alfred ever learned to write, although his children were taught to do so; we do know that the king later called upon Asser's services as a scribe to jot down striking passages in the works that they were studying together.[94]

No doubt a small number of laymen, like Alfred, went on to understand and even to read Latin. Alfred, in the preface to his translation of the *Pastoral Care* of Gregory, reminisces that there had previously been learned men (*wiotan*) both within and without the church (*ægðer ge godcundra hada ge woruldcundra*); it seems likely that he is referring to Latin learning.[95] Two seventh-century kings were given the accolade *doctissimus* (very learned) by Bede, although it must be admitted that both seem to have been educated abroad.[96] Other early Anglo-Saxon kings

---

[94] *Life of Alfred*, ed. Stevenson, pp. 20, 59–63, 73–5 (cc. 22–3, 76–8, 87–9); Keynes and Lapidge, *Alfred the Great*, pp. 75, 91–3, 99–100 (and p. 239 n. 46 for discussion).

[95] *Pastoral Care*, ed. Sweet, p. 2; Keynes and Lapidge, *Alfred the Great*, p. 124.

[96] Colgrave and Mynors, *Bede's Ecclesiastical History*, pp. 190 (Sigeberht of East Anglia),

showed enthusiasm for learning and literature, and the study of history, involving as it did the achievements of their ancestors and peers, was especially dear to their hearts. Bede implies that King Ceolwulf of Northumbria was actively interested in the progress of the *Ecclesiastical History* and indeed had asked for a copy of it.[97] We discover from a chance reference in a letter of Alcuin that King Offa of Mercia also owned a copy of Bede's most celebrated work.[98] A continuing royal interest in history is reflected in the fact that the first literary work to be produced in the vernacular in Alfred's reign seems to have been the Anglo-Saxon Chronicle.

Vernacular poetry and the Chronicle were secular literature and, even though clerics could and did appreciate the former and may have been responsible for the latter, probably imply a secular audience.[99] Asser provides the information that volumes of Saxon poetry and English books were available before Alfred gave a boost to the written vernacular. From the ninth century we have a significant number of vernacular charters and other documents which show laymen and women taking advantage of the medium of writing to record complex agreements and arrangements about property. It appears that, even before Alfred's time, certain sections of the laity were interested in writing and written material. We cannot tell if laymen in large numbers had acquired the mechanical skills of reading and writing: the details of Alfred's education remind us that in the early mediaeval period listening, reading aloud and extensive memorization were far more important adjuncts of learning than they are today. The strong element of professionalism in the skills of literacy might make it unnecessary for the higher classes of society to practise them; instead they could call on the services of a secretary to take dictation or to read aloud books and documents. In the last resort, the case for widespread literacy in the modern sense among the early Anglo-Saxon laity must remain unproven, and it is impossible even to approach the question of whether lay familiarity with runic writing laid the foundation for reception of conventional literacy or to any extent contributed to the strength of the vernacular written tradition. Nevertheless, it seems clear that already by the ninth century the written word had been accommodated within secular society. Keynes' chapter in

430 (Aldfrith of Northumbria) (III.15, IV.26). Sigeberht was educated in Gaul, Aldfrith in Ireland.

[97] *Ibid.*, p. 2 (Preface). See D.P. Kirby, 'King Ceolwulf of Northumbria and the *Historia Ecclesiastica*', *Studia Celtica* 14/15 (1979–80), 163–73.

[98] Levison, *England and the Continent*, pp. 245–6.

[99] See discussion by P. Wormald, 'Bede, *Beowulf* and the conversion of the English aristocracy', in *Bede and Anglo-Saxon England*, ed. R.T. Farrell, BAR, British Series 46 (Oxford, 1978), pp. 32–95, at pp. 42–9.

this volume demonstrates that by the later Anglo-Saxon period the royal adminstration and the upper reaches of society were using writing, and especially vernacular writing, on a routine basis. No doubt this state of affairs at least in part reflects the success of Alfred's plans for lay education and his wisdom in promoting English rather than the less accessible Latin as a basis for instruction. But Alfred did not initiate the use of vernacular writing in England; rather he attempted to enlarge the scope of books available in English in order to promote learning and philosophy and to improve the calibre of the nobility. English had been used since the seventh century to record material of lay interest. The foundation for the outstanding literary activity of the later Anglo-Saxon period already existed.[100]

[100] I should like to thank David Dumville, Rosamond McKitterick and Simon Keynes for their comments and criticism.

3

Administration, law and culture in Merovingian Gaul

Ian Wood

Merovingian Gaul was, in certain respects, a bureaucratic society; it was 'a society used to, needing and demanding, documents'.[1] This is not to say that documents were used equally by everyone, or in all parts of the Merovingian realm, but that they were regarded as useful by those classes of people for whom we have any quantity of evidence. And while most of the people who feature prominently in the sources were members of the secular or ecclesiastical elite, it is clear from administrative and legal texts that literacy was not confined to the highest stratum of society.

Certainly lay and ecclesiastical magnates had literate administrators, servants and slaves on their estates and in their households. In his account of the trial of Bishop Egidius, Gregory of Tours refers both to a diocesan and to a royal archive in which copies of correspondence were preserved, the former at Rheims and the latter at Chelles.[2] Fragments of financial records from Tours show something of the complications of estate management, and also of the need for documentation.[3] The agents of a great monastery or of a secular magnate must have been able to keep such accounts, although there would have been no need for them to have been as learned as the slave of the senator Felix, Andarchius, who was said by Gregory of Tours to be well versed in Vergil and the Theodosian Code.[4] Felix may have been an exception, but if he was it was because of the extent of his learning, not because of his literacy.

For the use of the written word outside the major institutions and estates

---

[1] P. Fouracre, '"Placita" and the settlement of disputes in later Merovingian Francia', in *Settlement of Disputes*, pp. 23–43, at p. 26.

[2] Gregory of Tours, *Liber Historiarum* X c. 19, ed. B. Krusch and W. Levison, *MGH SS rer. merov.* I.1, pp. 510–13; E. James, *The Franks* (Oxford, 1988), p. 181.

[3] *ChLA* XVIII, no. 659, pp. 3–61.

[4] Gregory of Tours, *Liber Historiarum* IV c. 46, ed. Krusch and Levison, *MGH SS rer. merov.* I.1, p. 181.

of the Merovingian kingdom it is possible to look at diplomatic evidence, although not at the surviving charters, which almost all related to a handful of important monasteries, but rather at the Formularies. These collections of model documents survive largely in manuscripts of the ninth century, but in the case of that of Marculf, the compilation clearly dates from the Merovingian period.[5] Further, individual *formulae* in the other collections can be shown to have been modelled on sixth- or seventh-century documents; for instance, precise historical references in the Auvergne Formulary suggest that one of the texts was based on a document drawn up shortly after Theuderic's attack on Clermont in the mid-520s.[6] It is possible, therefore, to examine some, but not all, of the *formulae* as evidence for the use of written records in Merovingian Gaul.

In certain respects even the Formularies which cannot be shown to have been compiled in the Merovingian period may provide better evidence for the sixth and early seventh centuries than for the eighth and ninth, despite the date of the manuscripts. For instance, the *gesta municipalia*, or local archives, are well attested in Merovingian sources, whereas most Carolingian references to them are to be found in the *formulae*, where they may be no more than outmoded survivals from earlier documents.[7] This is not to say that the Formularies themselves were no longer used at that time, but that their detailed information on local government is not necessarily relevant to ninth-century conditions. It is, indeed, possible that the compilation of the Formularies themselves is a mark of decline; the act of drawing up a volume of blue-prints might suggest that scribal activity had become somewhat spasmodic, and that, in place of a local administrative staff well versed in the diplomatic traditions of the later Roman Empire and the successor states, clerics now had to consult a manual before drawing up a new document. In the case of the Angers Formulary the compiler apparently drew on diplomas in the archives of the city's basilican church, for the most part omitting specific details, in order to create an appropriate handbook.[8] A similar case could be argued for Marculf's work, which presupposes the need for a collection of models, and which was commissioned by a bishop, probably of Paris, Landericus.[9]

---

[5] Fouracre, ' "Placita" and the settlement of disputes', p. 24.

[6] *Formulae Arvernenses* 1, ed. K. Zeumer, *MGH Formulae*, p. 28; I.N. Wood, 'Disputes in late fifth- and sixth-century Gaul: some problems', in *Settlement of Disputes*, pp. 7–22, at pp. 12–13.

[7] P. Classen, 'Fortleben und Wandel spätrömischen Urkundenwesens im frühen Mittelalter', in *Recht und Schrift im Mittelalter*, ed. P. Classen, Vorträge und Forschungen 23 (Sigmaringen, 1977), pp. 13–54, at p. 44.

[8] Wood, 'Disputes in late fifth- and sixth-century Gaul', p. 9 and n. 11.

[9] Marculf, *Formulae, praef.*, ed. Zeumer, *MGH Formulae*, p. 36.

For the sixth and at least for the first half of the seventh centuries, however, the Formularies provide a vivid insight into a society where all sorts of transactions had to be set down in writing, and to be registered in the local archives, which could in theory be consulted in the case of disputes. How easy it was to use the archives in practice is, however, an open question. Even finding a reference to a particular estate in a single document like the will of Bertram of Le Mans is no easy matter, since references to some places occur explicitly as afterthoughts, tacked on as and when they came to mind.[10] It may not have been any easier to find the document itself in the first place. Nevertheless, the will of Bertram, like other wills, deeds and grants, was entered in the *gesta municipalia*.[11] In addition there were plenty of other documents which were not publicly registered, or which nobody expected to be able to find in the public archives; hence the Auvergne *formula* dating apparently to the 520s, which deals with the problem of making good the destruction of deeds.[12] Similar *formulae* in the Angers collections deal with the theft of documents, and with the processes by which men justified their claims to land before two *cartae* could be drawn up, one for the landowner and the other to be kept *in foro publico*, which may be another way of referring to the *gesta*.[13]

Most of the Formularies are concerned primarily with providing models of documents which would be of use to local administrators, although by no means all envisage registration in the *gesta municipalia*. Indeed, they are not simply concerned with land and property, even if deeds of gift, dowry and sale do form a substantial portion of the *formulae*. There are in addition models for documents of protection, dependence, and manumission as well as blue-prints for legal judgements, apparently appropriate for local courts. Not all of these can be dated to the Merovingian period; nevertheless those preserved by Marculf show that many of these types of document were in existence by the early eighth century.[14]

Marculf is not only important in showing the variety of *formulae* which were definitely known in the Merovingian period, but he is also unique in providing numerous specimen orders addressed by the king to his agents. There are royal requisitions, gifts, grants of protection, responses to

---

[10] Bertram of Le Mans, *Testamentum*, in *Actus Pontificum Cenomannis in urbe degentium*, ed. G. Busson and A. Ledru (Le Mans, 1901), for example pp. 114 (*Pene michi in oblivione fuit positum*), and 139 (*Adhuc parva memoravi quod valde in oblivione tradidi*). On making alterations to wills, see Marculf, *Formulae* II.17, ed. Zeumer, *MGH Formulae*, pp. 86–8.

[11] Bertram, *Testamentum*, p. 141.

[12] *Formulae Arvernenses* 1, ed. Zeumer, *MGH Formulae*, p. 28.

[13] *Formulae Andecavenses* 32, ed. Zeumer, *MGH Formulae*, pp. 14–15.

[14] Marculf, *Formulae* I.18, 22, 24, II.5, 28, 32, 33, 34, 39, 40, ed. Zeumer, *MGH Formulae*, pp. 55, 57, 58, 77–8, 93, 95–6, 98–100.

petitions, orders for the appointment of bishops, for the execution of justice and arrangements of redress, as well as model replies to announce the arrival of the king's command.[15] Although no other source gives a comparable idea of the range of written orders emanating from the Merovingian court, Marculf's evidence suggests that royal government should be considered as being tied firmly to the written word.

It is worth approaching the legislation of the Merovingian kings with this in mind. Most obviously related to this tradition of written law are the edicts appended to the *Pactus Legis Salicae*, the *Pactus pro tenore pacis*, the *Edictus Chilperici* and the laws of Childebert II,[16] but there is also legislation within *Lex Ribuaria* which must have originally been issued as edicts, as can be seen from the phraseology of individual clauses.[17] In this respect the general profile of the major Merovingian codes, which do not claim to be the legislation of individual monarchs, is misleading. Hidden within the texts are unascribed edicts, giving further emphasis to the written nature of sixth- and seventh-century government. In the minor courts of the Merovingian kingdom the lawmen may have been illiterate,[18] but there was, nevertheless, a strong tradition of written legislation and of written instruction, which would have worked most smoothly when officials could read; at the very least they required a literate household.[19]

That the leading officials of the Merovingian kingdom could write is shown by the signatures of mayors and counts of the palace to be found on original charters which survive from the Merovingian period. Some officials, indeed, were able not only to sign their names in cursive, but also to attest documents in the short-hand system known as tironian notes.[20] Nor were they the only people to subscribe to Merovingian charters. Among the surviving originals is a document of 673, in which Chrotildis installs her niece as abbess of Bruyères-le-Châtel; ratifying this action are twenty-four signatures, including those of clerics and laymen.[21]

---

[15] *Ibid.*, I, *passim*; for several of the relevant texts in translation, and a discussion, see James, *The Franks*, pp. 186–9.

[16] *Pactus legis Salicae, capitulare legi salicae addita* II, IV, VI, ed. K.A. Eckhardt, *MGH Leges nat. germ.* IV.1, pp. 250–4, 261–3, 267–9.

[17] See the use of the verb *iubere* in *Lex Ribuaria* 61.i, vii, 91.i, ii. ed. F. Beyerle and R. Buchner, *MGH Leges nat. germ.* III.2, pp. 108–9, 111, 133–4.

[18] For the courts of the *rachymburgi* see Fouracre, ' "Placita" and the settlement of disputes', pp. 39–41.

[19] Compare Asser, *De rebus gestis Alfredi*, c. 106, in *Asser's Life of King Alfred*, ed. W.H. Stevenson (Oxford, 1904), pp. 92–5.

[20] D. Ganz, 'Bureaucratic shorthand and Merovingian learning', in *Ideal and Reality in Frankish and Anglo-Saxon Society*, ed. P. Wormald (Oxford, 1983), pp. 58–75, at pp. 61–2.

[21] *ChLA* XIII, no. 564, p. 63.

Other documents carry the autographs of kings, including those of Chlothar II, Dagobert I, Clovis II, Childebert III and Chilperic II.[22] The ability of the seventh- and eighth-century kings to sign their own names may not tell us as much about their literary skills as do the poems of Chilperic I,[23] or even Gregory of Tours' concise description of Gundovald, brought up as is the custom of kings, long-haired and literate, *litteris eruditus*,[24] but it does suggest that members of the royal family were able to read and write throughout the seventh and early eighth centuries.

It appears, therefore, that literacy was not uncommon in Merovingian Gaul, and it is likely that many members of the royal court, from the king downwards, were able to read and write. This last point can be supported not just by charter subscriptions, but by the *Vitae* of those saints who spent the early parts of their careers in royal service, although here there is reference not to basic literacy but to learning in general, and in particular to legal knowledge. Thus Desiderius of Cahors learnt Roman law,[25] and Bonitus of Clermont knew the Theodosian Code.[26] Leodegar was handed over by his uncle, Dido of Poitiers, *ad diversis studiis, quae saeculi potentes studire solent*, and we are told specifically that he had a knowledge of secular and canon law.[27] The second *Passio* of Leodegar describes him as being learned in *litterarum studiis*.[28]

That a knowledge of law, both secular and ecclesiastical, was common, at least among those royal servants for whom we have detailed information, is not surprising; at times both Desiderius and Bonitus had to exercise secular judicial functions,[29] and as bishops they and Leodegar had legal roles to fill. Not all learning and culture, however, was so directly utilitarian, and yet almost all of the most literate figures of the Merovingian age were administrators of note. Parthenius, who had a particularly bad press from Gregory of Tours because of his rapacity, which eventually prompted his murder at the hands of the people of Trier, was the grandson of Ruricius of Limoges,

[22] *Ibid.*, nos. 551, 552, 554, 555, pp. 10, 16, 22, 26; *ibid.* XIV, nos. 583, 587, 588, 593, pp. 38, 55, 58, 80.

[23] Gregory of Tours, *Liber Historiarum* V c. 44, ed. Krusch and Levison, *MGH SS rer. merov.* I.1, p. 254; see D. Norberg, *La Poésie latine rythmique* (Stockholm, 1954), pp. 31–40.

[24] Gregory of Tours, *Liber Historiarum* VI c. 24, ed. Krusch and Levison, *MGH SS rer. merov.* I.1, p. 291.

[25] *Vita Desiderii* c. 1, ed. B. Krusch, *MGH SS rer. merov.* IV, p. 564.

[26] *Vita Boniti* c. 2, ed. B. Krusch, *MGH SS rer. merov.* VI, p. 120.

[27] *Passio Leudegarii* I c. 1, ed. B. Krusch, *MGH SS rer. merov.* V, pp. 283–4.

[28] *Passio Leudegarii*, II c. 1, ed. B. Krusch, *MGH SS rer. merov.* V, p. 324.

[29] *Vita Desiderii* c. 7, ed. Krusch, *MGH SS rer. merov.* IV, p. 568; *Vita Boniti* cc. 2–3, ed. Krusch, *MGH SS rer. merov.* VI, pp. 120–1.

and was related to Sidonius Apollinaris.[30] He received an education at
Ravenna and was clearly a man of literary pretensions. Childebert II's
tutor, Gogo, seems to have regarded Parthenius as a rhetorician to be
emulated, and he himself was the author of a number of florid letters
preserved in the collection known as the *Epistulae Austrasiacae*, which may
have been compiled as a set of exemplars.[31] In this same collection there are
letters of other magnates of the period, most notably the patrician
Dynamius. Like Parthenius, he came from a family which could boast a
number of distinguished men of letters, and he numbered among his
correspondents Gregory the Great and Venantius Fortunatus.[32] He also
played a significant, if not altogether praiseworthy, role in the Provençal
politics of his time. Numerous other politicians are commemorated in the
poems of Venantius Fortunatus, which provide the fullest insight into the
court circles of late sixth-century Francia.[33] Granted the known cultural
aspirations and achievements of these men, it is not surprising that
Asclepiodotus, who drafted legislation for both Guntram and Childebert
II, was a man of some literary skill.[34]

The letters of the *Epistulae Austrasiacae* and the poems of Venantius
Fortunatus belong firmly to the sixth century, but the literary traditions
which they represent continue well into the seventh, as can be seen in
another letter collection: that of Desiderius of Cahors.[35] From a Gallic
point of view the traditions begin in the fifth century with Sidonius
Apollinaris, who was explicitly considered to be a model writer by his
relatives, Avitus of Vienne and Ruricius of Limoges.[36] Ferreolus of Uzès is
also said to have written books of letters in the manner of Sidonius,[37]
although these have not survived. The opening letters in the *Epistulae*

[30] Gregory of Tours, *Liber Historiarum* III c. 36, ed. Krusch and Levison, *MGH SS rer.
merov.* I.1, pp. 131–2; K.F. Stroheker, *Der senatorische Adel im spätantiken Gallien*
(Tübingen, 1948), no. 283, p. 199.

[31] *Epistulae Austrasiacae* 13, 16, 22, 48, ed. W. Gundlach, *MGH Epp. merov. et karol.* I, pp.
128, 130, 134–5, 152–3.

[32] *Ibid.*, 12, 17, *ibid.*, pp. 127, 130–1; Stroheker, *Der senatorische Adel*, no. 108, pp. 164–5.

[33] R. Koebner, *Venantius Fortunatus* (Berlin, 1915), pp. 28–39; D. Tardi, *Fortunat* (Paris,
1927), pp. 113–32.

[34] Stroheker, *Der senatorische Adel*, no. 38, p. 149; C.P. Wormald, 'The decline of the
Western Empire and the survival of its aristocracy', *Journal of Roman Studies* 66 (1976),
217–26, at 224.

[35] Desiderius of Cahors, *Epistulae*, ed. W. Arndt, *MGH Epp. merov. et karol.* I.

[36] Avitus, epp. 43, 51, ed. R. Peiper, *MGH AA* VI.2, pp. 72–3, 79–81; Ruricius, ep. II.26, ed.
B. Krusch, *MGH AA*, VIII, pp. 332–3.

[37] Gregory of Tours, *Liber Historiarum* VI c. 7, ed. Krusch and Levison, *MGH SS rer. merov.*
I.1, p. 276.

Austrasiacae were written by Remigius of Rheims, a contemporary and a correspondent of Avitus,[38] and, while the collection contains no letters which can be securely dated to the 520s and 530s, continuity in the tradition of letter-writing can be inferred from the works of Arator, friend and fellow student of Ruricius' grandson Parthenius, whom Gogo cited in the next generation as a master of rhetoric.[39] By the time of Gogo, however, the art of letters had received a further fillip with the arrival of Venantius Fortunatus. Although there is a gap of some thirty years between the last letter in the *Epistulae Austrasiacae* and the first in the correspondence of Desiderius of Cahors, both belong to the same tradition of letter-writing. How far the tradition survived Desiderius is more difficult to determine. There are a handful of Merovingian letters later in date than the last in his collection, but they are isolated examples and do not have to be seen in the same context as those written by him or his literary forebears.[40] As for the letters of Boniface, despite the fact that they share certain characteristics with those of Sidonius, the *Epistolae Austrasiacae* and Desiderius, it is clear from his more private letters, which are directed largely to Anglo-Saxon friends and well-wishers,[41] and also from the letters of Aldhelm,[42] that a tradition of letter-writing was already established in England, and it was that, rather than the survival of late antique culture in Francia, which lay behind Boniface's own style of correspondence.

The Gallic and Frankish letters deal with a wide range of topics, and do so in a variety of styles. It is, nevertheless, possible to talk about them as belonging to a coherent genre of letter-writing because throughout the various collections are to be found letters whose chief concern is the cultivation of friendship, of *amicitia* in the earlier collections, or of *dulcedo* (sweetness) in the writings of Venantius Fortunatus.[43] That such letters were written, despite the apparently insignificant nature of their contents, is an indication, on the one hand, of the strength of literary tradition within court circles, and, on the other, of the continuing value of such letters for sixth- and seventh-century society.

---

[38] *Epistulae Austrasiacae* 1–4, ed. Gundlach, *MGH Epp. merov. et karol.* I, pp. 112–16; Avitus, ep. 98, ed. Peiper, *MGH AA* VI.2, p. 103.

[39] Arator, *Epistola ad Parthenium*, ed. A. McKinlay, CSEL LXXII (Vienna, 1951), pp. 150–3; *Epistulae Austrasiacae* 16, ed. Gundlach, *MGH Epp. merov. et karol.* I, p. 130.

[40] *Epistulae Aevi Merovingici Collectae* 16, 17, ed. W. Gundlach, *MGH Epp. merov. et karol.* I, pp. 461–7.

[41] Boniface, *Epistolae*, ed. M. Tangl, *Die Briefe des heiligen Bonifatius und Lullus, MGH Epp. sel.* I.

[42] Aldhelm, ed. R. Ewald, *MGH AA* XV; see also *Aldhelm: The Prose Works*, trans. M. Lapidge and M. Herren (Ipswich, 1979).

[43] J.M. Wallace-Hadrill, *The Frankish Church* (Oxford, 1983), p. 83.

In the late Roman period the exercise of friendship, especially through letter-writing, was important in ensuring that a senator had a range of contacts on whom he could call to assist him in any eventuality; the classic example of this is to be found in the correspondence of Symmachus.[44] Similar concerns underlie the writings of Venantius Fortunatus, who, as a foreigner, was dependent on the kindness of others.[45] Desiderius of Cahors presents an analogous case; having served at court as treasurer to Chlothar II, he was sent to Marseilles as count by Dagobert I, and was subsequently appointed to the bishopric of Cahors.[46] His letters date largely from this last period of his life, and represent a determined attempt to keep up contacts so that, geographically separated though he was from court politics, he might still be able to call on old friends when he needed their help. Among his correspondents were Dagobert I, Sigibert III, Grimoald, the mayor of the palace and a number of powerful bishops, including Eligius of Noyon and, above all, Audoin of Rouen, to whom he addressed a famous letter, reminding him of times past, when the two of them and Eligius, amongst others, were all present at the court of Chlothar II.[47]

Equally remarkable are a group of letters addressed to Desiderius from his mother, Herchenafreda.[48] These are not preserved along with those written by the saint, but are included in the *Vita Desiderii*, whose author clearly had access to a larger collection than that which now survives. Herchenafreda's letters cast particular light on two further points; first, on the role of letter-writing within the family – a point that can also be paralleled in the works of Sidonius, Avitus, Ruricius and Ennodius;[49] and second, on the important part a woman could play in this aspect of the maintenance of family cohesion. Other literate women are known from the seventh century,[50] but these letters provide a unique example of such a woman manipulating traditions of culture and communication to preserve

[44] J.F. Matthews, 'The letters of Symmachus', in *Latin Literature of the Fourth Century*, ed. J.W. Binns (London, 1974), pp, 58–99, at p. 64.

[45] Koebner, *Venantius Fortunatus*, pp. 30–1.

[46] *Vita Desiderii* cc. 2–15, ed. Krusch, *MGH SS rer. merov.* IV, pp. 564–74.

[47] Desiderius, epp. I. 2–6, 10, II.6, 9, 17, ed. Arndt, *MGH Epp. merov. et karol.* I, pp. 194–6, 199, 206, 207–8, 212.

[48] *Vita Desiderii* cc. 9, 10, 11, ed. Krusch, *MGH SS rer. merov.* IV, pp. 569–70.

[49] The genealogies included in Stroheker, *Der senatorische Adel*, depend precisely on this.

[50] Apart from the *Vita Radegundis* by Baudonivia, ed. B. Krusch, *MGH SS rer. merov.* II, pp. 377–95, it might reasonably be assumed that the lives of two other queens edited in the same volume by Krusch, the *Vita Balthidis*, pp. 482–508, and the *Vita Geretrudis*, pp. 453–64, were also written by women. See also n. 107 below, p. 78.

the status of her family, despite the death of one son and the murder of another.[51]

The friendship letters of the Merovingian period, like those of the fifth century, tend to be written in a style which has been identified in the writings of Sidonius Apollinaris as the *stylum pingue atque floridum*.[52] It was the style thought appropriate for correspondence between friends, and its elaborate ornamentation was intended to delight the reader. The importance of choosing an appropriate style was well known to anyone with a proper rhetorical training. Avitus of Vienne explicitly tailored his style to his audience,[53] and it is probable that Caesarius of Arles cultivated literary *rusticitas* not because of any rhetorical incompetence, but because he regarded the simple style as appropriate for sermons which were intended to attract large congregations drawn from all classes of society.[54] That an appreciation of style remained is apparent from Gogo's comment on the *rethorica dictio* of Parthenius.[55] The letters of Gogo, Desiderius and their correspondents must have been deliberately florid.

This awareness of style is in apparent contradiction to Gregory of Tours' comment that 'the exercise of the liberal arts is in decline, or rather is dying, in the cities of Gaul',[56] an opinion which the bishop's own Latin is sometimes thought to substantiate. Problems of the textual transmission of Gregory's *Histories*, however, make it difficult to determine the exact nature of this Latin; it may well be that the earliest manuscript is not a good guide to what Gregory actually wrote, and that he should be credited with the more classicizing language of later manuscripts.[57] Besides, there is a further point: it is quite wrong to confuse questions relating to the use of classical grammar with those concerned with adherence to stylistic traditions, especially in a period of linguistic change, like that of the sixth, seventh and eighth centuries, when Latin developed slowly into a variety of proto-Romance forms.

---

[51] *Vita Desiderii* c. 11, ed. Krusch, *MGH SS rer. merov.* IV, p. 570.

[52] A. Loyen, *Sidoine Apollinaire et l'esprit précieux en Gaule* (Paris, 1943), pp. 129–34.

[53] Avitus, *De spiritalis historiae gestis, prologus*, ed. Peiper, *MGH AA* VI.2, pp. 201–2.

[54] M.-J. Delage, *Césaire d'Arles: sermons au peuple*, Sources Chrétiennes 175 (Paris, 1971), pp. 180–208.

[55] *Epistulae Austrasiacae* 16, ed. Gundlach, *MGH Epp. merov. et karol.* I, p. 130.

[56] Gregory of Tours, *Libri Historiarum, praefatio*, ed. Krusch and Levison, *MGH SS rer. merov.* I.1, p. 1.

[57] W. Goffart, 'From *Historiae* to *Historia Francorum* and back again: aspects of the textual history of Gregory of Tours', in *Religion, Culture and Society in the Early Middle Ages*, ed. T.F.X. Noble and J.J. Contreni (Kalamazoo, 1987), pp. 55–76.

Gregory's own writings not only display a great gift for narrative,[58] but also an awareness of appropriate style, despite the bishop's protestations of incompetence. Indeed the protestations are themselves an indication of such an awareness, and in general the prefaces to the *Histories*, especially that to book 5 denouncing civil war, employ rhetoric with some skill. Gregory also uses rhetorical tricks to dramatic effect in his condemnation of Chilperic I as 'the Nero and Herod of our time', appropriately placed to provide a survey of the king's life, after the account of his murder.[59]

A similar sense of correct form can be found in the *Vita Columbani* of Jonas of Bobbio, which is prefaced by a dedicatory letter, whose Latin is remarkable for its obscurity. Two factors combine to make this so: on the one hand Jonas' grammar and orthography are far from being classical, on the other he deliberately chose a florid style as being appropriate to his purpose. True to tradition he reserves his most elaborate writing for an expression of his own unworthiness, contrasting his celtic nard with the balsam of earlier writers.[60] The mixture of seventh-century grammar and the tricks of late antique rhetoric make the passage well-nigh incomprehensible, but it does show a commitment to appropriate literary form, and an awareness that a hagiographical preface has a specific function in that it provides the author with an opportunity to place himself, or herself, in a particular relationship with subject, patron and audience. The narrative section of a saint's life is concerned with other matters, and fortunately in the main body of the work Jonas resorts to a clearer style, fit for the task in hand.

Jonas' works might be claimed as a monument to Lombard culture, since although he came from Susa, which was in Merovingian hands,[61] he was educated at Columbanus' Italian monastery of Bobbio. Such national distinctions, however, are of little significance; the third abbot of Bobbio was Bertulf, a relative of Arnulf of Metz.[62] In any case, other Merovingian

---

[58] Gregory's narrative skills have generally been recognized; for two recent surveys of traditional interpretations of Gregory's art see G. de Nie, *Views from a Many-Windowed Tower* (Amsterdam, 1987), pp. 1–26, and W. Goffart, *The Narrators of Barbarian History* (Princeton, 1988), pp. 112–19. Both authors go on to offer major new interpretations of Gregory's writings.

[59] Gregory of Tours, *Liber Historiarum* VI c. 46, ed. Krusch and Levison, *MGH SS rer. merov.* I.1, pp. 319–21.

[60] Jonas, *Vita Columbani*, ep. to Waldebert and Bobolenus, ed. B. Krusch, *MGH SS rer. merov.* IV, pp. 61–3.

[61] Fredegar, *Chronica* IV c. 45, ed. J.M. Wallace-Hadrill, *The Fourth Book of the Chronicle of Fredegar* (London, 1960), pp. 37–9.

[62] Jonas, *Vita Columbani* II c. 23, ed. Krusch, *MGH SS rer. merov.* IV, p. 114.

saints' lives are also prefaced with letters of dedication which are written in a style more elaborate than the rest of the work, but which nevertheless invoke the traditional disclaimer of incompetence; Audoin, in his preface to the *Vita Eligii* emphasized the rusticity of his Latin,[63] as did the author of the first *Passio Leudegarii*;[64] the author of the life of Wandregisil stressed his incompetence,[65] and the man who wrote the *Vita Boniti* announced his unworthiness.[66] This awareness of the idea that certain styles were regarded as appropriate to particular tasks is, thus, to be found throughout the Merovingian period, and has its palaeographical counterpart in the use of *litterae elongatae* for kings' names in original charters.[67]

The appropriate use of style raises interesting questions about education in the sixth and seventh centuries. The schools of rhetoric which had existed in late antique Gaul seem to have come to an end in the sixth century at the latest,[68] although it is possible that some form of secular education was still available during the reign of Chilperic I, since he ordered all the *civitates* to teach young boys an alphabet with an extra four letters.[69] Some of the early Merovingian writers whose letters are contained in the *Epistulae Austrasiacae* could have had access, therefore, to a traditional Roman education. For the most part, however, we are probably dealing, even in the sixth century, with the products of a very much less developed educational system, dominated by local schools, such as that in Avallon attended by Germanus of Paris,[70] or that in the Auvergne, where Leobardus learnt the

---

[63] Audoin, *Vita Eligii, praef.*, ed. B. Krusch, *MGH SS rer. merov.* IV, pp., 663–5.

[64] *Passio Leudegarii* I, ep. to Herminarius, ed. Krusch, *MGH SS rer. merov.* V, p. 282.

[65] *Vita Wandregisili* c. 1, ed. B. Krusch, *MGH SS rer. merov.* V, p. 13.

[66] *Vita Boniti, prol.*, ed. Krusch, *MGH SS rer. merov.* VI, p. 119.

[67] *ChLA* XIII, nos. 565–8, 570, pp. 68, 71, 76, 78; *ChLA* XIV, nos. 572–7, 579, 581, 584–91, 593, pp. 8, 11, 15, 23, 32, 42, 46, 49, 55, 58, 63, 66, 68, 80; compare the lack of *litterae elongatae* in the charters of Pippin III before his usurpation; *ChLA* XIV, nos. 595–6, pp. 3, 8. This should perhaps be set in the wider context of the notion of a hierarchy of scripts, which was established 'by the beginning of the eighth century'; see R. McKitterick, 'The scriptoria of Merovingian Gaul: a survey of the evidence', in *Columbanus and Merovingian Monasticism*, ed. H.B. Clarke and M. Brennan, BAR, International Series 113 (Oxford, 1981), pp. 173–207, at p. 189; and see D. Ganz, 'The preconditions for caroline minuscule', *Viator* 18 (1987), 23–44, at 32, where the full development of the technique is placed in the context of the Carolingian renaissance.

[68] P. Riché, *Education et culture dans l'occident barbare, vie–viiie siècles* (3rd edn, Paris, 1962), pp. 69–75.

[69] Gregory of Tours, *Liber Historiarum* V c. 44, ed. Krusch and Levison, *MGH SS rer. merov.* I.1, p. 254.

[70] Venantius Fortunatus, *Vita Germani* c. 2, ed. B. Krusch, *MGH AA* IV.2, p. 12; Riché, *Education et culture*, pp. 324–6.

psalms.[71] In the seventh century there are records of similar local establishments; Filibert was educated in the city of Aire,[72] while Praeiectus received his schooling at Issoire in the Auvergne.[73] These seventh-century schools, moreover, may well have been ecclesiastical; Aire was, after all, an episcopal city[74] and Issoire had a major church dedicated to the cult of Austremonius.[75] Equally, the subjects taught may suggest that the education was an ecclesiastical one; this is indicated not just in the case of Leobardus, but also of that of Eucherius of Orleans, who learnt the church canons before embarking on the monastic life.[76]

In addition to the schools already mentioned, it is possible that the royal court had some role to play in the education of the children of the nobility. Certainly there was a royal tutor, of whom the most famous was Gogo, *nutritor* of Childebert II, as well as friend of Venantius Fortunatus, and contributor to the *Epistulae Austrasiacae*.[77] The existence of such an official, however, did not necessarily mean that the children of magnates were brought up in the royal household. In the case of Audoin and his brothers, we are told that they were sent to the king, who handed them over to be educated by members of the aristocracy (*ab inlustris viris*).[78] More revealing is the information in the second *Passio* of Leodegar, which tells of how the saint was sent by his parents to Chlothar II, who handed the boy over to Dido, bishop of Poitiers, for his education.[79] The first *Passio* actually makes no reference to the palace, but simply recounts the boy's education in Poitiers, organized by Dido,[80] who was also his uncle. It seems as if the palace acted as a clearing house, placing the sons of officials and magnates in appropriate households for their upbringing.

Parallel to this is the role of the court as a focus for talent. There are

---

[71] Gregory of Tours, *Liber Vitae Patrum* XX c. 1, ed. B. Krusch, *MGH SS rer. merov.* I.2, p. 741.

[72] *Vita Filiberti* c. 1, ed. W. Levison, *MGH SS rer. merov.* V, p. 584.

[73] *Passio Praeiecti* c. 2, ed. B. Krusch, *MGH SS rer. merov.* V, p. 227.

[74] *Vita Filiberti* c. 1, ed. Levison, *MGH SS rer. merov.* V, p. 584. On episcopal schools see Riché, *Education et culture*, pp. 328–31.

[75] *Passio Praeiecti* c. 9, ed. Krusch, *MGH SS rer. merov.* V, p. 231.

[76] *Vita Eucherii* c. 3, ed. W. Levison, *MGH SS rer. merov.* VII, p. 48.

[77] Gregory of Tours, *Liber Historiarum* V c. 46, ed. Krusch and Levison, *MGH SS rer. merov.* I.1, p. 256; on his successor see VI c. 1, *ibid.*, p. 265; *Epistulae Austrasiacae* 13, 16, 22, 48, ed. Gundlach, *MGH Epp. merov. et karol.* I, pp. 128, 130, 134–5, 152–3. Riché, *Education et culture*, pp. 267–8, 283–4.

[78] *Vita Audoini* c. 1, ed. W. Levison, *MGH SS rer. merov.* V, p. 554.

[79] *Passio Leudegarii* II c. 1, ed. Krusch, *MGH SS rer. merov.* V, pp. 324–5.

[80] *Ibid.*, pp. 283–4.

examples of boys being sent to court after they had received an education, among them Filibert, Geremar, Bonitus, Wulfram and Ermeland.[81] There is also some evidence that members of the royal court kept an eye open for promise. Thus Patroclus, who came from a landed family, but scarcely a wealthy one, since as a child he had to look after his father's flocks, was commended to Childebert I's adviser Nunnio, as a result of his prowess at school.[82] After his schooling Arnulf, later bishop of Metz, was sent to the household of the *rector palatii* Gundulf.[83]

The role played by the court makes it difficult to discuss Merovingian culture in regional terms. Many of the leading individuals, especially in seventh-century Francia, came from the provinces to the palace and subsequently returned to the provinces again. Thus, Eligius was born in the Limousin, but after he had received his training as a goldsmith, he made his way to Neustria, where he was noticed by Chlothar II's treasurer, Bobo, who gave him his entrée to court. In later life, however, he became bishop of Noyon.[84] At court he belonged to the same circle as Desiderius of Cahors, Audoin of Rouen, Paul of Verdun, Sulpicius of Bourges, Arnulf of Metz and Grimoald, all of whom, bar the last, had similar career structures.[85]

In the light of this it is important not to overemphasize regional variations in Merovingian culture, although there undoubtedly was variety. Certainly the famous anecdote illustrating the cultural superiority of the south, Domnolus' refusal to accept the see of Avignon from Chlothar because he would be tired out by sophistic senators and philosophical judges, can be made to bear too much weight.[86] After all, the first reason for refusing the southern diocese which Gregory attributes to Domnolus is the man's desire not to be exiled from court, a sentiment close to the heart of Desiderius of Cahors a century later.[87] As for the philosophers of the Rhône valley, they should not be allowed to obscure the very strong bureaucratic traditions of Le Mans, the city where Domnolus finally did become bishop. Domnolus'

[81] *Vita Filiberti* c. 1, ed. Levison, *MGH SS rer. merov.* V, p. 584; *Vita Geremari* c. 3, ed. B. Krusch, *MGH SS rer. merov.* IV, p. 628; *Vita Boniti* c. 2, ed. Krusch, *MGH SS rer. merov.* VI, p. 120; *Vita Vulframi* c. 1, ed. W. Levison, *MGH SS rer. merov.* V, p. 662; *Vita Ermelandi* c. 1, ed. W. Levison, *MGH SS rer. merov.* V, p. 684.

[82] Gregory of Tours, *Liber Vitae Patrum* IX c. 1, ed. Krusch, *MGH SS rer. merov.* I.2, pp. 702–3.

[83] *Vita Arnulfi* c. 3, ed. B. Krusch, *MGH SS rer. merov.* II, p. 433.

[84] *Vita Eligii* I cc. 1–3, ed. B. Krusch, *MGH SS rer. merov.* IV, pp. 669–71.

[85] Desiderius, ep. I.10, ed. Arndt, *MGH Epp. merov. et karol.* I, p. 199.

[86] Gregory of Tours, *Liber Historiarum* VI c. 9, ed. Krusch and Levison, *MGH SS rer. merov.* I.1, p. 279.

[87] Desiderius, ep. I.10, ed. Arndt, *MGH Epp. merov. et karol.*, I, p. 199.

own church was later to be responsible for the preservation of various
Merovingian episcopal acts, most notably the will of Bishop Bertram,
admittedly in the somewhat suspect *Gesta episcoporum Cenomanensium*.[88]
Moreover, the diocese could boast another centre of note, the royal
monastery of St Calais.[89] It might, indeed, have been the political importance of the district which made Le Mans acceptable to Domnolus, when
Avignon had not been.

While the centrality of the Merovingian court in the late sixth and seventh
centuries modifies the distinction between a romanized south and a barbarian north-east, at the same time the evidence relating to the education of
the leading men of the kingdom weakens the divide between secular and
ecclesiastical learning.[90] Although most of our evidence concerns the lives
of saints, many of them only entered the church late in life, after they had
already had secular careers. Despite his family's connections with Columbanus, and despite his own piety, Audoin remained a layman until his
appointment as bishop of Rouen in 640. Indeed, because he was a layman he
insisted on spending a year going through the required grades of the church
canonically, before his consecration.[91] His education was as much that of a
secular magnate as of a churchman, and the same will probably have been
true of his two brothers, the treasurer Rado and the ascetic Ado.[92]
Desiderius of Cahors also had a secular career before he became bishop, as
did Arnulf of Metz and Bonitus of Clermont.[93] These men were by no
means unfit for episcopal office. Equally Leodegar, although his master,
Dido bishop of Poitiers, wished him to become a churchman, was versed in
secular letters and the law, as well as the canons.[94] In any case most
education would probably have had a strong religious component.

---

[88] In general see W. Goffart, *The Le Mans Forgeries: A Chapter from the History of Church Property in the Ninth Century* (Cambridge, Mass., 1966); on the authenticity of the will of Bertram, pp. 263–4.

[89] For an indication of its importance see Gregory of Tours, *Liber Historiarum* V c. 14, ed. Krusch and Levison, *MGH SS rer. merov.* I.1, p. 207.

[90] For an alternative reading of this evidence see Ganz, 'Bureaucratic shorthand', pp. 62–3. I take the same evidence to imply an overlap between secular and ecclesiastical culture, rather than a clerical chancery.

[91] *Vita Audoini* c. 7, ed. Levison, *MGH SS rer. merov.* V, p. 558; compare *Vita Eligii* II c. 2, ed. Krusch, *MGH SS rer. merov.* IV, pp. 695–6.

[92] Jonas, *Vita Columbani* I c. 26, ed. Krusch, *MGH SS rer. merov.* IV, p. 100; *Vita Audoini* c. 1, ed. Levison, *MGH SS rer. merov.* V, pp. 554–5.

[93] *Vita Desiderii* cc. 2, 6, 7, ed. Krusch, *MGH SS rer. merov.* IV, pp. 564–8; *Vita Arnulfi* c. 4, ed. Krusch, *MGH SS rer. merov.* II, p. 433; *Vita Boniti* cc. 2–3, ed. Krusch, *MGH SS rer. merov.* VI, pp. 120–1.

[94] *Passio Leudegarii* I c. 1, ed. Krusch, *MGH SS rer. merov.* V, pp. 283–4.

Leobardus was taught the psalms not because he intended to embark on the religious life, but because it was part of a boy's basic education.[95] The sources do not suggest that there was any distinction to be drawn between the culture of a secular magnate and that of a bishop; both needed to be literate and for both the cultivation of letters had its social and political advantages. Nor was there much difference between the ambitions of lay aristocrats and senior clergy; churchmen were often in open competition for power in the late seventh century, and more than one bishop died a death as violent as any layman.

The clear overlap of religious and secular education may also explain why it is so difficult to determine whether Fredegar was a layman or an ecclesiastic. The continuators of his Chronicle acted on the orders of two members of the Carolingian family, Counts Childebrand and Nibelung.[96] Of Fredegar himself we know nothing except what can be deduced from his writings. Apart from geographical indications which seem to place him in Burgundy,[97] what is most striking is the odd mixture of secular and religious information. Although he has more to say about non-ecclesiastical matters, he was well acquainted with Jonas' *Vita Columbani* within a short period of its composition,[98] and also seems to have known Sisebut's life of Desiderius of Vienne.[99] His Chronicle is a peculiar mixture of information, and yet it is one that fits well with that element of aristocratic society influenced by Luxeuil, where noble patronage blended with Hiberno-Frankish asceticism.[100]

The overlapping culture of lay and clerical magnates, which was apparently a feature of Merovingian Gaul in the sixth and seventh centuries, suggests a remarkably literate aristocracy. The cultural standards implied are less surprising for the clergy, but there may also have been a greater tradition of clerical learning than is usually recognized. There are

---

[95] Gregory of Tours, *Liber Vitae Patrum* XX c. 1, ed. Krusch, *MGH SS rer. merov.* I.2, p. 741.

[96] Fredegar, Continuations 34, ed. Wallace-Hadrill, *Chronicle of Fredegar*, pp. 102–3; I follow Wallace-Hadrill, *ibid.*, pp. xxv–vi, in seeing Childebrand and Nibelung as being the patrons and not the authors of the text.

[97] Wallace-Hadrill, *Chronicle of Fredegar*, p. xxii.

[98] Fredegar IV c. 36, ed. Wallace-Hadrill, *Chronicle of Fredegar*, pp. 23–9; compare Jonas, *Vita Columbani* I c. 18, ed. Krusch, *MGH SS rer. merov.* IV, p. 86; I. N. Wood, 'The *Vita Columbani* and Merovingian hagiography', *Peritia* 1 (1982), 63–80, at 68.

[99] The juxtaposition of the reference to Desiderius' martyrdom with an account of the accession of Sisebut in Fredegar IV cc. 32–3, ed. Wallace-Hadrill, *Chronicle of Fredegar*, pp. 21–2, is suggestive.

[100] F. Prinz, 'Columbanus, the Frankish nobility and the territories east of the Rhine', in *Columbanus and Merovingian Monasticism*, ed. Clarke and Brennan, pp. 73–87.

references to lost works of theology, particularly from the pen of Bonitus of Clermont,[101] and it is known that there were church councils which debated matters of doctrine, whose canons have not survived.[102] This information, however, relates to the seventh century, and not to the church castigated by Boniface, whose gloomy evaluation of the prelates of his day has tended to make the last half-century of Merovingian rule appear like a cultural and spiritual desert.[103]

Any assessment of this impression is severely hampered by the state of the evidence; Milo may not have been typical of the Merovingian episcopate as a whole,[104] and as for the priest who baptized *in nomine patria, filia et spiritus sanctus*,[105] he need not represent the norm for Francia, since he was working in Bavaria. He is more likely to illustrate the declining standards of learning amongst Christian communities established a century earlier by missionary groups, such as those sent out from Luxeuil by Eustasius, and perhaps subsequently neglected.[106]

Turning away from the straitjacket imposed by Boniface's assessment of the situation, there are some general points which can be made; in particular the culture of the early eighth century can more easily be discussed in regional terms than that of previous generations. Thus, it is possible to argue for significant continuity in the north, but it is very much harder to do so in the south. The major historical work of this period, the *Liber Historiae Francorum*, was written somewhere in the Ile de France, probably in Soissons, in 727.[107] The life of Audoin was apparently composed in the previous generation,[108] and the *Vita Wandregisili* must date

---

[101] *Vita Boniti* c. 17, ed. Levison, *MGH SS rer. merov.* VI, p. 129.

[102] *Vita Eligii* I c. 35, ed. Krusch, *MGH SS rer. merov.* IV, p. 692.

[103] P. Riché, 'Le Renouveau culturel à la cour de Pépin III', *Francia* 2 (1974), 59–70, at 59.

[104] Boniface, ep. 87, ed. Tangl, *MGH Epp. sel.* I, p. 198; E. Ewig, '*Milo et eiusmodi similes*', in *Spätantikes und fränkisches Gallien* II (Munich, 1979), pp. 189–219.

[105] Boniface, ep. 68, ed. Tangl, *MGH Epp. sel.* I, p. 141.

[106] Jonas, *Vita Columbani* II c. 8, ed. Krusch, *MGH SS rer. merov.* IV, pp. 121–2.

[107] R. Gerberding, *The Rise of the Carolingians and the Liber Historiae Francorum* (Oxford, 1987), pp. 1, 150–9; for the possibility that the work was written by a nun of Notre Dame at Soissons see Janet L. Nelson, *Times Literary Supplement*, 11–17 March 1988, p. 286; the suggestion could be defended on the grounds that, although Gerberding's case for the work being composed in Soissons is persuasive, the failure of the *Liber Historiae Francorum* to make much of the cult of St Medard makes composition in that house unlikely; a nunnery dedicated to the Virgin, however, would have had no interest in promoting a particular Frankish cult, and might well have produced a work lacking allegiance to a specific local saint.

[108] W. Wattenbach and W. Levison, *Deutschlands Geschichtsquellen im Mittelalter, I: Vorzeit und Karolinger*, ed. W. Levison (Weimar, 1952), p. 128 n. 307.

from approximately the same period.[109] Other indications of cultural continuity can be seen in the production of manuscripts at such centres as Corbie and perhaps at Chelles.[110] Further south the evidence is less impressive; the Auvergne can boast a solitary saint's life, that of Bonitus, but there is little else from Aquitaine or from Provence and the Rhône valley. Vienne, which had supplied Benedict Biscop with manuscripts,[111] has nothing to offer in the early eighth century. Indeed, its bishop, Wilicharius, retired to Agaune because of the disasters inflicted on his see by Charles Martel.[112] Carolingian writers saw this as a period of destruction in the Rhône valley with Islamic invasions and Frankish counterattacks.[113] The significance of the military threat to cultural traditions is perhaps confirmed by the history of book production of Luxeuil, which appears to have been interrupted when the monastery was sacked by the Saracens in 732.[114]

This history of devastation in the south and continuity in the north makes possible some observations on the question of culture or its absence in certain centres of late Merovingian Gaul, but the nature of the evidence is such that it is not easy to make general comparisons between the sixth and seventh centuries on the one hand and the eighth on the other. What is most obviously absent in the later period is any information which allows the historian to build up a picture of a court circle, such as can be observed in the *Epistulae Austrasiacae* and the letters of Desiderius of Cahors. There is nothing to suggest that the court acted as a focus for talent. This may be no more than the reflection of a lacuna in the evidence, but it is possible that there was a genuine change in the significance of the royal court in the last years of the seventh and the first years of the eighth centuries.

The evidence for a court circle made up of men who were drawn into

---

[109] *Ibid.*, p. 138.

[110] D. Ganz, 'The Merovingian Library of Corbie', in *Columbanus and Merovingian Monasticism*, ed. Clarke and Brennan, pp. 153–72; McKitterick, 'The scriptoria of Merovingian Gaul', pp. 194–6, and see also her arguments for a scriptorium at Jouarre in the early eighth century: 'The diffusion of insular culture in Neustria between 650 and 850: the implications of the manuscript evidence', in *La Neustrie: les pays au nord de la Loire de 650 à 850*, ed. Hartmut Atsma, Beihefte der Francia 16, 2 vols. (Sigmaringen, 1988), II, pp. 395–432, at pp. 406–12.

[111] Bede, *Historia Abbatum* c. 4, ed. Plummer, *Baedae Opera Historica*, p. 367.

[112] Ado, *Chronicon, PL* 123, col. 122.

[113] Fredegar, Continuations cc. 14, 18, 20–1, ed. Wallace-Hadrill, *Chronicle of Fredegar*, pp. 91, 93–5; see I.N. Wood, 'A prelude to Columbanus: the monastic achievement in the Burgundian territories', in *Columbanus and Merovingian Monasticism*, ed. Clarke and Brennan, pp. 3–32, at p. 19.

[114] R. McKitterick, 'The scriptoria of Merovingian Gaul', p. 188.

royal service at the palace, and who subsequently held episcopal and secular office elsewhere, is more or less unbroken until the 670s. Thereafter, the evidence for such a group is negligible for half a century or more. According to Paul the Deacon, Chrodegang of Metz was brought up in the household of Charles Martel,[115] but Charles sent his own sons to be educated at St Denis and at the court of the Lombard king, Liutprand.[116] It would only be in the days of Pippin III that the Carolingians established a court anything like that of the sixth- and seventh-century Merovingians.[117]

Chronologically the absence of a cultured court circle coincides with Ebroin's struggles for power, and subsequently with Carolingian attempts to dominate the Merovingian kings. It is possible that during these struggles for power, the palace ceased to provide the chief focus for talent in the kingdom; politics at a court level were too dangerous, and with increasing polarization between a small number of factions, which were no longer dominated by the king, the chances of preferment were restricted. Thus, whilst individual families still maintained contacts throughout Francia,[118] these no longer depended on the friendships established by young courtiers early in their administrative careers. The impact of this on royal government would have been considerable; for the continuity of regional and local administrative traditions and culture in individual centres, it would have been of little significance.

Whatever the explanation for the difference between the evidence for the court before the days of Ebroin and afterwards, the sources relating to the first century and a half of Merovingian rule suggest that the administrative classes, both within the cities, and more particularly at court, were largely literate. Members of the aristocracy and of the royal family were expected to be able to read and write, and those destined for secular office received the same education as those intended for the church. Some may have been educated at court, but the majority were educated in the provinces and joined the royal household subsequently; in time most were sent out to positions elsewhere in the kingdom, where, separated from their peer group, they cultivated the friendship of their sometime colleagues by the exchange of letters, whose form and content were circumscribed by a set of literary traditions going back to the late Roman period. At the same time, situated in the provinces, they were the recipients of royal missives, which

---

[115] Paul the Deacon, *Gesta Episcoporum Mettensium*, ed. G.H. Pertz, *MGH SS* II, p. 267; Riché, 'Le Renouveau culturel à la cour de Pépin III', 63–4.

[116] Riché, 'Le Renouveau culturel à la cour de Pépin III', 69.

[117] *Ibid., passim.*

[118] See, for example, P. Geary, *Aristocracy in Provence* (Stuttgart, 1985), pp. 144–8.

were based on models, such as those preserved by Marculf, and they had to deal with the equally formulaic writings of local administration. In this blending of social and governmental literacy the administrative classes of sixth- and seventh-century Francia continued the traditions of their Gallo-Roman predecessors until the days of Ebroin, Pippin II and Charles Martel.

4

Literacy and the
papal government in late antiquity
and the early middle ages

Thomas F. X. Noble

It would be entirely legitimate to investigate many of the roles played by literacy in the story of the rise of the Roman church and of the papal administration. Wilken has seen the dawning of 'proto-catholic' tradition as a major stage in the rise of the Roman church, and he identifies the quest to define canon, creed and authority as distinguishing marks of that tradition.[1] The ability to write, to read and to understand texts played a major role in that process. It is true that Rome played a small role in the definition of the scriptural canon – apart perhaps from providing some impetus to the preparation of the Vulgate translation – but the papal role in struggles over creeds and authority was large and long-standing.[2] Early Christianity saw the development of many written rules for living, some of which were ascetic, or monastic, and of little interest in Rome – initially at least – but others of which, embodied in almost countless conciliar enactments, were or became subjects of intense concern at the papal court. Finally, many Christian communities, but none more so than that of Rome, generated abundant records of the routine minutiae of ecclesiastical administration.

Treating the subject of literacy in the papal administration, then, requires a focus that will rest essentially on the kinds of records which that administration produced and conserved. In some instances it is easy to see why certain kinds of records appeared, but in other cases it is more difficult. Sometimes we shall be able to see exactly who produced the records, but

---

[1] Robert Wilken, *The Christians as the Romans Saw Them* (New Haven, 1984).

[2] On Jerome's commission from Pope Damasus, see: H.F.D. Sparks, 'Jerome as a biblical scholar', in *The Cambridge History of the Bible*, ed. P.R. Ackroyd and C.F. Evans, 3 vols. (Cambridge, 1970), I, pp. 513–16. The papal roles in the great trinitarian and christological controversies can be read in almost any standard and substantial church history. There is no point in citing a list of them here. I confine myself to drawing attention to the appropriate, individually signed chapters in *History of the Church*, II: *The Imperial Church from Constantine to the Early Middle Ages*, ed. Hubert Jedin and John Dolan (New York, 1980).

sometimes we do not know. Strategies for conserving and using documents, while occasionally apparent, are often undetectable. Basically, there are two major categories of evidence. For purposes of discussion they can be labelled intellectual, and jurisdictional or bureaucratic (though sharp lines cannot always be drawn).

At the outset I should clarify some of the terms I shall be using in pursuing my subject. When I speak of the 'Roman church' I mean essentially the church in the province of which the pope was ordinary bishop. This means Rome and its suburbicarian dioceses, or roughly the Roman and Byzantine duchy of Rome. Viewed from this angle, the pope was much like other bishops, and his institutional needs and responsibilities were similar to theirs. One could well compare the papal administration to that of, say, the patriarchs of Alexandria, Antioch or Constantinople. But this study cannot range so far afield and, in any event, the Roman church province represents a formidable object of study.

Perhaps it will be objected that the papal administration had responsibilities that extended far beyond the environs of Rome. The objection would be just, but can be met by observing that, first, Rome's 'universal' responsibilities emerged only slowly and, second, the institution that came in time to administer the universal church of the Christian middle ages was fundamentally the old bureaux and branches of the early papal administration refined for new tasks. In other words, the emphasis here will be on the introduction to the story of literacy and the papal government. Another way to counter that objection would be to say that in looking at some intellectual and jurisdictional questions I shall indeed break out of the confines of the Roman region.

In the context of the papal administration I have three basic notions of literacy in mind. The first concerns institutional record keeping of every kind that has left a trace in the surviving evidence. I shall attempt to describe the major kinds of records, tell who produced them, how, and for what purposes. Second, I hope to say something about who was literate and what levels of literacy were attained. It must not be forgotten that the people and institutions I shall be describing constituted a relatively small clerical elite that used literacy to carry out its own business and to promote its own interests. Literacy in papal Rome had a great deal to do with the acquisition, retention and exercise of power.[3] My approach is very much a functionalist one. I will argue that Rome had, or developed, the kinds of literacy it needed to do what it wanted to do. It was only incidentally that papal Rome made any contributions to the literary culture of Europe or to the levels of

---

[3] Jack Goody, 'Introduction', in *Literacy in Traditional Societies*, ed. Jack Goody (Cambridge, 1968), pp. 2, 11–14.

literate attainment in my period. Third, at the end of this essay, and necessarily only summarily, I shall draw attention to the broad realm of intellectual history and mention theology and ecclesiology as two areas where at least some popes made durable contributions.

The early history of papal records, and of papal record keeping, is shrouded in obscurity. The first faint rays of light appear in the notice concerning Pope Fabian (236–50) in the *Liber Pontificalis*.[4] There we read that this pope installed notaries in each region of the city and gave them the charge of recording the deeds of the martyrs. We shall see below that this brief remark sheds some light on the beginnings of institutional history writing in Rome but for the moment it is the appearance of the papal administration, in the shape of the notaries, that must be pursued.

Pope Fabian appears to have divided Rome into seven ecclesiastical regions and to have placed at the head of each region a deacon and subdeacon. The regional deacons began as ministers for charitable services and they soon acquired responsibility for the administration of church properties in their regions. The regional deacons became powerful officers of the church. They had their headquarters in the Lateran and functioned as the pope's chief personal representative in each region of the city. If these officers truly appeared in the third century, their duties and visibility grew greatly after the time of Constantine and continued growing for centuries. By the late eighth century the seven regional deacons came to be called 'cardinal' deacons and they were both electors and eligible for election as pope.[5] The deacons were the chief figures in the administrative side of the papal government and they worked alongside but independently of the pastoral administration whose chief representatives were the titular priests. The archdeacon appears to have been the head of the ecclesiastical personnel as a whole.[6]

Under the deacons the key officers were the notaries and the defensors. The notaries may have had some duties as historians in early times but from the fifth century onwards they had different and more important tasks. Perhaps the notaries functioned by analogy to the Roman *notarii* and *tabelliones* as the preparers and keepers of records out in the regions and it is reasonable to suppose that they or their subordinates – we have no idea how

---

[4] *LP* I, p. 64. Harry Bresslau, *Handbuch der Urkundenlehre für Deutschland und Italien*, 2 vols. (4th edn, Berlin, 1969), I, pp. 191–2.

[5] T.F.X. Noble, *The Republic of St. Peter: The Birth of the Papal State, 680–825* (Philadelphia, 1984), pp. 217–18. Much of what follows depends upon this book and because it is fully documented I do not always cite all literature and sources here.

[6] *Ibid.*, p. 218 and n. 30.

many notaries there were – never lost this role. Still, we eventually find notaries writing papal documents, keeping the papal archives, and serving as the secretariat in papal synods.[7] By the pontificate of Gregory I the notaries were organized into a *schola*, a corporation, within which the seven regional notaries held first rank. Two of these, the *primicerius* and the *secundicerius*, were among the greatest officers of the church.[8]

The *primicerius* not only supervised the notaries who produced documents but also directed the papal archives, and, for a time, the library, where documents were conserved. By 649 the archives were in the Lateran whereas before then they may have been kept at the basilica of St Lawrence in Damaso.[9] The *primicerius* remained chief archivist throughout our period but his relationship with the papal library is more difficult to fix precisely. In the seventh century the sources make no sharp distinction between a library and an archive and I am inclined to think that bureaucratic records as well as various codices were kept in the same place under the charge of the *primicerius*.[10] In the early eighth century we meet for the first time a *bibliothecarius*[11] and then under Pope Hadrian I (772–95) three more *bibliothecarii* appear by name.[12] By 829 this office had achieved

---

[7] On the *tabelliones* see A.H.M. Jones, *The Later Roman Empire*, 2 vols. (Baltimore, 1986), I, pp. 515–16. On the notaries, see Rudolf von Heckel, 'Das päpstliche und sicilische Registerwesen in vergleichender Darstellung mit besonderer Berücksichtigung der Ursprünge', *Archiv für Urkundenforschung* 1 (1908), 398–400.

[8] Gregory I, *Registrum*, 8.16, ed. Dag Norberg, CCSL 140–140a (Turnhout, 1982), 140a, pp. 534–5. Giuseppe Palazzini, 'Primicerio e secundicerio', *Enciclopedia cattolica*, 12 vols. (Vatican City, 1953), X, cols. 20–2.

[9] Noble, *Republic of St. Peter*, pp. 219–21 and n. 39. Martino Giusti, 'The Vatican secret archive', in *The Vatican: Spirit and Art of Christian Rome* (New York, n.d.), p. 299, thinks it impossible to locate the archives in San Lorenzo in Damaso. I think he is correct to challenge the traditional meaning of the inscription that has long been cited as proof that Damasus installed the archives in San Lorenzo: Giovanni Battista De Rossi, *Inscriptiones Christianae Urbis Romae Septimo Saeculo Antiquiores*, II, pt 1 (Rome, 1857), p. 151, no. 23. The inscription only proves that Damasus' father had been a notary at that church and that Damasus himself had grown up there.

[10] Noble, *Republic of St. Peter*, pp. 219–22 nn. 29–51. Pierre Riché, *Education and Culture in the Barbarian West Sixth through Eighth Centuries*, trans. John J. Contreni (Columbia, South Carolina, 1976), pp. 175–6, 419–20. Joan Peterson, ' "Homo omnino Latinus"? The theological and cultural backgrounds of Pope Gregory the Great', *Speculum* 62 (1987), 529–51, at 533, has criticized me for assuming that the library and archives were alike transferred from San Lorenzo to the Lateran before 649. I had actually meant to say only that, before the eighth century, there was one collection of materials, and not a distinct library. Now I am less sure than I was about the transfer from San Lorenzo but I do think that Peterson, Riché and I all basically agree on the development of the library.

[11] *LP* I, p. 396; Noble, *Republic of St. Peter*, pp. 221–2.

[12] Philippus Jaffé, *Regesta Pontificum Romanorum*, 2 vols. (Graz, 1956), I, nos. 2401, 2431, 2457. Leo Santifaller, *Saggio di un elenco dei funzionari, impiegati e scrittori della cancellaria pontificia dall'inizio all'anno 1099*, 2 vols. (Rome, 1940), I, pp. 36–47.

sufficient prestige and differentiation from the notarial administration that it was usually filled by one of the suburbicarian bishops.[13] I have elsewhere offered the suggestion that a rising volume of business may have occasioned the separation of the archives from the library.[14] Although almost nothing can be known about the holdings of the early mediaeval papal library, or about its development, and also because nothing certain is known about the principles of archival management that were employed in Rome, there is a limited amount that can confidently be said about the way in which books and documents were conserved.

Two kinds of documents, papal letters and bureaucratic enactments, were probably enregistered in some way from the late fourth or the early fifth centuries. Walter Ullmann believed that registers of letters may have been compiled from the beginning of the fifth century if not perhaps before. He argued that as the papacy came to have a greater sense of itself as a public, legal, authoritative institution it needed to keep its records as evidence of the positions that it had taken and that it might wish or need to refer to in the future.[15] Other scholars think papal letters may have been registered as early as the pontificate of Liberius (352–66),[16] while some think that no evidence from before Leo I (440–61) can be regarded as conclusive.[17] Finally, it has been suggested that registers could have been kept almost immediately after the Constantinian 'Peace of the Church' inaugurated by the Rescript of Milan in 314.[18]

The difficulty in determining when papal registers began being kept is almost entirely attributable to the nature of the surviving evidence. Before the time of Innocent III in the thirteenth century no complete or partial register survives in its original form. We are wholly dependent upon copies. The oldest surviving part of an original papal document is a fragment of a letter of Hadrian I from 788, and the oldest complete document is a letter of

---

[13] Percy Ernst Schramm, 'Studien zu frühmittelalterlichen Aufzeichnungen über Staat und Verfassung', *Zeitschrift der Savigny-Stiftung für Rechtsgeschichte*, 62, *germanistische Abteilung* 49 (1929), 167–232, at 205; Bresslau, *Urkundenlehre*, I, p. 211. But Schramm thinks that 829 saw the first permanent *bibliothecarius* whereas, like Santifaller, I hold for Hadrian's pontificate.

[14] Noble, *Republic of St. Peter*, pp. 221–2.

[15] Walter Ullmann, *Gelasius I (492–496): Das Papsttum an der Wende der Spätantike zum Mittelalter*, Päpste und Papsttum 18 (Stuttgart, 1981), pp. 35–44.

[16] Harold Steinacker, 'Über das älteste päpstliche Registerwesen', *Mitteilungen des Instituts für Österreichische Geschichtsforschung* 23 (1902), 1–49, at 7. See Jaffé, *Regesta Pontificum Romanorum*, I, no. 216.

[17] Othmar Hagender, 'Papstregister und Dekretalenrecht', in *Recht und Schrift im Mittelalter*, ed. Peter Classen, Vorträge und Forschungen 23 (Sigmaringen, 1977), pp. 320–1.

[18] Steinacker, 'Registerwesen', 7–8.

Paschal I from 819.[19] For the whole period before these letters were written there survive some 2,500 papal letters of one kind or another but all of them are transmitted through copies. For example, two early canonical collections – collections, that is, of papal letters treated as having authoritative legal status – the *Quesneliana* and the *Collectio Avellana* point to the existence of fifth-century registers and give some hints about their contents. In a related vein, the eleventh-century canonist Deusdedit of Milan incorporated into his collection of canons substantial blocks of material that point directly to registers for Honorius I (625–38), Gregory II and III (715–41), Leo IV (847–55), Nicholas I (858–67) and John VIII (872–82). The closest thing we have to a complete register is that of Gregory I (590–604) containing more than 850 letters. But even this represents only about sixty letters per year for what was a busy and eventful pontificate. Much has been lost. We have almost one hundred papal letters from Gregory III to Hadrian I dispatched to the Frankish court, the so-called *Codex Carolinus*. This collection is invaluable to historians but as it was prepared in 791 at the Frankish court on the order of Charlemagne it tells us very little about the procedures of the papal chancery and archives. From the fourth century to the late ninth, nevertheless, we have an impressive array of register fragments and from them a good deal can be learned.[20]

Roman imperial practice provided the basic model for papal registers in two distinct respects. First, the imperial rescript provided the model for the actual form of the papal letters.[21] Second, imperial *commentarii*, that is, annually organized and chronologically arranged collections of letters, provided the actual model for the registers.[22] Down to the time of Gregory I papal registers were like the imperial in that they included both in-coming and out-going letters. In Gregory's time the number of in-coming docu-

---

[19] Reginald Lane Poole, *Lectures on the History of the Papal Chancery down to the Time of Innocent III* (Cambridge, 1915), p. 37. Cf. Jaffé, *Regesta Pontificum Romanorum*, I, nos. 2462, 2551.

[20] Poole, *Papal Chancery*, pp. 29–30; Hagender, 'Papstregister', pp. 320–1; Jaffé, *Regesta Pontificum Romanorum*, I, nos. 285–327 (Innocent I), 398–551 (Leo I), 619–743 (Gelasius I), 2153–228 (Gregory II), 2674–888 (Nicholas I), 2889–953 (Hadrian II), 2954–3386 (John VIII). For the *Codex Carolinus* see the *MGH* edition by Wilhelm Gundlach (Berlin, 1892). For the register of Gregory I the new edition by Norberg (cited above n. 8) has replaced the *MGH* edition by P. Ewald and W. Hartmann.

[21] Peter Classen, *Kaiserreskript und Königsurkunde. Diplomatische Studien zum Problem der Kontinuität zwischen Altertum und Mittelalter*, Byzantine Texts and Studies 15 (Thessalonika, 1977), pp. 99–101.

[22] Harry Bresslau, 'Die Commentarii der römischen Kaiser und die Registerbücher der Päpste', *Zeitschrift der Savigny-Stiftung für Rechtsgeschichte*, 19, *romanistische Abteilung* 6 (1885), 242–60, especially 255–60. This old study was incorporated into his *Urkundenlehre* and remains the basis for all subsequent work.

ments included in the registers appears to have declined dramatically and by the ninth century they had all but disappeared. It is possible, however, that the persons responsible for excerpting various registers may have left out the in-coming material and in the process distorted our understanding of the structure of the registers.[23] In the ninth century John the Deacon, in a biography of Gregory I, says, with neither emphasis nor surprise, that this pope left a volume of letters for each year of his pontificate.[24] It is likely, therefore, that papal registers were always organized annually. Through the ninth century papal documents were always written on papyrus, a material whose very high perishability helps to account for the disappearance of so many documents.[25] It appears that the papyri were put in the archive one by one, in chronological order, and then bound or bundled together in annual *volumina* according to indiction years. Steinacker sensibly proposed years ago that some indexing system must have been used but no one has been able to figure out from the surviving copies what that system was, and there has been some reluctance to embrace Steinacker's own hypotheses. He guessed that rubrics in a different script, probably uncial, and in a different colour, probably red, served as a kind of running index. He even imagined double columns with the texts in one and the rubrics in the other.[26] This is both possible and unprovable. There has been some controversy over whether originals or copies were enregistered. The present state of the evidence really makes it impossible to answer this question satisfactorily. Basic elements of the processes of composition and compilation do not seem to be in doubt. A notary took dictation from the pope or other high Lateran official and then went to the *scrinium* where at least two complete copies were prepared. One went to the archives to be enregistered and one went to the addressee. By the late ninth century there is some evidence that only extracts were going into the registers and this may be yet another indicator of the change in chancery standards that Lohrmann and others have noted and characterized as decline.[27] But it may be that a rising volume of business led to excerpting as a practical matter.

[23] Steinacker, 'Registerwesen', 8–9.

[24] *Vita Gregorii*, 4.71, *PL* 75, cols. 223A–B.

[25] Naphtali Lewis, *Papyrus in Classical Antiquity* (Oxford, 1974).

[26] Steinacker, 'Registerwesen', 45–6.

[27] The later period has been studied by Dietrich Lohrmann, *Das Register Papst Johann VIII*, Bibliothek des deutschen historischen Instituts in Rom 30 (Tübingen, 1968). Some general insights can be gleaned from a study that is most valuable for the later middle ages: M. Giusti, *Studi sui registri di bolle papali*, Archivi vaticani 1 (Vatican City, 1968). Steinacker, 'Registerwesen', 10–36, still has much of value. The annual structure is made clear by John the Deacon in the *Vita Gregorii*.

The papal registers, indeed the papal archives, were accessible for consultation. This had always been true with Roman archives because under the Roman system it was only the public, archived copy of a document that had probative value. Many times, it seems, parties to an action or dispute did not personally receive copies of documents pertaining to their case. The truly official copies were available in the archives for consultation or for copying when an *aide-memoire* seemed desirable. Even when the preparation of a document proceeded more from private will than from public action, the roles of the archives and of the documents were the same. For example, a person might present himself to one of the *tabelliones* for the purpose of having a will drawn up. The individual would then take that will, after having had it properly authenticated, to the archive where it was enregistered. The copy in the archives then became the valid one. One of the characteristics of the transition from Roman to mediaeval times was a shift in the nature and use of documents. Basically, one can say that the shift involved a change in probative value from the public doument in the archives to the private copy in the hands of a recipient.[28]

As we move across the period from the fourth to the ninth centuries we can see that only the papal archives survived as a major public repository. But others had existed, especially in the earlier part of this period. Cassiodorus' *Variae* and the Ravenna papyri provide valuable insights into the Ostrogothic and Byzantine archives at Ravenna. The former represent extracts made by Cassiodorus from the palace archives, perhaps registers, at Ravenna during or just after his own period of service,[29] and the latter constitute a good number of examples of the exercise of public authority under the Exarchate of Ravenna.[30] For a time public archives continued in all the germanic kingdoms but by the sixth, or at the latest the seventh, century they seem to have faded out everywhere largely because of the 'privatization' of modes of documentary proof noted above.[31]

If we wish to know what happened to the many papal registers that must

---

[28] This is one of the principal themes of Classen's *Kaiserreskript und Königsurkunde*. See also von Heckel, 'Registerwesen', 395–9, and Bruno Hirschfeld, *Die Gesta Municipalia in römischer und frühgermanischer Zeit* (Marburg, 1904), pp. 23–49.

[29] Cassiodorus, *Variae*, ed. A.J. Fridh, CCSL 96 (Turnhout, 1973). See also James J. O'Donnell, *Cassiodorus* (Berkeley, 1979), pp. 55–102.

[30] See J.O. Tjäder, *Die nichtliterarischen lateinischen Papyri Italien aus der Zeit 445–700*, I (Lund, 1955).

[31] Hirschfeld, *Gesta Municipalia*, pp. 61–81, discusses the fate of archives, but Classen, *Kaiserreskript und Königsurkunde*, pp. 107–37, does so more fully and capably. See also concerning Gaul: Ian Wood, 'Disputes in late fifth- and sixth-century Gaul: some problems, in *Settlement of Disputes*, pp. 7–22, especially pp. 12–15. And see Nelson's chapter in this volume, below, pp. 258–96.

once have existed, then, I think we can point to three or four factors in their disappearance. The use of papyrus will certainly have been responsible for some losses. A decline in standards or a deliberate change in policies in the later ninth century may have caused some material to disappear. The papal administration may have behaved like other archives and chanceries in that it gradually exhibited more concern for the documents it was sending out than for the ones it was keeping. Finally, papal Rome was often a turbulent, violent place. Riots and rebellions associated with internal strife and foreign attacks by Lombards, Byzantine officials and Arabs may be responsible for the loss of some documents.

Just as we modern historians are grateful for what does survive, so too people in the early middle ages appear to have been much attached to the papal archives. From as early as the pontificates of Innocent I (401–17) and Boniface I (418–22) popes made reference to the consultation of their archives. Phrases such as 'in sacro scrinio nostro', 'sicut in scriniis nostris legimus', 'testimonium nostri declarat scrinii', or 'ut scrinii nostri monumenta declarant' are met again and again.[32] It is not surprising that papal officers made frequent use of the archives but it is important to see that 'outsiders' did as well. Jerome, for example, was once accused of misrepresenting a papal letter and he wrote that anyone who wished to verify his statements could go and look for the pope's letter 'in Romana Ecclesiae chartario'.[33] Although this is the only case I know of the use of 'chartario', Jerome's meaning is perfectly clear and the case serves as a splendid example of what I would call the 'public' side of the archives. The registers of Gregory I were regularly consulted. Bishop Braulio of Saragossa (*ob. c.* 651) asked a priest, Taio, who had 'by his zeal and sweat' brought to Spain codices of Gregory's writings 'not yet known there' to transcribe copies and send them on to him.[34] He does not state his exact reason for wanting these works, which appear to have included some of Gregory's letters. Taio may, therefore, have visited the archives.

Much better known is the case of Nothelm, a contemporary of Bede, who sent the great Northumbrian author documents concerning Pope Gregory's English mission that had been uncovered in researches in the archives in Rome.[35] While Bede had scholarly interests in the archives his

---

[32] Jaffé, *Regesta Pontificum Romanorum*, I, nos. 300, 350, 369, for example. See also: von Heckel, 'Registerwesen', 410, and Hartmann in his preface to the *MGH* edn of Gregory's register, *MGH Epp.* II, pp. vii–viii.

[33] Jerome, *Epistula adversus Rufinum*, c. 20, ed. P. Lardet, CCSL 79 (Turnhout, 1982), p. 91.

[34] Braulio to Taio, *PL* 80, col. 690B.

[35] Bede, *Venerabilis Baedae Historiam ecclesiasticam gentis anglorum*, ed. Charles Plummer

countryman Boniface had more practical, ecclesiastical aims in mind in requesting from the cardinal-deacon Gemmulus a copy of some letters of Gregory I.[36] And, on another occasion, Boniface wrote to Pope Stephen II to ask for a copy of Pope Sergius' original instructions to Willibrord concerning the rights of the bishopric of Utrecht.[37] Finally, the Frankish court requested from Hadrian I in 794 a copy of the register of Gregory I and got some 684 letters. This collection provides the basis for all modern editions of the register but it is hard to know whether it is itself an extract or whether by the end of the eighth century only 684 letters survived from what must have been a much larger collection.[38] Many more examples could be cited but they would only serve to reinforce the same points. People all over Europe, over a long period of time, turned to the papal archives for documents that could be used in local situations. There is an irony here in that the dispatch from Rome of documents for local cases shows the 'privatization' of evidence which was discussed above but if the 'public' papal archive had not been there no such evidence would have been available. Here again there is evidence for several kinds of bureaucratic literacy and for some of the uses to which it was put. Private individuals like Taio or Nothelm could go to Rome to do research but we have to assume that there were competent officials there to help them. And Boniface could write to Rome for documents and act as if he were doing a perfectly normal thing. How many more such requests have simply vanished? Finally, of course, it should be stressed that it was written documents on all manner of subjects that were at issue in these cases.

Surviving letters display vividly the wide range of activities and interests of the papal administration. Extant texts were addressed to emperors, kings, prominent laymen, patriarchs, archbishops and bishops, abbots, missionaries and Roman ecclesiastical administrators. People from the north of England to Spain, from Gaul and Germany to Sicily, from North Africa to Constantinople and Jerusalem received missives from the popes. The subjects treated in these letters are numerous. Emperors were instruc-

---

(Oxford, 1896), p. 6. This is not the place for a full discussion of the complicated matter of what Bede actually got from Nothelm. For thorough discussion, with references, see Paul Meyvaert, *Bede and Gregory the Great* (Jarrow Lecture, 1984), pp. 8–13, 23–4, and *idem*, 'Bede's text of the *Libellus Responsionum* of Gregory the Great to Augustine of Canterbury', in *England before the Conquest: Studies in Primary Sources Presented to Dorothy Whitelock*, ed. P. Clemoes and K. Hughes (Cambridge, 1971), pp. 15–33.

[36] *Die Briefe des heiligen Bonifatius und Lullus*, no. 54, ed. Michael Tangl, *MGH Epp. sel.* I, pp. 96–7.

[37] *Ibid.*, no. 109, p. 236.

[38] Hartmann, in the preface to his and Ewald's edn, *MGH Epp.* II, p. viii, and Norberg, in the preface to his edn, CCSL 140–140a, p. v.

ted on proper relationships between secular and ecclesiastical officials. Synods were told what topics could be debated, and in what terms. Missionaries were encouraged and advised. Points of biblical exegesis were discussed. Routine matters of church administration were often raised. One could, I think, open Jaffé's *Regesta Pontificum* at any point and read, say, three pages of its brief entries and in so doing form a good impression of the kinds of letters produced in the Lateran and of the kinds of people to whom they were sent. And, of course, these documents show clearly the many uses to which literacy was put, ranging from the simple matter of actually writing the letters to the larger and more complex intellectual, legal, spiritual and other matters which had to be understood in order for the letters to respond adequately to the circumstances attending their composition.

A second type of material that was certainly archived and enregistered consists of a huge array of administrative documents that were for the most part very local in scope and significance. Some of these documents survive in the remaining fragments of papal registers, especially that of Gregory I, but most have disappeared. For bureaucratic enactments there are two possible Roman models. Major Roman officials had notaries and archives attached to their offices and these notaries both wrote and kept public records.[39] Here, certainly, we have an example of the kind of work that, in the papal government, resulted in the preparation and preservation of so many documents relating to everyday matters of administration. Rome also had public *tabelliones* who were 'public' notaries in the sense that they were licensed by the government and accessible to ordinary citizens who needed documents, say wills or deeds, drawn up, but 'private' in the sense that they were not attached to the *officium* of a Roman officer or archive. The *tabelliones* were supervised by the *magister censuum*.[40] In 758 and again in 821 the *magister* is mentioned at Rome so there were still, evidently, public notaries and thus a model for the papal notariate right through our period.[41] By 861 a new officer appears, the *protoscriniarius*, who was not a member of the *schola* of the notaries and who was on occasion a layman. He may have been a papal appointee who took over leadership of the public notaries.[42] From the fifth century onwards it is impossible to determine the relationship between the public and papal notaries but as the former were much the older of the two, they undoubtedly exercised influence on the work of the

---

[39] Hirschfeld, *Gesta Municipalia*, pp. 23–65; von Heckel, 'Registerwesen', 396–9, 406–9; Classen, *Kaiserreskript und Königsurkunde*, pp. 92–8.

[40] Jones, *Later Roman Empire*, I, pp. 515–16, 691–2.

[41] Bresslau, *Urkundenlehre*, I, pp. 205–8.

[42] Noble, *Republic of St. Peter*, p. 221.

latter. Another possible model for the papal notariate, and especially for the enregistering and archiving of bureaucratic records, may have been the *gesta municipalia*, which were enregistered accounts of public business, especially judicial matters. Contemporary evidence from Ravenna, and also from the Frankish and Burgundian kingdoms, shows, as we have already seen, that these *gesta* continued, at least through the sixth century, and it may be, although there is no certain testimony from Rome, that they were influential in the development of the papal collections of more or less public, administrative records.[43]

In other words, Roman practices provided many models for the preparation and preservation of records and there can be no doubt, in view of the obvious parallels, that the Roman church adopted and adapted numerous Roman structures and techniques. For example, papal registers look much like both imperial *commentarii* and *gesta municipalia* in that they contain both formal letters and routine bureaucratic enactments. But under the Roman regime these were two different kinds of records and they were handled in two different ways. Roman *notarii* and *tabelliones* played different but complementary roles, and they may have continued doing so under the papal government but we cannot tell for sure and, even if they did, it appears that all documents went into the one set of papal archives. Furthermore, every major Roman *officium* – as we might say ministry or department – had its own notarial staff and an archive in the form of an annual register. Did the papal government have department registers, or did everything come together in the one series of papal registers? Looking at the way the papal regime adapted the Roman system in other respects does not permit an unambiguous answer to this question. In any event, only the general papal registers survive in any form and, as already noted in a different context, they have a decreasingly bureaucratic flavour. This might mean that in the eighth and ninth centuries there was increasingly specialized record keeping and that, as a result, bureaucratic records were kept in departmental registers that have vanished. Or it may be that, because all surviving registers come down through non-official extracts, we have only a reflection of the interests and needs of the copyists; presumably major papal pronouncements and not administrative minutiae seemed worth copying.

Judicial records, which might have been among those kept separately from the general registers, were produced by the second *schola* of officers who worked in the regions alongside the notaries and under the deacons. These were the *defensores*. Just when the *defensores* first appeared is not known, but Gregory I organized them into a *schola* in 598. It seems that they emerged by analogy to the Roman *defensores civitatis* who had been

---

[43] Hirschfeld, *Gesta Municipalia*, remains the basic study but it is much in need of updating.

minor officials charged to protect citizens from mistreatment by Roman officials, and to handle small-scale judicial business.[44] Under their chief, the *primicerius defensorum*, another of the great officers of the church, the *defensores* appear to have functioned as the legal staff of the Lateran. A fair amount is known about the kinds of judicial records that had been prepared in secular Rome, so it is quite reasonable to suppose that the papal *defensores* were responsible, like their secular counterparts, for the creation of a good many documents. Unfortunately, not a scrap of this putative evidence survives. This is especially unfortunate because these records would have provided details on how the papal courts worked, on what kinds of business went before them, on the quality of justice that was supplied and on the kind of law that was applied. These records might have told us a great deal indeed about some of the major kinds of literacy that existed in papal Rome and about the uses to which that literacy was put. There is no warrant to speculate about details, but it is not illegitimate to point out that there had to have been considerable knowledge of law and legal procedure, and also of the kinds of record keeping appropriate to the smooth functioning of a legal and judicial system. The actual disappearance of the records is probably attributable to the fact that they will in the great majority have concerned no more than the local and mundane affairs of daily life; they lacked, in other words, great historical or theoretical significance for those who came along in later years and made copies of, for example, the papal registers.

Another category of records produced in the Lateran and conserved in the archives derived from the office of the *vestararius*. This official, one of the seven major figures in the papal government, had charge of the fabric of all the churches and monasteries in Rome that belonged to the papal administration and also responsibility for the vestments, sacred vessels and other precious possessions of the church.[45] No actual records from this Lateran department survive for study but some impression of what they might have been like comes from several notices in the *Liber Pontificalis* in which the building, remodelling, or refurbishing activities of several popes, most notably Hadrian I, Leo III (795–816), Paschal I (817–24) and Gregory IV (827–44), are recounted in considerable detail.[46] The compilers of the *Liber Pontificalis* clearly made use of the records of the *vestararius*. Because there exists nothing in the surviving register fragments like the *vestararius* records transmitted by the *Liber Pontificalis* these records,

[44] Balthasar Fischer, 'Die Entwicklung des Instituts der Defensoren in der römischen Kirche', *Ephemerides Liturgicae* 48 (1939), 443–54; Noble, *Republic of St. Peter*, p. 222 and n. 52.

[45] Noble, *Republic of St. Peter*, p. 226 and n. 77.

[46] *LP* I, pp. 499–515(Hadrian), II, pp. 1–4, 3–34(Leo), 53–63(Paschal), 74–83(Gregory).

even at second hand, may well provide a hint about the existence of separate departmental archives and registers that could not be demonstrated on the basis of the general registers alone.

The financial administration of papal Rome was directed by two major Lateran officers, the *sacellarius* and the *arcarius*, the former having been the paymaster and the latter, the treasurer. Both had subordinates.[47] The greatest single source of revenue was the papal patrimonies, a vast complex of large and small estates scattered throughout Italy. While much can be learned about patrimonial administration from, above all, the letters of Gregory I, little can be known for certain about the relationship between the financial and patrimonial administrations.[48] Thus, although strictly speaking no financial records survive, one can suggest without being reckless that financial records were produced and kept in the archives. The existence of a financial administration, plus the presumed existence of its records, points to yet another kind of literacy, or, rather, to two related kinds: the knowledge necessary for the actual work and the ability to make and keep the records. Where financial records are concerned, moreover, we have a hint of numeracy in the papal administration

At this point we must depart from our account of the particular branches of the papal government and the evidence which they produced to turn to four other kinds of evidence. These are the *Liber Diurnus*, the *Liber Pontificalis*, the liturgical books and the law books of the Roman church. Each of these bears an ambiguous relationship with one or more branches of the papal administration, and each throws light on one or more branch. These materials are revealing of several independent and interrelated kinds of literacy.

First, there is the *Liber Diurnus*.[49] This is a collection of *formulae* that was once thought to represent the actual formula book of the papal chancery. Santifaller then broke with that view and argued that it was a 'school and exercise book' for the training of notaries in the chancery. Confronted with the fact that all surviving manuscripts are north Italian in

---

[47] Noble, *Republic of St. Peter*, p. 225 and nn. 68–76.

[48] Edward Spearing, *The Patrimony of the Roman Church in the Time of Gregory the Great* (Cambridge, 1918); Vincenzo Recchia, *Gregorio Magno e la società agricola*, Verba seniorum, NS 8 (Rome, 1978); Peter Partner, *The Lands of St. Peter* (Berkeley, 1972), pp. 1–10; Noble, *Republic of St. Peter*, pp. 242–8.

[49] *LD*. The best place to get a sense of all the controversies surrounding this book, and to find the basis for most current thinking, is in Leo Santifaller, *Liber Diurnus: Studien und Forschungen von Leo Santifaller*, ed. Harald Zimmermann, Päpste und Papsttum 10 (Stuttgart, 1976). Shorter studies are: Giulio Batelli, 'Liber Diurnus Romanorum Pontificum', *Enciclopedia cattolica*, 12 vols. (Vatican City, 1951), VII, cols. 1262–7; Hans Foerster, 'Liber Diurnus Pontificum Romanorum', *New Catholic Encyclopedia*, 17 vols. (New York, 1967), VIII, p. 694.

origin, private, and without demonstrable connection to Rome, Santifaller abandoned his earlier position. He did establish, however, that the surviving version of the book does in fact contain many *formulae* that were actually used in Rome, and that a book like the *Liber Diurnus* must have been used both to train notaries and to prepare actual documents.

The *formulae* in the *Liber Diurnus* reveal many of the same kinds of things as the bureaucratic records. For example, let us begin at the beginning of Foerster's edition and see what we find: *Formata quam accipit episcopus; Synodale ut episcopus alterius civitatis in alia ecclesia possit incardinari; Preceptum de adunandis ecclesiis; Petitio dedicationis oratorii; Responsum oratorii dedicandi; Responsum de speranda sanctuaria.*[50] The second example, the one relating to the transfer of a bishop, can only refer to the pope but the other *formulae* listed here could have been used in almost any episcopal church. Thus it is easy to see why the surviving copies of the *Liber Diurnus* come from north Italian bishoprics. Portions of the *Liber* were copied and used outside Rome because Roman administrative practices, and the documents that accompanied those practices, were both useful and influential. But as with the *formula* for episcopal transfers, so in many other cases the *formulae* were only relevant to Rome and the pope. Perhaps the best example of this is the series of *formulae* pertaining to the adminstration of the church during a vacancy in the papacy and the documents relating to the election of a new pope.[51] As noted, then, the *Liber Diurnus* reveals much about several dozen kinds of actual documents, about the preparation of those documents, and about the administrative practices associated with those documents.

Second, there is the *Liber Pontificalis*.[52] In the last years of the fifth or the first years of the sixth century the lives of all the early popes were written up and collected. Then from Boniface II to Leo III (530–816) each pope received a contemporary *vita*. These differ a great deal in length, style and amount, or quality, of information. There are several indications that the *Liber Pontificalis* was produced in the papal chancery. Its language regularly echoes that of other documents written in the *scrinium*, especially papal letters.[53] Just as importantly, however, virtually every *vita* bears marks of research in the archives. It is easy to spot references to or even quotations from letters, administrative records, synodal enactments and

---

[50] *LD*, pp. 81–4. [51] *Ibid.*, pp. 113–21.

[52] The major source of information on the *LP* is formed by the hundreds of pages of notes in Duchesne's edition. I have expressed myself on this text in 'A new look at the *Liber Pontificalis*', *Archivum Historiae Pontificiae* 23 (1985), 347–58, at 347–8 n. 3, I cite much of the relevant literature.

[53] Erich Caspar, *Das Papsttum*, 2 vols. (Tübingen, 1933), II, pp. 732, 795.

liturgical sources.[54] It cannot be a mere coincidence that notarial language and notarial sources are so liberally strewn throughout the pages of the *Liber Pontificalis* and that the notaries and archivists, or librarians, worked in one bureau under the *primicerius notariorum*.

The *Liber Pontificalis* is, of course, a history of the popes. It is, indeed, an official history that provides a clear indication of how the papacy wanted its history told.[55] The work is distinguished neither by elegance of style nor sophistication of philosophical conception. Instead, it relentlessly, monotonously recounts basic facts about each of the popes. The book also follows certain basic themes, such as relations between the papacy and the Byzantine court, or Lombard pressure on Rome. The whole point of the *Liber Pontificalis* appears to have been to show how traditional the papacy was and to describe, but never to analyse in detail or to apologize for, the traditions that the papacy embraced. The book was widely copied outside Rome, and highly influential for the development of other ecclesiastical histories such as those of Ravenna, Metz, St Wandrille and St Gall.[56]

Certain characteristics of the *Liber Pontificalis* suggest the possibility that it may have played a role in the education of young Roman clerics. The book says that Stephen III was *ecclesiasticis traditionibus inbutus*.[57] It is hard to imagine a better means of accomplishing that end than by a careful reading of the *Liber Pontificalis*, the papacy's own official version of papal history, that is of 'ecclesiastical traditions'. There are also quasi-*formulae* at the beginning of each *vita* that look like the kind of mnemonic devices one would expect to find in an elementary textbook. For example, popes who were especially solicitous of Rome's poor were always called *mansuetus*, or *mitissimus* or something similar, and popes who were involved in doctrinal controversies were named *eruditus*, or *instructus* or the like.[58] Sot has argued that all ecclesiastical histories were addressed to a *public des clercs*[59] and one such history, that of Agnellus for Ravenna, contains explicit reference to *auditores*, to 'hearers', to an audience, who heard the text read out.[60] Riché has drawn attention to a Lucca codex that contains a variety of

---

[54] Noble, '*Liber Pontificalis*', Appendix, pp. 357–8.

[55] Walter Ullmann, *Short History of the Papacy* (corr. edn, London, 1974), p. 30.

[56] Herbert Grundmann, 'Geschichtsschreibung im Mittelalter', in *Deutsche Philologie im Aufriss* (2nd edn, Berlin, 1967), cols. 2253–4; Michel Sot, *Gesta episcoporum, gesta abbatum*, Typologie des sources du moyen âge occidentale 37 (Turnhout, 1981). See also Noble, '*Liber Pontificalis*', 348–9.

[57] *LP* I, p. 468.

[58] Noble, '*Liber Pontificalis*', 351.   [59] Sot, *Gesta episcoporum*, pp. 45–6.

[60] Agnellus, *Liber pontificalis ravennatis ecclesiae*, c. 79, ed. O. Holder-Egger, *MGH SS rerum Langobardicarum*, p. 331. I wish to thank Tom Brown for first drawing my attention to the importance of this passage.

historical works, including the *Liber Pontificalis*, 'which must have figured in the study program of young clerics'.[61] The nature of the text itself and the uses to which it was put outside Rome suggest strongly that, to some extent at least, the *Liber Pontificalis* was a school text in papal Rome. If this hypothesis is valid then the *Liber Pontificalis* represents both a kind of historical writing and a use of literacy to provide an historical record, and an actual book that was written and read to serve those very purposes.

The *Liber Pontificalis* has value for modern historians because it shows some of the kinds of records that were kept in papal Rome and because it adds weight to other evidence to the effect that the papal archives were used by various branches of the papal government. But even more significant is what the *Liber Pontificalis* reveals about the papacy's historical memory and its commitment of that memory to writing. As the title of his important book shows, Clanchy has detected, in high mediaeval England, a crucial transformation from communities where memory sufficed for the conduct of public business to communities where written records came to have a dominant role.[62] The *Liber Pontificalis* provides two reasons to suppose that Clanchy's theme will not fit papal Rome in the early middle ages. First, the written *Liber Pontificalis* was based throughout on careful research in the written memory, in the archives, of the papal government, and, second, it was the written *Liber Pontificalis* that helped to form the individual and the collective historical memory of clerics in training for the papal government. One might well say that in papal Rome one proceeded from written record to memory.

Third, there are the liturgical books of the Roman church.[63] The Roman liturgy was a long time taking shape but for the period before the fourth century there exist only scattered bits of evidence.[64] From the fifth century onwards, however, the record is quite full, and also very controversial. The technical details of liturgical history are of little concern to us here. Our

---

[61] Riché, *Education and Culture*, trans. Contreni, p. 408.

[62] I refer, of course, to Michael Clanchy, *From Memory to Written Record: England 1066–1307* (London, 1979).

[63] Good general accounts are: Theodor Klauser, *A Short History of the Western Liturgy*, trans. John Halliburton (2nd edn, Oxford, 1979), pp. 5–77; Cyrille Vogel, *Introduction aux sources de l'histoire du culte chrétien au moyen âge* (Spoleto, 1975), pp. 20–57. Older but still valuable are Ludwig Eisenhofer and Joseph Lechner, *The Liturgy of the Roman Rite*, trans. A.J. and E.F. Peeler (London, 1961) (prepared from the 6th German edn of 1953), especially pp. 241–70, and Gregory Dix, *The Shape of the Liturgy* (2nd edn 1945; repr. New York, 1983), especially pp. 546–612.

[64] Eisenhofer and Lechner, *Liturgy of the Roman Rite*, pp. 252–6, is a good account of the very early period but see also Klaus Gamber, *Codices Liturgici Latini Antiquiores*, 2 vols. (2nd edn, Freiburg, 1968), I, pp. 93–105.

intention is only to notice the kinds of books produced in the Roman church for the purpose of organizing its public, ritual celebrations.

The most important of Rome's liturgical books was the sacramentary, a volume containing the mass prayers *per circulum anni*. A full sacramentary needed collects, secrets, propers and prefaces, all of which could change for each celebration, along with the canon and post-communion which were relatively constant. By the eighth century, in Italy and elsewhere, there were *missalia plenaria* containing not only mass prayers but also readings, antiphons and responses.[65] In Rome, however, it appears that the various kinds of liturgical books tended to remain distinct.

It is difficult to say just when the Roman church produced its first comprehensive sacramentary. The so-called 'Leonine Sacramentary' contains a great deal of clearly Roman material from the period 450 to 560 but the oldest surviving manuscript was written in Verona about 600. Several popes, Leo I, Gelasius I and Vigilius, certainly made important contributions to what became the 'Leonine Sacramentary' but not one of them can be called its author.[66] The *Liber Pontificalis* says that Gelasius wrote *sacramentorum praefationes et orationes*[67] and Gennadius speaks of a *liber sacramentorum* in connection with this pope.[68] In the eighth century some writers picked up these remarks and began to attribute a sacramentary to Gelasius, and the famous manuscript Vaticanus Reginensis 316 is widely but somewhat misleadingly called the 'Gelasian Sacramentary'. Actually, liturgical scholars are not sure that Gelasius wrote a sacramentary. Chavasse thinks the 'Gelasian' is really a mass book from the seventh-century title churches while Gamber believes that the book was written in sixth-century Ravenna.[69] No one, in any case, doubts that the book is full of genuinely Roman material from the fifth and sixth centuries. The most likely candidate for the authorship, if that is not too strong a word, of a *Liber sacramentorum anni circuli Romanae ecclesiae* is Gregory I but, as Deshusses has pointed out, the traditions attributing a complete sacramentary to Gregory are no older than the eighth century and, even though it is almost certain that Gregory made huge contributions to the 'Gregorian

[65] Gamber, *Codices*, II, pp. 527–8.

[66] David M. Hope, *The Leonine Sacramentary: A Reassessment of its Nature and Purpose* (Oxford, 1971); Gamber, *Codices*, I, pp. 292–9; Vogel, *Introduction*, pp. 31–42.

[67] *LP* I, p. 255.

[68] Gennadius, *De viris illustribus*, c. 96, *PL* 58, cols. 1115B–1116A.

[69] Antoine Chavasse, *Le Sacramentaire gélasien (Vaticanus Reginensis 316). Sacramentaire presbytérial en usage dans les titres romains au viie siècle*, Bibliothèque de théologie, ser. 4, no. 1 (Paris, 1958). See also Gamber, *Codices* I, pp. 292–318, especially pp. 299–300, and Vogel, *Introduction*, pp. 48–57.

Sacramentary', it is also true that from Leo II (682–3) to Hadrian I (772–95) there were important modifications.[70] Taken together, the evidence of the 'Leonine', 'Gelasian' and 'Gregorian' Sacramentaries shows that the fifth and sixth centuries were rich ones for the development of the Roman liturgy.

Rome's other liturgical books can be treated more briefly. First, there is the lectionary. Before the fourth century there was *lectio continua* from Bible codices and then, in the fourth and early fifth centuries, pericopes, selected passages, were marked out for reading. The first evidence for an epistolary, a *Liber comitis*, dates from around 450 and shortly after that the first *Capitulare evangeliorum*, or evangelistiary, made its appearance. By the middle of the sixth century *lectionaria plenaria* began to appear in central Italy. It is not known where the *Liber comitis* first appeared and the *Capitulare evangeliorum* may have had its origin in Ravenna or Carthage. Leaving origins aside, one can say that by the end of the sixth century Rome had developed its lectionary, its book of biblical readings selected to accompany every major liturgical celebration *per circulum anni*, to a very high and precise state.[71]

The Roman antiphonary in the early middle ages contained both the antiphons for the divine office and the responses for the mass. In later times these were divided into the antiphonal and the gradual, respectively. Tradition attributes the antiphonary to Gregory I but the books most widely used in Rome and elsewhere seem to have taken shape by about 500. A good deal of older material went into them, of course, for example, the *Introitus* attributed to Celestine I (422–32).[72] Probably Gregory I did make a major contribution to reorganizing the antiphonary.[73]

Finally, there are the *ordines*, the rites for almost every conceivable kind of liturgical ritual celebrated in the Roman church. *Ordo Romanus I* is a remarkably detailed set of instructions for a major papal mass, while other *ordines* survive for different masses and also, to cite but a few examples, for ordinations of clergy, for the consecration of altars, for the installation of

---

[70] Jean Deshusses, *Le Sacramentaire grégorien*, 3 vols. (2nd edn, Freiburg, 1979), especially I, pp. 50–6. Gamber, *Codices*, II, pp. 325–47; Vogel, *Introduction*, pp. 67–83. I have not discussed the so-called 'eighth-century Gelasian sacramentary' because it is a hybrid book, formed in the Frankish world out of essentially 'Gelasian' and 'Gregorian' elements according to a design and purpose that are not yet fully understood. It provides no independent evidence for Rome. See Bernard Moreton, *The Eighth-Century Gelasian Sacramentary* (Oxford, 1976).

[71] Gamber, *Codices*, II, pp. 429–39, 446–83; and, more fully, Vogel, *Introduction*, pp. 239–88, 309–20.

[72] *LP* I, p. 230.

[73] Gamber, *Codices*, II, pp. 492–526; Vogel, *Introduction*, pp. 328–32.

relics and for a host of other rites. The oldest surviving Roman *ordines* date, in their preserved forms, from the seventh century but it is clear that their basic material is often much older, reaching back to at least 500 and probably even earlier.[74]

Rome's liturgical books provide evidence of several kinds of literacy. They show how a particular historical sense, a feeling for the continuity of worship, could be committed to writing and transmitted through time and across space. They represent the writing down of a splendidly Roman sense of order and decorum and solemnity in the conduct of public life. They betray an ability to articulate a sense of form and purpose in the administration of worship that is no less impressive than the articulation of much else in the papal administration. Finally, liturgy and, within the liturgy, one particular set of books, the lectionaries, show that as the Word of God was proclaimed and spread, other words laid out the context in which the Word would be heard and responded to. People around Europe did indeed turn to Rome for guidance on liturgical matters. Pope Vigilius (538–55) sent a sacramentary to Bishop Profuturus of Braga[75] and Hadrian I sent a 'Gregorian Sacramentary' to Charlemagne.[76] Roman antiphonaries were sent, among other places, to England in the time of Egbert of York and to Francia in the time of Pippin III.[77] This activity represents a very important use of literacy.

Fourth, and finally, there are Rome's law books. From at least the time of Pope Celestine I in 429 the Roman church had insisted that all clergy know the canons: *Nulli sacerdotum suos licet canones ignorare.*[78] It was only in the fifth and sixth centuries, however, that Rome began showing a real interest in collecting its law. In fact, the period from about 400 to 600 was an extraordinarily rich one in the history of law throughout the old Roman world. This age saw two major compilations of Roman law, those of Theodosius II and Justinian, a large number of germanic codes, dozens of monastic rules which are, after all, law-codes of a certain kind, and the earliest papal collections.[79] Papal law was based above all on synodal

---

[74] Michel Andrieu, *Les Ordines Romani du haut moyen âge*, 5 vols., II, Spicilegium Sacrum Lovaniense 23 (Louvain, 1971); Vogel, *Introduction*, pp. 127–81.

[75] *PL* 69, cols. 15–19.

[76] Charlemagne had charged Paul the Deacon to secure the sacramentary in Rome and in about 785/6 Hadrian complied: Jaffé, *Regesta Pontificum Romanorum*, I no. 2473 (=*codex Carolinus*, no. 89); Vogel, *Introduction*, pp. 72–8.

[77] Gamber, *Codices*, I, pp. 494–5.

[78] Jaffé, *Regesta Pontificum Romanorum*, I, no. 371.

[79] Classen, 'Fortleben und Wandel spätrömischen Urkundenwesens im früheren Mittelalter', in *Recht und Schrift*, ed. Classen, pp. 19–20.

enactments and papal decretals, which were authoritative pronouncements by the popes.[80] The most influential early synodal collections were those of Nicaea (325) and Chalcedon (451) but canons from many other local and regional councils found their way into the collections. The oldest papal decretals were issued by Siricius (384–99) and as time passed many decretals entered the collections; but not all of them because some were lost and because some were deliberately excluded.

The *Liber Pontificalis* says of Gelasius I that he 'made a constitution concerning the whole church'.[81] It is very hard to know what this means because Gelasius is not known to have issued a general code of church law although he did address a decretal in twenty-eight chapters to the bishops of southern Italy and Sicily.[82] More important and better known is the work of the Scythian monk Dionysius Exiguus who came to Rome in the time of Anastasius I (496–8) and produced, around 500, the first major Roman *corpus canonum*. It has come to be called the *Collectio Dionysiana* and with its careful selection of conciliar canons and papal decretals it was meant to reflect the law of the church as it was understood and applied in Rome and its environs.[83] For nearly three centuries this collection grew by the addition of new decretals and by the incorporation of canons from various Roman synods, especially those of 649, 721, 743 and 769. In 774, or shortly thereafter, Hadrian I sent a copy of the *Collectio Dionysiana*, henceforth called the *Dionysio-Hadriana*, to Charlemagne.[84] In other words, the period from 500 to 800 was a rich one in the history of canon law and a comparably important period, in Rome, would not be seen again until the eleventh century.

A knowledge of law, and of legal traditions, along with the ability to produce sophisticated legal collections, is evidence of several kinds of

---

[80] Hagender, 'Papstregister', pp. 320–2; Hans Erich Feine, *Kirchliche Rechtsgeschichte* (5th edn, Cologne, 1972), pp. 89–91; Paul Fournier and Gabriel Le Bras, *Histoire des collections canoniques en occident depuis les fausses décrétales jusqu'au Decret de Gratien*, 2 vols. (Paris, 1931), I, pp. 10–13; Alfonsus M. Stickler, *Historia Iuris Canonici Latini*, I : *Historia Fontium* (Rome, 1950; repr. 1974), pp. 42–52.

[81] *LP* I, p. 255.

[82] Duchesne in *ibid.*, I, p. 256 n. 7.

[83] Fournier and Le Bras, *Histoire des collections canoniques*, I, pp. 13–25; Feine, *Kirchliche Rechtsgeschichte*, pp. 90–6. Hubert Mordek, *Kirchenrecht und Reform im Frankenreich, Die Collectio Vetus Gallica*, Beiträge zur Geschichte und Quellenkunde des Mittelalters 1 (Berlin, 1975), pp. 2–9.

[84] For the transmission of the *Collectio Dionysiana* see H. Mordek, 'Kirchenrechtliche Autoritäten im Frühmittelalter', in *Recht und Schrift*, ed. Classen, pp. 237–55, especially pp. 238–41. Controversial but still valuable as an assessment of legal foundations is the first chapter of Walter Ullmann, *The Growth of Papal Government in the Middle Ages* (3rd edn, London, 1970), pp. 1–43.

literacy. Above all, however, I would draw attention to the ability to articulate, and to write down, precise rules for the daily ordering of an ecclesiastical polity. For centuries the church had managed without much written law and then, in a period when so many laws were being written, the church was fully able to participate in the legal activity of the time.

These four kinds of evidence help to round out the picture that was sketched earlier from the administrative records. The *Liber Diurnus*, the *Liber Pontificalis*, the liturgical books and the legal collections are exceptionally revealing documents. They provide insights into the workings of various branches of the administration that we otherwise would not have. The *Liber Pontificalis*, in particular, shows how some administrative records in the church were actually used. The *formulae* in the *Liber Diurnus* reveal the existence of many kind of documents for which there are no surviving examples. All of these books, in different but complementary ways, reveal a remarkable sense of history, and a perception that history needed to be written down and acted upon. The legal and liturgical books show a profound sense of order and precision that had come increasingly to depend on written instructions. Indeed, everywhere that one looks in the papal administration one finds the use of the written word.

The use and growth of literacy depended, after all, on the existence of trained personnel and on the presence of institutions capable of providing the necessary training. It is well, therefore, to say a little about education in papal Rome. There is a lot that simply cannot be known, but two points seem reasonably clear. Papal bureaucrats received training in the specific area of their administrative competence within the *scholae* and all clerics received a broader education. Because Gregory I had a potent dislike for laymen serving in the church's government, it seems that after his time, but with the possible exception of some of the lesser patrimonial administrators, all key figures were clerics who were both trained and educated.

Explicit testimony shows that Gregory II (715–31) was educated 'from earliest youth in the *patriarchium*',[85] and the same was true of Leo III (795–816),[86] and Sergius II (844–7).[87] Evidently, then, there was some kind of a school in the Lateran complex but not all aspiring clerics were educated there. Hadrian I (772–95),[88] and Nicholas I (858–67)[89] were educated privately, probably by tutors hired by their families, and Stephen III (768–72) was educated in the Greek monastery of St Chrysogonus.[90] Primarily the education was scriptural but we do hear that Sergius II learned *communes artes*[91] and that Nicholas I had a father who was a *liberalium artium amator*.[92] It is impossible to say exactly what the liberal arts might

[85] *LP* I, p. 396.   [86] *LP* II, p. 1.   [87] *LP* II, p. 86.   [88] *LP* I, p. 498.

[89] *LP* II, p. 151.   [90] *LP* I, p. 468.   [91] *LP* II, p. 86.   [92] *LP* II, p. 151.

have meant in papal Rome. Guillou has evidence that is not easily datable from Ravenna, pointing to the study of grammar, rhetoric, dialectic, morals, physics, arithmetic, geometry, music, astronomy, theology, history, chant and computus.[93] This list of subjects looks suspiciously ideal and comprehensive, and Brown has observed that, even in Ravenna, the liberal education of the sixth century declined badly in the seventh.[94] It is possible that clerical schools in Rome too gradually eclipsed the public ones, but the persistence, noted above, of public *tabelliones* into the ninth century suggests that some public education remained available for laymen. And because so many judicial, financial and patrimonial documents issued by the papal government were addressed to laymen, it seems possible to infer that some degree of lay literacy was present.

The needs of the papal regime were essentially ecclesiastical and administrative, and, in consequence, such schools as might have existed were there for very specific purposes. Boys entered the papal administration through either the *cubiculum* – the pope's chamber – or the *schola cantorum* – the agency charged with providing singers for the liturgy.[95] Just as the *schola cantorum* taught chant, and thus was not really a school in any large or comprehensive sense, so too the other *scholae* taught, not academic subjects, or even *communes artes*, but law or the notarial art. Certainly clerics in training learned the liturgy as we meet it in the *ordines* and there is evidence that the *Liber Pontificalis* may have figured in clerical education.[96] Somewhere in the Lateran palace there must have been a school for the boys who entered young into the papal government but the education provided there was appropriate for boys and young men who were going to live and work in an ecclesiastical setting. Illmer has reminded us that early mediaeval monastic and cathedral schools must not be idealized; that is, we must not exaggerate the level of learning attained in Rome. Schools existed to teach young men to be able to function and to succeed in a particular kind of religious community. If those schools turned out scholars then that was an inadvertent by-product of a quest for different goals.[97]

[93] André Guillou, 'L'Ecole dans l'Italie byzantine', *Settimane* 19 (Spoleto, 1972), 291–311.

[94] T.S. Brown, *Gentlemen and Officers: Imperial Administration and Aristocratic Power in Byzantine Italy A.D. 554–800* (Rome, 1984), pp. 79–81, especially p. 79.

[95] Georg Heinrich Hörle, *Frühmittelalterliche Mönchs- und Klerikerbildung in Italien* (Freiburg, 1914); Michel Andrieu, 'Les Ordres mineurs dans l'ancien rite romain', *Revue des Sciences religieuses* 5 (1925), 232–74; Riché, *Education and Culture*, trans. Contreni, pp. 417–19; Noble, *Republic of St. Peter*, pp. 228–9.

[96] See above n. 60.

[97] Detlef Illmer, *Formen der Erziehung und Wissensvermittlung im frühen Mittelalter: Quellenstudien zur Frage der Kontinuität der abendländischen Erziehungswesens*, Münchener Beiträge zur Mediävistik und Renaissanceforschung 7 (Munich, 1971).

Were we not so ill-informed about the holdings of the papal library and about the contours of education in papal Rome, we might be able to say more about the body of information that was available for transmission and consultation. Let me cite two cases where our ignorance of basic issues complicates our understanding. Before the sixth century Rome did not have a complete set of the canons of the ecumenical councils, and Dionysius Exiguus was set the task of ordering and completing the material and perhaps also of translating it from Greek into Latin.[98] Under such circumstances, it is very difficult to say how much was known in Rome before the sixth century about the history of the councils, and about their actual decisions. Another problem concerns the theology of the Greek east. Right through our period there were popes and papal administrators who knew Greek, but we do not know how many Greek books they had, or how well they understood the arguments of eastern churchmen, or how hard they tried to understand. A reader of Cassiodorus' *Institutes* will be familiar with the large number of Greek theological works that had been translated into Latin. But we cannot with confidence place many of those translations in Rome. Ambrose and Augustine played key roles as mediators between Greek and Latin but it is difficult to move from that perfectly valid generalization to a concrete statement about theological knowledge in papal Rome.[99]

I am inclined to take a rather positive view of the amount of knowledge that was available in Rome. I do not think that ignorance, let us say of Greek or of Greek thought, accounts for what some have seen as intellectual sterility. Far from being sterile, early mediaeval papal Rome shows us the gradual emergence of Latin, western and papal traditions which were afterwards gripped tenaciously. One kind of literacy involves understanding. The popes understood their world and its issues very well but they chose not to contend and instead to defend. Gregory II (716–31) and Gregory III (731–41) are good examples. The former refused to accept in Rome the canons of a major Byzantine church council held under imperial auspices in 692, and he solemnly rejected Byzantine iconoclasm. The latter continued to reject iconoclasm and also spoke bravely about the inappropriateness of imperial intervention in dogmatic issues.[100] The popes, in other

---

[98] Peterson, 'Gregory the Great', 572; Judith Herrin, *The Formation of Christendom* (Oxford, 1987), pp. 85, 104–5.

[99] The great study of Greek is Walter Berschin, *Griechisch-Lateinisches Mittelalter* (Munich, 1980), especially pp. 113–18. I have examined a few aspects of the problem in 'The declining knowledge of Greek in eighth- and ninth-century papal Rome', *Byzantinische Zeitschrift*, 78 (1985), 56–62.

[100] *LP* I, pp. 396–410, 415–21.

words, knew what they needed to know to rule over and through their church and to respond in the many and complex issues that confronted them. It is hard to see what more could be asked of them.

Because of the particular demands of the papal government, it is arguable that literacy in the papal administration was more widespread than anywhere else in the mediaeval west and also that, more so than anywhere else, it was necessary to almost every aspect of the functioning of the papal system; that is, that certain functions of the system assumed and depended upon the written word for success. But literacy did not mean scholarship, higher studies or learning for the sake of learning. Someone from the *schola cantorum* was 'literate' when he knew how to chant. Someone from the *schola notariorum* was 'literate' when he could draw up a document correctly. Both of these people were also literate in the sense that they could share in the divine office and probably read their psalms and gospels. The schools in the papal government, that is, taught people exactly what they needed to know to do the work and to live the life for which they were intended.

At the upper level of the papal administration there were the popes and the major administrators, men who were themselves *papabili*, and these people were literate in every imaginable sense of the word. At the lowest levels of the administration there were simple clerics in minor orders whose literacy was pretty much confined to the possession of certain bureaucratic skills and to the ability to act on rudimentary written instructions. The majority of papal administrators were probably able to read and write and they will have had to have made frequent use of all manner of written materials in their daily tasks. The whole administration may, however, have formed one or more of what Stock has expressively called 'textual communities'. He says that 'what was essential to a textual community was not a written version of a text, although that was sometimes present, but an individual who, having mastered it, then utilized it for reforming a group's thought and action'.[101] It is fruitful to think of the *Liber Pontificalis* as one book around which a textual community might have formed and where the essential understanding would have been historical. The liturgical books are another example. The liturgy contained written and spoken parts but celebrants and worshippers always had different roles to play. Nevertheless, words and movements bound a whole community together in a profound and shared experience. I can only repeat that people knew what they needed to know; they were as literate as they needed to be.

---

[101] Brian Stock, *The Implications of Literacy: Written Language and Models of Interpretation in the Eleventh and Twelfth Centuries* (Princeton, 1983), pp. 88–151; the quotation is from p. 90.

Although I have concentrated my attention on administrative literacy, I wish to acknowledge one or two other aspects of the issue. The popes were routinely involved in theological controversies, the great majority of which were not of their own making. For the most part, therefore, the popes did not seek to make distinguished or original contributions to theology. Instead, as with the *Tome* sent by Leo I to the Council of Chalcedon (451) we see a document that 'reflects and codifies with masterly precision the ideas of his predecessors'.[102] An exception might appear to be Gregory I, a prolific and, for centuries, deeply influential writer. But this pope was, in his theology as in his administration, practical above all else. He was a conservative traditionalist who sought to synthesize, to teach and to disseminate more than to speculate and to innovate.[103] As with theology, so too with ecclesiology and political thought. Leo I, Gelasius I, Gregory I and several ninth-century popes made lasting contributions to the mediaeval understanding of the nature of ecclesiastical authority, and the relationship between the sacred and the secular.[104] I can do no more here than note, therefore, that other kinds of literacy than administrative, historical, liturgical and legal existed in the papal government in the early middle ages. As in so many other cases so too here as well, this 'intellectual' literacy depended upon both a broad understanding of precise issues and, even more importantly, an ability to reduce that understanding to writing and to disseminate the writings thus produced.

Indeed, there are some remarkable convergences in the development of literacy in the papal government. The period from roughly 400 to 600 saw the first great elaboration of the papal administration, with all that this entailed for the preparation, dissemination and conservation of documents. But this was also the first great age for Roman liturgical and legal books. The official papal history, the *Liber Pontificalis*, was begun in this period. Major decretals, such as those of Leo I on the petrine theory of papal primacy, or of Gelasius I on proper relations between *imperium* and *sacerdotium*, were written in this period, as were tremendously significant books such as Gregory's *Dialogues*[105] and *Pastoral Care*. All of this seems to

---

[102] J.N.D. Kelly, *Early Christian Doctrines* (2nd edn, New York, 1960), p. 337.

[103] G.R. Evans, *The Thought of Gregory the Great*, Cambridge Studies in Medieval Life and Thought, Fourth Series, 2 (Cambridge, 1986).

[104] Walter Ullmann devoted his life to studying the ideological foundations of papal activity. One can look with profit at the appropriate sections of any of his stimulating and controversial works. For a reasonably balanced summation on the early middle ages, see Jeffrey Richards, *The Popes and the Papacy in the Early Middle Ages, 476–752* (London, 1979), pp. 9–28.

[105] I am impressed but not persuaded by the massive circumstantial case built against Gregorian authorship of the *Dialogues* by Francis Clark, *The Pseudo-Gregorian Dialogues*, 2 vols. (Leiden, 1987).

me attributable to the spread and elaboration of ecclesiastical administration after the Constantinian peace, to the patronage of the Roman government, to the entry in large numbers into the clerical ranks of educated Roman nobles and to the assumption of responsibility by the church for so much formerly secular administrative work. Then in the eighth century, the assumption of temporal rule by the popes brought a second efflorescence of literate activity. Administrative structures were refined, new structures were created, the library and archives grew in importance and, apparently, more documents were produced. Papal Rome, moreover, became a source for authoritative books – legal and liturgical ones, for example – all over Europe.

Modern scholars have commented in detail on how hard it is to determine just what literacy means.[106] Today one hears talk of 'cultural literacy', or of 'computer literacy'. The former involves reading, notably the reading of the classics, but the latter has nothing at all to do with reading or writing and much to do with the possession of a certain kind of skill or knowledge. It is this kind of literacy, or knowledge, that I have been emphasizing in connection with the papal government. The literary attainments of Gregory I were very high, and this appears to have been true of a number of the popes if we can assume that their letters – no more – were their own compositions. But the level of literary achievement of the *rectores* and *actionarii* on the papal patrimonies had to have been slight. A papal notary may have learned *communes artes* but he needed only to read his psalter and to draw up a contract or a letter. There existed a number of different kinds of literacy in papal Rome and there were many literate people. But the literacy was overwhelmingly practical in use and the literate were primarily a clerical, governing elite. Words – God's – had empowered a church to exist and other words, tightly kept and formally applied, empowered that church to act in the world. For that is how the papal administration used literacy: to act in the world, to rule, to govern.

[106] See, for example, Harvey J. Graff, 'Introduction', in his *Literacy and Social Development in the West: A Reader* (Cambridge, 1981), pp. 1–13, especially pp. 1–5.

5

Literacy and the laity
in early mediaeval Spain

Roger Collins

In the early seventeenth century the Morrocan author Al-Maqqarî, looking back on the departed glories of Al-Andalus, recalled that:

rich men in Cordova, however illiterate they might be, encouraged letters, rewarded with the greatest munificence writers and poets, and spared neither trouble nor expense in forming large collections of books; so that, independently of the famous library founded by the Khalif Al-hakem [961–76], and which is said by writers worthy of credit to have contained no less than four hundred thousand volumes, there were in the capital many other libraries in the hands of wealthy individuals, where the studious could dive into the fathomless sea of knowledge and bring up its inestimable pearls. Cordova was indeed in the opinion of every author the city in Andalus where most books were to be found, and its inhabitants were renowned for their passion for forming libraries.[1]

His words may seem ambivalent. On the one hand he hints that some of these avid collectors may not have been able to read the books they sought so hard to acquire, whilst on the other he implies that the substantial libraries that they formed were accessible to scholars more studious if less rich than themselves. Al-Maqqarî's principal source here would seem to have been the thirteenth-century author Ibn Sa'îd, whose own purposes were both satirical and moralizing.[2] He was criticizing the wealthy collectors who were interested only in the outward show of their books: the rarity value of the works and the fame of their calligraphers. Some modern bibliophiles might find his words uncomfortable. This was obviously a recognized target of criticism, and Al-Maqqarî quotes another passage from Ibn Khaldûn (1332–1406) to the effect that the antics of these philistine collectors were driving the price of books beyond the financial reach of those who really

---

[1] Al-Maqqarî, *Naf̣ at-Ṭîb*, trans. P. de Gayangos, *The History of the Mohammedan Dynasties in Spain*, 2 vols. (London, 1840), I, p. 139.

[2] Ibn Sa'îd al-Maghribî, quoted by Al-Maqqarî, trans. Gayangos, *Mohammedan Dynasties*, I, pp. 139–40.

needed them and appreciated them for their contents rather than their appearances.[3]

Despite the didactic character of the information there are reasonable grounds for believing that not only book buying but also book reading played an important role in the society of late Umayyad Al-Andalus, above all in Cordoba. Although the precise figures should not be trusted, Al-Maqqari's report of the great library of the Caliph Al-Ḥakam II and his extensive literary patronage can be corroborated from other sources. The fragment of the *Hasty Notes* of Sa'īd ibn Aḥmad of Toledo, written in 1067/8, records the Caliph's use of agents throughout Egypt, Syria and Iraq in hunting out books for his library, which in the author's view at least was more extensive than that of the 'Abbāsid caliphs in Baghdad.[4] Traditionally it is reported that the scientific and philosophical collections in this library were destroyed after the Caliph's death on the order of the dictator Al-Manṣūr (d. 1002) to appease religious fundamentalists, though this may have as little accuracy in it as the comparable story of the dispersal of the palace library of Charlemagne.[5] However, whatever the truth of that, it must be assumed that the Umayyad caliphal library was wholly or largely destroyed when the palace complex of Medina Azahara was sacked and destroyed in 1010.[6]

A distinction between lay and ecclesiastical literacy makes little sense in an Islamic society in which no separate priestly class exists. Even distinctions between what may be considered to be more narrowly religious literature, which would include the Koran itself, collections of traditions, and exegetical works, and other literary genres that could be classed as secular are not always easy to make. Works of history, for example, could be written for didactic and triumphalist religious ends.[7] For present purposes what is significant is that there is a considerable amount of evidence available to indicate that there existed a fairly substantial though unquantifiable urban market for books in late Umayyad Spain, and, as both a number of extant works and the recorded titles of others that are lost

---

[3] Ibn Khaldūn, quoted by Al-Maqqarî, trans. Gayangos, *Mohammedan Dynasties*, I, p. 140.

[4] Sa'īd ibn Aḥmad ibn Sa'īd of Toledo, trans. Gayangos, *Mohammedan Dynasties*, I, appendix C, pp. xl–xlii.

[5] Sa'īd ibn Ahmad, *ibid.*, p. xli, and Einhard, *Vita Karoli* ed. O. Holder-Egger, *MGH SS i.u.s.* XXV.

[6] For the sack of 1010 and the events leading up to it see E. Lévi-Provençal, *Histoire de l'Espagne musulmane*, 3 vols. (Paris and Leiden, 1951), II, pp. 291–320.

[7] For Arab historiography see D.M. Dunlop, *Arab Civilization to AD 1500* (London and Beirut, 1971), pp. 70–149; for some of the problems to be faced see R. Collins, *Early Medieval Spain: Unity in Diversity, 400–1000* (London and Basingstoke, 1983), pp. 146–9.

indicate, this was also reflected in the considerable output of new works in a variety of genres in the same period, basically the second half of the tenth century.

There are, as seen in the case of Al-Maqqarī's use of his earlier sources, a number of problems to be encountered in evaluating this evidence, and most of the information is later in date than the period it purports to describe. However, a useful control can be applied in the form of an examination of the literature and literary output of the minority elements in the society of Islamic Al-Andalus: the Jews and the Christians.[8] Both groups enjoyed a period of considerable literary and intellectual activity in the late tenth century, at least in Cordoba. Although relatively few new works were composed by Christian authors, the process of the translation of a number of standard late antique Latin texts into Arabic, which had been underway since perhaps as early as the eighth century, received considerable impetus from the patronage of the Caliph Al-Ḥakam II, for whom a *History of the Franks* was composed by a Bishop Godmar of Gerona and who commissioned a translation of Orosius.[9] The text of the former has been lost, but it is possible that it underlay some of the surprisingly detailed and accurate information on a number of topics that it might have dealt with which are to be found in the works of later Arab authors, such as Ibn al-Athīr, writing in the east.[10] The Arabic Orosius is still extant, and the degree of indebtedness to it of various Andalusi authors is becoming increasingly clear.[11] It may also have initiated a renewed interest in historical composition among Christian literati, who by that time wrote exclusively in Arabic.[12]

The impression of an active literary culture existing in the capital of Umayyad Al-Andalus in the last three-quarters of a century of the dynasty's rule is thus not too difficult to document, even on the basis of the few examples given here. What it implies in terms of the extent and dissemina-

---

[8] For Jewish learning in Spain, not be treated here, see C. del Valle Rodríguez, *La escuela hebrea de Córdoba* (Madrid, 1981); also M.E. Varela Morena, 'La escuela de gramáticos hebreos de Córdoba, in *Los Judios en Córdoba (ss. X–XII)*, ed. J. Peláez de Rosal (Cordoba, 1985), pp. 103–18. But compare Reif, below, pp. 134–55.

[9] For the translations of Christian works into Arabic see G. Levi della Vida, 'I Mozarabi tra Occidente e Islam', *Settimane* 12 (Spoleto, 1965), 667–95.

[10] For example Ibn al-Athīr is better informed on the regnal succession of the Visigothic kings than any of the Spanish Arab historians.

[11] See in general G. Levi della Vida, 'La traduzione araba delle storie di Orosio', *Al-Andalus* 19 (1954), 257–93; for its use by Arab authors see L. Molina, 'Orosio y los geógrafos hispanomusulmanes', *Al-Qántara* 5 (1984), 63–92.

[12] G. Levi della Vida, 'Un texte mozarabe d'histoire universelle', in *idem*, *Etudes d'orientalisme dédiées à E. Lévi Provençal*, 2 vols. (Paris, 1962), I, pp. 175–83.

tion of literacy, however, is not so easy to pin down. A learned court certainly existed, which could embrace the rulers and a wide range of Muslims, Christians and Jews who served the caliphs in a variety of capacities that were not mutually exclusive. The Jewish *Nasi* and scholar Ḥasdai ibn Shaprut served Abd ar-Raḥmān III and Al-Ḥakam as doctor and as diplomat, even in his cure of the obesity of the Leonese King Sancho the Fat combining the two in a single exercise.[13] Several Christian doctors are recorded as having been attached to the caliphal court at this time too.[14]

There existed a learned class from whose ranks the caliphal bureaucracy was drawn, in some cases providing dynasties of office holders.[15] Some of these men, such as the prolific Ibn Ḥazm, vizier to one of the more ephemeral Umayyads, were authors themselves; others were patrons of poets and scholars.[16] But their literary skills also served immediate practical needs. Throughout the central government of the Umayyad state writing played a dominant part. Unfortunately none of the administrative documents of Umayyad Al Andalus has survived, though it has been claimed that fragments of two diplomatic letters in Latin, dating to the mid-tenth century are preserved in Barcelona.[17] Certainly this period saw numerous diplomatic exchanges involving not only the Arab-speaking world and Constantinople, but also the newly created Ottonian monarchy in Germany, for which a variety of linguistic and document drafting skills would have been required.[18]

Regrettably, the Barcelona letter fragments have not yet been published, and their discoverer has even kept their precise location within the voluminous collections of the Archivo de la Corona de Aragón concealed. However, some deductions can be made on the basis of the partial photographs of them that are available. One at least of the letters is addressed to the Counts Miro and Borrell, whose period of joint rule in Barcelona is dated to 950–66. The claim that this text represents a formal

---

[13] On Ḥasdai ibn Shaprut, see Rodríguez, *Escuela hebrea*, pp. 59–85; J. Peláez de Rosal, 'Hasday ibn Shaprut en la corte de Abderrahmán III', in *Los Judios en Córdoba*, ed. Peláez de Rosal, pp. 63–77.

[14] Some of the Christian doctors will be found in J. Vernet, 'Los médicos andaluces en el *Libro de las Generaciones de Médicos* de Ibn Ŷulŷul', *Anuario de Estudios Medievales* 5 (1968), 445–62.

[15] For dynasties of office holders see, for example, *Historia de la conquista de España de Abenalcotía el Cordobés*, ed. J. Ribera (Madrid, 1926), p. 78.

[16] For Ibn Ḥazm, see M. Cruz Hernández, *Historia del pensamiento en Al-Andalus*, 2 vols. (Seville, 1985), I, pp. 65–103.

[17] A. Mundó, 'Notas para la historia de la escritura visigótica en su periodo primitivo', in *Bivium: Homenaje a Manuel Cecilio Díaz y Díaz* (Madrid, 1983), p. 187 and plate 6.

[18] Collins, *Early Medieval Spain*, pp. 196, 201, 203, 205.

caliphal epistle, composed for the Umayyad ruler by court scribes, must be rejected completely. In comparison with other examples of Arab chancery production the sheer baldness and lack of the necessary protocols evidenced in this letter makes such a supposition inconceivable. No such document would start without the full enunciation of the ruler's titles, and for a caliph to address Christians, and not even royal ones at that, as *Karissimos meos fulgentissimos et amantissimos sincerissimos* is beyond the bounds of the possible.[19] This is clearly correspondence between Christians and one with a marked ecclesiastical ring to it. A suspicion that the author of one or probably both of these letters is Bishop Reccimund of Cordoba (fl. 960), the friend of Liutprand of Cremona, is not unreasonable.[20] Thus, if impossible as evidence of the Latin secretariat of the Caliph, these fragments at least add testimony to the latinity of the Cordoban episcopate.

It is more difficult to visualize the degree to which literacy played a role beyond Cordoba. It is notorious how overly centralized the Umayyad state became, and it is interesting to see that its collapse was followed by a considerable flourishing in literary culture in most of the former provincial cities which became capitals of the short-lived kingdoms of the Ṭāifa period.[21] These regimes needed the same sort of skilled bureaucracy that had been drawn on so extensively by the Umayyads, and it is at least a reasonable surmise that they were able to depend on local resources. Here too a useful indicator may exist in the form of the practices of the Christian communities. Despite the unchallenged dominance of Arabic as the literary language of Al-Andalus, a considerable number of Christians continued to erect Latin funerary inscriptions. What is striking is not so much the continued use of Latin, which remained the language of the Christian liturgy, as the quality of the epigraphy and the sophistication of many of the texts employed in these inscriptions.[22] A skilled stone cutter may not have to be able to read what he was carving, but the interest of his clients in such monuments presupposes the continued existence of people capable of

---

[19] Mundó, 'Notas', p. 187, the text is legible in plate 6; for Arab regnal titles see *Rusūm Dār al-Khilāfah* of Hilāl al-Ṣābi', trans. E.A. Salem (Beirut, 1977), pp. 81–90: 'The rules of caliphal correspondence' and 'The rules of writing letters'. For some examples, see S.M. Stern, *Fāṭimid Decrees* (Oxford, 1964), nos. 3–10.

[20] On Bishop Reccimund, see F.J. Simonet, *Historia de los Mozárabes de España* (repr. Madrid, 1984), pp. 603–18.

[21] For the overly centralized nature of Umayyad rule, see Collins, *Early Medieval Spain*, pp. 183–200; D. Wasserstein, *The Rise and Fall of the Party Kings* (Princeton, 1985), pp. 15–81.

[22] These Christian Latin inscriptions are still surprisingly little known. The greater part of them are to be found in E. Hübner, *Inscriptiones Hispaniae Christianae* (Berlin, 1871), *appendix titulorum recentiorum*, inscriptions 210–28. Compare the San Vincenzo al Volturno inscriptions discussed by Mitchell, below, pp. 186–225.

reading them. These inscriptions, which continue on into the middle of the eleventh century, are neither exclusively dedicated to members of the Christian clergy nor do they confine themselves to mere statements of name, age and date of death. Furthermore, they are found throughout at least the heartlands of Al-Andalus, from Granada and Malaga to Cordoba and Seville, testifying to a more than metropolitan phenomenon.

Although some of the points of detail may be unfamiliar, the general picture here presented will probably occasion little surprise. Expectations of the level of sophistication of Muslim Spain are generally high; sometimes exaggeratedly so.[23] It is necessary, for example, not to read back the attainments of the later tenth century into the early eighth. In terms of a literary production and a readership in Arabic it is wise to be cautious and to envisage a gradual and measured advance. The earliest known Arab texts composed in Al-Andalus only date from the ninth century.[24] The rise in literacy in Arabic and composition in the language may indeed parallel the growth in the number of indigenous converts to Islam, a phenomenon that also can be said to have taken off in the tenth century, at least insofar as it is possible now to assess it.[25] Methodological disagreements and limitations of evidence make this an area particularly difficult to delineate precisely.

However, allowing that there is a rough correlation between the rise of both the adoption of Islam and of an increasingly Arabized intellectual and material culture in Spain, it is of some interest to take an inquiry such as this back into earlier stages of the process. Indeed, any study of the dissemination of literacy in the peninsula under Arab domination should consider to what degree the ground had been prepared in the preceding Visigothic period and how far there existed a real continuity in learning across the notional divide of the Arab conquest. Thus it is necessary to start this inquiry at a point earlier than the invasion of 711, and to form some assessment of the nature and extent of literacy in the Visigothic period. Furthermore, it may also prove instructive to look beyond the shifting frontiers of Al-Andalus to take comparative note of what was happening in the Christian states in the north of the Iberian peninsula in the eighth to tenth centuries.

The evidence for lay literacy in the ranks of the upper levels of society in

[23] For example, A.J. Cheyne, *Muslim Spain, its History and Culture* (Minneapolis, 1974).

[24] The earliest work to have survived, though only now in a Portuguese translation of *c.* 1300 is that of Ar-Razi (*c.* 925); see *Crónica del Moro Rasis*, ed. D. Catalán and M. Soledad (Madrid, 1975). The existence of some ninth-century authors can be established, even if their works survive only in the form of brief (and possibly interpolated) extracts in later texts.

[25] See the arguments of R. Bulliet, *Conversion to Islam in the Medieval Period* (Cambridge, Mass., 1979), pp. 114–27.

the period of the Visigothic kingdom is qualitatively if not quantitatively good.[26] Two of the kings look to have been capable of poetic composition. In the case of the earlier of them, Sisebut (612–21), this is evidenced by his *Epistola missa ad Isidorum de Libro Rotarum*, which, even if in excerpted form, shows evidence of its author's previous reading of classical poetic and scientific texts.[27] The case of the other royal versifier, Chintila (636–9), is less clear-cut in that the evidence takes the form of a brief dedicatory inscription on some gift sent by the king to the (unnamed) pope, and this could just as easily have been composed for him as by him.[28] In the case of Sisebut the existence of other works attributed more or less certainly to him, notably the remnants of his collection of letters and the *Vita Desiderii*, seem to justify belief in his own compositional powers.[29]

Aristocratic libraries also appear to have been a feature of Visigothic society. Isidore's pupil Braulio of Saragossa (d. 651) wrote in the 640s to an Abbot Aemilian in Toledo, who was one of the leading figures of the court of Chindasuinth, to ask him to obtain for him a copy of the *Commentary on the Apocalypse* of Apringius of Beja, having failed to find it closer to hand. He suggested that a copy had once existed in the library of a Count Laurentius, who is otherwise unknown. In his reply Aemilian regretted his inability to find the book in question, pointing out that the count's library had been dispersed on his death. He had, however, though equally unsuccessfully, searched the king's library for a copy.[30]

In the case of the Visigoths it is important to appreciate that dynastic succession was relatively rare, and in all of the cases mentioned above, including the reference to the library of Chindasuinth, the kings concerned were the first of their lines to hold the throne. They were thus not educated as future monarchs, but as members of the Gothic nobility, and these scattered examples suggest a broader and more literary side to such an education than might have otherwise have been anticipated. Evidence on schooling is not so easy to discover. One short text that would seem to belong to seventh-century Spain, the pseudo-Isidoran *Instituta Dis-*

---

[26] See in general P. Riché, *Education et culture dans l'occident barbare, vie–viiie siècles* (3rd edn, Paris, 1962), pp. 331–6, 339–50, 401–9.

[27] For the poem of Sisebut, see *Isidore de Seville: Traité de la Nature*, ed. J. Fontaine (Bordeaux, 1960), pp. 328–35 (text), pp. 151–62 (study); also V. Recchia, 'La poesia cristiana: introduzione alla lettura del Carmen de Luna di Sisebuto di Toledo', *Vetera Christianorum* 7 (1970), 21–58.

[28] *Anthologia Latina*, ed. A. Riese, I. 2 (Leipzig, 1906), no. 494.

[29] For the other writings attributed to Sisebut, with account of their manuscript transmission, *Miscellanea Wisigothica*, ed. J. Gil (Seville, 1972), pp. ix–xx, 3–28, 53–68.

[30] *Epistolario de San Braulio*, ed. L. Riesco Terrero (Seville, 1975), letters XXV, XXVI, pp. 122, 124.

ciplinae, gives an indication of some of the values that might have been sought to have been inculcated, and later Arabic sources hint at the existence of a palace school in Toledo, to which scions of the office holding aristocracy of the late Visigothic kingdom might have been entrusted.[31]

Unfortunately, this information comes from a very insecure context: the stories of how Count Julian of Ceuta revenged himself on the Visigothic King Roderic by aiding the Arabs to cross the straits. This story of the king's seduction of the count's daughter when sent to Toledo to be educated forms part of an interrelated group of legends concerning the events of the conquest, virtually no element of which can be found to have any historical foundation.[32] So at best the palace school in Toledo has to remain an interesting possibility. More probable is the education of the sons of the nobility in episcopal households. A number of monasteries also provided schooling, but in all cases where this is referred to it is in the context of aspiring monastic or clerical pupils. There do exist a number of texts that may have been composed for educational purposes. These include not only the grammar ascribed to Bishop Julian of Toledo, but also the rhetorical set pieces appended to his *Historia Wambae*.[33] Likewise, Bishop Eugenius II of Toledo's short versifications of sections of Isidore's *Etymologiae* might be expected to fit such a context, and the small corpus of poetic texts constituting the *dubia et spuria* in the Monumenta edition of Eugenius has recently been characterized as a '*Speculum* per un nobile visigoto'.[34]

Although it may have been common practice in late antiquity for letters to be read aloud to the recipients, their family and households, a presumption of literacy may be attached to lay correspondents in seventh-century Spain as much as in fifth- and sixth-century Gaul. As in the latter the literary exchanges of upper-class society were not just confined to families of Roman origin but seem to have been as avidly pursued by the Visigothic aristocracy. Few letter collections of this period have survived and none in anything like complete form. That of Braulio of Saragossa is the most substantial Spanish example, and as well as with clerics he exchanged letters with a number of lay correspondents, almost all of whom had germanic

---

[31] P. Riché, 'L'Education à l'époque wisigothique: les *Institutionum Disciplinae*', *Anales Toledanos* 3 (1971), 171–80.

[32] On the Arab legends, R. Brunschvig, 'Ibn 'Abd al-Ḥakam et la conquête de l'Afrique du Nord par les Arabes', *Al-Andalus* 40 (1975), 129–79, is judicious.

[33] *Ars Iuliani Toletani Episcopi*, ed. M.A.H. Maestre Yenes (Toledo, 1973); see the review by L. Holtz, *Revue des Etudes Latines* 52 (1975), 75–82; on the purposes of the appendices to the *Historia Wambae*, see R. Collins, 'Julian of Toledo and royal succession in late seventh-century Spain', in *Early Medieval Kingship*, ed. P.H. Sawyer and I.N. Wood (Leeds, 1977), p. 39.

[34] N. Messina, *Pseudo-Eugenio de Toledo, Speculum per un nobile visigoto* (Santiago de Compostela, 1983).

names.[35] Unfortunately none of their letters to him has survived in the collection.

Although it has been strangely fashionable amongst its own modern historians to decry it, the Visigothic state preserved several of the administrative and legal practices of its Roman predecessor. In all of these the role of writing was of considerable importance. The earliest extant charter of the Visigothic period is a document of donation of property made by the deacon Vincent to the monastery of Asán in Aragon on the 29th of September of either 550 or 551.[36] The original does not survive but the text was copied on to the first folio of a twelfth-century Bible preserved in the Pyrenean see of Huesca. Despite the considerable temporal gulf between the time of the donation and its record there are no good grounds for doubting the authenticity of the document thus preserved. The procedure of writing such a text into a Bible is unusual but has parallels elsewhere.[37] More significantly, not only do the *formulae* employed in the donation seem to authenticate it, but also its use of a citation of Roman law, in this case *Lex Aquilia*, is not anachronistic. This last point is significant in that in a small number of ninth- and tenth-century instances charters make a token reference to the same law. However, in all such cases the citation is purely formulaic and has no relationship to the known content or purpose of the original *Lex Aquilia*.[38] In the case of the document of 550/1 the reference relates to the second part of the *Lex*, which was abrogated by Justinian, but which was described in the *Institutes* of Gaius, a text known in abbreviated form in Visigothic Spain.[39]

Although few other such texts have survived that date to the Visigothic period, there are a small number of fragmentary originals, and one

[35] Letters of Braulio to lay correspondents: nos. XV, XVI, XIX, XX, XXVIII, XXIX, XXX, XXXIV, of *Epistolario*, ed. Riesco Terrero. Compare the discussion of letter-writing in Gaul by Wood, above, pp. 68–71.

[36] The Asán charter is published in *Diplomática Hispano-Visigoda*, ed. A. Canellas López (Saragossa, 1979), no. 14, pp. 126–8; see also P. Díaz Martínez, 'La estructura de la propriedad en la España tardoantígua: el ejemplo del monasterio de Asán', *Studia Zamorensia Historica* 6 (1985), 349–62.

[37] For example the Book of Durrow: R. Sharpe, 'Dispute settlement in medieval Ireland: a preliminary inquiry', in *Settlement of Disputes*, pp. 170, 173–4. See also Kelly's chapter in this volume, above, pp. 44–5.

[38] For an anachronistic use of a citation of *Lex Aquilia*: L. Barrau-Dihigo, ed., 'Chartes de l'église de Valpuesta', *Revue Hispanique* 7 (1900), no. VII, pp. 302–4, of Nov. 894.

[39] For the real *Lex Aquilia*: *Imperatoris Iustiniani Institutionum Libri Quattuor* IV.iii, ed. J.B. Moyle (Oxford, 1955), pp. 526–34; the part of the *Lex* most pertinent to its use in the Asán charter is the second chapter, declared obsolete by Justinian, and for that it is necessary to have recourse to Gaius: *Gai Institutionum Commentarii Quattuor* III.215–16, *Fontes Iuris Romani Antejustiniani*, ed. J. Baviera (Florence, 1968), p. 145; see also W.W. Buckland, *A Text-Book of Roman Law* (3rd edn, corr., Cambridge, 1975), pp. 585–6.

palimpsest, which looks very much as if it were the product of a royal writing office.[40] Its style and format have been compared with those of some of the Merovingian royal documents. Unfortunately, it is too damaged to yield up either its exact date or the name of the king who issued it.[41] Alongside these texts written on parchment, however, can be placed the celebrated if still mysterious slate documents, discovered lying in open countryside in a number of locations in the region of Salamanca.[42] Like the Albertini tablets from North Africa, a number of these seem to be locally made records of legal transactions, notably deeds of sale. Others seem to have a magical purport, and there are yet others that have been described as school exercises in writing and composition. There are also a small number that have exclusively numerical markings, the purposes of which are unclear.

The urban and rural courts of the Visigothic period produced a considerable amount of documentation. The settlement of disputes seems, from the prescriptions of the *Forum Iudicum*, generally to have turned on the production of written evidence of title, although additional procedures were employed to counteract the obvious dangers of forgery, and legal hearings were prolific in the production of written records in the form of sworn statements by witnesses, judges' declarations and renunciations on the part of the losers.[43] A notariat was clearly envisaged by the law code for the immediate enscribing of such documents in the court. The limitation in the evidence available for the Visigothic period proper makes it difficult to specify whether such notaries were lay or clerical. In subsequent centuries, when the procedures that originated in the time of the Visigothic kingdom were still employed in both Christian- and Muslim-ruled parts of Spain, the writing of such documents in court was carried out largely by scribes who described themselves as priests or deacons, and in Catalonia at least beneficiary production replaced a court notariat.[44] However, it is conceivable that lay notaries had functioned in the Visigothic period proper.

---

[40] Mundó, 'Notas', p. 179; for the text see *Diplomática Hispano-Visigoda*, ed. Canellas López no. 119, p. 198.

[41] A. Millares Carlo, *Tratado de paleografía española*, 3 vols. (3rd edn, Madrid, 1983), I, p. 42 and n. 29.

[42] First published in M. Gómez-Moreno, *Documentación goda en pizarra* (Madrid, 1966); some additions have been made to the corpus since then: M.C. Díaz y Díaz, 'Los documentos hispano-visigóticos sobre pizarra', *Studi medievali* 7 (1966), 75–107. See now the new and complete edition in I. Velázquez Soriano, *El Latín de las pizarras visigóticas*, 2 vols. (Madrid, 1988). This includes a study of each text.

[43] On the classification of these documents, see R. Collins, '*Sicut lex Gothorum continet:* law and charters in ninth- and tenth-century León and Catalonia', *EHR* 100 (1985), 489–512.

[44] *Ibid.*, 505–6.

The Arab conquest and the various civil wars fought in the peninsula in the 740s and 750s caused considerable damage and imposed a number of radical discontinuities on Spanish society.[45] Yet probably even more striking were the survivals, and some modern research has started to stress the continuities across the divide of this period of upheaval, particularly in respect of administrative structures and practices.[46] For the Christians, who provided the majority population probably throughout the whole of the period under consideration, although certain restrictions were imposed on them and they lost their previous monopoly of political power, the processes of change were slow. Indeed the change in their standing and the challenge presented by Islam and a no longer persecuted Judaism led to both conservatism and a treasuring of their traditions. This was reflected almost immediately in the first resurgence of historiographical composition since the early seventh century.[47] It has been assumed that the authors of the two anonymous chronicles, known for convenience as those of 741 and 754, were clerics, though this is not certain.

In some respects Christian learning, liturgy and lifestyles became fossilized in Al-Andalus, or so it is often asserted.[48] In comparison with the developments north of the Pyrenees, particularly in the Carolingian Empire, this is perhaps true. On the other hand, absorption into an Arab world that stretched the whole length of the Mediterranean and beyond opened the church in Muslim Spain to new currents of influence from Christian communities in the east. This could take the form of movements of both personnel and of texts.[49] Moreover, it is possible that the current ran more than one way, as the veneration of Spanish saints and certain palaeographical indications from manuscripts found in the library of St Catherine's monastery at the foot of Mount Sinai seem to suggest.[50]

The political geography of the church in Al-Andalus was not slow to

---

[45] For a reassessment of this overly neglected period see R. Collins, *The Arab Conquest of Spain, 710–797* (Oxford, 1989).

[46] J. Vallvé, 'España en el siglo VIII: ejército y sociedad', *Al-Andalus* 43 (1978), 51–112.

[47] The chronicles may be found in *Corpus Scriptorum Muzarabicorum*, ed. J. Gil, 2 vols. (Madrid, 1973), I, pp. 7–54; there is a more recent edition of that of 754 in *Crónica mozárabe de 754*, ed. J.E. López Pereira (Saragossa, 1980).

[48] M. Márquez-Sterling, *Fernán González First Count of Castile* (Mississippi, 1980), pp. 28–32, sees the Mozarabic influx into León as a further cause of its judicial conservatism.

[49] Levi della Vida, 'I Mozarabi', 677–8, on the possibility of Nestorian texts circulating in Al-Andalus.

[50] E.A. Lowe, 'An unknown Latin psalter on Mount Sinai', 'Two new Latin liturgical fragments on Mount Sinai', and 'Two other unknown Latin liturgical fragments on Mount Sinai', reprinted in *Paleographical Papers 1907–1965*, ed. Ludwig Bieler, 2 vols. (Oxford, 1972), II, pp. 417–40, 520–45, 546–74.

follow the realignments of the structures of power in the peninsula. Toledo, which had secured for itself an unchallenged predominance as both the *urbs regia* and primatial see for the whole church of the Visigothic kingdom, retained few traces of its former material glory and intellectual preeminence by the end of the eighth century. This, of course, may be more a reflection of the vagaries of the evidence than of contemporary reality. The city itself, though, appears to have become a frontier fortress, and was to be much plagued by inter-communal tension between the indigenous population and various Berber garrisons.[51] However, the shift of emphasis under the Arab rulers to the south and particularly to the Guadalquivir valley greatly benefited the great cities of Seville and Cordoba.

It may seem paradoxical that better evidence of lay literacy can be found in the surviving small corpus of Christian Latin writing produced in the south of the peninsula in the period of the rule of the Arab Umayyad dynasty than in the voluminous literary remains of the preceding Visigothic period. However, this is the case. The quantity of such Latin writing produced by the minority Christian culture is small, and is concentrated in the ninth century.[52] By the tenth century Arabic had achieved a predominant role. A small number of short works in Latin have survived from the eighth century; almost all being the products of clerical authors. The Voluntary Martyr Movement that flourished briefly in Cordoba in the mid-ninth century produced a sudden resurgence in the composition of Christian Latin writing. This largely resulted from the need for the principal protagonists of the movement to defend the actions of those who sought martyrdom by deliberately confronting the Muslim authorities and reviling their Prophet against the criticisms of fellow Christians, who objected to this disturbance of the *modus vivendi* that had been created between the two communities.[53] A number of accounts of the martyrdoms were written by the priest and titular Metropolitan of Toledo Eulogius.[54] He was also responsible for the bringing of a small corpus of Latin poetic texts to Cordoba from the region of Pamplona, on the basis of which there occurred a minor revival of verse composition in the Umayyad capital.[55]

---

[51] On the problems in Toledo see Lévi-Provençal, *Histoire de l'Espagne musulmane*, I, pp. 107–9, 154–9, 291–6.

[52] All in *Corpus Scriptorum Muzarabicorum*, ed. Gil.

[53] On the Martyr Movement there exists a useful description of the sources in E.P. Colbert, *The Martyrs of Cordoba* (Washington, 1962), especially chapters VII–XIV; the classic account is that of Simonet, *Historia de los Mozárabes de España*, pp. 319–472; a recent attempt at an assessment is K. B. Wolf, *Christian Martyrs in Muslim Spain* (Cambridge, 1988).

[54] Eulogius, ed. Gil, *Corpus Scriptorum Muzarabicorum*, I, pp. 363–503.

[55] R. Collins, 'Poetry in ninth-century Spain', *Papers of the Liverpool Latin Seminar*, 4 (1984), 181–95.

Interesting as Eulogius may be in his own right, for present purposes his friend and later biographer Paul Alvar is even more significant. For he was a layman. Under the instruction of Eulogius, who devoted a brief spell of imprisonment to the study of metrics, he became the most productive of the Cordoban poets. He also composed a considerable corpus of prose works.[56] The most substantial of these is his *Indiculus Luminosus*, a spirited defence of the martyrs. As well as his *Vita Eulogii*, he wrote a *Confessio*, an extended lament on his own sinfulness, and has left part of a substantial collection of letters. Not the least interesting of the latter are his epistolary exchanges with Flavius John of Seville, a fellow layman otherwise unknown.[57] Another lay correspondent was the doctor Romanus.[58] Of the six letters that passed between him and John four are by Alvar, and relate to a series of theological issues the two men were discussing. These included the Christian's attitude to the study of rhetoric, the immortality of the soul and a Christological debate.

To some extent it may be thought that Alvar at least was self-consciously trying to recreate the kind of learned *Amicitia* expressed through exchange of letters that he would have found in his reading of patristic letter collections.[59] Of these he certainly knew some of those of Jerome, Fulgentius, Gregory and Braulio. Even if he was being rather too demonstratively learned and with an eye on a readership beyond his correspondent, the range of texts that he was able to quote from is impressive, and includes a variety of exegetical texts by Ambrose, Jerome, Augustine and Isidore. He was also up to date on recent controversies, at least within Spain, providing the first citations of Beatus' letter to Elipandus condemning Adoptionism, and, it has been claimed, of the *Commentary on the Apocalypse*. Even John, who is more restrained in both the number and size of his letters, managed to include quotations from Origen in Rufinus' translation, Sedulius, Gregory the Great and the letters of Jerome and Leo.[60] Even if some of these works were available only in excerpted or abbreviated form, and there is no evidence to suggest this, the impression that considerable libraries of Christian learning were available to these two laymen in their respective cities is hard to deny.

What, then, of the education that underlay such interest in Christian literature and theological discussion? Of John of Seville nothing more can

---

[56] Paul Alvar, ed. Gil, *Corpus Scriptorum Muzarabicorum*, I, pp. 143–361.

[57] *Ibid.*, pp. 144–201; on the correspondence, see C.M. Sage, *Paul Alvar of Cordoba: Studies on his Life and Writings* (Washington DC, 1943), pp. 43–81.

[58] *Alvari Epistula IX*, ed. Gil, *Corpus Scriptorum Muzarabicorum*, I, pp. 211–14.

[59] As suggested by Sage, *Paul Alvar*, pp. 43–4.

[60] See the references given to the citations in the edition of Gil.

be said, but Alvar does reveal something of his own debt to his master the Abbot Speraindeus. In his *Vita Eulogii* Alvar records the beginning of his friendship with Eulogius when they were both pupils of the abbot.[61] His somewhat elliptical references seem to suggest that Eulogius himself was being taught elsewhere, quite possibly in the Basilica of St Zoilus, one of the patrons of Christian Cordoba, to which he was to be attached as a priest, but came to Speraindeus for additional instruction. Such an impression fits in with what is known of teaching in the Visigothic period, in which urban basilicas served as places of instruction for oblates later enrolled in the ranks of the clergy.[62] Monasteries likewise provided instruction.[63] But it is not possible to be certain that such facilities were extended to members of the laity who had no intention of accepting ordination or the monastic life. It is possible that Alvar had been so destined but had changed his mind, but the clear evidence of a learned laity in both the Visigothic kingdom and in ninth-century Al-Andalus cannot be explained away on the grounds of a number of such last-minute changes of heart. It does look as if the educational resources of the church were extended to the laity. In all cases this presumes a certain social level. If then there appears to be an essential continuity in practices from the Visigothic period in the south after 711, what of the north?

A search for lay literacy in the Christian states that began to develop in the north of the Iberian peninsula from the end of the first quarter of the eighth century onwards is considerably harder to pursue than the comparable study of conditions in the Muslim-dominated south.[64] For one thing new literary production, of the kind to be associated with such Cordoban clerics and laymen as Eulogius and Alvar, is not to be found in the north. The only large-scale new work to be composed in these regions before the turn of the millennium comes in the form of the *Commentary on the Apocalypse* of the Asturian monk Beatus (fl. 785) and the polemical letter that he wrote in association with Bishop Eterius of Osma attacking the Adoptionist theology of Elipandus of Toledo.[65] To these may be added the short chronicles and

---

[61] *Vita Eulogii* 2, ed. Gil, *Corpus Scriptorum Muzarabicorum*, I, p. 331.

[62] For boys attached to the basilica of St Eulalia in Mérida: *Vitas Patrum Emeretensium* I.1, ed. J.N. Garvin, *The 'Vitas Sanctorum Patrum Emeretensium'* (Washington DC, 1946), p. 138. See also n. 104 below.

[63] For the monastery of Cauliana near Mérida as a school in the early seventh century, see the anecdote recorded in *The 'Vitas Patrum Emeretensium'*, II.14, ed. Garvin, p. 152.

[64] For the history of these Christian states see J. Pérez de Urbel and R. del Arco, *Historia de España, VI: España Cristiana: 711–1038*, ed. R. Menéndez Pidal (Madrid, 1956).

[65] *Beati Liebanensis et Eterii Oxomensis, Adversus Elipandum Libri Duo*, ed. B. Löfstedt, CCSL Continuatio Medievalis 49 (Turnhout, 1984); *Beati in Apocalipsin Libri Duodecim*, ed. H. Sanders (Rome, 1930).

chronological collections associated with the court of the Asturian King Alfonso III (866–910).[66] In general the search has to be confined to a small corpus of inscriptions and, in valuable distinction to the Visigothic period, a substantial body of charters.[67]

Of Beatus remarkably little is known. Certain embroidering of his biography has been possible on the basis of late traditions but these give few grounds for confidence.[68] Even his authorship of the *Commentary* has to be regarded as no better than a strong possibility, though that of the *Epistula* is certain.[69] Beatus was possibly not a priest, but in the absence of any certain indicator of his place of origin it would be unwise to make too many assumptions as to the evidence his writing provides for his education. What is striking are the resources that Beatus or the author of the *Commentary* had at his disposal for the compiling of the work. In itself it is largely a piecing together of excerpts taken from earlier commentaries on the same book, but the variety of such sources including works that otherwise seem rare, such as the comparable commentary of the African Donatist Tyconius, argues for the existence of a significant library at his disposal.[70] Was such a thing really to be found in an Asturian monastery or even in its royal court? Were the author of the *Commentary* not to be Beatus then the whole question of his geographical location would have to be reopened.

The Asturian kingdom came into being around the years 718/22 as a realm without towns, a feature that was only intensified by the reported depopulation of the urban settlements of the Duero valley by one of the earliest kings, Alfonso I (739–56).[71] On the other hand, this process brought a fresh influx of population into the mountain kingdom that had been used not only to town life but also to the legal and governmental system of the Visigothic monarchy. By about 800 the Asturian kingdom had developed a new permanent court centre in Oviedo, which grew rapidly into

---

[66] M. Gómez-Moreno, ed., 'Las primeras crónicas de la Reconquista', *Boletín de la Real Academia de la Historia* 100 (1932), 600–28.

[67] The charters of the Asturian period are conveniently collected in *Diplomática del periodo astur*, ed. A.C. Floriano, 2 vols. (Oviedo, 1949, 1951); for the inscriptions see Hübner, *Inscriptiones Hispaniae Christianae*, nos. 229–88.

[68] On the almost absolute lack of information relating to the biography of Beatus see L. Vázquez de Parga, 'Beato y el ambiente cultural de su epoca', in *Actas del Simposio para el estudio de los códices del 'Comentario al Apocalipsis' de Beato de Liébana*, 3 vols. (Madrid, 1978), I, pp. 35–45.

[69] The question of the authorship has remained closed for too long; it was usefully reopened by Professor Díaz y Díaz in the discussion following the paper cited in n. 68: *ibid.*, p. 47.

[70] *Beati in Apocalipsin, praefatio* I.5, ed. Sanders, p. 1.

[71] *Chronicle of Alfonso III* 8, ed. J. Prelog, *Die Chronik Alfons III* (Berne and Cirencester, 1980), pp. 32–9 (versions A and B).

a recognizable town, and, what is more, in art, architecture, governmental forms and self-presentation it was seeking to make itself look like the heir and perpetuator of the former Visigothic kingdom.[72]

The earliest extant royal charter of the Asturian monarchy only dates to 774, but by the reign of Alfonso II (791–842) such documents had proliferated.[73] Furthermore the quality of their drafting had been greatly improved.[74] In general the legal procedures and norms of the Visigothic law were preserved in the Asturian kingdom and then in its southwards extension into León, not least in the emphasis on the importance of written title to property, the use of written evidence and the production of documentation in the course of the settlement of legal disputes.[75] Unlike the contemporary Catalan counties, then under Frankish suzerainty, the Asturian and Leonese documents do not always bear the names of the scribes who wrote them. This makes it difficult to generalize about the kind of notariat that is responsible for the production of this substantial corpus of texts, not all of which is yet published.[76] However, it does seem likely that such notaries were ecclesiastics. No certain evidence of any form of lay notariat, as may have existed under the Visigothic kingdom, can be detected in its self-proclaimed successor.

The existence or otherwise of a royal chancery in these centuries has aroused surprisingly little interest, particularly in the light of the lively debate on this question in respect of the Anglo-Saxon kingdom.[77] Admittedly, although the quantity of charter materials from the Asturian and Leonese kingdoms is considerable, the proportion of royal documents is relatively small. A full-scale investigation would require more space than is available here. However, an indicator could be taken from just one reign that is comparatively well represented in the production of royal diplomas,

---

[72] C. Sánchez-Albornoz, 'La restauración del orden gótico en el palacio y en la iglesia', in his *Orígenes de la nación española*, 3 vols. (Oviedo, 1972–5), II, pp. 623–40.

[73] León, Archivo de la Catedral, doc. 1; A. Millares Carlo, 'Consideraciones sobre la escritura visigótica cursiva', no. 15 and plate, in *idem*, *León y su Historia* II (León, 1973), p. 355.

[74] For drafting, see the discussions accompanying the documents in *Diplomática del periodo astur*, ed. Floriano.

[75] Collins, '*Sicut lex Gothorum continet*', 489–512.

[76] Although some of the main bodies of documents and cartularies have been published, notably in *Documentación de la Catedral de León (siglos IX–X)*, ed. G. del Ser Quijano (Salamanca, 1981), and *Colección diplomática del Monasterio de Sahagún (siglos IX y X)*, ed. J.M. Mínguez Fernández (León, 1976), certain major collections, such as those relating to Lugo and the cartulary of Celanova, have never been edited in full.

[77] On the debate over the Anglo-Saxon chancery see S.D. Keynes, *The Diplomas of Aethelred 'the Unready', 978–1016* (Cambridge, 1980), pp. 14–83, and the bibliography cited there; also the chapters by Kelly and Keynes in this volume, above, pp. 39–46, and below, 232–48.

that of Ramiro III of León (966–84). For this period at least it can be asserted that all of the known documents produced in the name of this king were written by scribes otherwise found in the context of the household of the bishops of León.[78] It looks as if the episcopal scriptorium served the purposes of the royal chancery. It should be noted that this is not a case of beneficiary production, as the bulk of the documents were drawn up for third parties. Such a conclusion is probably not a surprising one, other than for those who would regard the existence of a court-based chancery as the natural presumption. In the case of the Spanish kingdoms it may well be that not until the twelfth century would such an assumption be justified.[79]

Such an ecclesiastical monopoly of the production of governmental and private documents is certainly indicative of a more limited dissemination of literacy, but does not necessarily indicate a lack of it in the upper levels of secular society, where it might most be expected. The problem is that of obtaining the evidence. Signatures to charters may be revealing, though this is by no means a sure test of literacy, as the use of stencils enabled otherwise illiterate laymen to write their own names on documents.[80] Even this form of evidence, though, is often denied the inquirer, in that unlike most of the Catalan collections the greater part of the Asturian and Leonese materials have survived not as originals but as later cartulary copies. Many of the 'originals', too, turn out on inspection to be early copies. Thus the copious bodies of charters that can be associated with some of the leading figures in the tenth-century aristocracy of the kingdom of León do not help to determine the educational attainments of their owners.[81]

On the other hand, the latter's books might be expected to provide better information, and some knowledge of these can be obtained through some of the same charters in which they are bequeathed or donated. Two collections of all such references to books in documents from the Leonese kingdom

---

[78] This becomes clear from a study of the extant charters of Ramiro III in relation to those of the bishop of León; most of the published texts will be found in *Colección diplomática de Sahagún*, ed. Mínguez Fernández and *Documentos de la Catedral de León*, ed. del Ser Quijano; a full study of this is to follow.

[79] See now B.F. Reilly, 'The chancery of Alfonso VI of León-Castile (1065–1109)', in *Santiago, Saint-Denis and St. Peter*, ed. B.F. Reilly (New York, 1985), pp. 1–40.

[80] There exist several apparently fluent signatures by counts of Barcelona in the Catalan charter collections, e.g. Barcelona, Archivo de la Corona de Aragón, pergaminos: Miro. 3 (sig. of Count Sunyer), Archivo de la Catedral de Urgell, consagracions 12 (sig. of Count Miro).

[81] In particular the two great Galician monasteries of Celanova and Sobrado, founded by the greatest of the noble dynasties of the region. For Sobrado see *Tumbos del monasterio de Sobrado de los Monjes*, ed. P. Loscertales de García de Valdeavellano, 2 vols. (Madrid, 1976), and for Celanova the unpublished *Tumbo*: Madrid, Archivo Histórico Nacional, sección de códices 986B.

dating to before the turn of the millennium have been made, one of which relates exclusively to charters from Galicia.[82] A wide and various range of books has emerged from these trawls. Unsurprisingly, the greater part of the donors were ecclesiastics, but a number of laymen do feature. Of the twenty-eight relevant Galician documents dating to before the year 1000 only seven contain gifts of books by laymen, and two of these qualify themselves as *confesus*.[83] The lay donors are generally figures of considerable local significance and include Ilduara Eriz, wife of Count Hermenegildo and mother of Bishop Rosendo of Santiago, Count Hermenegildo of Presaras and his wife Paterna, the Countess Mummadona Díaz, and Count Osorio Gutiérrez.[84]

Consideration of the books actually given and the contexts in which the donations were made suggests that considerable caution is necessary in using such materials to suggest anything about their owners' literacy. In most cases the gifts of books were made as part of the endowment of a newly founded monastery. This is true of the donation of exclusively liturgical books to the monastery of San Fiz and the Macchabees made by Osorius and his wife Argilona in 933, and of the gifts made by Count Hermenegildo and his wife to their foundation at Sobrado in 952, and of the provision of books for his newly created monastery of Lorenzana on the part of Count Osorio Gutiérrez in 969.[85] Of all the books included in these various donations, other than that of Mummadona Díaz, only one is not liturgical or a book of monastic rules, and that is a copy of the Visigothic law-code, the *Forum Iudicum*, here called *Liber Goticum*, given to the family monastery of Celanova by Ilduara Eriz in 938.[86] It is only sensible to assume that in all but the last case the books were specially made or bought for the purpose of providing the newly founded monasteries with the necessary texts for the carrying out of liturgical observance.

The donation made in 959 by the Countess Mummadona Díaz to the monastery she founded at Guimarães, formerly the monastic see of Dumio, is exceptional in the context of the other documents in that she provided her new house with a substantial library. This included, as well as the

---

[82] C. Sánchez-Albornoz, 'Notas sobre los libros leidos en el Reino de León', *Cuadernos de Historia de España* 1/2 (1944), 222–38; M.R. García Alvarez, 'Los libros en la documentación gallega de la alta edad media', *Cuadernos de Estudios Gallegos* 20 (1965), 292–329.

[83] García Alvarez, 'Los libros', nos. 20 and 26, pp. 310, 312.

[84] *Ibid.*, nos. 17, 21, 23, and 25, pp. 309, 310–11, 312.

[85] *Ibid.*, nos. 15, 21, and 25, pp. 308, 310–11, 312.

[86] Tumbo de Celanova: Madrid, Archivo Histórico Nacional, sección de códices 986B, fols. 5v–6v.

mandatory liturgical books and a considerable collection of monastic rules, some Isidore, Ildefonsus and Gregory the Great, the *Vita Martini*, a *Historia Ecclesiastica* (Rufinus' translation of Eusebius?), Ephrem Syrus and a *Troyano*, probably indicating Dictys Cretensis. Such a collection, located in what was at the time a remote frontier region of the kingdom, is surprising, and some of the items find no parallels in other evidence relating to the monastic libraries of northern Spain.[87] How the countess acquired such books remains uncertain, though an ultimately southern Spanish or Cordoban origin for some of them at least might be postulated. One possible line of transmission would be through the episcopal monastery of Abeliare in León, founded and endowed by Bishop Cixila in 927, where copies of these texts are known to have existed.[88] As the 'milk-sister' of King Ramiro II (931–51) Mummadona and her family were powerful and influential, and her obtaining of copies of such otherwise rare books as the Ephrem Syrus from Abeliare may explain their appearance in Guimarães.[89] In any case no certainty exists that she would have read all or any of them herself.

Thus it looks as if at best there is no evidence on which any secure assessment of lay literacy in the Christian kingdoms of the north of the peninsula can be based. These small, under-urbanized states could be regarded as being essentially frontier societies that developed largely on the basis of raiding and opposition to their larger and more powerful Muslim neighbour to the south. Their royal courts were small and relatively poor and the aristocracy newly emerged and concerned with developing profits from war and from land. Their needs for education were limited. Even their often extensive monastic patronage could be suspected of having an economic purpose to it in helping to develop the under-populated and waste frontier regions.[90]

Yet it would be unwise to write off the Christian kingdoms of the Asturias and León, let alone their diminutive eastern counterpart, centred on Pamplona, that came into being early in the ninth century, as being in this

---

[87] University of Coimbra, Archivo, doc. 1 (twelfth-century copy of lost original). On Mummadona Díaz see J. Mattoso, 'As famílias condais portucalenses dos séculos X e XI', *Studium Generale* 12 (1968/9), 59–115, no. IVB, reprinted in his *A Nobreza medieval portuguesa* (Lisbon, 1981), pp. 101–57, especially pp. 139–40.

[88] For Cixila's library at Abeliare see M. Gómez-Moreno, *Iglesias mozárabes*, 2 vols. (Madrid, 1919), I, pp. 347–8.

[89] On Mummadona's relationship with the Leonese royal house, see J. Rodríguez, *Ramiro II rey de León* (Madrid, 1972), pp. 32–4.

[90] On the economic and social role of monasteries, see, *inter alia*, M. Pallares Méndez, *El monasterio de Sobrado: un ejemplo del protagonismo monástico en la Galicia medieval* (La Coruña, 1979).

respect unworthy heirs of the Visigoths.[91] Perhaps the most striking testimony to a level of lay literacy and an interest in learning in these societies, otherwise so largely concealed by the limitations of the evidence, comes in the form of the principal historical composition of the Asturian kingdom, the *Chronicle of Alfonso III*. This now survives in two distinct but related versions, and argument continues as to the priority to be ascribed to one or other of them, and their relationship to an original first form of the text.[92] But, whatever the nature of the beliefs held as to the precedence, place of origin and authorial milieu of the two extant recensions, there is still a general unanimity as to the royal authorship of the original Chronicle. The *Chronicle of Alfonso III* was in its first state actually written by and not just for the Asturian King Alfonso III, probably around the year 883.[93] Arguments that would make of him too busy a ruler to have contemplated such an undertaking have proved as ill-founded as if applied to the literary work of Alfonso's contemporary, the West Saxon King Alfred.[94] Both were monarchs facing formidable military and administrative problems, and both found the desire and the time to write. In the case of the Asturian king his Chronicle might have been little more than a history of the reign of his father, Ordoño I (850–66), but it is no mean achievement.[95]

Alfonso III may have generated too many successors in respect of the practical and military aspects of kingship: he was deposed by a conspiracy of his own sons in 910. But he failed to pass on his model of the royal participation in scholarship. The kingdom created by his heirs with its centre in León has been seen as intellectually arid and failing to develop the seeds of the revival of learning produced by the court of Alfonso.[96] This is perhaps not entirely fair. Scholars may have been few, but for certain very

---

[91] On the literary culture of the kingdom of Pamplona in the ninth century, see R. Collins, *The Basques* (Oxford, 1986), pp. 145–51. For the tenth century, see S. de Silva y Verastegui, *Iconografía del siglo X en la Reina de Pamplona-Nájera* (Pamplona, 1984).

[92] For the fullest discussion of the manuscripts, together with an edition of the two earliest extant (together with two other later) versions of the text, see *Die Chronik Alfons III*, ed. Prelog; for some of the arguments as to priority, see M. Gómez-Moreno, 'Las primeras crónicas de la Reconquista', *Boletín de la Real Academia de la Historia* 100 (1932), 5–628, and *Crónica de Alfonso III*, ed. Ubieto Arteta (Valencia, 1971), pp. 8–12.

[93] Ubieto, *Crónica*, pp. 12–15; *Crónicas asturianas*, ed. J. Gil Fernandez, J.L. Moralejo and J.I. Ruiz de la Peña (Oviedo, 1985), pp. 38–41, 60–80.

[94] L. Barrau-Dihigo, 'Remarques sur la Chronique dite d'Alphonse III', *Revue Hispanique* 46 (1919), 323–81, and on Alfred, see Kelly, above, pp. 52–5, and Keynes, below, pp. 230–4.

[95] As argued by Gil, in *Crónicas asturianas*, ed. Gil *et al.*, p. 75.

[96] J.I. Ruiz de la Peña, in *ibid.*, p. 42, here following the verdict of L. García de Valdeavellano.

practical things the ability to read was increasingly necessary, and not just for clerics. The most obvious example of this comes with the role of the judge. The considerable number of judicial documents produced in the course of the settlement of legal disputes that have survived from the kingdom of León testify to the continued application in practice as well as theory of the legal procedures of the Visigothic kingdom.[97] As has been mentioned, in most cases those who wrote such documents, the production of which was enjoined on the courts by the law itself, were clerics. However, most of the judges whose names are known were laymen.[98]

Such judges can be sub-divided in terms of their status. In many of the peripheral regions of the kingdom, particularly in Galicia and the county of Castille, which emerged in the late ninth century, the counts, initially royal appointees but from their landed base effectively hereditary regional nobles, presided over the courts.[99] Obviously such men could be thought of as eminent presidents but dependent on the skills of other better trained subsidiary judges. This is perhaps the case, but at least two donations of copies of the code, the *Forum Iudicum*, or 'Gothic Book' as it came increasingly to be called, might indicate that such counts were themselves possessors of the law book.[100] As well as such great men, who filled the presidential role that the king himself could undertake in León, there did exist a body of what may be termed professional judges. Not only do such men feature in making up the panels who sat in judgement at the hearings, but, significantly, they can also be found using *iudex* as a title and mark of their status in private charters in which they feature and which have no relationship to their performance of their judicial responsibilities.[101]

As the records of several of the hearings indicate, the role of the judge involved more than just the application of common sense and a spirit of compromise to the solution of disputes. It was necessary that proceedings and above all rules of evidence, both in respect of written testimony and of

---

[97] R. Collins, 'Visigothic law and regional custom in disputes in early medieval Spain', in *Settlement of Disputes*, pp. 85–104, especially pp. 85–8.

[98] For lay judges, see, in the absence of comprehensive listing, the various cases cited and discussed in Collins, '*Sicut lex Gothorum continet*', and *idem*, 'Visigothic law and regional custom'.

[99] Collins, '*Sicut lex Gothorum continet*', 498, 508.

[100] Madrid, Biblioteca Nacional MS 18387, fol. 240, gift of Adosinda Gudestéiz; Madrid, Archivo Histórico Nacional, sección de códices 986B, fol. 6, gift of Ilduara Eriz.

[101] For example, 'Abozehar iudez' and 'Bello iudex' who signed as witnesses to the donation made to the monastery of Santiago in León in 959 by the *conversa* Justa: *El Monasterio de Santiago de León*, ed. M. Yánez Cifuentes (León and Barcelona, 1972), doc. 13, pp. 147–8.

witnesses, should be obeyed and should follow the norms stipulated in the code.[102] Thus at various points it is clear from surviving documents that the *Forum Iudicum* was openly consulted by the judges. 'Perquisivimus et legimus in librum gothicum' is a standard *formula* in the judicial transcripts of hearings for the stage at which the judges consulted the code for such rules, and in a number of instances the relevant text itself was cited and included in the document, even with the precise reference to the law, title and book of the *Forum Iudicum* being provided.[103]

It should be stressed that there is a strong element of the formulaic in this. Such citations were generally concerned with the procedures rather than with the interpretation of law. To some extent, then, this was intended as a public display of the fact that things were being done properly; indeed, were being done 'by the book'. However, this does not detract from the clear implication of these records that the judges themselves, and in the main they were laymen, could read the book they thus resorted to. Such a deduction is strengthened by the evidence of the surviving manuscripts of the *Forum Iudicum* themselves. These are almost all what could be regarded as being working codices.[104] They are generally quite small, not necessarily written on the finest vellum, and with a highly restrained ornamentation that detracts in no way from the readability of the text. Indeed the ornamental element, which shows signs of standardization and may derive from Visigothic prototypes, looks intended to enhance the ease of access to the contents of the book.[105] All of this is in contrast to the manuscripts of the conciliar collections, none of which seems to have been intended for ease of portability or frequent reference. Admittedly, there exists one grand manuscript of the code, written in the mid-eleventh century for the abbot and judge Froila, but there are grounds for suspecting that this was copied from the authoritative exemplar of the law book preserved in the royal monastery and *Infantado* of San Salvador in León.[106] It may well have come to serve a similar purpose itself in the royal house of San Isidoro in the same city.

---

[102] For the rules of evidence, see Titles iv and v of book II of the *Forum Iudicum*, ed. K. Zeumer, *MGH Leges nat. germ.*, I.1, pp. 94–120.

[103] The citations of the *Forum Iudicum* in Catalan documents are tabulated in M. Zimmermann, 'L'Usage de droit wisigothique en Catalogne du IXe au XIIe siècle: approches d'une signification culturelle', *Mélanges de la Casa de Velazquez* 9 (1973), 240–53; no such survey of the Leonese materials has been carried out.

[104] For the MSS see M.C. Díaz, 'La *Lex Visigothorum* y sus manuscritos – un ensayo de reinterpretación', *Anuario de Historia del Derecho Español* 46 (1976), 163–223.

[105] Common decorative schemes may be found in the majority of the MSS and fragments listed in *ibid.*

[106] Madrid, Biblioteca Nacional, MS Vitr. 14–15.

Such considerations obviously raise the question of where, if anywhere, such judges received their training.[107] To which the immediate answer must be that no evidence has yet emerged with a bearing on the matter. Charter references make it clear that many of the principal monasteries and episcopal churches of the kingdom owned copies of the code.[108] Several of their abbots feature as judges, and in cases not apparently involving their houses. For the lay judges it is probably safe to assume that no such thing as a specialized training in law existed. At best they may well have learned their profession in the execution of it or by personal instruction from other practitioners.

In general such education as existed in the Christian regions of Spain after 711 appears to have been centred on monastic schools. Again this is hardly surprising, as this may well have been the norm in the preceding Visigothic period, and was also to be found in the Muslim-ruled south in these centuries. The only appreciable difference in structural terms is that there seems to have been no equivalent in the north to the schools based in the major martyrs' basilicas that had existed under the Visigoths and still could be found in ninth-century Cordoba.[109] These, though, were essentially urban foundations. The discontinuities in town life in the north meant that any such institutions as may have existed in these regions before 711 failed to survive.

One other element that may be new or indeed may be a revival of a Visigothic practice is the existence of what may be presumed to have been court schools. In charters of the late tenth and early eleventh centuries from both León and Pamplona the presence of an ecclesiastic at court holding the title of *magister* can be noted.[110] From such references the existence of a *schola regis* has been deduced.[111] This may be being overly optimistic, and it is important to recall that this same period saw the writing of royal

---

[107] R. Gilbert, 'La enseñanza del derecho en Hispania durante los siglos VI a XI', *Ius Romanum Medii Aevi*, Pars I, 5b (Milan, 1967), pp. 3–54.

[108] Sánchez-Albornoz, 'Notas sobre los libros', 281, lists the evidence of monastic ownership of copies of the code. To this should be added the donation of Ilduara Eriz cited above, nn. 86 and 100. No such list exists for the monasteries of Catalonia.

[109] See some of the accounts of the lives of the mid-ninth-century martyrs given by Eulogius, which include some references to their training: for example the priest Perfectus *sub paedagogis basilicae sancti Aciscli clara eruditione nutritus*, *Eulogi Memoriale Sanctorum* II.i.1, ed. Gil, *Corpus Scriptorum Muzarabicorum*, I, p. 398.

[110] For example, Madrid, Biblioteca Nacional, MS 18387 ('Cartulario de Samos'), doc. 156, fol. 272 r/v of 983 includes the signature of 'Froyla Hamitiz magister regis'; Abbot Galindo, 'Magister regis' to King Sancho II Garcés of Pamplona: Madrid, Archivo Histórico Nacional, sección de clero, carpeta 1404, doc. 5. Such references can be multiplied.

[111] Gibert, 'Enseñanza del derecho', p. 35.

documents by the episcopal scriptorium. Certainly no major centres of learning should be envisaged in the existence of what might at best have been a tutor to the royal family.

Cautious as it is necessary to be, there are features of the conditions in the north that suggest that in the matter of lay literacy, despite differences in both economy and social structure, the Christian kingdoms did not let go entirely of their Visigothic inheritance. Certainly it appears to have been intensely practical in character, and a really disinterested revival of concern for scholarship was slow in coming in Christian Spain; perhaps not to be looked for much before the thirteenth century. Even the monasteries appear to have been great landowners and centres of liturgical observance before being places of learning. But some of them were able to combine all three purposes, and in so doing served the purposes of their lay founders.

One other dimension that should not be overlooked is the continuing impact of the south on the Christian north, especially from the beginning of the tenth century. In 882 a corpus of books, ones that had probably once belonged to or were copies of those of Eulogius, reached Oviedo from Cordoba, very probably as part of a diplomatic exchange. Their subsequent fate is unknown, though the possibility exists that some of them, or copies, featured in Bishop Cixila of León's gift to his monastery of Abeliare in 927.[112] Cixila himself has been seen as a 'Mozarab' or Arabized Christian refugee from Muslim Al-Andalus; if so he could have brought his books with him.[113] As has been seen above his monastery's library looks a possible source for the subsequent donation of books to her new foundation for nuns at Giumarães on the part of Mummadona Díaz. Whatever the truth be as to the origins of Cixila, certainly some southern Christians did come north and establish themselves above all in the frontier regions of León. They founded monasteries with the backing of the kings and the Leonese aristocracy, and they brought more books with them.[114]

The limited nature of the evidence relating to early mediaeval Spain remains a permanent problem, and there are features that have not been discussed here, such as the possible impact of developments north of the Pyrenees, above all on Catalonia. However, it may be hoped that some impression may have been formed of continuities across the supposed chasm of the Arab conquest of the peninsula. Most obviously these can be seen in the continuing hold of the learning, liturgy and law of the Visigothic period on the Christian population throughout the peninsula

---

[112] On the list, see M.C. Díaz y Díaz, *Códices visigóticos en la monarquía leonesa* (León, 1983), pp. 42–53.

[113] Collins, 'Poetry in ninth-century Spain', 189 and n. 39.

[114] On the books of the Mozarabs see Gómez-Moreno, *Iglesias mozárabes*, I, pp. 345–64.

after 711. But such a clinging to tradition in threatening circumstances occasions small surprise. What is more notable is the survival in the south of a literate laity in, of course, the upper levels of society. To a more restricted degree the same is true of the Christian-ruled north as well.

This continuity in the existence of what may be termed a reading public needs to be underlined when the flowering of the patronage of scholarship and the collecting of books in late Umayyad society be recalled. The two have never been associated, largely due to the existence of assumptions that the cultural floresence of Arab Spain needs no explanation. In fact it would be quite fallacious to assume that conditions were identical throughout the Arab world. Why not just the Umayyad court but also the upper classes in general in the major cities of Al-Andalus were avid readers needs some positive explanation. This was a population whose last major influx from outside the peninsula had occurred in the mid-eighth century. In other words, it was largely composed of increasingly Arabized but indigenous elements. Although the question has to be answered in a fuller and more complex way, it is not unreasonable to suggest that some part in it should have been played by this survival of the existence of an educated laity from the period of the Visigothic kingdom onwards.

6

Aspects of mediaeval Jewish literacy

Stefan C. Reif

The purpose of this essay is twofold. Unlike the remainder of the contributions, it sets out to describe cultural developments that occurred within a non-Christian tradition and that seem first to have flourished in an environment dominated by Islam. The geographical area in question ranges from Muslim Spain, through North Africa, Egypt and the Syro-Palestinian territories, to what is today Iraq and Iran, and the chronological limits are from the sixth to the eleventh centuries of the Christian era. This departure from Europe for more oriental climes is not a matter of scholarly choice but is dictated by a dearth of evidence in that continent for the chronological span just defined that frustrates current research and contrasts with the wealth of sources emanating from the Jewish communities of the Arab world. The description here being offered will serve to complement the other essays not only by providing an external yardstick against which to measure the significance of literary trends in the world of European Christianity but also by drawing attention to certain parallel developments, the accurate evaluation of which will become possible only when scholarly research increases knowledge of the beginnings of Jewish settlement in Christian Europe.[1] Its second aim, which has more in common with the other subjects treated in the volume, is to assess the degree to which literacy penetrated various societies around the Mediterranean area and to the east of it in the latter half of the first Christian millennium and thereby to dispel some of the myths that have led to the overall representation of that period in terms of 'the dark ages'. By means of such an assessment a more accurate picture will emerge of what was innovative and what long-standing in the matter of Jewish literary achievement in the post-mediaeval and early

---

[1] It is clear from A. Grossman's Hebrew volume on *The Early Sages of Ashkenaz* (Jerusalem, 1981) – cf. also his *The Early Sages of France* (Jerusalem, 1989) – that little may be said about developments prior to the tenth century. In the volume *A History of the Jewish People*, ed. H.H. Ben-Sasson (London, 1976), the chapter by him entitled 'Jewish social and cultural life until the end of the eleventh century', pp. 439–61, devotes only three pages out of twenty-three to Jews in the non-Islamic environment.

modern periods. The need for the picture to include many themes and to deal with the totality of a religious culture rather than with a single element in it will of necessity entail the painting of a broad canvas rather than an intense and detailed miniature. The treatment will commence with some general points about Jewish attitudes to language and text and then move on to the nature of the Jewish literary experience between the sixth and eleventh centuries.[2] The period has been chronologically defined in this way in order to match the Jewish periodization of history. The concept of literacy will here be understood as referring to the commitment of traditions to writing, the technical process of scribal activity and the popular acquaintance with what can be done with an alphabet.

To explain the nature of developments in the 500 years of the post-talmudic or geonic period (that is, the age when the leaders or *ge'onim* of the talmudic academies in Babylon guided Jewish cultural trends), it is necessary to make mention of the part played by the transmission of the written word in the Jewish religious heritage. Both internal and external evidence demonstrates a substantial use of the written word in ancient Israel for archives, inscriptions and the establishment of religious authority. To that latter end a significant element in codification appears to have been textualization, which was regarded as a means of ensuring the permanence of knowledge, guidance and edification for the faithful. Committing a text to writing lent it an impressive spiritual status and the acts of copying and reciting texts that ultimately became part of the Hebrew Bible were established practices by the beginning of what is known to Jewish historians as the second temple period (515BC–AD 70), that is, late in the sixth pre-Christian century. As the people's record of what is regarded as its special revelation and its religious history, this body of texts was looked upon as sacred, attracted various forms of veneration and declamation and also came to be used for theurgical purposes. Central as it was to the faith, it also became the primer from which children would familiarize themselves with both the written language and the religious message.[3] It is indeed difficult to

---

[2] Although this period is the subject of a good deal of current scholarship, especially in Israel, this specialized research and its conclusions have yet to be consolidated in a general history of the period in either English or Hebrew. In the meantime, more general scholarly interest is served by S.W. Baron, *A Social and Religious History of the Jews*, 18 vols. (New York, 1952 – New York, London and Philadelphia, 1983), III–VIII (New York, London and Philadelphia, 1957–8); Cecil Roth, *The World History of the Jewish People. Medieval Period. The Dark Ages* (London, 1966); and the work edited by H.H. Ben-Sasson and cited in n. 1 above.

[3] Typical examples of illustrative texts in the Hebrew Bible are Exodus 17:14, Deuteronomy 17:18, Isaiah 8:1, Jeremiah 17:1 and the whole of chapters 32 and 36, Ezekiel 37:20 and Habakuk 2:2. See E. Würthwein, *The Text of the Old Testament* (4th edn, London, 1980), pp. 3–11; Y. Kaufmann, *The Religion of Israel from its Beginnings to the Babylonian Exile*

disentangle the intertwined strands of text, language and religion in the Judaism of the late biblical period and Hebrew itself became so identified with the sacred ideology that, whatever its later fate as a spoken vernacular, it was ultimately given a special status as the sacred, cultic or perhaps even divine language in Jewish tradition.[4] At the same time, however, Greek language and literature issued a serious challenge to the Jews, particularly in the communities of the diaspora, and tensions were created between the desire for written communication in the language of the national heritage, or in one closely associated with it, namely, Aramaic, and the exciting prospect of adopting a more universal medium for the transmission of Jewish religious ideas.[5]

As the second temple period gave way to the early rabbinic period, just before and after the time of Jesus, the concept of sacred scripture took on a meaning much wider than the transmission of the words in text or recitation. If the revealed word represented the will of God, then all theological developments must originate there and its ideology must be transmitted by way of popular expansions, interpretations and adjustments of the original text that paradoxically incorporated novel ideas into ancient canon. The Hebrew Bible was thus credited with being the source of many of the apocryphal, pseudepigraphical, Qumranic, Hellenistic and rabbinic traditions of the late pre-Christian and early Christian centuries and renderings of its text spawned various Aramaic and Greek translations and paraphrases that themselves contributed to a considerable expansion of Jewish (and, ultimately, Christian) literature.[6] The early rabbinic liturgy

---

(London, 1961), pp. 174–5, 354–62; R. de Vaux, *Ancient Israel: Its Life and Institutions* (London, 1965), pp. 48–50; and J.L. Crenshaw, 'Education in ancient Israel', *Journal of Biblical Literature* 104 (1985), 601–15.

[4] S. Esh, *'HQBH. Der Heilige Er Sei Gepriesen.' Zur Geschichte einer Nachbiblisch-Hebräischen Gottesbezeichnung* (Leiden, 1957), pp. 82–3, explaining the term 'tongue of holiness' used in the Mishnah, *Soṭah* 7.2.4 and *Yevamoth* 12.6. See also, for the history of Hebrew in the late biblical period, E.Y. Kutscher, *A History of the Hebrew Language*, ed. R. Kutscher (Jerusalem and Leiden, 1982), especially pp. 81–114; J. Naveh, 'Hebrew and Aramaic in the Persian period', in *The Cambridge History of Judaism*, ed. W.D. Davies and L. Finkelstein (Cambridge, 1984), I, pp. 115–29; and C. Rabin, 'Hebrew and Aramaic in the first century', in *The Jewish People in the First Century*, ed. S. Safrai and M. Stern, 2 vols. (Assen and Philadelphia, 1974–6), II, pp. 1007–39.

[5] See S. Lieberman, *Greek in Jewish Palestine* (New York, 1942); M. Hengel, *Judaism and Hellenism* (London, 1974); G. Mussies, 'Greek in Palestine and the Diaspora', in *The Jewish People*, ed. Safrai and Stern, II, pp. 1040–64; and the attempt by L.H. Feldman to offer a corrective in his 'How much Hellenism in Jewish Palestine?', in *Hebrew Union College Annual* 57 (1986), 83–111.

[6] E. Schürer, *The History of the Jewish People in the Age of Jesus Christ (175 B.C.–A.D. 135)*, ed. G. Vermes and F. Millar, 3 vols. (Edinburgh, 1973–87), I (Edinburgh, 1973), pp. 17–122, and III (Edinburgh, 2 parts, 1986–7), pp. 177–889; *The Jewish People*, ed. Safrai and Stern, I, pp. 1–61; and *Jewish Writings of the Second Temple Period*, ed. M.E. Stone (Assen and Philadelphia, 1984).

incorporated elements of both the biblical and the post-biblical forms of the Hebrew and Aramaic languages and the tannaitic traditions were incorporated into the Mishna, Tosefta and Talmud in the same contemporary Hebrew language that was used by Bar Kokhba to write his army orders in AD 132–5.[7] Jewish culture of the early Christian period consequently made use of three languages, namely, Hebrew, Aramaic and Greek, not only in the vernacular, as the evidence of inscriptions makes abundantly clear, but also in the formulation of its transmitted traditions.

It must not, of course, be assumed that all these traditions were committed to textual form. In some cases the content of the biblical text underwent a popular transformation and emerged as oral teaching while, in others, orally transmitted lore acquired a more formal, literary structure at the hands of generations of transmitters and evolved into authoritative text. It may well be fair to say that the halakhic (legal) and aggadic (other religious) traditions of the rabbis became predominantly oral while their equivalents among other Jewish groups, ranging from the Hellenistic to what for ease of reference may be referred to as the sectarian, were consigned to the written form. What remained basic to all groups were the veneration and recitation of biblical scroll-texts, and a linguistic knowledge sufficient to understand them or their translations, a respect for the written word as the source of religious teachings and the medium for conveying at least some of them, the use of legal documents to impose the requirements of the Mosaic code as they understood it, and an educational system that furnished members of the community with the ability to adhere to these values. It is not by some semantic quirk that the sum total of Jewish religious theory and practice came to be known by the talmudic rabbis as *torah*, the Hebrew word for 'teaching'. Similarly, the epithet *qara'* could mean 'reader', 'scholar' or 'expert in Bible', and the titles of a number of classical rabbinic works, including the Mishnah and the Talmud, carried the basic sense of 'learning' or 'teaching'. The whole learning and teaching process lay at the centre of Judaism and is incapable of comprehension outside the linguistic and literary context just described.[8]

A glance at the world of rabbinic religious traditions in the sixth century

[7] Kutscher, *Hebrew Language*, pp. 115–47; J. Heinemann, *Prayer in the Talmud: Forms and Patterns* (Berlin, 1977), pp. 123–38, 159, 190–2, 265–6, 278 and 287; Y. Yadin, *Bar Kokhba: The Rediscovery of the Legendary Hero of the Second Jewish Revolt against Rome* (London, 1971), pp. 124–39; and J.C. Greenfield, 'Languages of Palestine 200 b.c.e.–200 c.e.', in *Jewish Languages: Theme and Variation*, ed. H.H. Paper (Cambridge, Mass., 1978), pp. 143–54.

[8] In addition to the relevant sections of the literature cited in n. 6 above, see *The Literature of the Sages. First Part: Oral Tora, Halakha, Mishna, Tosefta, Talmud, External Tractates*, ed. S. Safrai (Assen, Maastricht and Philadelphia, 1987), especially the chapter by the editor on 'Oral Tora' (pp. 35–119), and H. Dimitrovsky's collection of reprinted essays *Exploring the Talmud, I: Education* (New York, 1976).

and an examination of the phonetic spelling in which they were recorded in later manuscripts reveal that the method of transmitting many of them still remained predominantly an oral one. While scrolls of the Hebrew Bible were carefully copied, and there were surely some texts of the Aramaic versions (*Targumim*), of the early third-century corpus of Jewish law (Mishnah) and of synagogal poetry and biblical commentary in existence, the massive body of rabbinic (more accurately, talmudic–midrashic) teachings, covering the whole field of textual interpretation and legal discussion and the liturgical formulations of some five centuries, were gradually acquiring a more formal structure but were yet to be committed in any substantial degree to writing.[9]

Texts of such works were, unlike their biblical antecedents, for private recall rather than public circulation and edification and were never familiar to any more than an influential minority. Not only is there no evidence of widespread copying of rabbinic traditions, there are clear indications in the statements of some of the talmudic rabbis of an aversion to the possible results of a misguided equation with the authoritative biblical texts and a neglect of the oral method of education. The oral transmission of these traditions is described as a special feature of the revelation to Israel and of Jewish education and 'there is no authority for committing oral sayings to writing'.[10] Since the earlier evidence of the late second temple period has been seen to point to something of a textual explosion, it is not unreasonable to see the oral trend of the rabbis as the defence of a more populist philosophy and the choice of an alternative and less formal medium for its transmission.

The course of the next 500 years of Jewish history ensured a major change in this situation. While under Parthian and Byzantine hegemony, the Jewish communities of the Near East and the Mediterranean area had been prone to periods of tolerance interchanging with times of persecution and had been unable to rely on any degree of political stability, their position in

---

[9] M.L. Klein, *Genizah Manuscripts of Palestinian Targum to the Pentateuch* (Cincinnati, 1986), introduction to the first volume, especially pp. xxxiv–xxxvi; A. Goldberg, 'The Mishna – a study book of Halakha', in *Literature of the Sages*, ed. Safrai, pp. 211–62; T. Carmi, *The Penguin Book of Hebrew Verse* (Harmondsworth, 1981), introduction, pp. 13–20, based largely on the Hebrew volume of E. Fleischer, *Hebrew Liturgical Poetry in the Middle Ages* (Jerusalem, 1975); J. Heinemann and J.J. Petuchowski, *Literature of the Synagogue* (New York, 1975); G.G. Porton, *Understanding Rabbinic Midrash* (Hoboken, New Jersey, 1985); D. Weiss-Halivni, *Midrash, Mishnah and Gemara* (Cambridge, Mass., 1986), especially p. 83; and S.C. Reif, 'Some liturgical issues in the talmudic sources', *Studia Liturgica* 15 (1982–3), 188–206.

[10] Babylonian Talmud, *Giṭṭin* 60b and cf. Palestinian Talmud, *Pe'ah* 2.6 (17a) and *Megillah* 4.1 (74d). See *Literature of the Sages*, ed. Safrai, and B. Gerhardsson, *Memory and Manuscript: Oral Tradition and Written Transmission in Rabbinic Judaism and Early Christianity* (Uppsala, 1961), especially pp. 113–70.

general society underwent a considerable revolution with the conquest of that mass of territory by the Arabs and its subsequent domination by Islam. The Jew remained a second-class citizen but his status was legally established; the religio-political system under which he lived held sway from Afghanistan to Spain; and the Arab absorption of the finest achievements of the peoples they conquered led to a flourishing of what was perhaps the broadest culture yet known to man. This not only led to the emergence of a variety of religious and heretical trends from both within Islam and outside it, but also provided an example of centralization, authority, standardization and intellectual progress that the Jews were not slow in adapting to their own communal, religious and literary requirements. The major Jewish communities that were subject to the various caliphates of the geonic period were located in Babylon, the Holy Land, North Africa and Spain and it was in these centres, each in its own heyday, that the various components of Jewish literature gradually acquired the forms that later became familiar to Jews and non-Jews and instrumental in the formation of their respective ideas. The various literary achievements of these communities must now be separately considered.[11]

Whether inspired by the example of the Koran or the Syriac Christian tradition, or the result of the schism between Rabbanites, who upheld the authority of the talmudic tradition, and Karaites,[12] who looked to a literal interpretation of the Hebrew Bible for their religious guidance, a new expertise was developed in the orthography, punctuation, vocalization and cantillation of the Hebrew Bible and subsequently transferred to other areas of Hebrew linguistic expression. These experts, known as Masoretes (from the Hebrew *masorah* meaning 'traditional transmission' or possibly at an earlier stage, 'counting the letters'), introduced a number of divergent systems for protecting the authenticity of the textual tradition, one of which ultimately became standard in the majority of important manuscripts, and, by peppering the biblical text with their comments and instructions, laid the foundations for the later emergence of Hebrew philological studies beginning in the tenth century.[13] The earliest exponents of these studies

---

[11] S.D. Goitein, *Jews and Arabs: Their Contacts through the Ages* (2nd edn, New York, 1964); E.I.J. Rosenthal, *Judaism and Islam* (London and New York, 1961); N.A. Stillman, *The Jews of Arab Lands: A History and Source Book* (Philadelphia, 1979); and B. Lewis, *The Jews of Islam* (London, 1984).

[12] For further details of the Karaite movement and ideology, see L. Nemoy, *Karaite Anthology* (New Haven and London, 1952), and P. Birnbaum, *Karaite Studies* (New York, 1971).

[13] Würthwein, *Old Testament*, pp. 12–41; A. Dotan, 'Masorah', *EJ* XVI, cols. 1401–82; and the more dated but historically useful material assembled by S.D. Leiman in *The Canon and Masorah of the Hebrew Bible: An Introductory Reader* (New York, 1974).

were not slow in detecting the linguistic affinities between Hebrew,
Aramaic and Arabic and in composing dictionaries, grammars and theoretical principles to explain their structure and relationship. Almost inevitably,
an intellectual backlash was also created and written efforts were made to
defend an imagined Hebrew purity against the onslaught of the early
mediaeval equivalent of the comparative semiticist.[14]

Since neither the Hebrew nor the Aramaic versions that were traditionally recited in the synagogue were necessarily and consistently understood
without difficulty by sections of the Jewish community, it then became
customary to add a rendering in Arabic to the traditional, earlier versions
and to use the Hebrew script which, significantly, was assumed to be widely
familiar, for its written transmission. In the earlier part of the geonic
period, it is clear that a variety of Aramaic and Judaeo-Arabic versions
circulated. As with the vocalized text itself, however, standard versions of
both the Aramaic and the Arabic were promoted and ultimately became
accepted at the end of that period and this inevitably had a major influence
on the way in which the biblical text was understood.[15] As the rational
interpretation of the Hebrew Bible took on new significance in the theological struggles within the Jewish community and with Muslims, Christians
and heretics outside it, so the fanciful, poetic and colourful exegesis of
midrashim, which had had their origins in the synagogue and academy,
gradually gave ground to the more literal, clinical and philological commentaries that were to grace the folios of the manuscripts newly being produced
at the time. While one must be careful not to overdo the characterization of
one whole community as committed to the idea of the authoritative version
and another to the preservation of diversity there is little doubt that the
Babylonian *ge'onim* were more prone to the former tendency while their
Palestinian counterparts generally favoured the latter. The spread of
Babylonian influence as far as Spain, and later to Provence and France, and

---

[14] D. Téné has written on such early comparative study in the volume of Hebrew essays
Hebrew Language Studies Presented to Professor Zeev Ben-Hayyim, ed. M. Bar-Asher, A.
Dotan, G.B. Sarfatti and D. Téné (Jerusalem, 1983), pp. 237–87. See also A. Maman, 'The
comparison of the Hebrew lexicon with Arabic and Aramaic in the linguistic literature of the
Jews from Rav Saadia Gaon (10th cent.) to Ibn Barun (12th cent.)' PhD dissertation in
Hebrew with English summary, Hebrew University of Jerusalem, 1984, pp. vii–xxvii and
7–11.

[15] On the Aramaic translations see R. Le Déaut, *Introduction à la Littérature Targumique*
(Rome, 1966); J.W. Bowker, *The Targums and Rabbinic Literature* (Cambridge, 1969);
and Y. Komlosh, *The Bible in the Light of the Aramaic Translations* (Tel-Aviv, 1973). For
an explanation of the development of Judaeo-Arabic literature see J. Blau, *The Emergence
and Linguistic Background of Judaeo-Arabic* (1st edn, Oxford, 1965; 2nd edn, Jerusalem,
1981), pp. 19–50.

the final eclipse of the Palestinian Jewish presence through appalling slaughter at the hands of the Crusaders, or flight to Egypt or Syria to avoid it, subsequently strengthened the move towards standardization and authority not only in the field of biblical exegesis but in other areas of the Jewish religious tradition.[16]

While the trend in the evolution of the talmudic traditions during the first few Christian centuries had been towards the intellectual, the dialectical and the search for the authoritative source, the position was forced to alter when the general form and content of the Babylonian Talmud was decided and much of the editorial process concluded in the sixth century. From that period onwards the aims of the rabbis had to be geared as much to the practical as to the theoretical and they saw as their function not only the arrangement of higher talmudic education but also the provision of guidance for the communities who looked to them for leadership. Consequently, the exposition of the talmudic text, the response of the expert to the specific halakhic question addressed to him and the more systematic and extensive codification of Jewish religious law in general came to stand as much at the centre of the talmudic tradition as the argumentation about its own origin that was so typical of its earlier method of transmission. Edited texts of the Babylonian talmudic tractates were disseminated throughout the Jewish world. Written *quaestiones et responsa*, sometimes exchanged between cities in Spain and Mesopotamia, and dealing with textual as well as exegetical and legal problems, were received and issued by such leaders as Yehudai ben Naḥman (eighth century), Amram ben Sheshna (ninth century) and Saadya ben Joseph (tenth century) of Sura, and Sherira ben Ḥananiah (tenth century) and Hai ben Sherira (eleventh century) of Pumbedita. Collections of decisions, including the *Halokhoth Pesuqoth* attributed to Yehudai, and the *Halakhoth Gedoloth* now assumed to be the work of Simeon Qayyara (ninth century ?) were composed and circulated.[17] This is not to say that oral discussion was replaced by written debate during

---

[16] These developments are discussed in detail by Baron, *History of the Jews*, particularly in VI, pp. 152–313. On the history of Palestinian Jewry until the Crusades, see M. Gil, *Palestine during the First Muslim Period (634–1099)*, 3 vols. (Tel-Aviv, 1983), and for an edited collection of the most important sources about the leadership of Babylonian Jewry see A. Grossman, *The Babylonian Exilarchate in the Gaonic Period* (Jerusalem, 1984).

[17] Baron, *History of the Jews*, VI, pp. 3–151; S. Abramson, *Bamerkazim Uvatefuṣoth* (Jerusalem, 1965), and *idem*, *'Inyanoth Besifruth Hage'onim* (Jerusalem, 1974), both in Hebrew; Weiss-Halivni, *Midrash*; and A. Goldberg, 'The Babylonian Talmud', in *Literature of the Sages*, ed. Safrai, pp. 323–45, followed by an appendix on manuscripts of the Babylonian Talmud by Michael Krupp, pp. 346–66. The work of L. Ginzberg in English and S. Assaf in Hebrew may be consulted for more detail and earlier interpretations: *Geonica*, 2 vols. (New York, 1909), and S. Assaf, *Gaonica* (Jerusalem, 1933).

the geonic period. The educational value and the historical authenticity of the former was still argued in the time of Sherira (tenth century) and there continued to be an oral system of advanced adult education at the Babylonian academies for two short terms twice a year, during which time the scholars were expected to present to a more popular audience a comprehensive digest of their studies.[18] The foundations had, however, been laid for the wider use of the written word and the later collapse of the Babylonian centres did not therefore spell disaster for the transmission of their talmudic learning.[19]

In the field of liturgy, too, what had previously been specifically designated as an orally transmitted medium was first committed to writing in the ninth century. With the arrival of the prayer book, authoritative instruction on the precise nature, function and wording of the various prayers finally emerged victorious from its age-old battle with spontaneity and pluralism. Those who had embraced the view of the second-century scholar Eliezer ben Hyrcanus[20] that fixed prayer can never be supplicatory saw the erosion of their ideal and its replacement with a more practical commitment to a defined text. While various rites continued to enjoy parallel existence, certain fundamental principles came to be accepted by them all and firmly controlled the extent to which variation was possible. Attempts were made to define the basic nature of the Jewish prayer and benediction and thereby to exclude what could then be regarded as excessively innovative.[21] The element of pure creativity in the realm of prayer was channelled into the mystical and poetic streams of the tradition and even there it continued to attract virulent criticism whenever the rabbinic authorities identified what they regarded as departures from what had become the established norm. As far as liturgical poetry (*piyyut*) is concerned, this was, at its earliest stage in the late talmudic and early geonic periods, the province of the composer and the reciter and had no popular application or educational significance. If texts were copied, they were

---

[18] *Iggeret R. Scherira Gaon in der französischen und spanischen Version*, ed. B. Lewin (Haifa, 1921), p. 71; A. Neubauer, *Mediaeval Jewish Chronicles* (Oxford, 1887), pp. 83–5; Baron, *History of the Jews*, VI, pp. 36, 213, 430–1; and a Hebrew paper delivered by R. Brody at the Ninth World Congress of Jewish Studies in Jerusalem in 1985, entitled 'The testimony of geonic literature to the text of the Babylonian Talmud' and scheduled for publication in a collection of essays by the Talmud department of the Hebrew University of Jerusalem.

[19] For the transfer of that learning to the North African centre see M. Ben-Sasson, 'The Jewish community of medieval North Africa: society and leadership', PhD dissertation in Hebrew with English summary, Hebrew University of Jerusalem, 1983.

[20] *Mishnah*, Berakhoth 4.4.

[21] L.A. Hoffman, *The Canonization of the Synagogue Service* (Notre Dame and London, 1979).

copied by or for the liturgical poets themselves and the public's knowledge was limited to what they heard recited between and within the standard prayers. By the tenth century, however, it is clear from the nature and extent of the manuscript evidence that *piyyuṭim* were emerging as a less technical and more independent literary genre and texts were being transcribed and circulated not only by the experts and the learned but also by a wider body of interested laymen for educational and aesthetic reasons as well as for liturgical purposes.[22] The basis of the change lay in the adaptation of Hebrew poetry to the dominant Arabic forms and Dunash ibn Labrat's contribution to this process has been described by T. Carmi as 'one of the most drastic operations in the history of Hebrew poetry'. As he expresses it, 'The complexion of Hebrew poetry – one is tempted to say its physiognomy – was dramatically transformed in the tenth century with the emergence of the Andalusian school . . . and the appearance of secular poetry.'[23]

The situation regarding developments in mysticism and philosophy is of a different nature from that applying to the more dominant rabbinic traditions just described. The written dimension was obviously a familiar one to the mystic in the early talmudic period and stress was laid on the theurgical power of texts, names, letters and numbers, as recorded on papyrus and on artefacts, throughout the geonic period. Interpretation and formulation were by definition restricted to initiates although clients for practical application were never in short supply.[24] Conversely, the study of systematic philosophy among the Jews of the early mediaeval period was not a direct continuation of its Hellenistic forerunner but the result of influences emanating from Christian and Muslim theological circles. The composition of texts on this subject was inevitably, therefore, a novel development. No change from the oral to the written is then detectable in the history of Jewish mysticism and philosophy in the period under discussion but it is clear that there were moves towards the creation of systems, forms and conventions here no less than elsewhere and that these were recorded in the ever-increasing number of manuscripts being written and circulated.[25]

---

[22] Fleischer, *Hebrew Liturgical Poetry*, pp. 333–421.

[23] Carmi, *Hebrew Verse*, pp. 19–20.

[24] G. Scholem, 'Kabbalah', in *EJ* X, cols. 508–12; I. Gruenwald, *Apocalyptic and Merkavah Mysticism* (Leiden, 1980), pp. 98–234; and N. Sed, *La Mystique Cosmologique Juive* (Paris, 1981), pp. 75–261.

[25] C. Sirat, *A History of Jewish Philosophy in the Middle Ages* (Cambridge, 1985), pp. 1–13; see also I. Husik, *A History of Medieval Jewish Philosophy* (New York, 1916), introduction, pp. xiii–l, and J. Guttmann, *Philosophies of Judaism* (London, 1964), pp. 47–60.

The point has already been made that the literary achievements just described were a product of the Jewish communities living in the Islamic environment. There were also substantial Jewish communities in the Byzantine Empire, Italy and the Rhineland but the conditions there were certainly inferior to those enjoyed to the south and the east and the pressure from Christian authorities tended to be more pervasive than that of most of their Muslim counterparts. The two sets of Jewish communities were certainly in contact both personally and by correspondence, and ideas forged in the one must have been imported into the other. By the tenth century the Italian and Byzantine Jewries had already enjoyed a long, if chequered, history and had produced liturgical poets, talmudic scholars and chroniclers of their own, probably as a result of their close relationship with the Holy Land. For its part, the Franco-German centre was set to carry forward these Jewish cultural traditions but was still in its infancy. The limited scholarly knowledge that we do have of that community that later became known as Ashkenaz suggests a lower degree of literary productivity than its counterpart under Islam in the geonic period under discussion.[26] On the basis of later developments, however, we may assume that the influences of the oriental Jewish communities were already making themselves felt at that time and that foundations were being laid for similar cultural expansion when the communities of Christian countries also became more organized and comfortable. As is amply demonstrated in other contributions to this volume, there were internal developments in the early mediaeval Christian communities of the northern Mediterranean and western Europe that led to an expansion of literacy.[27] Whatever the political, religious, administrative or legal considerations that motivated that expansion, their relevance to the wider community appears to have been limited and they seem to constitute neither a necessary nor a related effect as far as the later history of European Jewish literacy is concerned. The precedents for that appear to have been established chronologically, geographically and culturally elsewhere. This is not to say that the influences of the western Christian world on Jewish religious culture were negligible. It is simply to stress that the trend towards a wider and more

---

[26] Baron, *History of the Jews*, III, pp. 3–74, IV, pp. 3–88; B. Blumenkranz, *Juifs et Chrétiens dans le Monde Occidental* (Paris, 1960), and his reprinted essays in *Juifs et Chrétiens Patristique et Moyen Age* (London, 1977); Roth, *World History*; A. Grossman, 'The Jews in Byzantium and medieval Europe', in *The Jewish World*, ed. E. Kedourie (London, 1979), pp. 168–77; A. Sharf, *Byzantine Jewry from Justinian to the Fourth Crusade* (London, 1971); and nn. 1–2 above.

[27] This is particularly well exemplified, for the purposes of comparison, in the chapters in this volume by Collins, Kelly, Keynes, Mitchell and Nelson.

intensive degree of Jewish literacy had originated at an earlier period, further south and east.

It is now necessary to pause in the presentation of elements in Jewish literary history and to assess their significance for any definition of Jewish mediaeval literacy. If, for the moment, such literacy is equated with the composition of literature, the spread of the written tradition among a substantial proportion of the population, and the part played by authoritative texts in shaping the lives and ideals of the community, it must be acknowledged that Jewish literacy, which had already existed at a fairly high level in earlier centuries, made substantial, further progress during the geonic period. Standard texts of the leading religious works were edited, rational methods of textual exegesis were initiated and written guidance was provided for both ritual and theology. In order to justify the claim that such developments affected a substantial proportion of the Jewish population rather than an elitist minority, some reminder is required of the literary nature of the Jewish religious tradition as it related to that population.

The text of the Pentateuch stood at the centre of the tradition and confronted the ordinary Jew in synagogue, home and school. It was not the rabbi who functioned as the intermediary between the people and its God but sacred scripture and the exegesis that was regarded as an integral part of it. If a liturgy, *qua* religious communion, existed in rabbinic Judaism, it was experienced through the learning process, so that education developed an almost cultic function. It was not a specially ordained priest who performed a symbolic ceremony to demonstrate the allegiance of the faithful but any Jew educated enough in the sources to be called *rabbi*, 'my teacher', and to lead his co-religionists through the intricacies of the traditions, the knowledge and practice of which demonstrated their commitment to religious continuity. Hebrew was a *sine qua non* of Jewish life and even the rare Jew who had for some reason remained illiterate was *malgré lui* caught up in its appearance, recitation and sound.[28]

What is equally important, and what seems to have received little recognition from those engaged in research on the period, is that it was a change in the medium of transmission that led to these achievements. The contents of scrolls were copied on to codices, where they attracted bountiful glossing, and oral traditions were committed to manuscript and thereby acquired a new degree of authority. The centralization and organization of the Jewish community under Islam made possible the wide distribution of

---

[28] For details of how the mediaeval Jewish community operated as a whole, see I. Abrahams, *Jewish Life in the Middle Ages*, ed. Cecil Roth (London, 1932); T. and M. Metzger, *Jewish Life in the Middle Ages* (New York, 1982).

such texts and their acceptance as authoritative. It ensured that, when the caliphate disintegrated and smaller independent Jewish communities emerged, they already had a corpus of written sources to which they looked for instruction and inspiration. Established Jewish familiarity with the religious function and authoritative nature of the written word helped to overcome any reticence about the novelty of such a medium in some traditionally oral disciplines. What is more, the fact that leading scholars chose to summarize the religious traditions in such published forms seems to indicate a conviction on their part that there existed a large enough body of literate Jews to make the whole exercise effective and influential.[29] This point will shortly receive further attention.

Turning to the evidence of Hebrew codicology, one finds an almost total absence of Hebrew manuscripts between the second and the ninth centuries and it is unlikely that this is to be attributed to historical accident. More convincing would be the theory that the dominant tendency during these centuries was the oral one and that it was only with the expansion of the use of the codex, for the reasons just described, that the trend was reversed. Texts other than Hebrew Bible scrolls then began to make a wide appearance. Although the number of complete Hebrew codices that have survived from the ninth and tenth centuries is still only in single figures and their content predominantly biblical, the evidence of the Cairo Genizah, shortly to be discussed, leaves little room for doubt that many of the fragments from that source originally belonged to codices of various types of literature dating from those centuries or even a little earlier and emanating from the oriental communities to which reference has already been made. Until Hebrew palaeographical research makes further progress it can only be surmised that the Hebrew codex made its appearance in the early geonic period, perhaps in the eighth century when there are traces of Islamic influence, and within three centuries became the standard medium for textual transmission. While the eighth-century post-talmudic tractate of Palestinian provenance, *Massekheth Soferim*, was, with the exception of one problematic reference,[30] primarily concerned with the writing of a biblical scroll, the position totally changed within two or three centuries by which time there were already standard practices for Jewish scribes copying all kinds of literature on to codices. With similar developments taking place among the Muslims, the Jews were gradually replacing papyrus with vellum

[29] The emergence of the Hebrew codex is touched upon by D. Diringer, *The Hand-Produced Book* (London, 1953), pp. 321–35, and by R. Posner and I. Ta-Shema, *The Hebrew Book: An Historical Survey* (Jerusalem, 1975), pp. 33–62.

[30] *Massekheth Soferim*, ed. M. Higger (1st edn, New York, 1937; 2nd edn, Jerusalem, 1970), 3.6, p. 125.

as the primary material for the transcription of texts and would soon begin to adopt paper. Quires were composed, catchwords included, sections numerated, lines justified, folios pricked and ruled, and the *masṭara* (ruling-board) was employed to facilitate the planning of the lines. Pride was taken in producing particularly beautiful codices of the Hebrew Bible.[31] The different Jewish communities followed their own customs in these scribal practices but the codex was unique in offering versatility, ease of reference and substantial capacity.[32] It was therefore widely adopted for the circulation of the literature created and expanded in the previous few centuries. It has indeed recently been demonstrated by Ben-Sasson that in the Jewish communities of North Africa in the ninth and tenth centuries texts were being widely copied and circulated and extensive libraries, both private and public, and covering various languages, were being amassed and sold. Such libraries included not only the classical Jewish sources but also the newest commentaries on the one hand and more general learning on the other. By creating and disseminating the contents of these libraries, the Maghrebi Jews of means introduced a wide variety of literary works to other communities and thereby exercised a powerful influence on the levels of Jewish cultural achievement.[33]

While literacy may justifiably be understood to refer to an acquaintance with literature, it may also convey, and indeed more often today conveys, the sense of linguistic knowledge, that is, the ability to read and write a language or more than one language. If we are to understand the Jewish situation in this connection during the period under discussion, it will be necessary to liberate ourselves from an exclusive concern with the history of literature and to attempt a consideration of the more mundane aspects of Jewish life more than a thousand years ago.

As in earlier generations, trilingualism was a feature of Jewish society, Hebrew, Aramaic and Arabic being used in a variety of contexts by different people for sundry reasons, with each of these languages exercising an influence on the others. While Hebrew obviously continued to be the

---

[31] M. Beit-Arié, *Hebrew Codicology* (1st edn, Paris, 1977; 2nd edn, Jerusalem, 1981); C. Sirat, *Ecriture et civilisations* (Paris, 1976), and *idem, Les Papyrus écrits en lettres hébraïques trouvés en Egypte* (Paris, 1981); M. Beit-Arié and C. Sirat, *Manuscrits mediévaux en caractères hébraïques*, 2 vols. (Paris, 1972–9).

[32] The significant advantages of the codex are outlined by C.H. Roberts and T.C. Skeat, *The Birth of the Codex* (London, 1983), pp. 45–61.

[33] M. Ben-Sasson, 'Maghreb libraries in the Genizah', a paper delivered at the third international congress of the Society for Judaeo-Arabic Studies held in Cambridge in July, 1987, and shortly to be published in the proceedings of that congress scheduled to appear in the publications of the Faculty of Oriental Studies at the University of Cambridge handled by Cambridge University Press, or, if not yet ready, in a later publication.

language of the biblical lectionaries, was adopted for masoretic notes on the biblical text (see p. 139 above), and was retained as the language of *midrashim*, of the statutory prayers (in a predominantly mishnaic form) and of liturgical poetry, it was Arabic that was chosen for biblical commentary and translation. This Arabic, usually written in Hebrew characters and preserving more vernacular forms than classical Muslim Arabic, and currently entitled Judaeo-Arabic, was also the language chosen for the earliest philological studies, philosophy, theology, science and more ephemeral documents of a social, political and economic nature. The language that had once been a vernacular in Roman Judaea, Aramaic, was restricted to a more scholarly role, being used for the Talmud and for commentaries on it and codes extracted from it. It was also employed for the *targumim* (the Aramaic biblical renderings that had once served to inform and edify Aramaic-speaking Jews but had since developed a literary life of their own) and for some parts of the liturgy. Arch-linguistic conservatives that they were, the Arabic-speaking Jews of the early middle ages did not elect for one language or another but composed trilingual versions in which the Hebrew, the Aramaic and the Judaeo-Arabic appeared side-by-side on each verse.[34]

But the situation was never quite so clear-cut. Mundane letters were also written in Hebrew,[35] poems were composed in Aramaic,[36] rubrics for the Hebrew prayers were couched in Judaeo-Arabic[37] and Hebrew vowel-points were attached to Judaeo-Arabic texts.[38] Sometimes the same work was composed in both Hebrew and Judaeo-Arabic.[39] The Karaites, in fact,

---

[34] Cambridge University Library, MSS T-S B1.1–25; the articles on Hebrew and Judaeo-Arabic by J. Blau, and on Aramaic by J.C. Greenfield, in *Jewish Languages*, ed. Paper, pp. 1–13, 121–31 and 29–43; and W. Chomsky, *Hebrew: The Eternal Language* (Philadelphia, 1964), pp. 93–183.

[35] Examples may be found in J. Mann, *Texts and Studies in Jewish History and Literature*, I (Cincinatti, 1931), and *idem*, *The Jews in Egypt and in Palestine under the Fatimid Caliphs*, ed. S.D. Goitein (original edn, 2 vols., Oxford, 1920, 1922; repr. New York, 1970), and throughout the publications of S.D. Goitein, listed in the bibliography compiled by R. Attal, *A Bibliography of the Writings of S.D. Goitein* (Jerusalem, 1975 and 1987).

[36] M. Sokoloff and J. Yahalom, 'Aramaic Piyyuṭim from the Byzantine period', *Jewish Quarterly Review* 75 (1985), 309–21.

[37] J. Mann, 'Genizah fragments of the Palestinian order of service', *Hebrew Union College Annual* 2 (1925), 269–338, reprinted in *Contributions to the Scientific Study of the Jewish Liturgy*, ed. J.J. Petuchowski (New York, 1970), pp. 379–448.

[38] J. Blau and S.A. Hopkins, 'A vocalized Judaeo-Arabic letter from the Cairo Genizah', *Jerusalem Studies in Arabic and Islam* 6 (1985), 417–76.

[39] R. Drory has dealt with this topic in a book shortly to be published by Tel-Aviv University entitled *The Emergence of Jewish-Arabic Literary Contacts at the Beginning of the Tenth Century*. She also has a paper entitled 'Words beautifully put – Hebrew v. Judaeo-Arabic in tenth century Jewish literature', scheduled for publication in the proceedings referred to in n. 33 above.

took to writing Hebrew texts in Arabic script with Hebrew vowel-points[40] and also composed a highly Arabicized Hebrew that would appear to have been comprehensible to nobody but themselves.[41] Some generations of Karaites preferred Arabic while others reverted to Hebrew.[42] This variety in the choice of the language written in particular contexts demonstrates that there was more at stake than the simple matter of comprehensibility. The choice may have amounted to a polemical statement, a way of demonstrating one's adherence to a particular tradition or one's departure from it.

One possible reason for the complicated language distribution just described may be sought in the tendency to treat new literature as deserving only of the vernacular while venerating older literature by continuing to use the ancient tongues in which it had long been transmitted. Another may have to do with the level of education available to those making most use of a particular genre. Alternatively, Drory may be justified in postulating the existence of a distinction in the Jewish mind of the period between the literary, aesthetic and solemn significance of Hebrew and the communicative value of Arabic as a widespread vernacular.[43] Whatever the reasons, this trilingual circumstance was a major factor in the blossoming of philological study among the Jews. Familiar as they were with the forms occurring in three Semitic languages, they were able to construct theories about the general form of these languages and how they related to one another and to use the characteristics of one to explain the anomalies of another.

It was not without good reason that the Arabs referred to the Jews as *ahl al-kitāb*, 'the people of the book'. The literary output and the linguistic competence just described pre-supposes an almost obsessive concern with the written word. While, as has been pointed out, that concern had its origins in the biblical period, it had to a large extent been transferred to the area of oral transmission in talmudic and immediately post-talmudic times insofar as the rabbinic traditions were concerned. Only with the passion of the rabbinic authorities to establish their whole ideology and practice as central and definitive did it return to its original form, or even to an extension of that form. Anxious as they also were to refute the accusation made by such theological opponents as the Karaites that their oral traditions

---

[40] G. Khan, 'The Medieval Karaite transcriptions of Hebrew into Arabic script', *Israel Oriental Studies* (forthcoming).

[41] S.A. Hopkins, 'Arabic elements in the Hebrew of the Byzantine Karaites', a paper scheduled for publication in the proceedings referred to in n. 33 above.

[42] Z. Ankori, *Karaites in Byzantium* (New York and Jerusalem, 1959), pp. 189–93, and Khan, 'Karaite transcriptions'.

[43] Drory, *The Emergence of Jewish-Arabic Literary Contacts*, and *idem* 'Words beautifully put'.

were a travesty of the original, sacred scripture, prone to error and alterations, the Rabbanites embraced the written medium once again and utilized it to publicize an ever-expanding variety of works that adopted the latest ideas to defend and promote their own theological position. The more catholic outlook that lay behind the complaint of the ninth-century head of the Sura academy, Natronai ben Hilai, that other disciplines were being neglected in order to concentrate on Talmud was fast becoming the norm by the end of the geonic period.[44]

This regeneration of wider interests, as in the golden age of Spanish Jewry, combined with an enthusiastic adoption of the codex to produce a wealth of new, scholarly texts. The question that remains to be answered is to what extent it may be assumed that the wider availability of such texts was paralleled by a broadly based knowledge of them on the part of what may be referred to as the Jewish masses.

While in respect of most cultures of the early mediaeval period there are few sources that may fairly be described as reflecting the reality of everyday existence, Jewish scholarship has for about a century been in the happy position of having the documentary evidence of the Cairo Genizah to call upon. These 200,000 fragments, almost three-quarters of which are in the possession of Cambridge University Library were, out of pious fear of destroying anything that might be considered sacred, amassed by the Jewish community of the Ben Ezra Synagogue in Cairo in its *genizah* (synagogal depository) from at least as early as the eleventh century and shed light on every aspect of Jewish life in the Mediterranean area from the ninth until the nineteenth centuries. Unscrupulous synagogue officials began to sell items to visitors and dealers about a hundred years ago and some fragments thus made their way to various academic institutions in Europe and America. It was Solomon Schechter, who was lecturer, and later reader, in talmudic literature at the University of Cambridge from 1890 until 1902, who persuaded the Chief Rabbi of Cairo to grant him permission to remove the bulk of the collection to Cambridge in 1897 and it was he who began the systematic and scientific exploitation of its contents. In the first decades of research the interest of scholars was primarily in the fragments' importance for the study of Jewish literary, religious and communal history but more recent work, especially that of Goitein and his students over the last quarter of a century, has concentrated on the unique information they contain about legal, commercial, social, political, scientific, educational and personal matters.[45]

---

[44] Baron, *History of the Jews*, VI, pp. 236, 313 and 441.

[45] *EJ* XVI cols. 1333–42; S.D. Goitein, *A Mediterranean Society*, I (Berkeley and Los Angeles, 1967), pp. 1–28, and *idem, Religion in a Religious Age* (Cambridge, Mass., 1974),

What the evidence from the Cairo Genizah convincingly demonstrates is that written material of a great variety of content existed in the Jewish community in and around Cairo from the tenth to the twelfth centuries. If some 200,000 manuscript fragments, yielding a total of about three times that number of discrete leaves, the majority of them dating from those centuries, have survived the ravages of time and the elements, one may with a fair degree of confidence assume that the original hoard deposited in the synagogue *genizah* was greatly in excess of that number and itself represented only a proportion of what was actually produced in the communities in and around Cairo. Also to be taken into account in assessing the evidence is the fact that Cairo was not renowned for being the most scholarly or literate of the Jewish societies of the period. Indeed, much of this material emanated from circles that were not primarily concerned with scholarship, religion or science. Its particular value lies in the fact that it represents what has been referred to as 'counter-history' rather than the views of the leadership, and as such it provides ample testimony to the whole gamut of education from elementary to advanced and from children's alphabetical exercises to adults' guest lectures. What is more, while explicit dates are not usually given, hundreds of the fragments may pre-date the tenth century, therefore bearing direct witness to the heart of the geonic age, while the customs reflected in the collection as a whole appear to be relevant to a wider geographical area than Cairo and its environs.[46] It will therefore be of value in the present context to summarize the research to date so that some sense of the wider literacy of that age in that area may be obtained and it may be convincingly demonstrated that the dissemination of texts was likely to have a major impact on large sections of the Jewish people.

Since it was degrading for a Jew to be unable to participate fully in those aspects of the synagogal service that involved simple recitation of Hebrew and a mark of some distinction to be knowledgeable enough to undertake the rarer and more difficult readings, the basic aim of elementary education

pp. 3–17, 139–51; S.C. Reif, *A Guide to the Taylor–Schechter Genizah Collection* (1st edn, Cambridge, 1973; 2nd edn, 1979); *idem*, 'Genizah collections at Cambridge University Library' (Hebrew) in *Te'uda*, I, ed. M. Friedman (Tel-Aviv, 1980), pp. 201–6; *idem*, 'The Taylor–Schechter Genizah Research Unit', in *Newsletter* 19 of the World Union of Jewish Studies (August, 1981), 17*–21*; *idem*, '1898 preserved in letter and spirit', *The Cambridge Review* 103, no. 2266 (29 January, 1982), 120–1; *idem* (with G. Khan) 'Genizah material at Cambridge University Library', *EJ Year Book 1983/85* (Jerusalem, 1985), pp. 170–1; and *idem*, *Published Material from the Cambridge Genizah Collections: A Bibliography 1896–1980* (Cambridge, 1988), introduction.

[46] S.D. Goitein, *A Mediterranean Society*, 5 vols. (Berkeley, Los Angeles and London, 1967–88), II, p. 173; Beit-Arié, *Hebrew Codicology*, pp. 9–19; and S.A. Hopkins, 'The oldest dated document in the Geniza?', in *Studies in Judaism and Islam Presented to S.D. Goitein*, ed. S. Morag, I. Ben-Ami and N.A. Stillman (Jerusalem, 1981), pp. 83–98.

was to set him on the road toward these achievements. Most of the male community achieved at least the simplest level of reading and writing Hebrew while the fewer more educated members became familiar with more difficult, biblical and rabbinic texts. Literacy in Hebrew also provided the opportunity to write Judaeo-Arabic, that is, to record their own vernacular in a script more familiar to them than Arabic. Not that Arabic itself was ruled out. Some Jews were taught the required calligraphy and such a competence could qualify them for those administrative, religious, medical and commercial professions for which it was required. If one may include numeracy under the general heading of literacy, references are also found to arithmetic although less frequently than to Hebrew and Arabic. Classes in those subjects took place in the synagogue, communal study-centre or in the teacher's home and were conducted by a professional teacher whose fees were paid either by parents or by the community if the parents lacked the means or the children were orphans. Reinforcement of these lessons, or education in wider religious practice, was the task of the father in the synagogue and of either or both parents in the domestic setting. Being largely phonetic, Hebrew could be taught analytically letter by letter, although there is evidence of a pedagogical innovator who preferred the global method. Scrap paper was used for practice and, copies of books being an expensive item, one text was often used for the whole class and pupils therefore had to acquire the ability to read the text from whatever angle at which they might be seated in relation to the script. Alphabet primers were among the few items of Hebrew literature that attracted illumination and individual wooden boards were in use. Naturally, the learning situation was not always ideal and there are cases of fathers expressing concern about corporal punishment and teachers demonstrating frustration at absence, lateness and unruly behaviour. For example, a scribbled note from a rather cross teacher informs the father of little Abu el-Ḥassan that his son had at first been most conscientious but that one of the class, egged on by the others, had soon put a stop to this by breaking the newcomer's writing board. Similarly, two little boys who came late to school brought a note explaining that the elder had been delayed by studying Arabic at home and the younger, who could not make his own way, had had to wait for his brother. The teacher is politely asked to refrain from spanking either for the tardiness of their arrival. Teachers did enjoy a respected position in the community and parents made efforts to maintain good relations with them, presumably to the advantage of their children's education.[47]

[47] Goitein, *Mediterranean Society*, II, pp. 173–83, 185–90; *idem*, 'Side lights on Jewish education from the Cairo Geniza', *Gratz College Anniversary Volume*, ed. I.D. Passow and S.T. Lachs (Philadelphia, 1971), pp. 83–110.

Girls did not automatically receive such an education but occasionally there were parents who made such arrangements for them, usually for biblical studies, and some succeeded so well that they became professional teachers themselves, while others developed skills as calligraphers. In one sad little manuscript a father bewails the loss of just such a daughter, mournfully remembering her intellect, her knowledge of the *Torah* and her piety, and poignantly recalling the lessons he used to give her. The fact that there are a number of letters in which wives are directly addressed by their husbands, as against others in which a male colleague is requested to pass on written information by word of mouth to the writer's spouse, appears to demonstrate that women were not universally illiterate. One such letter, written by Isaac ben Barukh from a small town in the Egyptian countryside to his wife in Cairo, and probably dating from the eleventh century, is typical of so many Genizah letters in the insights it provides and therefore deserves to be quoted extensively (in my own translation):

My greetings abound: may God's help soon be found, by the Jews all around. To my worthy and modest wife. I am aware of your admirable behaviour and there is no need for me to dwell on this here. In contrast to your own happy position, I am thoroughly miserable and miss you all, particularly the eyes of my beloved young son whom I adore and cherish. In tears and anguish, I look for consolation at every corner, day and night, but I expect none, other than from God. I know that there is no need for me to lay down the law but do please think of your religious duties and conduct yourself in a way that brings you honour. Take every care of our dear, beloved child and spare no effort on his behalf. This will be a sure sign of your love. Do not worry at all about me. If only I could catch a swift cloud I would return in record time. But with God's help I shall finish my business and come home quickly with a pocket that is less than full but with a happy heart.

Since there are also letters and documents from female hands it is clear that some women were acquainted not only with reading but also with writing, but it should be acknowledged that even these occurrences are in the legal, communal and personal spheres rather than in the literary. One mother was so anxious that her daughter should receive a sound education that she made a death-bed request in a letter written in her own hand to her sister, requesting that the latter should take on the responsibility for ensuring this, although she was aware that this would strain the family resources. At once moving and instructive, the text is worthy of citation, at least in part (in Goitein's translation):

This is to inform you, my lady, dear sister – may God accept me as a ransom for you – that I have become seriously ill with little hope of recovery, and I have dreams indicating that my end is near. My lady, my most urgent request of you, if God, the exalted, indeed decrees my death, is that you take care of my little daughter and make efforts to give her an education, although I know well that I am asking you for something unreasonable, as there is not enough money – by my father – for support,

let alone for formal instruction. However, she has a model in our saintly mother . . .
my lady, only God knows how I wrote these lines![48]

Those boys who advanced to higher scholarly levels developed a more
educated hand and the range of styles recorded among the Genizah texts
begins at the primitive and advances to the most expert. Some young men
spent many years at talmudic centres of learning both at home and abroad,
maintained by communal and individual subscriptions, and adults who
were engaged in making a living nevertheless devoted time, sometimes
daily, to studying the traditional sources, biblical and rabbinic, with
friends, or attending courses given by local scholars or lectures delivered by
specially invited authorities. The learning process often took place at night,
or during the night, and Maimonides makes a point of stressing how
important it is to use the dark hours profitably in this way. Communities
ensured that there was accommodation available for such devoted study,
usually on the synagogal premises. Book-lists are a common feature of the
Genizah discoveries and demonstrate the existence of reference literature
for such educational activities. Bibles, prayer books, talmudic texts and
commentaries, Jewish legal and theological tracts, as well as scientific and
philosophical works, are among the items that are regularly listed. Cairo
was better known among the communities of the Jewish world for its
economic activity than for its academic prowess and yet even there such
evidence of literacy abounds. Scholarly notes, invitations to lectures, details
of refresher courses – all point to an intense degree of educational activity
while the remainder of the evidence confirms that it was not an elitist or an
exclusivist preoccupation.[49]

By the eleventh century, then, literacy for the Jews of the communities
living under Islam constituted a fairly complex and sophisticated level of
education for a broad section of the community in a variety of Jewish and
non-Jewish subjects. By this time, too, their Jewish brethren in Christian
Europe were following their lead and had established a sound base for a later
flowering of Hebrew and Jewish letters in that centre that was to have
important cultural consequences for the modern western world. The
paradox is that while these centres to the north flourished, so their
counterparts to the south began to decline and a process got underway that
was to stand the geography of Jewish educational achievement on its head.

[48] Jewish Theological Seminary of America, New York, MSS ENA 2935.17 and Misc. 6*;
Cambridge University Library, MS T-S 13J20.9; Goitein, *Mediterranean Society*, II, pp.
183–5, III, pp. 220–1, 235; and Mann, *Jews in Egypt*, II, pp. 307–8.

[49] Goitein, *Mediterranean Society*, II, pp. 191–211; Maimonides, *Mishneh Torah, Talmud
Torah* 3.13, ed. M. Hyamson, *The Book of Knowledge* (Jerusalem, 1965), 60a; J. Mann,
'Listes de livres provenant de la Gueniza', *Revue des Etudes Juives* 72 (1921), 163–83, and
idem, Texts and Studies, pp. 643–84.

To refer to that process is, however, to anticipate and to move beyond the parameters of the subject here defined.[50]

[50] My friend, Professor Raphael Loewe, has kindly let me see an English version of a paper on Jewish attitudes to Hebrew ('Jews, language and Judaism: master and servant') that appeared in Hebrew in *'Am va-Sefer* NS, no. 4 (1987), 10–52, edited by Chaim Rabin in Jerusalem, and is relevant to various issues raised in this essay. I am indebted to the editor of this volume, to my fellow contributors, to my colleagues Dr G. Khan and Dr R. Brody, and to my dear friend Professor E. Fleischer of the Hebrew University of Jerusalem, for their helpful suggestions, and to my wife, Shulie, as always, for assistance with the final arrangement of the material.

7

Writing in early mediaeval Byzantium

Margaret Mullett

On 18 (or 12) July 836 the brothers Theodore and Theophanes, forever afterwards to be described as the Graptoi (the inscribed), were interrogated by the Iconoclast emperor Theophilos.

But when the saints remained silent, returned no answer, and bent their heads towards the ground, the Emperor said to his Prefect, 'Take away these impious men and tattoo their foreheads, inscribing these iambics, and hand them over to two of the sons of Hagar, that they may conduct them to their own country.' Near the Emperor there stood a man named Christodoulou who had composed the iambics and who had them at hand. The Emperor commanded him to read them aloud in the hearing of all and he added, 'Even if they are badly composed, never mind.' He said this, knowing how excellently they themselves practised accuracy in poetical composition, and how much they would be ridiculed by the champions of Christ. One of those present, wishing to please the Emperor, said, 'But they are not worthy, O Lord, of better iambics.'[1]

This passage epitomizes a view of Byzantine literacy widely current among both Byzantinists and western mediaevalists, of the supreme power of the written word, and of the ability of the Byzantines to appreciate it. Here, at least, the classical tradition was not dead, where simple monks could be shamed by the quality of versification of their tormentors, composed by a layman-about-court. Whatever the vicissitudes of literacy in the states which succeeded the Roman Empire in the west, Byzantium offers a clear foil of continuity in literary production and education, and of widespread lay, even female, literacy.[2]

This view has a certain amount to recommend it. There were women *litterati* at most periods of Byzantine history,[3] though there may well have

---

[1] *Life* of Michael the Synkellos, ed. and trans. M.B. Cunningham, BBTT 1 (Belfast, 1990), p. 84. For the date, see commentary, n. 162.

[2] R. Browning, 'Literacy in the Byzantine world', *BMGS* 4 (1978), 39–54, voices traditional assumptions; for a more sceptical view, see E. Patlagean, 'Discours écrit, discours parlé; niveaux de culture à Byzance au VIIIe-XIe siècle', *Annales ESC* 34 (1979), 264–78.

[3] To take the most famous examples: the empress Athenais-Eudokia under Theodosios II; the nun Kasia under Theophilos; Anna Komnene under John II and Manuel I Komnenos;

been fewer than in societies whose literacy practices are frequently compared with Byzantium.[4] And lay literacy, the concern of so many of the papers in this present volume, was never a problem in Byzantium, although clerical literacy (or lack of it) was.[5] (There was a strong strain in the monastic tradition which regarded books – even liturgical books – as luxury objects rather than repositories of the Word, and which scorned book-learning as not even the 'outer wisdom' of more mainline thought.)[6] Nor is there any problem about aristocratic literacy. Emperors composed literary works, hymns, orations, histories, and though they may not actually have set pen to paper there is no reason to believe that this is because they were unable to.[7] Their aristocracy, as in so many other matters, followed suit.[8] As for the rest of the population, it has been suggested that at least more were literate than in the west. The evidence of a declining number of inscriptions is set against the increase in use of personal lead seals at roughly the same time, and prolific signatures on documents of land tenure point the same way.[9]

But this view has for some time been under attack. A group of papers given at a Dumbarton Oaks symposium in 1971 agree in questioning the assumptions of the traditional viewpoint.[10] The elitist nature of book-ownership was pointed out, with elaborate compilations balancing the cost

Eirene-Eulogia Choumnaina Palaiologina under Andronikos III. See the remarks of J. Herrin, 'In search of Byzantine women: three avenues of approach', in *Women in Antiquity*, ed. A. Cameron and A. Kuhrt (London, 1983), pp. 167–93; on female patronage in the twelfth century see various studies by E. Jeffreys including 'The Sebastokratorissa Eirene as literary patroness: the monk Iakovos', *JÖB* 32/3 (1982), 63–71; for a cautionary view and a discussion of one woman's reading, see M.E. Mullett, 'The "disgrace" of the ex-Basilissa Maria', *BS* 45 (1984), 202–11.

[4] Classical Chinese is suggested by W.J. Ong, *Orality and Literacy: The Technologizing of the Word* (London and New York, 1982), p. 114. In fact female literacy seems less striking in Byzantium than in the mediaeval west, see A. Weyl Carr, *Byzantine Illumination 1150–1250: The Study of a Provincial Tradition* (Chicago, 1987), p. 205, on women's *ex libris*; P. Wormald, 'The uses of literacy in Anglo-Saxon England and its neighbours', *TRHS* 5th series 27 (1977), 95–114, at 98, on male and female literacy.

[5] Note the need for Alexios Komnenos' edict on the reform of the clergy, ed. P. Gautier, 'L'Edit d'Alexis Ier sur la réforme du clergé', *REB* 31 (1973), 165–201.

[6] See, for example, *The Sayings of the Desert Fathers*, Bessarion, 12, trans. B. Ward, SLG (London, 1975), p. 42.

[7] Leo VI, Constantine Porphyrogennetos, Manuel II are perhaps the most distinguished, Justin I and Basil I the least; for a discussion of Justinian's level of literacy, see A.M. Honoré, 'Some Constitutions composed by Justinian', *JRS* 65 (1975), 107–23, especially 122.

[8] See *The Byzantine Aristocracy IX–XIII Centuries*, ed. M.J. Angold, BAR, International Series 221 (Oxford, 1983), p. 8, and in many other papers in the volume.

[9] On all these indicators, see Browning, 'Literacy in the Byzantine world'.

[10] *Byzantine Books and Bookmen: A Dumbarton Oaks Colloquium* (Washington DC, 1975).

of books against what we know of civil service salaries. The cost of parchment alone, it was suggested, was enough to make literacy prohibitive to the average Byzantine.[11] Manuscript studies emphasize the scarcity of manuscripts and their apparent lack of use; studies of literary works[12] emphasize the elite nature of even so-called 'popular' literature[13] and in the wake of this symposium linguists suggest that even though Byzantium had no learned language accessible only to a literate class, the difference between rhetorical Greek and the vernacular may have been almost as wide as between Latin and the vernaculars in the west.[14] A figure of 200 at any one time receiving a rhetorical education has received enormous currency and has been widely quoted.[15] Work on levels of style, much heralded at the beginning as helping to define the audience of Byzantine literature, came up against difficulties which suggested that Byzantine *litterati* may not have directed their writings to a specific level of audience, but may have written in the highest style open to them while they aimed at reading in the lowest style available.[16] The Byzantine reading public vanished overnight.

There are various ways of casting doubt on the validity of this attack. For one thing book-ownership in mediaeval societies is a poor indicator of literacy;[17] for another, papyrus (cheaper than parchment) may have continued to be used even in tenth-century Anatolia;[18] work on levels of style is at present crude in the extreme;[19] analyses of Byzantine literary society are of little use in determining if there was widespread functional literacy in the

---

[11] N.G. Wilson, 'Books and readers in Byzantium', in *ibid.*, pp. 1–16.

[12] J. Irigoin, 'Centres de copie et bibliothèques', in *ibid.*, pp. 17–28; C. Mango, 'The availability of books in the Byzantine Empire, AD 750–850', in *ibid.*, pp. 29–45.

[13] H.G. Beck, 'Der Leserkreis der byzantinischen "Volksliteratur" im Licht der handschriftlichen Überlieferung', in *ibid.*, pp. 47–67.

[14] M.J. and E.M. Jeffreys, 'The literary emergence of vernacular Greek', *Mosaic* 8/4 (1975), 171–93.

[15] P. Lemerle, *Le Premier Humanisme byzantin* (Paris, 1971), pp. 155–7.

[16] H. Hunger, 'Stilstufen in der byzantinischen Geschichtsschreibung des 12 Jahrhunderts: Anna Komnene und Michael Glykas', *Byzantine Studies – Etudes Byzantines* 5 (1978), 139–70; I. Ševčenko, 'Levels of style in Byzantine literature', *XVI International Byzantine Congress* (Vienna, 1981), pp. 289–312.

[17] On book-sharing in the mediaeval west see M. Parkes, 'The literacy of the laity', in *Literature and Western Civilization: The Medieval World*, ed. D. Daiches and A.K. Thorlby (London, 1973), pp. 555–77, at pp. 556–7 and 571–2; M. Clanchy, *From Memory to Written Record: England 1066–1307* (London, 1979), p. 198; B. Stock, *The Implications of Literacy: Written Language and Models of Interpretation in the Eleventh and Twelfth Centuries* (Princeton, 1983), *passim* and p. 522.

[18] See Arethas, ep. 40, ed. L.G. Westerink, *Arethae Scripta Minora*, I (Leipzig, 1968), p. 297.

[19] For example the dictionary approach in Ševčenko, 'Levels of style', p. 291.

sense of 'acquiring the essential knowledge and skill to engage in all these activities in which literacy is required for effective functioning in the group and community'.[20] Indeed, the further the literary language is deemed to be from everyday speech the more likely it is that functional literacy operated on a different linguistic (and certainly stylistic) register.[21]

Another line of attack influential in recent years has been to emphasize orality in Byzantine society. Early attempts to apply the theories of Parry and Lord to some Byzantine literature were unsuccessful,[22] but more nuanced viewpoints have been far more persuasive. Work on the role of the vernacular and its emergence in the twelfth century as a literary option has made scholars more conscious of the differences between spoken and written speech;[23] distinctions between oral composition, transmission and performance[24] have opened up a considerable interest in the performance aspect of Byzantine literature. The place of rhetoric in Byzantine literature has ceased to be an example of a classical straitjacket[25] and become an indicator of orality: the prevalence of funeral orations, speeches to the emperor, rhetorical descriptions (*ekphraseis*), occasional speeches of all kinds and sermons have taken on new significance recently.[26]

It has become normal to ask questions unthinkable fifteen years ago, and about very different texts. Evidence for performance is sought for works like the satire *Timarion* and Theodore Prodromos' *Life* of Meletios; ceremonial settings are sought for Paul the Silentiary's *Ekphrasis* of Agia Sophia and some of Romanos' hymns.[27] The most uncompromisingly

---

[20] This is a definition made in a statement by UNESCO in 1962, see B.V. Street, *Literacy in Theory and Practice*, Cambridge Studies in Oral and Literate Culture 9 (Cambridge, 1984), p. 183.

[21] See R. Browning, 'The language of Byzantine literature', *Byzantina kai Metabyzantina*, I: *The Past in Medieval and Modern Greek Culture*, ed. S. Vryonis Jr (Malibu, 1978), pp. 103–33.

[22] M.J. and E.M. Jeffreys, 'Formulas in the Chronicle of the Morea', *DOP* 23 (1973), 163–95.

[23] R. Beaton, ' "De vulgari eloquentia" in twelfth-century Byzantium', ed. J. Howard-Johnston, *Byzantium and the West c. 850–c. 1200* (Amsterdam, 1988), pp. 261–8.

[24] See the discussion in R. Beaton, *Folk Poetry of Modern Greece* (Cambridge, 1980), pp. 179–92.

[25] R.J.H. Jenkins, 'The Hellenistic origins of Byzantine literature', *DOP* 17 (1963), 37–52, at 52: 'the paralysing grip of Hellenistic rhetoric, a strait-jacket which held its prisoner in a state of mental retardation'.

[26] For example in the exaugural lecture of M. Alexiou, Birmingham, 1985.

[27] S. Whiston, 'A reading of the Hades episode in the Timarion', MA dissertation, University of Birmingham, 1987, pp. 13–14; P. Armstrong, 'The lives of St Meletios by Theodore Prodromos and Nikolaos of Methone, introduction, translation and commentary', MA dissertation, University of Belfast, 1988, section III; M. Whitby, 'The occasion of Paul the Silentiary's Ekphrasis of S. Sophia', *CQ* 35 (1985), 215–28; R. Macrides and P. Magdalino,

literary works, it is now accepted, were written for performance in the *theatra* of Constantinople.[28] This viewpoint has been greatly facilitated by the work of social anthropologists and psychologists (as well as oral historians and the students of folk poetry); using this theoretical perspective it begins to look as if Byzantinists should identify as exceptional those texts which were *not* written for performance.[29] There are problems, though, on leaning too heavily on this body of theory. For one thing it in its turn leans heavily on theories of orality discredited among specialist scholars in specialist fields;[30] for another the attempt to privilege the oral only emphasizes the 'Great Divide' which characterized literacy studies in anthropology until recently.[31] It may still in some quarters be necessary to emphasize the orality of Byzantine society and literature, but much the most interesting work in literacy studies is at present being done in the area of mixed modes in residually oral societies,[32] and it is surely possible to view Byzantium in this light.

A third line of attack on the monolithic view of high Byzantine literacy is to open the diachronic perspective and point out that the Byzantine experience was not static. The early eighth century is a favourite point at which to evoke Byzantium in contrast to the west: unfortunately for those who do so we now have dated to precisely this period the curious text called the *Parastaseis Syntomoi Chronikai* which reveals that a group of people in Constantinopole, purporting to be scholars, had no access even to Procopius, an important text of only two centuries previously.[33] This is one

---

'The architecture of Ekphrasis: construction and context of Paul the Silentiary's Ekphrasis of Hagia Sophia', *BMGS* 12 (1988), 47–82; M.E. Mullett, 'Romanos's Kontakia on the XL martyrs; date and setting', *The XL Martyrs of Sebasteia*, BBTT 2 (Belfast, forthcoming).

[28] H. Hunger, *Reich der Neuen Mitte* (Graz, Vienna and Cologne, 1965), p. 341; M.E. Mullett, 'Aristocracy and patronage in the literary circles of Comnenian Constantinople', in *The Byzantine Aristocracy*, ed. Angold, pp. 173–201.

[29] Ong, *Orality and Literacy*, pp. 157–9; for guidance in the theoretical literature, see H.G. Graff, *Literacy in History: An Interdisciplinary Research Bibliography* (London and New York, 1981).

[30] Recent work on Homer, for example, has tended to view the work by Milman Parry and Albert Lord on oral composition as useful but not all-explanatory, see G. Kirk, *The Iliad, a Commentary* (Cambridge, 1985), p. 12; B.C. Fenik, *Homer, Tradition and Invention* (Leiden, 1978), p. 90; J. Griffin, *Homer on Life and Death* (Oxford, 1980), pp. xiii–xiv. The theoretical literature, on the other hand, depends heavily on the Parry–Lord approach.

[31] F. Finnegan, 'Literacy versus non-literacy: the great divide', *Modes of Thought: Essays on Thinking in Western and Non-Western Societies*, ed. R. Finnegan and R. Horton (London, 1973), pp. 112–44 offers analysis of the problem and an early attempt to avoid the trap.

[32] J. Goody, *The Interface between the Written and the Oral* (Cambridge, 1987); Street, *Literacy*, especially pp. 95–7.

[33] *Parastaseis Syntomoi Chronikai*, trans. A. Cameron and J. Herrin in conjunction with A. Cameron, R. Cormack and C. Rouché, *Constantinople in the Early Eighth Century* (Leiden, 1984), p. 46. On the reading of the author of the *Parastaseis*, see pp. 38–45.

reason why Byzantinists, unlike historians of the west, cling to the term 'Dark Ages' to describe the period from the 630s to the 790s, when literary activity appears to have been at a minimum and when profound changes transformed the eastern Empire. City culture came to an end; not only the old aristocracy but also the classical name system died out; education changed radically in purpose and after that became harder to get. These among other factors suggest that not just the high culture of the capital may have suffered but that province-wide disruption of practical literacy may have occurred.[34]

Clearly there is room for much discussion about the depth of darkness of the Dark Ages and the nature of the recovery from it: what was, for example, the implication of the change from uncial to minuscule – an attempt to recirculate lost works or a sizeable rise in demand which needed supply?[35] But it is clear that, if there is no question in Byzantium of a 'revival of literacy' in the eleventh and twelfth centuries,[36] there is a real sense in which literacy cannot be taken for granted over the whole span of its existence.

And, given the likelihood of the seventh and eighth centuries as a watershed or period of reduced literacy, an understanding of the ninth and tenth centuries becomes crucial. Byzantium in the ninth and tenth centuries, the 'Imperial Centuries', has been seen as being at its height.[37] A military recovery followed the scholarly recovery[38] and the Empire held a special place, maintaining diplomatic links with the west, the Arab world and the Steppes. It has been seen as a time of increasing wealth, confidence and security and conspicuous artistic activity.[39] It was a time when the

---

[34] C. Renfrew, 'Systems collapse as social transformation: catastrophe and anastrophe in early state societies', in *Transformations: Mathematical Approches to Culture Change*, ed. C. Renfrew and K.L. Cooke (New York and London, 1979), pp. 481–508, offers an alternative viewpoint; J.F. Haldon, 'Some remarks on the background to the iconoclast controversy', *BS* 38 (1977), 161–84, and *idem*, 'Some considerations on Byzantine society and economy in the seventh century', *Byzantinische Forschungen* 10 (1985), 75–112, offers the best survey of the Byzantine evidence.

[35] Mango, 'Availability of books', p. 45.

[36] There was, though, a revival of rhetoric in the eleventh century which leaned on rhetorical commentaries of the tenth century and facilitated the boldly original literary experiments of the twelfth century. See G.L. Kustas, *Studies in Byzantine Rhetoric*, Analecta Blatadon 17 (Thessalonika, 1973), pp. 21–6.

[37] R. Jenkins, *Byzantium: The Imperial Centuries* (London, 1966), or *idem*, 'The age of conquest', in P. Whitting, *Byzantium: An Introduction* (2nd edn, London, 1981), pp. 61–82.

[38] W. Treadgold, 'The revival of Byzantine learning and the revival of the Byzantine state', *AHR* 84 (1979), 1245–66.

[39] R. Cormack, 'Patronage and new programs of Byzantine iconography', *XVII International Byzantine Congress* (Washington DC, 1986), pp. 609–38, at p. 609.

Empire functioned most efficiently, an Empire which has been described as 'an achetypical bureaucratic state'.[40] Certainly it needed literacy: to facilitate communications between the capital and its decentralized local government (theme) system, and between the capital and the field offices of its centralized tax machine; to carry out the mass of diplomatic activity; and to record the intricacies of a society obsessed with order (τάξις).[41] Is it possible to determine these and other uses of literacy from the sources which have survived? Only to a limited extent, for the quantity of documentary (as against literary) sources which has survived is disappointingly small, and very selective. A tenth-century treatise on tax-collection may be put together with an eleventh-century cadaster and a group of charters which run throughout the period, but the paucity is remarkable for a bureaucratic state. The runnings of the central administration must be deduced from four seating plans for imperial banquets; we have law-codes from the period, but no case-law until the eleventh century with the *Peira* ('Rulings'). As for literary sources, histories rewrite previous reigns and maintain imperial authority; rhetoric eases the great occasions of everyday life; and records of imperial ceremonial lay down the greater occasions of less everyday life.[42]

Certainly there is enough evidence to argue that literate modes were normal in Byzantium.[43] If inscribed tombstones are not common for the period, personal lead seals are;[44] charters are preserved with rich arrays of peasant signatures;[45] wills are beginning to surface;[46] monasteries have

---

[40] A. Epstein, 'Art and hegemony in Byzantium, 9th to 12th century', *XXVI International Congress of the History of Art* (Washington DC, 1986), abstracts, p. 9.

[41] On Byzantine administration in the period, see J.B. Bury, *Imperial Administration in the Ninth Century* (London, 1911); N. Oikonomides, *Les Listes de Préséance byzantine des IXe et Xe siècles* (Paris, 1972); H. Ahrweiler, 'Recherches sur l'administration de l'empire byzantin au IXe -XIe siècles', *BCH* 184 (1960), 1–111.

[42] On the lack of surviving documentary evidence, see R. Morris, 'Dispute settlement in the Byzantine provinces in the tenth century', in *Settlement of Disputes*, pp. 125–7. Note, though, the neat detachment of widespread literacy from documentation in Kievan Russia in S. Franklin, 'Literacy and documentation in mediaeval Russia', *Speculum* 60 (1985), 1–38.

[43] At least in the terms of Clanchy, *From Memory to Written Record*, pp. 2–4.

[44] J.S. Allen and I. Ševčenko, *The Dumbarton Oaks Bibliographies Based on Byzantinische Zeitschrift*, 2nd series, I: *Epigraphy* (Dumbarton Oaks, 1985), offers the best survey at present of the epigraphic evidence; N. Oikonomides, *Byzantine Lead Seals* (Dumbarton Oaks, 1985), points to the seventh century (*boulloteria* in general use, p. 3) and the eighth century (use of seals increased, p. 21) as crucial periods.

[45] *Actes d'Iviron*, ed. J. Lefort, N. Oikonomides and D. Papachryssanthou, I (Paris, 1985), pp. 117–29.

[46] The will of Eustathios Boilas, ed. P. Lemerle, *Cinq études sur le XIe siècle byzantin* (Paris, 1977), pp. 15–63, is not only the most famous but also an early example.

foundation charters;[47] letter-bearers on major routes must have been a familiar sight. Even more familiar, and far less welcome, must have been the activities and presence of the officers of the fisc, equipped with their instructions, their cadaster, or notes therefor; one such officer is simply called the ἀναγραφεύς, the writer-up. Captions and books abound in wall-paintings; litugical books were necessary even if small villages could not boast the riches of early Byzantine Syria.[48] It would not have been easy for any Byzantine peasant to be unaware of the possibilities of writing.

Given the state of surviving evidence, however, it would be difficult to go further than this. Our sample of bureaucratic documents is insufficient to draw the kinds of conclusions open to Clanchy; still less can we discriminate between different kinds of literacies, ritual and functional,[49] or detect the personal literacy skills of an individual.[50] It seems unlikely that villages would escape evidence either of ritual or of functional literacy in terms of the church and the fisc, or that there was not a wide range of competence from the professional scholar or scribe downwards.[51] But it is hard to imagine our evidence yielding much more – except perhaps in the area of the Athos acts.[52]

[47] See K.A. Manaphes, *Monasteriaka Typika-Diathekai* (Athens, 1970), and the forthcoming Dumbarton Oaks Typikon Project. There are ninth- and tenth-century examples, but they increase noticeably after the mid-eleventh century.

[48] M. Mundell, 'Patrons and scribes indicated in Syriac manuscripts 411–800 AD', *JÖB* 32 (1982), 3–12.

[49] See J. Goody, 'Restricted literacy in Northern Ghana', in *Literacy in Traditional Societies*, ed. J. Goody (Cambridge, 1968), pp. 199–264; *idem, The Interface*, pp. 137–9, on 'restricted literacy'; Street, *Literacy*, pp. 130–1 and section 2 *passim* on distinctions in Persia between 'maktab', 'commercial' and 'debestan' literacies; Clanchy, *From Memory to Written Record*, pp. 258–60, for 'practical literacy'.

[50] J. Goody with M. Cole and S. Scribner, 'Writing and formal operation: a case study among the Vai', in Goody, *The Interface*, pp. 191–208, is an analysis of one man's writing. *An Approach to Functional Literacy* (Adult Literacy Resource Agency, 1981), pp. 24–8, gives a series of literacy skills ('find the main ideas in the text'; 'recording and communicating for others', etc.) which could be modified for use in mediaeval societies.

[51] On professionalism among Byzantine writers see P. Magdalino, 'Byzantine snobbery', *The Byzantine Aristocracy*, ed. Angold, pp. 58–78, at pp. 67–8, and A.P. Kazhdan and A.W. Epstein, *Change in Byzantine Culture in the Eleventh and Twelfth Centuries*, The Transformation of the Classical Heritage 7 (Berkeley and Los Angeles, 1985), p. 131 (exaggerated views), and on the working conditions of Byzantine scribes, see Wilson, 'Books and readers', pp. 9–11, and of illuminators, for example, R. Nelson, 'Theoktistos and associates in twelfth-century Constantinople: an illustrated New Testament of AD 1133', *J. Paul Getty Museum Journal* 15 (1987), 53–76. On the role of the scribe in organizing specific commissions, see Carr, *Byzantine Illumination 1150–1250*, p. 144; on *taboullarioi*, see Morris, 'Dispute settlement', pp. 140–1.

[52] See now N. Oikonomides, 'Mount Athos: levels of literacy', DOP 42 (1988), 167–78.

What may perhaps be managed is to look further at the special characteristics of the period and see what may be perceived in the area of literate
mentalities. The first is summed up in the term 'Macedonian Renaissance'[53]
or in the equally ambitious 'First Byzantine Humanism'.[54] Was the recovery
after the Dark Ages of such magnitude as to justify such terms? The
implications of classical learning in both terms may perhaps be disposed of
first; although classical texts were again available, read by Photios and
bought by Arethas and taught in the nebulous schools reestablished after
the mid-ninth century, it is not in this area that the tenth century excelled,
and in any case it is a crude and misleading indicator, only too familiar to
students of the mediaeval west.[55]

Even when we abandon classical yardsticks the literary achievement of
the tenth century does not impress: epistolography, which we shall examine
below in greater detail, is perhaps its acme. Historiography was centrally
orchestrated, hagiography less than innovative, rhetorical genres practised
in moderation. Occasional poems have been preserved. Nor does the
achievement in scholarship outstrip the period's creativity.[56] Wilson, for all
his enthusiasm for Photios' reading opportunities, makes it clear that none
of the activities of the learned men of the day approximates to our idea of
scholarship[57] any more than those of the 'scholars' of the *Parastaseis* who
looked at ancient statues and discussed their possession by evil spirits. And

[53] The 'Macedonian Renaissance' was invented by K. Weitzmann, see, for example, 'The
character and intellectual origins of the Macedonian Renaissance', in K. Weitzmann,
Studies in Classical and Byzantine Manuscript Illumination, ed. H.L. Kessler (Chicago
and London, 1970), pp. 176–223, queried by C. Mango, 'The date of Cod.Vat.Regin.gr. 1
and the "Macedonian Renaissance"', in *Acta ad Archaeologiam et historiam artium
pertinentia*, Institutum Romanum Norvegiae 4 (Rome, 1969), pp. 121–6, and relegated to a
postscript in Cormack, 'Patronage'. W. Treadgold, 'The Macedonian Renaissance', in
*Renaissances before the Renaissance: Cultural Revivals of Late Antiquity and the Middle
Ages*, ed. W. Treadgold (Stanford, 1984), pp. 75–98, is incisive on the question of
definitions, clear on the (lack of) original achievement of the period and positive in
defending Byzantine literary society against twentieth-century critics.

[54] Lemerle, *Premier humanisme*.

[55] M.E. Mullett and R. Scott, *Byzantium and the Classical Tradition* (Birmingham, 1981),
seek to free the study of Byzantine civilization from the inappropriate imposition of classical
norms.

[56] On the literary achievement of the period, see A.P. Kazhdan (with G. Constable),
Byzantine People and Power: An Introduction to Modern Byzantine Studies (Washington
DC, 1982), pp. 113, 135; realistically, Treadgold, 'Macedonian Renaissance', p. 94: 'it
seems as if literary research was in fashion and original composition was not'; 'the
Macedonian renaissance was much more a revival of knowledge than a revival of literature'.

[57] N.G. Wilson, *Scholars of Byzantium* (London, 1983), for example, p. 135 on Arethas and
ch. 7, pp. 136–47, though Photios is signalled as 'the most important figure in the history of
classical studies in Byzantium', because 'he must be presumed to have read more ancient
literature than anyone has been able to since his day' (p. 89).

for once these off-the-cuff value judgements may not be impossibly unfair to their subjects.

Where the period clearly did excel was in organization. It is the period par excellence of encyclopaedism.[58] Every possible class of material was collected, copied, sorted, preserved. Earlier emperors had codified law to make it more manageable and accessible;[59] emperors, churchmen and scholars in the ninth and tenth centuries processed their reading,[60] saints' lives,[61] literary terms and works,[62] recipes and agricultural lore,[63] liturgical information,[64] ceremonies,[65] diplomatic and ethnographic information,[66] tactics,[67] propaganda.[68] Rather than a renaissance or a flowering of humanism, it looks, as it was, like a society which had come close to losing its collective literacy and was building a bulwark against its ever happening again.[69]

So if we are trying to characterize the levels and uses of literacy in tenth-century Byzantium, it is hard to make a great case for achievement at the top of the ladder. There was a group of rhetorically educated people who were capable of writing in the highest-style Attic Greek and who among themselves amused each other with works of wordy brilliance. But they chose to put their abilities to a purpose unusual in the Empire, impressive in scale, but hardly of a sophistication worthy of the term 'Renaissance'. Of the composition of that group much has been written,[70] but I think that it is

---

[58] Lemerle, *Premier humanisme*, pp. 267–300.

[59] See N. Svoronos, *Recherches sur la tradition juridique à Byzance: la Synopsis major des Basiliques et ses Appendices*, Bibliothèque byzantine, Etudes 4 (Paris, 1964); Morris, 'Dispute settlement', pp. 126–9.

[60] For example, Photios, *Bibliotheca*, ed. R. Henry, 8 vols. (Paris, 1959–77).

[61] For example, Symeon Metaphrastes, *PG*, 114–16.

[62] *Suidae Lexicon*, ed. A. Adler, 4 vols. (Leipzig, 1928–38).

[63] Geoponica, *Geoponica sive Cassiani Bassi scholastici de re rustica eclogae*, ed. H. Beckh (Leipzig, 1895).

[64] For example, the *Typikon of the Great Church*, ed. J. Mateos, *OCA* 165–6 (Rome, 1962–3).

[65] *De cerimoniis*, ed. I.I. Reiske, CSHB, 2 vols. (Bonn, 1829–30).

[66] *De administrando imperio*, ed. G. Moravcsik and R.J.H. Jenkins, DOT 1=CFHB 1 (Washington DC, 1967).

[67] *Poliorcétique, Enée le Tacticien*, ed. A. Dain and A.M. Bon (Paris, 1967).

[68] Genesios, *Basileiai*, ed. K. Lachmann, CSHB (Bonn, 1834); Theophanes Continuatus, *Chronographia*, ed. I. Bekker, CSHB (Bonn, 1838).

[69] Compare the remarks of H. Hunger, 'The past in literature', *XVII International Byzantine Congress*, p. 519. On lists as 'elementary forms' of literacy, see Goody, *The Interface*, pp. 211–12.

[70] On the social composition of the literary elite in the period, see H.G. Beck, *Das literarische*

worth noting that in particular nothing excluded in Byzantium the military man from participation in literary and scholarly life.[71] And to characterize the lowest levels of literacy is if anything harder. To show the place of writing in everyday disputes in two different provinces of the Empire is possible, but it is not possible to be clear about the individual levels of literacy of the disputants. On issues like the provision (or lack of it) of education on a wide scale in the provinces,[72] and the existence (or not) of mass functional literacy, the greatest caution is advisable.

But there is one other characteristic of the period which suggests a particular approach to the problem of literacy. This is that Byzantium was not only emerging from the Dark Ages at this time; it was also emerging from 150 years of Iconoclasm. The contribution of Iconoclasm to the revival of learning has been much discussed, and it has been shown that the impetus to produce texts as backing for arguments led to the early rush to copy texts at the end of the eighth century.[73] But by the mid-ninth century the place of art in society and the relationship of art to words had been exhaustively discussed, and in any study of the ninth and tenth centuries it is difficult to ignore the place of the visual.[74] Religious art had been validated finally by texts and textual argument, and much literature of the ninth and tenth centuries is concerned with art, with inauguration sermons,[75] with epigrams designed to complement, adorn or mark a building or work of art;[76] with *ekphraseis*.[77]

Schaffen der Byzantiner (Vienna, 1976), pp. 11–15; Kazhdan, *People and Power*, pp. 101–3; compare the remarks of Mullett, 'Literary circles', pp. 18–20.

[71] For example, Nikephoros Ouranos and many correspondents of letter-writers, compare Kekaumenos, n. 54, ed. B. Wassilewsky (Vasily Grigor'evich Valisevsky) and V. Jernstedt, *Cecaumeni Strategicon et incerti scriptoris De officiis regiis libellus [Consilia et narrationes]* (St Petersburg, 1896), p. 19, and Cormack on the assumption that military emperors 'resented spending money on the arts': 'Patronage', n. 17.

[72] A. Moffatt, 'Schooling in the Iconoclast centuries', *Iconoclasm*, ed. A.A.M. Bryer and J. Herrin (Birmingham, 1977), pp. 85–92.

[73] Lemerle, *Cinq études*, pp. 105–7; Mango, 'Availability of books', p. 45; Treadgold, 'The revival of Byzantine learning'.

[74] Cormack, 'Patronage', p. 627. See now the excellent L. Brubaker, 'Byzantine art in the ninth century: theory, practice and culture', *BMGS* 13 (1989), 23–94.

[75] For example, the homilies X and XVII of Photios, ed. S. Aristarches (Constantinople, 1900), trans. C. Mango, *The Homilies of Photios, Patriarch of Constantinopole*, English Translation, Introduction and Commentary DOS 3 (Washington DC, 1958), pp. 184–90; 286–96.

[76] See, for example, P. Magdalino, 'The Bath of Leo the Wise', in *Maistor, Studies for Robert Browning*, ed. Ann Moffatt, Byzantina Australiensia 5 (Sydney, 1984), pp. 225–40, and the forthcoming PhD thesis of Valerie Nunn.

[77] See, for example, A.W. Epstein, 'The rebuilding and redecoration of the Holy Apostles in Constantinople: a reconsideration', *GRBS* 23 (1982), 79–92.

From first principles it might appear that art did not play a great part in Byzantine society: the status of the artist appears to be well below that of the writer. Works are not signed until well after our period; Constantine Porphyrogennetos is the exception to the rule that emperors may write but not paint; it is arguable that the patronage of works of literature and of works of (visual) art is different in kind as well as degree.[78] Mango in a classic article designed to show that the Byzantines were unappreciative of their classical heritage demonstrated also their apparent insensitivity to the visual;[79] descriptions of works of art make readers doubt that their authors had seen the work in question.[80]

Yet when Byzantines compare pictures and words, unlike their colleagues in the west,[81] it is usually to the detriment of writing. Three examples are famous. Theodore of Stoudios contrasts the Gospels (writing in words) with icons (writing in gold); the Patriarch Nikephoros emphasizes the vividness of deeds in pictures, and in Homily XVII Patriarch Photios clearly privileges pictures over words – they will teach better, have a greater effect, aid the memory, stimulate emulation of the martyrs. It is a pity that these judgements cannot be taken at face value, for all three churchmen had a vested interest in pictures. It is particularly disappointing in the case of Photios, for here we have an unrivalled opportunity to compare a Byzantine's reception of both known works of literature and known works of art.[82] But given a sensitive understanding of the differences of genre between the *Bibliotheca* and his inauguration sermons it might be possible to understand why his literary criticism is largely evaluative, while his treatment of art clearly commits the affective fallacy. But Photios' example also shows the assimilation of both writing and pictures in an age when forms of the verb γράφω were used for both.[83]

So instead of searching for statements by contemporaries on the relation between art and literature we should concentrate on finding a way to view the interface. Three models have been tried in recent years; many more will

---

[78] Cash on the nail seems to be the exception rather than the rule in the production of Byzantine literature; on the hard commercial facts of Byzantine art in the period, see Cormack, 'Patronage'. Much work remains to be done.

[79] C. Mango, 'Antique statuary and the Byzantine beholder', *DOP* 17 (1963), 53–75.

[80] H. Maguire, 'Truth and convention in Byzantine descriptions of works of art', *DOP* 28 (1974), 111–40. Some consolation may be found in Ong, *Orality and Literacy*, p. 127.

[81] See McKitterick, below pp. 297–301.

[82] Photios on literature: G.L. Kustas, 'The literary criticism of Photius', *Ellenika* 16 (1988–9), 132–69. Photios on art: R. Cormack, *Writing in Gold: Byzantine Society and its Icons* (London, 1985), pp. 142–58, and many of the contributors to the Birmingham symposium on the Byzantine Eye.

[83] For instance the word ἱστοριογράφος, is ambiguous.

no doubt emerge. One sees a 'great divide' between art and literature. Writing reaches the literate; art reaches the parts writing cannot and is 'a vehicle of consolidation and control of a largely oral but centralised and bureaucratic state'.[84] This view assumes a contradiction which is more apparent than real; to say that Byzantium was a residually oral society is not to deny the enabling function of literacy in its bureaucratic workings. And it also assumes that art is more transparent, more legible than words, an equally questionable assumption.[85] And it politicizes art in a way which reduces it to the function of propaganda, simplifying relations between centre and periphery.[86]

A second model assumes that writing and pictures say more or less the same thing, so that pictures seek to express words and the modern scholar can use words to explain pictures. This model is behind many manuscript studies which relate the words on a page with its illustrations,[87] and, more subtly, in recent attempts to persuade early Byzantine rhetoric to explain iconographic or stylistic peculiarities in middle Byzantine art. Here orality has a place also: the topoi of early Byzantine literature read by bishops educated in the schools of Constantinople were relayed in Sunday sermons to the faithful who included the painters who decorated the churches viewed by the faithful.[88] It also enables other scholars to deduce a public or a patron from a work of art,[89] a practice currently under just attack.[90] Much work is still necessary here to test the usefulness of the model: some help might be gained by studying the epigrams apparently commissioned at the same time as minor works of art to accompany them.

A final model assumes that pictures will not duplicate texts, and that we must look for functions that only pictures can perform. Art, it is suggested, does not only embellish and instruct; it offers a channel to the other world;

---

[84] Epstein, 'Art and hegemony', p. 9.

[85] Compare M. Camille, 'Seeing and reading: some visual implications of medieval literacy and illiteracy', *Art History* 8 (1985), 26–49.

[86] Epstein, 'Art and hegemony', p. 9, and in a series of articles on Byzantine political art, for example, 'The political content of the paintings of Agia Sophia at Ochrid', *JÖB* 29 (1980), 315–29.

[87] For example, S. Der Nersessian, 'The illustrations of the Homilies of Gregory of Nazianzus, Paris gr. 510; a study of the connections between text and image', *DOP* 16 (1962), 195–228.

[88] H. Maguire, *Art and Eloquence in Byzantium* (Princeton, 1981), especially pp. 109–11.

[89] For example, A. Cutler, 'The mythological bowl in the treasury of San Marco in Venice', *Near Eastern Numismatics, Iconography, Epigraphy and History: Studies in Honour of George C. Miles*, ed. D.K. Kouymjian (American University of Beirut, 1974), pp. 235–54; L. Brubaker, 'Politics, patronage and art in ninth century Byzantium: the Homilies of Gregory of Nazianzus in Paris BN Gr 510', *DOP* 39 (1985), 1–13.

[90] Cormack, 'Patronage'.

it is simultaneously a witness of the powers of the supernatural; it acts subliminally to predispose the viewer to accept the order of the universe; it confers authority on a dubious text; it involves the emotions; and, above all, it is able to say the unsayable.[91] This model has many attractions, though it may not be universally applicable: it assumes, for example, that text and image are equally available to the same audience, and it may have to make room for the use of text in images. But it avoids the easy answers of allowing texts to 'explain' images: theoretical and methodological problems of interpreting pictures must be faced.

Thus research has so far focussed on the reflection of pictures in writing, or on the particular importance of pictures. The representation of writing in pictures has not so far been studied to any great extent, except from the point of view of orality.[92] Looking at religious representation it is easy to see why. Artists appear to have been impressed by the opportunities of representing the technical equipment of the scribe in evangelist portraits; books appear open or closed in certain stereotyped situations; liturgical books are often represented as rolls.[93] Texts cited in particular programmes are recognized as being of particular importance, but they are usually more indicative of their context than of general problems of literacy. It is worth trying to look outside these possibilities and one obvious example offers itself.[94]

The Madrid manuscript of the *Synopsis Istorion* of John Skylitzes, one of the few pointers to the illustrated chronicle in Byzantine art, tells its story in three ways: in the text, in 574 narrative illustrations (one or two to the page and occupying its full width) and in red captions which identify major actors and events in the scenes.[95] Two major difficulties warn against its

---

[91] Cormack, *Writing in Gold*, p. 47: a channel to the other world; p. 94: a witness to the power of the supernatural; p. 153: the viewer and the order of the universe; p. 175: authority conferred on a dubious text; p. 150: the emotions involved; p. 242: saying the unsayable.

[92] For example, the paper given by Robert Nelson to the XXI Spring Symposium of Byzantine Studies: The Byzantine Eye, Word and Perception, Birmingham, 1987.

[93] Apart from evangelists, hymnographers are also shown in the act of composition and prophets carry their utterances. Bishops are equipped with codices in the early period and rolls in the middle. Moses receives the tablets of the law; the census is taken for Caesar Augustus in the days of Herod the King and the Book has a central place in the Last Days. A book is a constant companion of Christ in iconography, for example, as Pantokrator.

[94] J.C. Estopañan, *Skylitzes Matritensis*, I: *Reproducciones y miniaturas* (Barcelona and Madrid, 1965); A. Grabar and M. Manoussacas, *L'Illustration du manuscrit de Skylitzes de la bibliothèque nationale de Madrid*, Bibliothèque de l'institut hellénique d'études byzantines et postbyzantines de Venise 10 (Venice, 1979). In what follows I give first the folio number, then the serial number in Estopañan, then the reference to an illustration in Grabar and Manoussacas (abbreviated as GM hereafter) if there is one.

[95] On the manuscript tradition, see J. Thurn, *Joannis Scylitzae Synopsis Historiarum editio princeps*, CFHB 5 (Berlin and New York, 1973), pp. xx–xlvi; a Belfast project aims to tackle the problems of narrative in text, illustrations and captions.

indiscriminate use as an indicator of Byzantine attitudes and mentalities (or indeed of anything more concrete): first its production in twelfth-century Sicily raises the problem of milieu. It may not be a very Byzantine artefact, and it is certainly a twelfth-century representation of an eleventh-century narrative of ninth- and tenth-century events. Second, its very rarity value raises the problem of models; the artists may have been drawing on the specific conventions of secular illumination which has nowhere else survived. So we are looking at ninth- and tenth-century events viewed both from an earlier and a later perspective, a kind of fictionalized account, which needs to be checked in various ways from the inside. Even with these provisos, and moving with the maximum caution, I believe it can still offer us valuable insights.[96]

In the Madrid Skylitzes, literacy bulks large, shown in nearly forty of the 574 illustrations, twice the number of illustrations which concern themselves with moveable works of art, though fewer than the illustrations which show the spoken word. In only one case is the issue of literacy explicit: in the sad story of Patriarch Tryphon (928–31). Skylitzes tells us how the metropolitan of Caesarea, Theophanes Choirinos, in accord with Romanos Lekapenos' wishes, duped the patriarch into putting his name to his own resignation. On the pretext of accusations that the patriarch was illiterate (ἀγράμματος), Theophanes persuaded Tryphon to call a synod and then to prove his literacy by signing his name and titles (effectively a blank cheque) to which were added the words of resignation.[97] The Madrid manuscript shows the story in four pictures: the original interview between Theophanes and Tryphon,[98] Tryphon calling the synod,[99] and then a pair of scenes on the same folio showing Tryphon confronting the synod, signing his name (actually at the top of the sheet)[100] and the denouement: at the left Tryphon is being bundled out of the patriarchal palace while the emperor sits facing the synod while Tryphon's resignation is read aloud to him.[101] Writing and listening are visually opposed; the irony is in the orality

---

[96] On the milieu see N.G. Wilson, 'The Madrid Scylitzes', *Scrittura e civiltà* 2 (1978), 209–19; on using the illustrations, C. Walter, 'Raising on a shield in Byzantine iconography', *REB* 33 (1975), 133–75; *idem*, 'Saints of second iconoclasm in the Madrid Scylitzes', *REB* 39 (1981), 307–18; and most recently in C. Walter, *Art and Ritual in the Byzantine Church*, Birmingham Byzantine Series 1 (London, 1982), pp. 41–5.

[97] Skylitzes, ed. Thurn, pp. 226–7; on the letter 'of resignation' (=Grumel 786) and the relative veracity of the accounts in Skylitzes and in Theophanes Continuatus, see V. Grumel, *Les Régestes des actes du patriarcat de, Constantinople*, I: *Les Actes des patriarches*, II: *Les Régestes de 715 à 1043* (Chalcedon, 1936), I, p. 222.

[98] Fol. 128ra=E316=GM309, fig. 151.

[99] Fol. 128rb=E317=GM310, fig. 152.

[100] Fol. 128va=E318=GM311, fig. 153, pl. XXVI.

[101] Fol. 128vb=E319=GM312, fig. 154.

represented. Both these last scenes take place in public: reading and writing
was an issue at the heart of tenth-century politics. For Tryphon, at least, a
little literacy was a dangerous thing.

Elsewhere books are taken for granted, both in codex and roll form:
codices on the knees of the emperor Theophilos interrogating the Graptoi
(writing as a weapon);[102] rolls as part of the professional equipment of the
bishop.[103] Books are also part of the equipment of the schools started by
Constantine VII (teaching ratio of twelve pupils to six books to three
teachers: favourable),[104] and symbols of Christianity in the process of the
conversion of Rus; placed in a bonfire, Christian books are burnt but not
consumed.[105] Other documents (chrysobulls, pittakia)[106] appear also, and
documents are used to convey concepts like conversion,[107] appointment,[108]
administration[109] and diplomacy.[110] Various literate practices are represented: bishops sign decrees promulgated by Nikephoros Phokas and a
secretary offers them to him (an indication of their subservience to him);[111]
the plot of Basil against Leo VI is detected by secretaries hidden behind a
bed taking down a conversation verbatim (surely a clear case of silent
writing!)[112] and then reading the transcript back to the emperor.[113] Reading
is both public and private, oral and visual. The deposition of the empress
Zoë is marked by the reading of a declaration of the emperor publicly in the
Forum of Constantine by the Prefect of the City;[114] Leo V has read aloud in
front of the empress (who has asked for the pardon of Michael of Amorion)
the oracle predicting that Leo would be killed by someone called Michael;[115]
on the occasion of the conspiracy of Leo Phokas the *epi tou kanikleiou* reads
an imperial chrysobull to his soldiers.[116] Private reading is shown in two
cases, both exceptional: in one case Leo the Philosopher is shown worriedly

---

[102] Fol. 51=E127=GM121, fig. 50. The Graptoi do the talking.

[103] Fol. 21rb=E41=GM35.

[104] Fol. 134=E336=GM329, fig. 164.

[105] Fol. 103vb=E242=GM235, fig. 114.

[106] Fol. 125v=E306=GM299; fol. 56v=E141=GM fig. 60; fol. 157vb=E415=GM fig. 204.

[107] Fol. 103va=E241=GM234, fig. 113.

[108] Fol. 21rb=E41=GM35.

[109] Fol. 154r=E404=GM397.

[110] Fol. 210r=E517=GM510, fig. 245; fol. 96r=E224=GM217, fig. 97.

[111] Fol. 154=E404=GM397.

[112] Fol. 110ra=E259=GM252, fig. 127. On silent writing, see Clanchy, *From Memory to Written Record*, p. 218; Ong, *Orality and Literacy*, p. 26.

[113] Fol. 110rb=E260=GM253, fig. 128.   [114] Fol. 219va=E542=GM535.

[115] Fol. 24va=E50=GM44.   [116] Fol. 125v=E306=GM299.

poring in secret over the letter from the Caliph Mamoun, technically the enemy;[117] in another John Tzimiskes and Romanos Kourkouas receive offers of promotion if they join a revolt; exceptionally their letters are shown open and folded, underlining the secrecy and complicity of the context.[118]

A remarkably high proportion (over half) of the representations of literacy involve letters, perhaps not so remarkably, if it is true that while 'not in itself a spontaneous development of writing, [letter-writing] comes near to being a universal feature'.[119] In twenty cases, sometimes where explicitly called for in the text, sometimes to spell out a phrase like ἔγραψε πρὸς τὸν βασιλέα[120] or πέμπει μὲν πρεσβόντας, ἐξαιτῶν . . .[121] letter-exchange is represented. But the way in which it is spelt out is not by representing the moment of composition, either writing or dictating, or the moment of reading, either aurally or visually, but the process of letter-exchange, epitomized in the transaction of delivery, the primary reception of the text. The bearer, the *komistes*, hands over a scroll to the recipient. In some cases[122] the whole process is shown, from (from right to left) the handing over of the letter to the bearer by the sender, through the carrying of the letter, to the delivery of the letter to the recipient. In three cases[123] the swift horses of the bearer are shown; in two cases[124] the recipient waits patiently for his aide de camp to receive the letter and either hand it to him or read it aloud. The same formula is used for the translation to Constantinople after George Maniakes' capture of Edessa of the letter of Christ to Abgar, differentiated from other letter-deliveries only by the reverently covered hands of the *komistes*.[125] In all, the emphasis is on ceremony, on the transaction, on the public nature of letter-exchange, on the social and political importance of communication.

Tenth-century Byzantine letters which have survived[126] are rarely of this political importance, though some are more political than others. We have, for example, the vital correspondence between Nicholas Mystikos and

---

[117] Fol. 75=E191=GM184, fig. 75.

[118] Fol. 144ra=E370=GM363.

[119] Goody, *The Interface*, p. 231.

[120] For example, fol. 109ra=E256=GM249, fig. 124.

[121] For example, fol. 226rb=E560=GM553.

[122] For example, fol. 75v=E191=GM185, fig. 76.

[123] Fol. 19va=E35=GM29; fol. 19vb=E36=GM fig. 30; fol. 230rb=E569=GM362 fig. 270.

[124] Fol. 230rb=E569=GM563, fig. 270; fol. 78a=E197=GM191.

[125] Fol. 205rb=E508=GM501.

[126] See the list in M.E. Mullett, 'Theophylact through his letters: the two worlds of an exile bishop', University of Birmingham PhD thesis, 1981, fig. I, pp. 798–800.

Symeon of Bulgaria;[127] we have whole sets of letters revealing the abyss of synodal politics during the ninth and tenth centuries,[128] and the letters of Theodore of Stoudios are classic examples of the consolidating role of correspondence during the Second Iconoclasm.[129] But in general the letters which have survived from the period were preserved for another reason; they were preserved deliberately by the author or the recipient because of their literary merit,[130] and they were collected for posterity in manuscripts which unite admirable letters of all periods, or in manuscripts uniting rhetorical works of many genres, or as the collected works of a single writer. They were seen as having permanent value only in that they succeeded as works of art, and as such they have succeeded in drawing expressions of puzzlement and disgust from modern critics.

Byzantine letters lack all the normal characteristics of a letter.[131]

To us, a letter is a message accompanied by an expression of personal regard; a Byzantine letter is an impersonal flourish which either contains no message at all, or if it does, the message is couched in so obscure and allusive a fashion as to be nearly unintelligible.[132]

The Byzantine letter is about as concrete, informative and personal as the modern mass-produced greeting card. Just as we have a selection of illustrated cards suitable for every occasion so the Byzantine had his formularies of model letters.[133]

This reaction is common to all Byzantine letters, despite their wide difference over time; the tenth century has attracted most of this abuse because letters of that period have been seen in the context of a Macedonian Renaissance, because tenth-century letters have been more (if not better) studied than letters of earlier and later periods[134] and because the work that

---

[127] Epp. 3–31, ed. R.J.H. Jenkins and L.G. Westerink, *Nicholas I Patriarch of Constantinople, Letters*, DOT 2=CFHB 6 (Washington DC, 1973), pp. 17–215.

[128] See the collections of Alexander of Nicaea, Leo of Synada, Theodore of Nicaea, Theodore of Kyzikos in J. Darrouzès, *Epistoliers byzantins du Xe siècle*, Institut Français d'Etudes Byzantines. Archives de l'Orient Chrétien 6 (Paris, 1960).

[129] See P. Alexander, 'Religious persecution and resistance in the Byzantine empire of the eighth and ninth centuries – methods and justifications', *Speculum* 52 (1977), 238–64.

[130] For discussion of mediaeval letter collections generally, see G. Constable, *Letters and Letter Collections*, Typologie des sources du moyen âge occidental 17 (Turnhout, 1976).

[131] W. Schubart, *Einführung in die Papyruskunde* (Berlin, 1918), p. 212.

[132] Jenkins, 'Hellenistic origins', 45.

[133] G.T. Dennis, *The Letters of Manuel II Palaeologus, Text, Translation and Notes*, DOT 4=CFHB 8 (Washington DC, 1977), p. xix.

[134] There is no good study of tenth-century letters. In 1972–3 Antony Littlewood wrote a long and thorough article, 'Byzantine letter-writing in the tenth century', for *Aufstieg und Niedergang der römischen Welt* which is still, regrettably, unpublished.

has been done has concentrated on establishing chains of influence which readily give the impression of a dry and cliché-ridden genre.[135]

It is in fact possible to see the period as a golden age of Byzantine letter-writing. About one thousand letters have survived, in the major collections of Leo Choirosphaktes, Arethas, Theodore of Kyzikos, Theodore of Nicaea, Leo of Synada, Symeon Metaphrastes, Philetos Synadenos, Nicholas Mystikos and three anonymous collections, as well as many shorter collections. It is in a sense a real revival of the great days of patristic letter-writing, and letters of the period contrast both in quantity and nature with the bread-and-butter efforts of the Iconoclast centuries and the rich but isolated eleventh-century collections of John Mauropous and Michael Psellos. Theodore's letters were entirely political in purpose, and Photios' are those of a working patriarch, but in the letters of Ignatios topoi look back to antiquity and forward to the group of letter-collections which are preserved for the tenth century. Those letters stretch from the period of the Tetragamy and the Bulgarian wars through to the victories of Byzantium on the eastern frontier in the reign of Basil II and continue into the eleventh century.[136]

Despite the impression of homogeneity and boredom which one gains from the secondary works, from the letters themselves the impression is more of diversity and variety. In social origin, the letter-writers are more diverse than at any other period of Byzantine epistolography. Ambassadors, generals, literary figures, schoolmasters, rub shoulders with the great officials of church, bureaucracy and provincial administration, who are often thought of as the staple literary class of Byzantium. Writers famous for works in other genres (hagiography, historiography, rhetoric, tactics, occasional poetry) have all left their letter-collections. Some of these collections are more concrete than others, indeed tediously so; it is possible to reconstruct Alexander of Nicaea's entire campaign for reinstatement from the series of letters he has left,[137] and to isolate various political crises from the letters of Theodore of Nicaea.[138] The anonymous schoolmaster's letters deal with the day-to-day ups and downs of the job,[139] and Nikephoros

---

[135] See G. Karlsson, *Idéologie et cérémonial dans l'épistolographie byzantine: textes du Xe siècle analysés et commentés*, Studia Graeca Upsaliensis 3 (2nd edn, Uppsala, 1962). In its own terms it is excellent; a further work on the same subject is still needed.

[136] For full details see my thesis, 'Theophylact through his letters'. Since then see the edition of the letters of Leo of Synada by M.P. Vinson, *The Correspondence of Leo Metropolitan of Synada and Syncellus, Greek Text, Translation and Commentary*, DOT 8=CFHB 23 (Washington DC, 1985).

[137] Alexander of Nicaea, ep. 1, ed. Darrouzès, *Epistoliers byzantins*, pp. 67–9.

[138] On the various affairs touched on in these letters see *ibid.*, pp. 54–7.

[139] Anonymous Londiniensis, ed. B. Laourdas, Ἡ συλλογὴ ἐπιστολῶν τοῦ χώδιϰος BM

Ouranos[140] offers a most unsoldierly aperçu of the delights of campaign. The encomium of the apple and *ekphrasis* of his garden by John Geometres on the other hand are rhetorical set-pieces as well as epistolary gems.[141] Littlewood and Karlin-Hayter have each shown how individual treatments of the same circumstances can be in the period;[142] individuality is a real characteristic of these letters. There are many valuable rarities: in the letters of Theodore Daphnopates we observe the phenomenon (which is much commoner in the west) of letters written by a secretary in the name of the employer;[143] in the correspondence between Constantine Porphyrogennetos and Theodore of Kyzikos[144] we have not only the rare opportunity of following both sides of a conversation, but also of seeing the private life of a most public emperor in these charming letters, which are the friendliest of friendship letters.

This is something the collections have in common: they are letters of friendship, written between friends, or between enemies, rivals or fellow heads of state under a cover of letter-friendship, using a well-tried repertoire of writing about friendship incorporated into the letter at a very early stage. The topoi of the Aristophanes myth, the winged visit, the other self, the illusion of presence are all there;[145] it would have been astonishing if they had not been; they were expected and appreciated articulations for the enormous emotional need for communication and the function of letters as the shared outlook of a close group,[146] which marks out letters of this kind as an example of symbolic literacy in middle Byzantine society. But a word of caution is necessary here: I have shown recently[147] that friendship in

Add. 36749', *Athena* 58 (1954), 176–98; R. Browning, 'The correspondence of a tenth-century Byzantine scholar', *Byzantion* 24 (1954), 397–452; R. Browning and B. Laourdas, 'Τὸ χέμενον τῶν ἐπιστολ κώδικος BM 36749', *EEBS* 27 (1957), 151–212; 319–21; A. Steiner, *Untersuchungen zu einem anonymen byzantinischen Briefcorpus des 10. Jahrhunderts* (Frankfurt, 1987).

140 Nikephoros Ouranos, ep. 47, ed. Darrouzès, *Epistoliers byzantins*, p. 245.

141 John Geometres, five letters, ed. A.R. Littlewood, *The Progymnasmata of Joannes Geometres* (Amsterdam, 1972).

142 P. Karlin-Hayter, 'Arethas, Choirosphaktes and the Saracen Vizir', *Byzantion* 35 (1965), 282–92; Littlewood, 'Byzantine letter-writing in the tenth century', under the heading of 'Letters of friendship'.

143 For example, Symeon Magistros for the Patriarch Nicholas; Theodore Daphnopates for Romanos II. Byzantine letter-collections compared with their counterparts in the mediaeval west are remarkably free from this kind of letter.

144 Ed. Darrouzès, *Epistoliers byzantins*, pp. 317–32.

145 Karlsson, *Idéologie et cérémonial*, pp. 62–7, 57–8, 34–5.

146 See my thesis, 'Theophylact through his letters', II.4, pp. 270–308.

147 M.E. Mullett, 'Byzantium: a friendly society?', *Past and Present* 118 (1988), 3–24.

Byzantium should not be regarded as the exclusive vocabulary of an elite; it was also a functional form of social cohesion as essential as kinship. Symbolic literacy could turn out to be functional too.

The collections all share the constant concerns of the Byzantine letter, its recognizable subject-matter of sickness, death and exile.[148] Tenth-century epistolographers, like all Byzantine letter-writers, complain of illness, reply to complaints, send wishes for recovery, use sickness as an excuse for not writing, request medical assistance and regard sickness, like separation, as a trial wished by Providence, which can, however, be eased by letters. 'Gout oppresses us and every hair falls out of my head'[149] is Alexander of Nicaea's problem. 'I was prostrated by shivering as a report announcing your illness completely maimed my soul and my tongue' is Nikephoros Ouranos' response to news from a correspondent;[150] Symeon Magistros trusts that relief provided by Divine Providence will ensure that the pain arising from his correspondent's illness will not increase.[151] John of Mount Latros tries the sickness excuse: 'It is unkind to accuse me of forgetfulness, for I have an invisible malady.'[152] 'Get better,' writes Alexander of Nicaea, 'for if you do not I will die.'[153] Theodore of Nicaea thanks a friend for a comforting letter which had a calming effect on 'me who cannot bear the harshness of the shifting heat and the mosquitoes, and who am wasting away with stomach pains and lack of sleep'.[154]

Like all Byzantine letter-writers, tenth-century epistolographers dealt also with death.[155] About half are consolatory letters, for one of the original *typoi* was παραμυθητικός[156] and to many mediaeval letter-writers the letter was itself a *consolatio*.[157] Compared with other death genres and forms,[158] the *epitaphios logos*, the *paramythetikos logos*, the *threnos* and the

---

[148] On sickness and letters, see my 'Theophylact through his letters', II.3, pp. 223–69.

[149] Alexander of Nicaea, ep. 1, ed. Darrouzès, *Epistoliers byzantins*, p. 70.

[150] Nikephoros Ouranos, ep. 36, *ibid.*, p. 236.

[151] Symeon Magistros, ep. 37, *ibid.*, p. 125.

[152] John of Mount Latros, ep. 6, *ibid.*, p. 214.

[153] Alexander of Nicaea, ep. 8, *ibid.*, pp. 82–3.

[154] Theodore of Nicaea, ep. 37, *ibid.*, p. 303.

[155] On death and letters see my thesis, 'Theophylact through his letters', III.2, pp. 403–49.

[156] Demetrios Phalereus, *Typoi Epistolikoi*, 5, ed. R. Hercher, *Epistolographi graeci* (Paris, 1873), p. 2; Proklos, *Peri epistolimaiou charakteros*, 21, *ibid.*, p. 10.

[157] See Karlsson, *Idéologie et cérémonial*, pp. 45–7.

[158] On death genres in Byzantine literature, see M. Alexiou, *The Ritual Lament in Greek Tradition* (Cambridge, 1974), and (for the rhetorical side of the picture) my thesis, 'Theophylact through his letters', III.2, pp. 423–43, and fig. IIb, pp. 832–6.

epitaph, the letter is personal (one addressee), immediate (written as soon as the news is heard), closer in emotional time than a speech (delivered at some distance from the death) and habitually concerned with human emotion.[159] Tenth-century letter-writers took full advantage of the possibilities with remarkable originality.

On the theme of exile the tenth-century letter-writers have a great deal to say.[160] Karlsson has well analysed the themes of separation which are the obverse of friendship-thinking: the illusion of presence, the letter as consolation for absence, the letter as δεύτερος πλοῦς, the winged visit, the *unio mystica*.[161] Writers of our period add to the repertoire in terms of separation from a place as well as from people: Theodore of Stoudios' narration of his journey to exile follows the footsteps of John Chrysostom[162] and builds a role-model figure of heroic ecclesiastical exile. Four tenth-century collections pinpoint the conditions and mentalities of political exile: Leo Choirosphaktes, a casualty of the Tetragamy crisis, wrote eight letters to friends and patrons, detailing the conditions of his imprisonment and appealing for recall.[163] Niketas Magistros, who fell from favour in 927–8, was deported and tonsured and settled on his own property on the southeast shore of the Hellespont where he lived the life of a gentleman farmer for eighteen years, during which he wrote the thirty-one letters which survive to us.[164] Alexander of Nicaea was exiled in 944 for no clear reason, but he used letters, of which seventeen have survived, to secure the vote of this or that bishop for his return.[165] Theodore of Kyzikos was exiled shortly after the death of Constantine Porphyrogennetos in 959 to Nicaea where he wrote twelve letters, patient and resigned, with more of an eye to the next world

[159] A. Littlewood, 'An "ikon of the soul": the Byzantine letter', *Visible Language* 10 (1976), 218–19; *idem*, 'Byzantine letter-writing in the tenth century', contains these arguments in greater detail, first given at the VII Spring Symposium of Byzantine Studies, Birmingham, 1973.

[160] On exile and letters see my thesis, 'Theophylact through his letters', IV, pp. 551–653.

[161] Karlsson, *Idéologie et cérémoniel*, pp. 34–9, 45–7, 48–57, 57–8, 58–61.

[162] John Chrysostom, letters to Olympias, epp. 1, 2 (from Nicaea), 3, 4 (from beyond Caesarea), 5, 6 (Koukousos), ed. A.M. Malingrey, *Chrysostom, Lettres, à Olympias* Sources chrétiennes 13 (Paris, 1947), pp. 95, 96, 97, 98, 100, 102; Theodore of Stoudios, ep. I.3, *PG* 99, cols. 913–20.

[163] On Leo Choirosphaktes, see G. Kolias, *Léon Choirosphactès, magistre, proconsul et patrice, biographie-correspondance (texte et traduction)*, Texte und Forschungen zur byzantinisch-neugriechischen Philologie (Athens, 1939), pp. 15–20, 53–60, and for his psychological makeup, P. Karlin-Hayter, 'Arethas, Choirosphaktes and the Saracen Vizir'.

[164] For Niketas Magistros, see *Nicétas Magistros, lettres d'un exilé (928–946)* ed. L.G. Westerink (Paris, 1973).

[165] On Alexander of Nicaea, see P. Maas, 'Alexandros von Nikaia', *BNJ* 3 (1922), 333–6; *Epistoliers byzantins*, ed. Darrouzès, pp. 27–32.

than this.[166] But it is not in the letters of legal exiles, but in those of administrators like Philetos Synadenos, judge at Tarsos,[167] or Nikephoros Ouranos the general that we have the clearest impression of deprivation and loss, what it was to be cut off from the smoke of Constantinople and the magic circle of like-minded friends.[168]

Tenth-century collections share with all Byzantine letters the mysterious quality which so infuriates modern scholars, *asapheia* (lack of clarity), which has been described as 'a touchstone of Byzantine rhetoric'.[169] They are also particularly concerned with this characteristic, and the issues of levels of literacy, comprehensibility and the badge of rhetoricity which arise from it. All agreed that letters should be written with clarity;[170] one of the classic letter-types known from antiquity was the riddling letter (αἰνιγ-ματικη),[171] but an equally classic statement of letter style was that 'a letter is designed to be the heart's good wishes in brief; it is the exposition of a simple subject in simple terms'.[172] Letters were not thought of as a written conversation[173] but something more structured and formal; riddles, though, were explicitly excluded by Gregory of Nazianzus.[174] No Byzantine letter, however, was easily read, and over the centuries, of the three classic epistolary virtues, clarity, brevity and decoration, clarity was increasingly sacrificed to decoration.

It is in precisely this period that there is thought to be a change in the theorists of rhetoric, towards an acceptance of *asapheia* as a literary option. And there are frequent complaints in our tenth-century letters of obscurity: Symeon Metaphrastes wonders whether a certain metropolitan is being

---

[166] On Theodore of Kyzikos, see *Epistoliers byzantins*, ed. Darrouzès, pp. 58–61; for his letters, see S. Lampros, 'Epistolai ek tou Biennaiou kodikos phil gr. 3426', *Neos Ellenomnemon* 19 (1925), 269–96; *ibid.*, 20 (1926), 31–46, 139–57; *Epistoliers byzantins*, ed. Darrouzès, pp. 317–41.

[167] Philetos Synadenos, see *Epistoliers byzantins*, ed. Darrouzès, pp. 48–9, 249–59, especially epp. 11 and 12 on Tarsos and Antioch.

[168] Nikephoros Ouranos, ep. 47, *ibid.*, p. 246.

[169] Kustas, *Studies in Byzantine Rhetoric*, p. 93.

[170] Simplicius, *Eis tas Kategorias tou Aristotelous*, ed. C. Kalbfleisch, CAG 8 (Berlin, 1908), pp. 750–4; Demetrios, *Peri Ermeneias*, no. 223, ed. Rhys Roberts, *Demetrius on Style* (Cambridge, 1902), p. 172.

[171] Proklos, *Peri epistolimaiou charakteros*, ed. V. Weichert (Leipzig, 1910), p. 32.

[172] Demetrios, *Peri Ermeneias*, no. 231, ed. Roberts, *Demetrius on Style*, p. 176.

[173] Demetrios, *Peri Ermeneias*, no. 224, *ibid.*, p. 172, distinguishes the letter from the dialogue on precisely these grounds.

[174] Gregory of Nazianzus, ep. 61, ed. P. Gallay, *Grégoire de Nazianze, Lettres* (Paris, 1964), I, p. 67.

deliberately obscure;[175] Theodore, metropolitan of Nicaea, complains of
receiving a letter full of Pythagorean riddles;[176] Arethas' unaccustomed
simplicity in a letter to the emir of Damascus is explained in a marginal
annotation 'it is simply phrased for the understanding of the Arabs',[177] but
another letter shows him on much more usual form when he defends his
style against a friend who had sent back a work and complained that he
could not understand it.[178] Here, rhetoric, the most abstruse use of literacy
in tenth-century Byzantium, is used to create a badge of membership of an
elite club, so exclusive that it defeats its own purpose.

So the letters which have been preserved in manuscript collections are
very different from the letters which form part of the Skylitzes narrative;
they have been *collected*, which may in some cases mean homogenized (just
like saints' lives put through the process of encyclopaedism), just as the
letters described in the chronicle are those which affected crucially the
politics of the period. But in some ways the picture they present is very
similar. In both the moment of receipt is featured; in both the bearer is a
central concern; in both the practicalities of communication and literacy
practices are emphasized, and in both a sense of immense value placed on
the letter as a means of communication is conveyed.

Here is Symeon Metaphrastes receiving a letter:

When your letter reached me, these worries were dissipated like the shadows of
dreams after waking. When I got it into my hands, I loosed the fastening and
immediately looked at its length, just as the thirsty gaze at the size of the cup before
drinking, then slowly dwelling on each syllable, I read it, prolonging for myself the
pleasure and desiring not to stop the cause of my pleasure until I was satisfied.[179]

and here John Mauropous:

I thought that the season was already autumn and not spring. Where then did this
nightingale of spring come from to visit me now? Its voice did not resound from
some distant wood or grove, but – wonderful to tell – it flew into my very hands. And
here it sings to me of spring, and listening to the liquid notes close at hand, I stand
spellbound. Yet if I must speak the truth, it seems to me that though the voice of this
most beautiful bird is that of a nightingale, its form is that of a swallow. Its song is
clear and melodious like the nightingale's; but on its body two contrasting colours
are wonderfully blended together like the swallow's. The black words stand out on

---

[175] Symeon Metaphrastes, ep. 94, ed. Darrouzès, *Epistoliers byzantins*, p. 154.

[176] Theodore, metropolitan of Nicaea, ep. 7, *ibid.*, p. 277.

[177] Arethas, ep. 26, ed. Westerink, *Arethae Scripta Minora*, I, pp. 133–45; P. Karlin-Hayter,
'Arethas' letter to the Emir of Damascus', *Byzantion* 29 (1959), 282–92.

[178] Arethas, ep. 17, ed. Westerink, *Arethae Scripta Minora*, I, pp. 186–91.

[179] Symeon Metaphrastes, ep. 89, ed. Darrouzès, *Epistoliers byzantins*, p. 150.

the white paper like a rich purple embroidered on a shining and translucent material. But whether a nightingale or a swallow, this marvellous letter filled me with complete joy.[180]

One concentrates on the literal procedures of reception, the other on the oral and visual experience. The letter, it is clear, was thought of as both.

A similar impression arises from examining the value placed on the letter by contemporaries. Oral images are common – birdsong,[181] the bewitching song of the Sirens,[182] but so also are visual – the meadow of delightful flowers,[183] the icon of the soul.[184] (Scent and taste, Hymettos honey and precious perfumes, also have a place.) It seems that in the view of letter-writers there was no great conflict between writing and speech; the letter could be described in terms of both.

This is not because letter-writers were uninterested in questions of literate practice; far from it. Alexander of Nicaea's letters abound with literacy. When he was arrested at night his papers were searched, and confiscated, he was forced to write his will,[185] his whole consciousness focuses on who signed or did not sign various documents in the case.[186] He tells his correspondent that he would write in blood and tears if they were available and has to fall back on his usual ink.[187] Deprivation of writing materials[188] became a symbol of the conditions of his imprisonment, unaware (like Richardson's Pamela)[189] of the ironies of such description. Yet as in all our writers the opposite of communication is described in oral terms, σιωπή or σιγή, silence.[190]

Just as literacy is a common concern of letter-writers, so are the difficulties of communication, which only serve to enhance the enormous

---

[180] John Mauropous, ep. 1, ed. P. Lagarde, 'Johannis Euchaitorum metropolitae quae in codice vaticano graeco 676 supersunt', *Abhandlungen der königlichen Gesellschaft der Wissenschaften zu Göttingen* 28 (1881), 51.

[181] For nightingales and swallows see Karlsson, *Idéologie et cérémonial*, pp. 106–11.

[182] Symeon Metaphrastes, ep. 23, Nikephoros Ouranos, ep. 19, ed. Darrouzès, *Epistoliers byzantins*, pp. 114, 226.

[183] For example, Symeon Metaphrastes, epp. 23, 91, *ibid.*, pp. 114, 152.

[184] For example, Symeon Metaphrastes, epp. 85, 89, *ibid.*, pp. 147, 151; for full treatment see Littlewood, 'An "ikon of the soul" ', *passim*.

[185] Alexander of Nicaea, ep. 1, ed. Darrouzès, *Epistoliers byzantins*, pp. 68–71.

[186] *Idem*, e.g., epp. 12, 13, 14, *ibid.*, pp. 88, 89–90, 91–3.

[187] *Idem*, ep. 1, *ibid.*, p. 68.

[188] *Idem*, e.g., ep. 2, *ibid.*, p. 73; ep. 5, p. 77.

[189] Compare D. Kennedy, 'The epistolary mode and the first of Ovid's *Heroides*', *CQ* NS 34/2 (1984), 413–22, at 413.

[190] See my thesis, 'Theophylact through his letters', I.5, pp. 144–6.

value placed on letters which link the separated across great distances. The practicalities of weather and travel and bearers, requests for replies, apologies for not writing, loom large in most correspondences.

And just as the Madrid illustrations express the exchange of the letters in shorthand by a gesture of the bearer, so many letters of the tenth century also place him in the foreground. Not only recommendatory letters, which have as their purpose the delineation of the qualities and the validation of the *komistes*,[191] but also other letters give a cue to the bearer to elaborate on particular aspects of their issue, to expand or to confirm. Occasionally he conveys a message desired by the recipient but not articulated by the sender.[192] But we need to be careful in our interpretation of Byzantine statements on the role of the bearer. When John Mauropous writes: 'As useless as a lantern at midday or well water in midwinter are letters when you have a talkative and many-voiced bearer'[193] he does not mean that the letter carried no message and should be seen as mere wrapping paper for the message of the bearer. Most often it would seem that the letter and the oral report were meant to supplement each other, both bearing the same message but concentrating on different aspects of it. Note how in several letters Nicholas Mystikos opposes the two kinds of message.[194] Long before the tenth century, epistolographers had made literary capital out of this essential feature using various kinds of hyperbole. Julian pointed out how the letter of friendship is enriched when delivered by a third friend.[195] Basil describes a favourite bearer as a man who could take the place of a letter.[196] In general perhaps it is helpful to use Synesios' image of a double letter, the living and the lifeless,[197] rather than pursue Mauropous' idea of 'uselessness', itself in this tradition of hyperbole. The letter is then to be seen, in an ideal situation, when the available bearers met with the writer's approval and confidence, as comprising two parts, the written letter and the verbal

---

[191] On the recommendatory letter see Demetrios, *Typoi epistolikoi*, ed. V. Weichert (Leipzig, 1910), pp. 3–4; Libanios, *Epistolimaioi charakteres*, ibid., pp. 10, 22, 58; Steiner, *Untersuchungen*, pp. 62–5.

[192] For example, Nicholas Mystikos, ep. 182, ed. Jenkins and Westerlink, *Nicholas I*, p. 512.

[193] John Mauropous, ep. 1, ed. Lagarde, 'Johannis Euchaitorum', 52.

[194] Nicholas Mystikos, ep. 6, ed. Jenkins and Westerink, *Nicholas I*, p. 38; ep. 19, *ibid.*, p. 126. Sometimes the bearer was used as a safety net in case more detailed letters failed to arrive, ep. 77, *ibid.*, p. 330.

[195] Julian, ep. 61, ed. W.C. Wright, *The Works of the Emperor Julian*, III (London and Cambridge, Mass., 1923), p. 212.

[196] Basil, ep. 200, ed. R.J. Deferrari, *Saint Basil: The Letters*, III (London and Cambridge, Mass., 1934), p. 135.

[197] Synesios, ep. 85, ed. Hercher, *Epistolographi Graeci*, p. 691.

report. It is the built-in disadvantage of letter-writing study that half of the letter, the living half, is automatically missing, and the form in which the other half is preserved may be distorted by the process of collection. And, it should be remembered, many Byzantine letters have not been preserved at all.

But just as letters in literary letter-collections bear no resemblance to the majority of Byzantine epistolary exchanges, one may be sure, so the neat depictions of letter-exchange in the Madrid Skylitzes are equally far from the reality. For one thing few letters can have been a single sheet of rolled parchment, even if the *metron* of a letter (I estimate 400 words) has something to do with how many words can be got on a single sheet. The whole business must have been much more unwieldy, perhaps resembling the arrival of the widow Danelis or at least the handing over of captured gifts and prisoners[198] than the formula for letter-exchange. A large proportion of the letters we know of were intended to be accompanied by gifts, whether poems, books, works of art, lettuces or fish. The variety of objects sent with letters has frequently been noted,[199] but no satisfactory explanation is usually offered. Why should the supreme and elegant compression of literary art be marred by the banality of cabbages or sheepskins? One answer is that the letter was itself regarded as a gift;[200] another is that it was not viewed as a totally literary experience. All the senses are intended to be comforted, amused, inspired, informed by the act of communication involved. In our letters, John Geometres made a present of six apples which he accompanied with three encomia;[201] Symeon Metaphrastes receives butter and sends bread and wine;[202] Theodore, metropolitan of Nicaea, was only one of many Byzantine letter-writers to receive a gift of fish;[203] the correspondence of Theodore of Kyzikos and Constantine Porphyrogennetos is rich in gifts, the famous lettuce from Olympos, but also wine, cake,

---

[198] For example, fol. 200=E495; fol. 204ra=E504; fol. 102rb and c=E239 and 240=GM, figs. 111, 112.

[199] For example, by L. Robert, 'Les kordakia de Nicée, le combustible de Synnade et les poisson-scies. Sur les lettres d'un métropolite de Phrygie au Xe siècle. Philologie et réalités', *Journal des Savants* (July–Dec. 1961), 97–106 (Jan.–June 1962), 5–74; J. Shepard, 'Tzetzes' letters to Leo at Dristra', *Byzantinische Forschungen* 6 (1979), 191–239; A. Karpozelos, 'Realia in Byzantine epistolography, X–XII c', *Byzantinische Zeitschrift* 77 (1984), 20–37.

[200] Demetrios, *Peri Ermeneias*, no. 224, ed. Roberts, *Demetrius on Style*, p. 172; compare Karlsson, *Idéologie et cérémonial*, ch. 5, pp. 112–37.

[201] See Littlewood, *The Progymnasmata of Johannes Geometres*.

[202] Symeon Metaphrastes, epp. 72, 99, ed. Darrouzès, *Epistoliers byzantins*, pp. 141, 157.

[203] Theodore, metropolitan of Nicaea, ep. 18, *ibid.*, p. 286; Robert, 'Les Kordakia de Nicée', and Shepard, 'Ttetzes' letters', on some which went off.

fish, incense and an Arab goblet.[204] A letter of Symeon Metaphrastes underlines the value of such gifts (gifts of a friend, the product of holy hands, the quantity) to end amusingly with a suggestion that his correspondent had overdone it, sending not the first fruits but the harvest.[205] Number symbolism is often cited; rarely is there any suggestion that the gift itself is more important than the transaction. But there is no doubt that gifts were a standard and expected part of the letter-exchange.

One part of the visual component of the letter-experience does often survive.[206] It is estimated that 60,000 Byzantine lead seals are preserved world-wide, four times my own estimate of surviving letters.[207] The seal was at once the commonest and cheapest form of art visible throughout the Empire[208] and the vital validation of the written and oral parts of the letter. The letter was validated not by what the seal *said* but by being recognizable to the recipient as the sender's 'usual lead seal'.[209] This clearly has implications for literacy (using a seal becomes a sub-literate practice) but also for the role of the visual; the letter was validated by its seal as icons had been validated by written arguments during Iconoclasm. All letters needed this kind of validation; it has been suggested by Mango on the basis of a Coptic text that the globes carried by angels in Byzantine art are misunderstood seals; the approximation of angels and letters is also made in tenth-century texts.[210]

So a letter in ninth- and tenth-century Byzantium was not only a component of an abstruse literary genre, the letter-collection; it was a transaction, an act of communication between two people. It was written, oral, material, visual, and it had its own ceremony, lost for us totally except in the pages of the Madrid Skylitzes and allied representations. While we can gain some idea of the subsequent acts of performance and preservation of letters – such as reading aloud to the senior pupils, performance in a *theatron*, copying into a collection, showing to friends who would appreciate its literary qualities – from internal evidence, the letter-writers, 'men

---

[204] Theodore of Kyzikos, epp. 7, 10, 11, 12, 1, 3, 6, 12, ed. Darrouzès, *Epistoliers byzantins*, pp. 324, 327, 328, 320, 322, 329.

[205] Symeon Metaphrastes, ep. 29, *ibid.*, p. 119.

[206] W. Seibt, *Die Byzantinische Bleisiegel im Oesterreich*, I (Vienna, 1978), p. 34.

[207] See my 'Classical tradition in the Byzantine letter', in Mullett and Scott, *Byzantium and the Classical Tradition*, p. 75.

[208] See A. Cutler, 'Art in Byzantine society', *XVI International Byzantine Congress*, pp. 759–88.

[209] N. Oikonomides, 'The usual lead seal', *DOP* 37 (1981), 147–57.

[210] *Epistoliers byzantins*, Lettres diverses, ep. 17, ed. Darrouzès, p. 355, plays on the idea of γραμματᾰφόρος as ἄγγελος.

who had a love for learning, a love for beauty and a love for each other',[211] focussed on the moment after that recorded by the manuscript. The writers of letters are interested in the receipt, the holding in the hand, the unloosing of the seal and the perusal of the letter rather than the arrival of the *komistes* at the residence of the recipient, his reception, entertainment, ushering into the presence and handing over of the parchment and the gifts. What follows is clear from neither:[212] in some miniatures the recipient takes the letter himself; in others his household shields him from it; in no case is it clear whether the recipient reads the letter silently, whether a member of his household (as in the Tryphon story) or whether the bearer reads it to him, before the bearer offers his oral contribution; what it clear is that many rereadings must have been necessary before the *ainigmata* and *asapheia* gave up their meanings to the recipient. Communication theory which makes use of the concept of decoding (however challenging the implications of intentionalism here) may be of supreme use to the Byzantinist.

Two things here are worth noting: one is the reason for the puzzling, deconcretization of the letter-as-preserved-in-letter-collections: it may be deconcretized because of the circumstances of collection, but it is mostly so because it is only part of a much bigger whole. Writing in itself was not enough.[213] The other is the usefulness of the evidence of the Skylitzes, even with all its worrying problems of milieu and models. McCormick has recently warned against taking any picture of a ceremony as evidence for its performance;[214] what the Skylitzes representations can do for us is to point to a ceremonial context which might otherwise be totally neglected.

All our evidence is partial; letter-collections preserve (on literary grounds) a tiny part of the *written* part of letter-exchange; seals preserve (on random[215] survival) some elements of the *visual* part of the process; the emphasis on the *komistes* in the miniatures of the Madrid Skylitzes and their captions[216] points us to the *oral* part of the transaction. The exchange of

---

[211] J. Bryennios, ep. 82, ed. N. Tomadakes, Ὁ Ἰωσήφ Βρυέννιος καὶ η Κρήτη κατὰ το 1400 (Athens,1947), p. 126.

[212] It might be possible to get some idea from extrapolating from descriptions of diplomatic receptions in the same way that it is assumed that episcopal administrations were modelled on the patriarchal secretariat or that aristocratic palaces were scaled-down versions of imperial ones.

[213] Compare the importance of perambulation in the settlement of boundary disputes, see Morris, 'Dispute settlement'.

[214] M. McCormick, 'Analysing imperial ceremonies', *JÖB* 35 (1985), 1–20, at 9–10.

[215] On the circumstances of preservation of seals, see G. Zacos and A. Veglery, *Byzantine Lead Seals*, I/1 (Basel, 1972), p. vii, and Oikonomides 'Usual lead seal', 149.

[216] The *komistes* is frequently signalled in the captions; I have here simply avoided the topic of the captions but hope to take it up elsewhere.

letters in ninth and tenth-century Byzantium was a multi-media experience where oral, visual and written elements combined in an expected ceremonial. Sound, writing and pictures were complementary and essential elements in the process of communication.

Does this perception help at all towards an appreciation of the place of writing in Byzantine society? We have seen that letter-writing was regarded as being of functional as well as of ritual importance and that books were represented as a natural part of the ninth- and tenth-century environment. But it should now be clear that Byzantium cannot be viewed as a rich backdrop of high literacy against which to view the vicissitudes of the west; Byzantine literacy also had its ups and downs; it also had literacies rather than a single literacy. It too was a 'residually oral' society in which writing, pictures and speech each had a place. Patriarch Tryphon rather than the Graptoi may point the way to future research.[217]

[217] This paper was begun in the legendary favourable atmosphere of Dumbarton Oaks and completed in the mists of the Veneto. I am grateful to many Washington friends, to the Istituto di Studi Bizantini at Padova and the Istituto Greco di Studi Bizantini e Postbizantini at Venice and especially to Andreina Sartori.

8

Literacy displayed:
the use of inscriptions at the
monastery of San Vincenzo al Volturno
in the early ninth century

John Mitchell

(To the memory of Don Angelo Pantoni OSB)

The monastery of San Vincenzo on the Volturno is situated at the head of the Volturno valley, a little more than 1 kilometre distant from the source of the river. It lies some 25 kilometres north of the old Roman town of Venafrum, modern Venafro, and about 30 kilometres north-east of Montecassino, across the Mainarde range of mountains. Founded in the first years of the eighth century, by three young men of noble birth from Benevento, it grew in size and fame, and became, for a relatively short period, one of the great monasteries of Europe. Contemporary sources refer to the exceptional size of the community in the closing years of the eighth century.[1] In the later ninth century its fortunes began to decline, and in 881 it was sacked by an army of Saracens from North Africa, which had been harrying much of southern Italy for more than twenty years. The monks returned to San Vincenzo in 914, after thirty-three years of exile in Capua. The damaged buildings were gradually repaired and reconstructed, but the monastery never regained its former size and reputation. Finally, in the later eleventh century new monastic buildings were erected, and subsequently, under the

---

[1] Pope Hadrian I, in a letter to Charlemagne of 784, refers to the community at San Vincenzo as 'tam magnam congregationem', *Codex Carolinus: MGH Epp. merov. et karol.* I (=*MGH Epp.* III. 66, p. 594); and Paul the Deacon, in his history of the Lombards, composed at the neighbouring monastery on Montecassino, probably in the 790s, writes that the monastery of San Vincenzo 'nunc magna congregatione refulget' (Lib. 6, ch. 40), ed. G. Waitz, *MGH SS rerum Langobardicarum*, p. 179; Paul the Deacon, *History of the Lombards*, trans. W.D. Foulke (Philadelphia, 1907; new edn, Philadelphia, 1974), p. 283. In the early twelfth-century chronicle of San Vincenzo, it is recorded that either 500 or 900 souls were killed by the Saracen war-band which sacked the monastery in October 881. This number is said to have included the inmates of various monasteries and cells subject to San Vincenzo, who had gathered at the main monastery, presumably for protection (*Chron. Vult.*, I, p. 368).

Abbots Gerard and Benedict the main abbey church of San Vincenzo was completely rebuilt.[2]

Until recently it was assumed that the monastery of the eighth to the eleventh centuries occupied the same site as its successor of the eleventh to the twelfth centuries, a somewhat elevated position in a bow of the Volturno, protected by deep rock-cut ditches on two sides, and by the river gorge to the east, and that the material evidence for its principal church and buildings had been utterly destroyed in the process of reconstruction.[3] However, excavations carried out during the years 1980–5 have demonstrated conclusively that the early monastery was, in fact, situated about 300 metres to the west of the later abbey, on the opposite bank of the River Volturno, on the eastern slopes of a low hill, the modern Colle della Torre, and on the narrow strip of plain between the hill and the river (Fig. 1).

According to the Chronicle, the three founders established their monastery on the site of an abandoned settlement, where there stood an old oratory, dedicated to St Vincent, reputedly built by the emperor Constantine.[4] Three churches are recorded as having been constructed in the first half of the eighth century: San Vincenzo under the first abbot, Paldo (703?–20),[5] Santa Maria Maior under his co-founder Taso (729–39)[6] and San Pietro under Ato (739–60).[7] During the following fifty years the rate of growth increased. A generation after Ato, Abbot Paul (783–92) founded the church of Santa Maria Minor,[8] and some years later his successor Iosue (792–817) completely rebuilt the principal abbey church, San Vincenzo, as an aisled basilica with sixteen columns in each arcade.[9] Under the Abbots Talaricus (817–23) and Epyphanius (824–42), four further churches were built, so that by the second quarter of the ninth century there were in all eight churches within the confines of the monastery.[10] During this period of expansion, between the late 780s and 840s, in which six new churches were constructed, the number of donations and bequests made to the com-

---

[2] The new abbey church of Abbots Gerard and Benedict survived, radically altered and truncated, until the Second World War. It was completely rebuilt by the monks of Montecassino thirty years ago. Most of what is known of the early history of San Vincenzo al Volturno is contained in the chronicle of the monastery, which was compiled early in the twelfth century, and incorporates earlier material. There is an excellent modern edition: *Chron. Vult.* A good brief account of the early history of San Vincenzo is given by A. Pantoni, *Le chiese e gli edifici del monastero di San Vincenzo al Volturno* (Montecassino, 1980), pp. 17–25.

[3] Pantoni, *Le chiese, passim.*

[4] *Chron. Vult.*, I, pp. 111, 145–8.

[5] *Ibid.*, p. 145.

[6] *Ibid.*, p. 155.

[7] *Ibid.*, p. 162.

[8] *Ibid.*, p. 204.

[9] *Ibid.*, I, pp. 220–1. The date of its dedication is given as 808.

[10] *Ibid.*, pp. 287, 288.

188

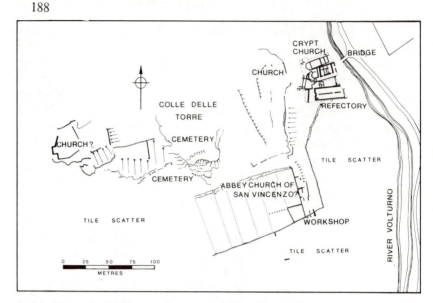

1 San Vincenzo al Volturno, the site of the early mediaeval
monastery *(a) (above)* overall plan *(b) (right)* detail of main
excavated buildings

munity, mostly gifts from the dukes of Benevento and from local Lombard
landowners, greatly increased,[11] and the new Frankish rulers of Italy,
Charlemagne, and his son, Louis the Pious, seem to have taken a direct
interest in San Vincenzo.[12]

The recent excavations have largely confirmed the evidence of the
Chronicle (Fig. 1).[13] The early ninth-century monastery was quite small,
and had been established among the ruins of a small fifth- to sixth-century
estate centre, a *villa rustica*, situated on the north-east slopes of the hill,
close to an old Roman bridge over the Volturno, which is still in use today.
A fifth-century funerary church, which had served this early Christian
community, was repaired and refurbished, perhaps as the first conventual
church dedicated to St Vincent. Various eighth-century phases of construction have been identified, but it was not until the last years of the century

[11] *Ibid., passim.*

[12] *Ibid.*, pp. 204–15, 218–43, 289–90; *Codex Carolinus: MGH Epp. merov. et karol.* I (=*MGH
Epp.* III. 66 and 67, pp. 593–7. See below, pp. 223–4.

[13] Interim reports on the excavations have appeared each year from 1981 to 1986 in
Archeologia Medievale. A volume of preliminary studies on various aspects of the project
was published in 1985: *San Vincenzo al Volturno: The Archaeology, Art and Territory of an
Early Medieval Monastery,* ed. R. Hodges and J. Mitchell, BAR, International Series 252
(Oxford, 1985). The Final Report on the excavations is in preparation.

that major changes took place in the layout and the appearance of the monastery. In two phases of activity, it was completely redesigned, with new construction taking place on a massive scale. The first of these phases has been associated with the Abbots Paul (783–92) and Iosue (792–817), and the second phase can be assigned to the time of Epyphanius (824–42), who erected two churches, and whose portrait is featured in the painted crypt of a small church at the northern end of the site, the crypt church, which was remodelled during the second phase of construction (Fig. 2). During this half-century of building activity the monastery expanded to something like ten times its original size.

In the first phase of expansion, the original nucleus was extended towards

the south, and a new abbey church, a columnar basilica, was built on an artificially constructed platform at the south-eastern corner of the hill, providing a new focus for the monastery. In the area of the late antique settlement to the north, an elevated guest hall, with a chapel at one end, was erected in the shell of the old funerary church, and immediately to the south of this an old garden atrium was remodelled with elegant columned porticos on two sides, and a refectory for distinguished guests on the side towards the river. Fronting this garden, to the west, was a splendid entrance hall, a building with arched and pilastered façade, containing a large staircase, which provided access to the raised guest hall and to ranges of buildings on the lowest slope of the hill behind. To the south, lay a great two-halled refectory, 33 metres long and 14 metres wide, with seating for about 450 monks. On the western side of this refectory, against the slope of the hill, was a long assembly room, with benches built against all its walls. This probably served as an ante-room for those about to dine, and may also have doubled up as a chapter-house. Beyond the refectory, in all probability, lay the kitchens, a large cloister, the dormitory and, to judge from extensive surface-scatter of building debris, a succession of further structures, all of which have yet to be excavated. In the second phase of construction, a long range of rooms and a substantial church were erected on the terraced slope of the hill overlooking these principal buildings, the guest hall at the northern end of the complex was rebuilt to a grander specification and provided with an inlaid marble floor and rich paintings on its walls, and the crypt church, to the north, was remodelled and embellished. On the middle slopes of the hill is the burial ground of the early mediaeval community, containing something in the order of 2,000 graves, and beyond this, on the summit, are the remains of another substantial structure, probably a church from the second phase. At the southern end of the hill, construction continued out on to the plain, and it was here that the monastery's workshops were located. Abundant evidence of the manufacture of vessel- and window-glass and enamel and of fine metal-working has been excavated in this area.[14] Surface-scatter indicates the presence of further extensive ranges of buildings far out on to the plain at this end of the complex. It is clear that, by the mid-ninth century, the monastery had evolved into a loosely structured concentration of churches, halls, cells, courts, passages and workshops extending over an area of about 6 hectares.

Two things would have struck a ninth-century visitor to San Vincenzo with particular force. The first of these would have been the brightly painted surfaces of the plastered walls. The extent of the painted decoration of the

---

[14] J. Moreland, 'A monastic workshop and glass production at San Vincenzo al Volturno, Molise, Italy', in *San Vincenzo al Volturno*, ed. Hodges and Mitchell, pp. 37–60.

monastery is remarkable. To judge from the recent excavations and survey of the site, it seems that nearly every interior wall-surface was painted, not only the walls of the churches and of the large communal rooms, like the monks' refectory, the assembly room and the guest hall, but also the covered passages and porticos, and the individual cells of the ranges on the lower slopes of the hill. Even a building in the industrial area of the monastery, dating from the middle years of the century, which has been identified as the dwelling of the glass-master or the fine-metalsmith, had plastered walls with a simple decorative scheme of bands of colour.[15]

In the great majority of the excavated rooms from both of the ninth-century phases of construction, the lower sections of the walls were ornamented with a dado painted in imitation of panels of polished stone revetment, with diagonal undulant veining endlessly repeating in sequences of stacked upright and inverted chevrons. This recalls the polished marble revetment of ancient Roman buildings, and of the more splendidly appointed early Christian churches. The upper surfaces of the walls carried figural subjects, in many of the rooms so far excavated are simple standing figures, prophets, apostles and saints, often set beneath elaborately painted arcades. Porticos and passages were also richly decorated. The rear wall of the eastern portico of the garden atrium had an elegant painted colonnade, with plants and shrubs in the intercolumniations, echoing the real colonnade of reused fluted ancient columns, and probably also real shrubs which once stood in pots between the columns. One of the long corridors, which are a feature of the plan of the monastery, conserves traces of its early ninth-century scheme of decoration, a sequence of panels, at dado level, painted to imitate *crustae*, cut pieces of polished stone, skilfully laid together to form elaborate repeating patterns, and on one end wall a great round multi-coloured disc.

The best-preserved painting at San Vincenzo is on the walls of the small crypt of a church at the far northern end of the complex, the crypt church.[16]

---

[15] Some painted plaster still adheres to the walls of the excavated rooms, but the greater part of it fell away in the decades following the Saracen sack of 881, and fragments of broken painted plaster were recovered in large quantities from most parts of the site. Considerable progress has been made in reassembling these fragments, and on the reconstruction of the various schemes of decoration. For a preliminary account of this material, see my chapter, 'The painted decoration of the early medieval monastery', in *San Vincenzo al Volturno*, ed. Hodges and Mitchell, pp. 125–76. A team of restorers working for the Istituto Centrale di Restauro in Rome has continued the recomposition of the pieces of fallen plaster, and a preliminary report of their progress has been published: G. Basile, 'Abbazia di S. Vincenzo al Volturno: restauri in corso', *Arte Medievale* 2nd series, 2, part 1 (1988), 153–6.

[16] H. Belting, *Studien zur beneventanischen Malerei* (Wiesbaden, 1968), pp. 24–41, 193–222, ills. 12–60; *San Vincenzo al Volturno e la cripta dell'abate Epifanio 824/842* (Montecassino, 1970), figs. 29–63.

2 Abbot Epyphanius (824–42), and inscription, crypt of crypt church, San Vincenzo al Volturno

Every surface of its interior was painted, during the abbacy of Epyphanius (824–42), with an elaborate iconographic scheme – images of Christ, Virgin Martyrs, Mary, Archangels, a brief infancy cycle, the martyrdoms of SS Lawrence and Stephen and the Crucifixion, with the Abbot Epyphanius kneeling at the foot of the cross (Fig. 2). The programme is intricate and the quality of the painting is high.

The excavations have shown that during the period of intense building activity at San Vincenzo in the closing decades of the eighth, and the first forty years of the ninth centuries, the greater part of the new structures were elaborately and brilliantly painted as soon as they were completed, and that this work was done by highly trained and skilled artists.

The second thing about the monastery, which would have struck a ninth-century visitor, was the display of script. An extraordinary number of inscriptions of various kinds were to be seen in the various parts of the complex. These were executed in a number of media, two of which were quite exceptional for the time. Each category merits our attention.

Many fragments of the painted inscriptions and *tituli* which accompanied the images on the walls of the various buildings were recovered during the excavations: inscriptions in white or black capitals on narrow coloured bands. Since only broken sequences of letters have been preserved, none of these has been deciphered and identified. However, their form and setting indicate that they ran along walls at major horizontal divisions in decorative schemes, presumably identifying or commenting on an adjacent image, spelling out an exhortation to the spectator or recording the names of the individuals responsible for the works. Other excavated fragments clearly come from small inscriptions set in fields of colour, evidently from short *tituli* written within scenes and images, which identified events, individuals and places. Both of these types of inscription are preserved *in situ* in the paintings of the crypt at the north end of the site (Fig. 2).[17] Inscriptions of these kinds were commonly employed by artists in western Europe in the early middle ages.

Somewhat less usual, however, was the practice of writing legible texts in books held open by individual painted figures. In the crypt, both Christ and Mary are represented with open books, the one with the words spoken by God to Moses from the burning bush: *Ego sum D[eus] Abraha[m]*, the other with a passage from the Magnificat.[18] These were clearly legible when they were newly written. While it is by no means unknown for figures to be depicted holding open books with legible texts in the early middle ages, it is certainly more usual for them to be shown with books which are closed, or which, if open, are either blank or covered with indecipherable script-like notations. The presence of two such fully inscribed books in a single small pictorial cycle, at this period, is exceptional. The written word was clearly a thing of some significance to the inventors of the pictorial scheme in the crypt.

This interest is more forcibly expressed in the painted imagery of the long west wall of the large assembly room, which adjoins the refectory. The decoration of this wall has been reconstructed from the excavated fragments of its fallen plaster.[19] A sequence of Prophets, almost life-size, stood, at intervals of about 1 metre, between the columns of a painted arcade. In his left hand each held a large scroll inscribed with a text, written in alternating lines of red and black capital letters (Fig. 3). The letters are about 5 centimetres high, and variant forms as well as inscript characters (small-

---

[17] Belting, *Studien*, ills. 19, 21, 23, 26, 32, 33, 38, 41, 49; *San Vincenzo al Volturno e la cripta dell'abate Epifanio*, figs. 34, 38–43, 45, 46, 51–4, 56, 60–2.

[18] Belting, *Studien*, ills. 21, 45; *San Vincenzo al Volturno e la cripta dell'abate Epifanio*, figs. 53, 54, 56, 62; F. de' Maffei, 'Le arti a San Vincenzo al Volturno: il ciclo della cripta di Epifanio', in *Una grande abbazia altomedievale nel Molise, San Vincenzo al Volturno: atti del 1 convegno di studi sul medioevo meridional (Venafro – S. Vincenzo al Volturno, 19–22 maggio 1982*, ed. F. Avagliano (Montecassino, 1985), pp. 274, 285.

[19] Mitchell, 'The painted decoration', pp. 143–50. figs. 6:17–6:25; Basile, 'Abbazia di S. Vincenzo al Volturno', 153–6, figs. 3–7. A detailed reconstruction of the scheme of decoration on this wall will be published in the Final Report on the excavations.

scale letters which are embraced by ones of full size) are employed, for the sake of variety and ornamentation. The one inscription which has, so far, been more or less fully reconstructed has eight lines of script, and the length of the complete scroll was something in the order of 30 centimetres. The text is: *In die illa dicit D[omi]n[u]s congregabo claudicantem et eam quam eieceram congregabo*, a variant reading of Micah 4.6. The convention of introducing writing on scrolls or books was employed in the middle ages as a means of incorporating the act of speech into the mute medium of painting, and here the Prophets were represented calling out their prophecies in succession. Fragments of *tituli* recovered from the other side of the room suggest that the Apostles faced the line of Prophets, from the long east wall, and they may have held answering texts in their hands.

Figures holding open scrolls bearing legible inscriptions are not commonly found in the mediaeval west before the eleventh century; and in the one outstanding surviving instance of their use the texts in question were carefully and purposefully chosen, and relate to a particular historical situation: the four church fathers painted on the walls flanking the main apse of Santa Maria Antiqua in Rome, in the middle of the seventh century. These four figures carry enormous scrolls inscribed with long texts in Greek, taken from the passages from their writings which were cited in refutation of monothelitism at the Lateran Council of 649. It was largely as a result of the decrees of this Council and of the staunchly anti-monothelite stance of the pope, Martin I, that the pope was abducted from Rome by the Byzantine exarch, transported to Constantinople, humiliated, tried and exiled to the Crimea. The images in Santa Maria Antiqua are usually interpreted as instruments of anti-Byzantine propaganda, commissioned after 649 and perhaps before Martin's removal in June 651.[20] In the west scrolls of this kind seem to have been of the utmost rarity before the eleventh century, and it was only in the twelfth century that they are often put in the hands of Prophets and other figures, in wall-paintings, mosaics, manuscript painting, ivory carving and in other media.[21] In the Byzantine east the motif

---

[20] G.M. Rushforth, 'The church of S. Maria Antiqua', *Papers of the British School at Rome* 1 (1902), 68–73; P. Romanelli and P.J. Nordhagen, *S. Maria Antiqua* (Rome, 1964), pp. 32–4; P.J. Nordhagen, 'S. Maria Antiqua: the frescoes of the seventh century', in *Acta ad archaeologiam et historiam artium pertinentia*, Institutum Romanum Norvegiae 8 (Rome, 1978), pp. 97–9, pls. III–XI. For an account of the events of these years, see P. Llewellyn, *Rome in the Dark Ages* (London, 1971), pp. 150–6. A second, earlier, isolated instance of an inscribed scroll of this kind, bearing the Greek word , is held by Christ at the Second Coming on one of the panels of the fifth-century wooden doors of S. Sabina, in Rome: G. Jeremias, *Die Holztür der Basilika S. Sabina in Rom* (Tübingen, 1980), pls. 68, 69.

[21] An early instance, dating from the 1070s, are the Prophets in Sant'Angelo in Formis, near Capua: O. Demus, *Romanesque Mural Painting* (New York, 1970), pl. 7.

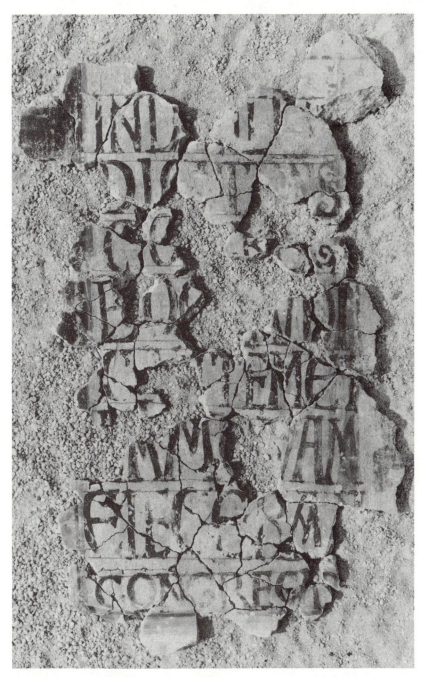

3 Scroll with text from Micah 4.6, held by the figure of the
Prophet, assembly room, San Vincenzo al Volturno, *c.* 800

is somewhat more common. It appears already in the fifth century, in the mosaic in the apse of St George, in Thessaloniki, where Christ holds a scroll bearing a long inscription,[22] and is found occasionally in the succeeding centuries: on pre-iconoclastic panel-paintings of the Virgin of Intercession, of St John the Baptist and Elijah, preserved in the monastery of St Catherine on Mount Sinai,[23] and on one of the ivory plaques of the so-called Grado Chair group, carved with the figure of the Prophet Joel.[24] From the tenth century onwards, the Prophets in monumental schemes of decoration, in the eastern Mediterranean, are often represented displaying their words on large open scrolls.[25]

It is possible that the idea for the motif was the result of the artists' acquaintance with Byzantine imagery[26] but, given its rarity in the west, the reason for the choice is likely to have been a desire to place special emphasis on the inscriptions held by the Prophets. The particular significance of the one text which has been fully reconstructed is not obvious, and it may be that it was the display of script, the very presence of lines of elegant letters on white fields, as much as the content of the texts, that interested the person who devised this scheme of decoration.

Painted inscriptions are also found in early mediaeval graves at San Vincenzo. A small percentage of the many block-built graves excavated in various parts of the site had plastered walls and painted decoration. In most cases the state of preservation was too poor for the schemes of decoration to

---

[22] R. Hoddinot, *Early Byzantine Churches in Macedonia and Southern Serbia* (London, 1963), colour pl. VI, pl. 48a; A Grabar, *Christian Iconography: A Study of its Origins* (Princeton, 1968), fig. 117.

[23] K. Weitzmann, *The Monastery of Saint Catherine at Mount Sinai: The Icons, I: From the Sixth to the Tenth Century* (Princeton, 1976), catalogue nos. B.4, B.11, B.17.

[24] These ivories are dated by Goldschmidt to the sixth century, and by Weitzmann to the eighth century: A. Goldschmidt, *Die Elfenbeinskulpturen aus der Zeit der karolingischen und sächsischen Kaiser*, 4 vols. (Berlin, 1914–26), IV, no. 121; K. Weitzmann, 'The ivories of the so-called Grado Chair', *DOP* 26 (1972), fig. 4.

[25] The earliest examples, for which material evidence survives, seem to be the figures of the four major Prophets on the northern and southern tympana in Hagia Sophia, in Istanbul: C. Mango, *Materials for the Study of the Mosaics of St. Sophia at Istanbul* (Washington DC, 1962), figs. 78, 80, 81, 85, 86. However, to judge from Photius' dramatic description, the Prophets in mosaic in the church of the Virgin of the Pharos, in the Great Palace, of 864, already held up scrolls inscribed with their prophecies: *The Homilies of Photius, Patriarch of Constantinople*, English Translation, Introduction and Commentary, ed. C. Mango, DOS 3 (Washington DC, 1958), p. 188; *idem, The Art of the Byzantine Empire 312–1453: Sources and Documents* (Englewood Cliffs, New Jersey, 1972), p. 186. The type is also found in manuscript illumination later in the tenth century, in a copy of the Major and Minor Prophets, in Rome, Vat. Chis. R. VIII.54: K. Weitzmann, *Die byzantinische Buchmalerei des IX. und X. Jahrhunderts* (Berlin, 1935), pl. XIII, fig. 61.

[26] Belting, *Studien*, pp. 200–2.

4 Inscription flanking the head-niche in a grave at the threshold of
the crypt church, San Vincenzo al Volturno, second quarter of the
ninth century

be reconstructed, but in the two instances in which the painted surface was
preserved on the walls, inscriptions figured prominently on the short wall
surface behind the dead man's head. One of these, the grave of a young man,
who died in the second quarter of the ninth century, is located before the
threshold of the crypt church. The wall surface surrounding the head-niche
carried an inscription in well-formed red capital letters, ending with the
formula ET VITAM ETERNAM (Fig. 4).[27] The inscription is in some of the
finest painted script found at San Vincenzo, although the quality of the
plaster on which it lies is extremely poor. A second painted grave, whose
plastered sides are well preserved, is located under an arcosolium in a
passage which ran beneath the great guest hall at the northern end of the
site. A large cross is painted in the middle of each of the four walls, and the
cross at the head is flanked by the protective inscription: CRVX XPI CONFVSIO
DIABOLI.[28] Plastered and painted graves were not uncommon in early
mediaeval Italy, and quite often they bear inscriptions. However, they
appear to have been more common in the north than in the south of the

---

[27] Mitchell, 'The painted decoration', p. 158, fig. 6:32.

[28] *Ibid.*, figs. 6:33 and 34.

peninsula.[29] Since the only two such graves at San Vincenzo to retain their painted decoration bear inscriptions, it seems likely that a high percentage of them would have been similarly inscribed.

A further category of inscription at San Vincenzo is found on gravestones. Some twenty-five of these, most of which are fragmentary, have survived (Figs. 5 and 6).[30] The majority date from the ninth century and are in variant forms of a single script.[31] The letters are tall and narrow in proportion and usually set quite closely together. Their individual strokes are clearly and deeply cut wtih slanting profiles, which meet at something approaching a right-angle in the trough, and create a lively play of lighted and shaded planes. Curving strokes expand and contract quite dramatically, while vertical strokes have almost parallel sides, which expand a little at their terminals into little wedge-serifs. The bars of letters such as 'T' and 'E' are formed of prominent triangular wedges. For the sake of variation and decoration variant forms of characters are used, for instance 'A' with straight or broken bar, and inscript letters are quite common. These inscriptions are clear and sharp, decorated with restraint and give an appearance of ordered, elegant precision. They are distinctly superior in quality to the general run of funerary inscriptions from early mediaeval Italy, and show that there was a carefully cultivated tradition of funerary calligraphy at San Vincenzo in the ninth century.

A number of stones carrying ancient Roman funerary inscriptions were reused in the construction of churches and monastic buildings at San Vincenzo, in the building phases of the later eighth and early ninth centuries (Fig. 7). They were almost always laid so that the inscribed surface faced outwards or upwards, visible to the passer-by.[32] Although the

---

[29] *Ibid.*, pp. 158–65; C. Fiorio Tedone, 'Tombe dipinte altomedievali rinvenute a Verona', *Archeologia Veneta* 8 (1985), pp. 251–88; *idem*, 'Dati e riflessioni sulle tombe altomedievali internamente intonacate e dipinte rinvenute a Milano e in Italia settentrionale', *Atti del 10. congresso internazionale di studi sull'alto medioevo, Milano 26–30 settembre 1983* (Spoleto, 1986), pp. 402–28.

[30] A. Pantoni, 'Epigrafi tombali di S. Vincenzo al Volturno', *Samnium* 36 (1963), 14–33; Pantoni, *Le chiese*, pp. 158–70: *San Vincenzo al Volturno*, ed. Hodges and Mitchell, frontispiece. The early mediaeval carved inscriptions from San Vincenzo will be described in the forthcoming Final Report on the excavations.

[31] The same script is also found on a number of other small fragments of carved inscriptions, found at San Vincenzo, which cannot with certainty be identified as deriving from funerary monuments.

[32] The examples found, to date, are situated in the following locations: in the north wall of the guest hall; in the refectory, set at the western end of the central spine-wall, forming the base of the western-most of the sequence of columns which support the roof; in the pavement of a walkway immediately to the south of the south wall of the refectory; in one of the treads of a flight of steps climbing up onto the first terrace, immediately behind the west wall of the

mediaeval masons did not always reuse these ancient gravestones in upright positions, with their texts correctly oriented, it is clear that they intended the lines of script to be seen.

There are two further instances of the display of script at San Vincenzo, both of which are exceptional and remarkable. The first of these are the inscribed tiles of fired clay with which the floors of the principal rooms, corridors and porticos of the monastery were paved, and the inscribed roof tiles used to cover the majority of the buildings (Figs 8, 9, 10 and 11).[33] Four types of flooring were employed at San Vincenzo in the building phases of the late eighth and early ninth centuries. The most prestigious buildings were paved with small, smooth, shaped sections of marble and coloured stone laid in repeating patterns – *opus alexandrinum*. This was used in the various churches constructed during the period, and in the great elevated guest hall at the northern end of the complex. Buildings of second rank were paved with large rectangular clay tiles. The third kind of floor, which is found in ranges of cells on the lower terraces of the Colle della Torre, and in other buildings of less significance, is of mortar. The simplest floors are of compacted earth, and are found in structures of a purely utilitarian nature, like the workshops.

The tiles which compose the second kind of floor, and which concern us, are of three sizes, all of them large: *c.* 54×40×4 cm; *c.* 50×36×4 cm; *c.* 38×30.5×4 cm. The roof tiles are large *tegulae* and *imbrices*, which were laid in alternating rows to form a continuous covering more or less resistant to the weather. Both floor and roof tiles were manufactured in one spate of production during the first phase of building operations which completely transformed the appearance of the monastery during the years around 800. The production was extensive, but short-lived. It had evidently ceased by the time of the following phase of construction, which took place a generation later. Tiles employed in this later phase were all old ones, reused.

Between 40 and 50 per cent of the floor tiles, and a similar proportion of the *tegulae* and *imbrices* from the roofs, were marked with inscriptions and decorative motifs before firing. These record the names of some fifty-six individuals, almost always in abbreviated form. The names are not evenly distributed among the tiles. More than 100 examples of some names have been found, while of others there are only one or two instances. Sixteen names are found on both the floor and the roof tiles, and show that both types were manufactured at the same time. The letters of the inscriptions

assembly room (Fig. 7). These inscriptions will be described and analysed by John Patterson in the forthcoming Final Report on the excavations.

[33] The tile industry at San Vincenzo will be described in some detail in the Final Report.

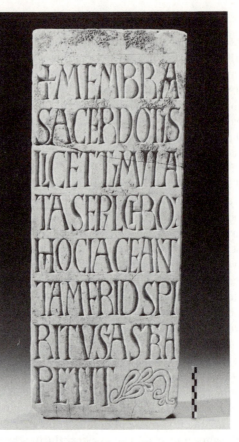

5   Epitaph of the priest Tamfrid, San Vincenzo al Volturno,
middle of the ninth century

6   Fragment of a funerary inscription, San Vincenzo al Volturno,
middle of the ninth century

are large and very legible. On the floor tiles and on the roof *tegulae* they vary in height from 2.5 to 48 centimetres, the majority being between about 6 and 25 centimetres tall, while on the smaller arched *imbrices* they vary from 2.5 to 8.5 centimetres, with a normal height of about 4 centimetres. The inscriptions are in letters of sufficient size to attract the eye, even to demand the attention, of any walking over them.

Only one of the tiles, laid in the floor of the assembly room, is inscribed with a full name: LIVTPERTI SVM (I am of Liutpertus) (Fig. 8). Other tiles marked with the name Liutpertus, and all of the other floor and roof tiles, carry abbrevated forms of names, with one, two, three or four letters. The abbreviated names include: ALIP (Alipertus), ge, GVN, LAN, me, sa, TEVP (Teupertus) and VR. Sometimes these inscribed tiles are embellished with compass-drawn designs of intersecting circles and arcs, or with reiterated undulating lines which apparently imitate the diagonally veined marbling of the painted dados of all the principal rooms of the monastery. When found *in situ*, the tiles with compass-drawn ornamentation are usually laid in prominent positions, at the thresholds of doorways, or before important features, such as the lector's pulpit in the refectory.

Tiles inscribed in this fashion, and dating from the early middle ages, are extremely rare. A few late Roman examples bearing abbreviated names in large letters have been found in Cividale, in the far north of Italy (two of these are displayed in the town archaeological museum), one dating from the fifth to the sixth centuries has been found in Naples, and a number of floor tiles from the church of San Giovanni at Canosa di Puglia carry the monogram of a sixth-century bishop of Canosa, Sabinus.[34] The only other site where quantities of similarly inscribed tiles have come to light in an early mediaeval context is Montecassino. There they have been found both beneath the eleventh-century church of Abbot Desiderius on top of the mountain, and in the town below in the church of Santa Maria delle Cinque Torri, constructed under Abbot Teodemar (778–97).[35] Both groups of tiles from Montecassino can be dated to the last quarter of the eighth century, that is, to approximately the same time as the production at San Vincenzo. Montecassino lies some 30 kilometres to the south-west; the two

---

[34] P. Arthur and D. Whitehouse, 'Appunti sulla produzione laterizia nell'Italia centro-meridionale tra il VI e XII secolo', *Archeologia Medievale* 10 (1983), figs. 3 and 7.

[35] E. Scaccia Scarafoni, 'La chiesa cassinese detta "Santa Maria delle Cinque Torri" ', *Rivista di Archeologia Cristiana* 22 (1946), 186; A. Pantoni, 'Su di un cimitero alto medioevale a Montecassino e sul sepolcro di Paolo Diacono', *Atti del 2. congresso internazionale di studi sull'alto medioevo. Grado 7–11 settembre 1952* (Spoleto, 1953), pp. 260–1; idem, *Le vicende della basilica di Montecassino attraverso la documentazione archeologica* (Monte-cassino, 1973), pp. 42, 84, fig. 40; idem, 'Santa Maria delle Cinque Torri di Cassino: risultati e problemi', *Rivista di Archeologia Cristiana* 51 (1975), 252–6, figs. 6 and 7; Arthur and Whitehouse, 'Appunti sulla produzione laterizia', 529, fig. 5.

7 *(above)* Roman funerary inscription reused as a tread in a flight of steps, San Vincenzo at Volturno, *c.* 800

8 *(below left)* Floor tile with the inscription LIVTPERTI SVM assembly room, San Vincenzo al Volturno, *c.* 800

9 *(below right)* Floor tile with the inscription LAN, assembly room, San Vincenzo al volturno, *c.* 800

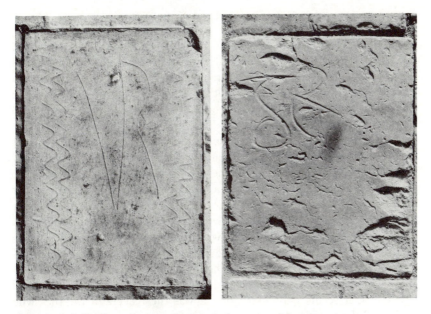

10 *(above left)* Floor tile with the inscription vr, and framing decoration of undulating lines, refectory, San Vincenzo al Volturno, *c.* 800

11 *(above right)* Floor tile with the inscription ge, assembly room, San Vincenzo at Volturno, *c.* 800

monasteries maintained close contact throughout the early middle ages, and their histories ran parallel courses. However, the tiles from the two neighbouring monasteries were not made by the same craftsmen. The inscribed names are, for the most part, different, and written by different hands, and those on the tiles from Montecassino tend to be either spelt out in full or to be in less abbreviated forms. This suggests that it was not the tilers themselves, but rather knowledge of the technology of tile-making, and the notion of inscribing the names, that travelled from the one place to the other.

Neither the identities of the men named on the tiles from San Vincenzo, nor the meaning of these names, is immediately obvious. The one fully legible tile on which a name is spelt out in full, the one in the assembly room with the inscription: LIVTPERTI SVM, gives the name in the genitive. The tile proclaims: 'I am the tile of Liutpert'. One possibility is that the inscriptions record the names of benefactors who had contributed towards the construction of the monastery. There was, in late antiquity, an established custom of individuals donating particular areas of mosaic paving in churches. An inscription recording the name of the donor, and sometimes the area paid for, would be worked into the mosaic of the floor. Instances of this practice are to be found at Grado, in the sixth-century pavement of the cathedral and in the fifth-century floor of the church of Santa Maria.[36] However, at San Vincenzo various factors suggest that the names are likely to be those of the men who made the tiles, and not those of friends of the monastery who contributed towards its rebuilding. First, tiles carrying a particular name are not laid in groups, as one would expect if a benefactor was involved, but are set among tiles bearing other names, in seemingly random sequence. Second, the bare record of the name, almost always in abbreviated form, makes it most unlikely that the names of donors are recorded here. Their identity would have been forgotten within a generation. Third, the manner in which a particular name is recorded on different tiles is not standard. A name can be abbreviated in various ways, for instance Liutpertus, which is abbreviated 'LI', 'LI', or 'L'. Fourth, each name, on all the tiles on which it is found, appears to be by a particular hand. To judge from the script, it does not seem that any one hand inscribed a number of different names on tiles. All in all, it seems most likely that it was the makers of the tiles who inscribed their own names into the clay before firing.

If we are right, and it was the tilers who drew the inscriptions into the tiles, it is clear that they were literate, at least to the extent of being able to write their own names. None of the hands responsible for the tiles is hopelessly unpractised, and some of them appear to be well trained, and fully conversant with the conventions of contemporary scribal practice – the abbreviations 'ge' (Fig. 11), 'me' and 'sa' were all written by men well acquainted with pre Caroline cursive script. It is most likely that the monks themselves were the tilers. All would probably have been able to read, many would have been able to write and some among them would have been trained scribes. The great number of names, probably fifty-six in all, the frequent incidence of some and the sporadic and rare occurrence of others, would be consonant with a situation in which a number of the monks were detailed to manufacture the tiles, while many of their brethren gave occasional assistance, or tried their hands at turning out half a dozen items, each man taking pride in inscribing his name.

A further question is why the men who made the tiles took such pains to record their names on them. A possible explanation might be that the inscriptions served to keep a tally of the number of items made by each individual, perhaps to facilitate the calculation of payment. However, if this had been the purpose of the names, one would have expected either every tile to be inscribed, or else every fifth or tenth, or so, so as to keep a record of

---

[36] G. Brusin, *Aquileia e Grado: Guida storico-artistica* (Padua, 1964), p. 269, fig. 159, pp. 247–8, fig. 143.

production. And, if it was the monks who made the tiles, it is almost inconceivable that they would have demanded or received payment.

It is possible that the makers inscribed their tiles as an act of humility and self-mortification, in the knowledge that their names were destined to be trodden over by future generations of monks, and by visitors to the monastery, year in and year out. However, the inscriptions and the ornamental motifs of the roof tiles, which appear with a frequency more or less equal to those on the floor tiles, clearly cannot be explained in this way. They would have been fully visible probably only to people engaged on repairing the roofs of the buildings. Besides, many of the names on the floor tiles are inscribed with considerable flourish in large characters, and a not inconsiderable number are grandly framed by undulating lines imitating the veining of marble, or by elaborate compositions of compass-drawn circles and arcs. All this is hardly compatible with a desire for self-abasement and mortification.

The fact that almost 50 per cent of the floor tiles and many of the roof tiles bear names, and that there is a very uneven distribution of the numbers of tiles carrying each name, indicates, on the one hand, a certain want of system and economy in the production of the tiles, and, on the other hand, a great interest in, even an infatuation with, writing, and perhaps also a concern to advertize mastery of the skills of literacy.

Undoubtedly the most exceptional and the most technically elaborate inscriptions at San Vincenzo were those composed of large gilded metal letters, which were set up on the façades of more than one of the principal buildings of the monastery in the early ninth century. Angelo Pantoni, the distinguished architect, archaeologist and antiquary of Montecassino, recognized two limestone slabs which had been reused in the *opus sectile* pavement of the Romanesque abbey church of San Vincenzo, constructed by the Abbots Gerard and Benedict on the new site in the years around 1100, as fragments of the setting of the gilded inscription which their predecessor Iosue is recorded as having placed on the façade of his own new basilica of San Vincenzo in the first decade of the ninth century.[37] These two pieces are at present set into the interior wall of the north aisle of the new abbey church of San Vincenzo, where the full text of the original inscription has been completed with painted characters (Figs. 12 and 13).

The larger of the two fragments measures 62.7×30.8 cm, the smaller, 18×17.5 cm, and both are about 4 cm thick. The first bears the letters RDO, the second, the remains of the letters ES. The letters themselves are lost, and what has survived are the shallow sunken settings cut to the shapes of the

...VI R.D.O MINI IOSVESTRVXIT...

AVANZI DELLA GRANDE
ISCRIZIONE POSTA
DALL'ABATE GIOSVÈ(797-817)
SVLLA FACCIATA DELLA
BASILICA DA LVI ERETTA

12 Fragment of setting for metal letters, from the inscription of
Abbot Iosue, San Vincenzo al Volturno, beginning of the
ninth century

metal characters, which were probably laid in flush with the surface of the
stone. None of these letter-settings is completely preserved, but enough
remains of the larger fragment to show that the letters were once between 29
and 30 centimetres in height, that is about 1 Roman foot (29.6 cm). The
material of the letters themselves was, in all probability, an alloy of copper,
a metal which is most suited for gilding.

That the fragments really are mediaeval, and are not from a Roman
imperial inscription, is clear both from the forms of the letters and from the
manner of attachment to the support. The letters are distinctly irregular in
execution: 'O' is asymmetrical about its vertical axis, and the vertical shaft
of 'D' bows out to the left; and two of them are noticeably un-Roman in
design: 'O' is vertically elongated and faintly pointed, and the leg of 'R' has a
reverse curve, forms which are typical of ninth-century carved and painted
inscriptions from San Vincenzo. Furthermore, the letters from San
Vincenzo do not have the delicate and prominent serifs which are so
characteristic a feature of ancient Roman monumental capitals. The settings are also uncharacteristic of Roman work. Roman metal letters are
usually quite substantial objects, and lie in deep sockets cut into the
underlying stone support. They are secured by means of small rectangular
lugs which project from their rear surfaces and are set in lead in corresponding rectangular cuts in the floors of the sockets. The letters at San Vincenzo,
by contrast, seem to have been very thin, their sockets being only between 2
and 4 millimetres deep, and they were held in place by round-sectioned
rivets which passed right through the thickness of the stone support. This
manner of fixing is apparently unparalleled on Roman monuments.

The surviving characters on the two fragments retrieved by Pantoni from

13 Fragment of setting for metal letters, from the inscription of Abbot Iosue, San Vincenzo al Volturno, beginning of the ninth century

the pavement of the Romanesque abbey church fit perfectly into the text of the inscription which is recorded as having been set up in golden letters on the façade of the abbey church of San Vincenzo, by Abbot Iosue, in the first years of the ninth century:

> Quaeque vides ospes pendencia celsa vel ima
> Vir Domini Iosue struxit cum fratribus una.[38]

The overall length of the inscription on the front of Iosue's San Vincenzo can roughly be calculated from the two fragments re-used in the floor of new abbey church. The mean width of a letter, to judge from the three preserved on the larger fragment, was about 15 centimetres, and the mean interval

[38] *Chron. Vult.*, I, p. 221. The passage in which the erection of this inscription is referred to, reads as follows: 'Ita autem virtus Domini cor regis [Louis the Pious] in huius operis amore convertit, et fratrum devocionem ac laborancium manus iuvit, ut non multo tempore preclaro opere et maximis columpnis ecclesia levaretur, in cuius ecclesie fronte ita, deauratis litteris, legebatur: Quaeque vides, ospes, pendencia celsa vel ima, Vir Domini Iosue struxit cum fratribus una' – 'The power of the Lord so affected the heart of the king with love of this work, and strengthened the devotion of the monks and the hands of the labourers, that in a short time the church was constructed with outstanding workmanship and with great columns: and on the façade of this church there could be read, in gilded letters: "Whatever lofty structures you see here, traveller, extending from low on high, were built by the servant of the Lord, Iosue, and his brother monks".' I am grateful to Michael Lapidge for help with this translation.

between them 5 centimetres. Consequently, the length of the inscription would have been something like 14.5 metres. It is likely that an inscription of these proportions would have run across the façade of the nave of the church, high up, under the base of its gable, in the manner of an inscription on the front of a Roman temple. The width of the nave of Iosue's church can roughly be calculated. The overall width of the building is recorded in the Chronicle of the abbey as 16 *passus*.[39] The *passus* of 5 standard Roman feet of 29.6 centimetres had a length of 1.48 metres, which if applied to Iosue's church would make its overall width 23.68 metres. But in the pre-metric period the length of the *passus* varied greatly from area to area. The *passus* which seems geographically most relevant to usage at San Vincenzo, one which is recorded as having been widely used in Campania and southern Abruzzo, measures 1.846 metres.[40] The antiquity of this particular local standard is uncertain, but local norms of measurement are likely to be fixed by tradition and to have long ancestries, and it is at least possible that this one, which was in use in the early modern period, was in origin far older. The application of this local standard for the *passus* to the measurements of the basilica recorded in the Chronicle would give a width of 29.536 metres for the full church, nave and aisles. Assuming that this *passus* of 1.846 metres is the one referred to by the chronicler, and assuming that the proportions of Iosue's church were similar to those of a contemporary columnar basilica, whose dimensions are known, San Salvatore in Cassino, at the foot of Montecassino, in which each aisle was roughly half the width

---

[39] *Chron. Vult.*, I, p. 221.

[40] Various lengths of *passus* in use in Italy, including the *passus* of 1.846 metres, are collected by R.E. Zupko, *Italian Weights and Measures from the Middle Ages to the Nineteenth Century* (Philadelphia, 1981), pp. 187–8. Pantoni, *Le chiese*, p. 21, briefly discusses the lengths of foot and *passus* current in Italy in the middle ages, in connection with the dimensions of Iosue's church, and opts for a short *passus*, consisting of 5 Liutprandian feet of 28.5 centimetres each. This would give a width of 22.80 metres for Iosue's church. Pantoni's choice of the Liutprandian foot is determined by his observation that the dimensions given in the chronicle would more or less accord with those of the rebuilt abbey church of *c.* 1100 if calculated on the basis of this standard, and by his belief that this new edifice, whose dimensions have been recovered by excavation, was constructed directly over Iosue's earlier church, and that the two buildings were more or less of the same size. However, the recent excavations have shown that the site of the new church of San Vincenzo was not settled by the monks before the late eleventh century, and that Iosue's church was almost certainly located at the original site of the monastery on the other side of the river. Archaeological excavation has so far thrown no light on the dimensions of the earlier building.

  A. Pantoni, citing F. Guillaume, *Essai historique sur l'abbaye de Cava* (Cava dei Tireni, 1987), p. xiv, also refers to a long *passus* of 5.5 feet, varying between 1.87 and 1.96 metres, which he says was widely used in the middle ages. This long *passus* is close in length to the Campano-Abruzzan *passus* of 1.846 metres, which we have identified as a possible candidate for the *passus* refered to in the Chronicle of San Vincenzo.

14 Fragment of setting for metal letters, San Vincenzo al Volturno, excavations

of the nave, the width of the nave of Iosue's San Vincenzo would have been about 14.75 metres.[41] In this case, the two verses of the inscription would probably have been laid out in a single long line of script, something like 14.5 metres in length, fitting quite precisely the width of the façade of the nave.

Three further fragments of settings of large metal letters have been found during the survey and excavation on the site of the early mediaeval monastery: the straight sloping member of a letter, perhaps the leg of an 'A'; the terminals of two adjacent, unidentifiable characters (Fig. 14); and a small fragment of the straight member of a further letter. All three of these settings are pierced by the characteristic round rivet holes found on the two sections reused in the floor of the Romanesque abbey church. Two of the pieces were found at the northern end of the monastery, one in a late mediaeval fill in the area of the vestibule, the other in an eleventh-century

---

[41] San Salvatore, which was erected in the time of Abbot Gisulf of Montecassino (797–817), is now destroyed, but it survived into the eighteenth century when an accurate plan and elevation was made by Erasmo Gattola. See G. Carbonara, *Iussu Desiderii: Montecassino e l'architettura campano-abruzzese nell'undicesimo secolo* (Rome, 1979), ill. 2.

destruction layer over the garden atrium. The third was picked up on the surface, on the plain at the south-eastern corner of the Colle della Torre, immediately in front of the pilastered façade of a prominent structure of *c.* 800, which has been tentatively identified as Abbot Iosue's abbey church of San Vincenzo. However, the settings on these fragments, and those recovered from the pavement of the Romanesque abbey church by Pantoni, differ in their cutting and in the diameter of their rivet-holes. The shafts of the letters of the fragments found in the floor of the new abbey church seem to have been narrower than those of the second and third fragments found on the site of the early monastery, and the rivet-holes of the former fragments have a somewhat wider bore than those found during the excavations. The settings in the first and second fragments from the old site are sharply cut with steeply sloping sides. Those of the third fragment and of the two pieces from the floor of the abbey church are less exact in their cutting. There is a distinct possibility that different craftsmen were responsible for these various pieces, and that more than one of the early ninth-century buildings at San Vincenzo carried inscriptions in large gilded-copper letters on their façades.

These letter-settings are remarkable on two counts. First, inscriptions of large metal letters were employed only very rarely in the middle ages, and, second, the practice of setting monumental inscriptions of any kind up on the façades of buildings was more or less totally abandoned in late antiquity. In Roman antiquity, inscriptions in large metal characters had been common, and had been used, throughout the Empire, in a variety of contexts, on the façades of temples,[42] on triumphal arches,[43] on city gates,[44]

---

[42] For example, on the Augustan Maison Carrée at Nîmes: R. Amy and P. Gros, *La Maison Carrée de Nîmes*, 38th supplement to *Gallia*, 2 vols. (Paris, 1979), I, pp. 177–95, II, pls. 41, 74a, b and c; on the temple in the main square at Assisi, and in Rome, on the Pantheon: W.L. MacDonald, *The Architecture of the Roman Empire, I: An Introductory Study* (rev. edn, New Haven and Connecticut, 1982), pls. 96, 102; on the Temple of Hadrian: E. Diehl, *Inscriptiones Latinae* (Bonn. 1912), pl. 17; and on the Temple of Antoninus and Faustina in the Forum Romanum: R. Cagnat, *Cours d'épigraphie latine* (Paris, 1914), pl. XI, 2.

[43] For example, on the Arch of Cottius at Susa: J.E. Sandys, *Latin Epigraphy* (Cambridge, 1919), p. 122; on that of Augustus at Aosta; and, in Rome, on those of Claudius: E. Nash, *Pictorial Dictionary of Ancient Rome*, 2 vols. (rev. edn, London, 1968), I, figs. 106 and 107; of Titus: Cagnat, *Cours d'épigraphie*, pl. VIII, 2, Nash, *Pictorial Dictionary of Ancient Rome*, I, fig. 143; of Septimius Severus: R. Brilliant, 'The Arch of Septimius Severus in the Roman Forum', *Memoirs of the American Academy in Rome* 29 (1967), pls. 14, 15a, 16a and b; and of Constantine: Cagnat, *Cours d'épigraphie*, pl. XX, 1, Nash, *Pictorial Dictionary of Ancient Rome*, I, fig. 112; and on that of Trajan at Benevento: M. Rotili, *L'Arco di Traiano a Benevento* (Rome, 1972), pls. III, VII. For comparative illustrations of inscriptions on arches, see Diehl, *Inscriptiones Latinae*, pl. 26.

[44] For example, on the Claudian Porta Maggiore, at Rome: Nash, *Pictorial Dictionary of Ancient Rome*, II, fig. 968; and on the triple gate at Pisidian Antioch, erected by Gaius

on public buildings,[45] on the bases of columns and statues[46] and even set flat into the pavements of fora and other public spaces.[47] However, metal inscriptions seem to have gone out of fashion in the fourth century. One of the last instances of their use on a major monument was on the Arch of Constantine in Rome, dedicated in   315. For more than thirteen centuries they almost completely disappeared; and it was not until the seventeenth century that they began to be reintroduced.[48]

Apart from San Vincenzo, they are met with only once on an early mediaeval building: in the framed inscription set high up on the façade of the Westwerk at Corvey, a late Carolingian structure, erected between 873 and 885.[49] There, the inscription, which calls on God and his angels to protect the monastery, is in metal letters 11 centimetres high, four short lines within a frame 84 centimetres high and 168 centimetres wide. The script is in well-proportioned square classicizing capitals.

The small scale of the letters of two metal-letter inscriptions known from the twelfth century makes them essentially different in kind from the ones from San Vincenzo. Abbot Suger, in his *Liber de rebus in administratione sua gesta*, and in his *Libellus alter de consecratione ecclesiae Sancti Dionysii*, records a dedicatory inscription in gilded copper letters, which he ordered for his new church of St Denis.[50] In the latter work he gives its

Julius Asper, consul in AD 212: D.M. Robinson, 'Roman sculptures from Colonia Caesarea (Pisidian Antioch)', *Art Bulletin* 9, no. 1, (1926), 45–6, figs. 1 and 67. I owe this reference to Stephen Mitchell of University College, Swansea.

[45] For example, on the basilica in the forum at Silchester, in Britain: G.S. Boon, *Silchester, the Roman Town of Coleva* (2nd edn, Newton Abbot, 1974), p. 116.

[46] For example, on the base of the column of Antoninus Pius, erected in AD 161, now in the Vatican: Sandys, *Latin Epigraphy*, p. 128; and an inscription with a dedication to the emperor Tiberius, from the base of an equestrian monument in the forum at Saepinum, in the Biferno valley, north of Benevento.

[47] For example, the inscription which spans the forum at Saepinum, and the inscriptions on the dial of the great *solarium* of Augustus in Rome: E. Buchner, *Die Sonnenuhr des Augustus* (Mainz am Rhein, 1982), pls. 134–41, *Nachtrag*, pls. 1, 3–6.

[48] It appears that it was in Paris, in the mid-seventeenth century, that monumental inscriptions in metal letters were first reintroduced in modern times. Two early examples can be seen on Lemercier's portal at the Sorbonne of 1641, and on the façade of the church of the Val-de-Grâce, erected in the mid-1640s (M. Fleury, A. Erlande-Brandenburg and J.-P. Babélon, *Paris Monumental* (Paris, 1974), figs. 164, 225. For this information I am indebted to James Mosley, of the St Bride Printing Library in London, and to David Thomson, of the University of East Anglia.

[49] W. Effmann, *Die Kirche der Abtei Corvey* (Paderborn, 1929), p. 11, pl. 30,2; *Kunst und Kultur im Weserraum 800–1600, Ausstellung des Landes Nordrhein-Westfalen*, 2 vols. (Corvey, 1966), I: *Beiträge zur Geschichte und Kunst*, p. 20, II: *Katalog*, no. 378, p. 645; H. Thümmler, *Weserbaukunst im Mittelalter* (Hameln, 1970), figs. 2 and 32.

[50] E. Panofsky, *Abbot Suger on the Abbey Church of St.-Denis and its Art Treasures*, ed. G.

location as *super portas . . . deauratas*, that is, over the golden historiated doors in the central portal of the west front. Thus it was set low down on the façade, so as to be readily visible to any person entering the church, and the letters were probably quite modest in size. This is certainly the case with the mid-twelfth-century metal (leaden?) inscriptions on two brackets supporting sculpted groups of figures which flank the west portal of the cathedral at Termoli, in Molise.

The only other ninth-century phenomenon which is in any way comparable to the inscriptions in metal letters at San Vincenzo and at Corvey is a series of gravestones from Saint-Martin at Tours, of the second quarter of the century, with legends in lead letters in quite well-formed romanizing capitals, between 5 and 6 centimetres high, let into the surface of the stone;[51] and a fragment of an epitaph preserved in one of the cloisters at the abbey of Farfa, which has been identified as that of the Abbot Ingoald, who died around 830.[52] The latter, which is badly damaged, carried an inscription in two lines of metal letters about 10 centimetres high.[53]

In setting a great gilded-copper inscription on his new church at San Vincenzo, Abbot Iosue was clearly reviving Roman practice. His action was highly original, even idiosyncratic, seemingly without exact parallel in the years around 800, a period in which interest in Roman antiquity was becoming more intense in western Europe. Not only the idea of using large metal letters was taken from Roman usage, but also certain details of the

---

Panofsky-Soergel (2nd edn, Princeton, 1979), pp. 46–7, 98–9. Paul Williamson, of the Victoria and Albert Museum, drew my attention to Suger's accounts of this inscription. Another instance of the use of metal letters in the twelfth century is to be found in the prominent inscription which runs round the main entablature of the ciborium over the high altar in San Nicola in Bari: see C.A. Willemsen and D. Odenthal, *Puglia, Terra dei Normanni e degli Svevi* (Bari, 1959), pl. 183.

[51] P. Descamps, 'Paléographie des inscriptions de la fin de l'époque mérovingienne aux dernières années du XIIe siècle', *Bulletin Monumental* 88 (1929), pp. 5–86, pl. II, fig. 2; M. Vieillard-Troiekouroff, 'Les Sculptures et les objets préromans retrouvés dans les fouilles de 1860 et de 1886 à Saint-Martin de Tours', *Cahiers Archéologiques* 13 (1962), 112–13, figs. 33–5; N. Gray, *A History of Lettering: Creative Experiment and Letter Identity* (Oxford, 1986), fig. 69.

[52] David Whitehouse, of the Corning Museum of Glass, has tentatively identified Ingoald as the subject of this epitaph.

[53] Gray, *A History of Lettering*, p. 86, apparently refers to this fragment. The metal characters have been removed by robbers, but the settings give the outlines of rather irregularly formed classicizing square capitals, with rectangular cuttings to take the fixing lugs. This inscription, like the well-known epitaph of Ingoald's successor, Sicardus (C.B. McClendon, 'An early funerary portrait from the medieval abbey at Farfa', *Gesta* 22/1 (1983), 13–26, fig. 9), has an enframing moulding which does not project to protect the lettering, as is almost invariably the case with framed classical inscriptions. Instead the moulding is sunk into the surface of the slab.

fragmentary inscriptions from San Vincenzo seem to reveal a close acquaintance with Roman exemplars.

No complete letter from the San Vincenzo inscriptions survives, but enough remains of the two fragments which can be certainly associated with Iosue's inscription to show that the letters were originally about 29 to 30 centimetres tall. This is close to 1 Roman foot (29.6 cm). The precise measurements of the characters of inaccessible inscriptions on Roman monuments are hard to come by, but in two instances where I have been able to ascertain the size of the letters, they are exactly, or close to, 1 Roman foot in height: the inscription on the front of the Maison Carrée at Nîmes, where the letters of the two-line inscription are precisely 29.6 centimetres high,[54] and the inscriptions on the attic of the Arch of Constantine in Rome, where they are slightly larger, between 30 and 32 centimetres. It is possible that the foot-high letter was a size regularly employed on Roman buildings, and that the measurements of the inscription on Iosue's church of San Vincenzo were taken from standard Roman practice.

A second feature of the fragments seems to show that the makers of the inscription may have taken a particular accessible Roman example as their model. As was said above, Roman metal letters were usually anchored to their support by small rectangular lugs which projected from their rear surface and were set in lead in corresponding rectangular sockets cut into the stone. The inscriptions from San Vincenzo are remarkable in that they were held in position by round-sectioned rivets which passed right through the thickness of the stone support. Occasionally Roman metal letters were held in place by round-sectioned lugs, or nails. One instance of this is a gilded bronze letter 'V' found at Colchester, which was secured by two nails which passed through its arms.[55] Another inscription with metal letters held in place by small round-sectioned dowels has been found at a site closer at hand. This bears a dedication to Tiberius, and comes from the base of an equestrian statue which stood on the south-west side of the forum at Saepinum, the Roman town on the road between modern Boiano and Benevento, about 60 kilometres to the south-east of San Vincenzo.[56] The holes for the dowels do not pass right through the stone slab, but the sockets for the letters, their copper fillings long-since removed to reveal the small round holes for attachment, could well have provided the makers of the San

---

[54] Amy and Gros, *La Maison Carrée de Nîmes*, I, pp. 177–95, especially p. 187, and II, pls. 41, 74a, b, and c.

[55] R.G. Collingwood and R.P. Wright, *The Roman Inscriptions of Britain*, I (Oxford, 1965), p. 64, no. 198.

[56] It is now kept in one of the two small museums at the site.

Vincenzo inscriptions with the idea of using long rivets to tie their letters to their stone supports.[57]

The gilded metal inscriptions from San Vincenzo were remarkable also in another way. Dedicatory inscriptions in large carved letters are found on the façades of ancient Roman buildings in all provinces of the Empire. They are one of the characteristic features of any major Roman settlement. On mediaeval monuments, however, they are very rare indeed. As was the case with metal letters, so also the practice of setting a large carved inscription on the façade of a building was abandoned in late antiquity; and the tradition was not revived until the middle of the fifteenth century, when Leone Battista Alberti ran the dedicatory inscription, in large Roman capitals, across the façade of his temple, the Tempio Malatestiano, at Rimini.[58]

In mediaeval Italy the normal position for an inscription recording the foundation or dedication of a church was outside, immediately over or flanking one of the principal doors, or inside, usually in the main apse. The few cases in which an inscription of large letters was set in a prominent position high up on the front of a building are instructive. There are only a handful of instances. The first are the inscriptions on the front and on the side-porches of the Tempietto sul Clitunno, near Spoleto. This is a small Christian oratory, constructed by the local Lombard aristocracy, probably in the second half of the seventh century, but so classicizing in its form and ornamentation, and using Roman spolia so successfully, that Palladio published it as an ancient temple,[59] and modern scholars have sometimes been tempted to date it centuries too early.[60] The inscription which runs across the front of the building under its main pediment is in elegantly cut romanizing capitals, 15 centimetres tall. The reason for the extraordinary classicizing appearance of this building has never been satisfactorily explained. But the inscriptions play a crucial role in the Roman language of its architecture.[61] A second instance of a large inscription on the front of an early mediaeval church is on the cathedral at Salerno, which was con-

---

[57] To judge from the published photographs, the letters of the inscriptions at Corvey may also have heen held in place by small round dowels, rather than by rectangular lugs: Thümmler, *Weserbaukunst im Mittelalter*, fig. 32.

[58] L.H. Heydenreich and W. Lotz, *Architecture in Italy 1400 to 1600* (Harmondsworth, 1974), fig. 19; A. Bartram, *Lettering in Architecture* (London, 1975), figs. 15 and 16.

[59] A. Palladio, *I quattro libri dell'architettura*, 8 vols. (Venice, 1570), IV, pp. 98–102.

[60] The most recent publication on the Tempietto, in which the earlier literature is cited, is *I dipinti murali e l'edicola marmorea del tempietto sul Clitunno*, ed. G. Benazzi (Spoleto, 1985).

[61] The inscriptions on the Tempietto sul Clitunno served as the inspiration for the ones on the façades of two other twelfth-century buildings in the vicinity, the cathedral at Foligno, and the church at Bovara.

secrated in July 1084.[62] This also runs directly beneath the gable of the façade, and is in large and carefully designed Roman capitals. These record that Robert Guiscard paid for the construction of the building from his own purse. Robert, who in 1084 had entered Rome, liberated the pope, Gregory VII, and had driven out the emperor Henry IV, is given the title: ROBBERTVS DVX. R. IMP. MAXIM[V]S TRIVMPHATOR, which has been completed 'Robbertus Dux Romani Imperii Maximus Triumphator'.[63] Robert is identified as a triumphator of or over the Roman Empire, and this may have been the reason for the decision to lay the inscription across the front of the building, in imitation of ancient Roman imperial usage.[64] Prominent inscriptions were also set on the façades of three churches of the late twelfth and the early thirteenth centuries: in elegant carved letters on the architraves of the porches of Ss. Giovanni e Paolo and San Giovanni in Laterano, in Rome, and in mosaic on the arch and porch on the front of the cathedral of Città Castellana. All three were the work of Roman *marmorarii*, who, in a broad climate of reform, drew heavily on ancient Roman and early Christian architecture and sculpted ornament.[65]

---

[62] E. Bertaux, *L'Art dans l'Italie méridional* (Paris and Rome, 1903), p. 318; M. de Angelis, *Nuova guida del Duomo di Salerno* (Salerno, 1937), pp. 23–5; A. Carucci, *Il Duomo di Salerno e il suo Museo* (Salerno, 1962), p. 27; H. Bloch, *Monte Cassino in the Middle Ages*, 3 vols. (Rome, 1986), I, p. 83. A. Thiery, in his commentary on Bertaux's text in the *Aggiornamento dell'opera di Emile Bertaux sotto la direzione di Adriano Prandi* (Rome, 1978), p. 554, seems to have the wrong inscription in mind. Bertaux, *L'Art dans l'Italie*, stated that the inscription was not put up in the eleventh century, but did not give his reasons.

[63] Carucci, *Il Duomo di Salerno*, p. 27; Bloch, *Monte Cassino in the Middle Ages*, I, p. 83 n. 2. The full text of the inscription runs as follows: 'M(atthaeo) A(postolo) ET EVA(n)GELISTAE PATRONO VRBIS ROBBERTVS DVX. R(omani?) IMP(erii?) MAXIM(U)S TRIVMPHATOR DE AERARIO PECVLIARI'.

[64] The implications of the titles given to Robert Guiscard in the inscription are obscure. They may refer to his entry into Rome and his effective victory over the recently crowned emperor, Henry IV. However, if the inscription is later than the consecration of the cathedral, as Bertaux believed, the titles may be no more than a fanciful tribute to the great duke who was responsible for its rebuilding. For Robert's activities in the 1080s, see: F. Chalandon, *Histoire de la domination normande en Italie et en Sicilie*, 2 vols. (Paris, 1900), I, pp. 258–84; H.E.J. Cowdrey, *The Age of Desiderius: Montecassino, the Papacy, and the Normans in the Eleventh and Early Twelfth Centuries* (Oxford, 1983), pp. 136–76.

[65] The porch of the Lateran basilica, which was demolished in the early eighteenth century, bore the name of the mason Nicolaus de Angelo, and the porch of Ss. Giovanni e Paolo has been attributed to the same master. Both were erected probably around 1180. The inscriptions on the central arch of the porch of Città Castellana give the names of master Iacobus and his son Cosmas and the date 1210. The work of the Roman *marmorarii* is the subject of an excellent recent book, which covers the subject in exhaustive detail: P.C. Claussen, *Magistri Doctissimi Romani: Die römischen Marmorkünstler des Mittelalters* (Stuttgart, 1987), pp. 22–6, fig. 17 (San Giovanni in Laterano), pp. 32–3, figs. 35, 36 (Ss.

It is clear that not only the gilded metal letters, but also the very presence of a long dedicatory inscription on the façade of the abbey church of San Vincenzo, were extraordinary in an early mediaeval context. In both aspects of the inscription, specific reference is made to imperial Roman practice.

The ninth-century visitor to San Vincenzo would have been confronted by script wherever he looked. As he approached the monastery, his eye would have been caught by the great inscription set high up on the front of the principal church, glinting golden in the sunlight. Once inside the complex, *tituli* accompanying painted images would have spoken to him from every wall, and as he entered the assembly room the line of Prophets, almost life-size, would have cried out to him the words written on their long scrolls.[66] Walking through the rooms, his feet touched script at almost every step, the names of the tilers written on the tiles in large letters. Periodically he would come across an ancient Roman funerary inscription incorporated into the new monastic structure, and in the areas reserved for the burial of the monks stone slabs carved with epitaphs in the incisive and elegant script practised by the monastery's masons were set into the floor over the individual inhumations. If our traveller's visit had happened to coincide with the burial of one of the members of the community, just before the grave was closed he would probably have caught a glimpse of a protective *formula* written in neat capitals on the plaster behind the deceased man's head. The quantity of lettering at San Vincenzo, the care which was taken over it, and the variety of the media and forms in which it was executed, are remarkable.

The various means of exhibiting script employed in the churches and the other buildings derive from disparate traditions. It would appear that a purposeful effort was made by the men coordinating the expansion and the reconstruction of the monastery to feature lettering of various kinds on a

---

Giovanni e Paolo), pp. 82–91, figs. 98, 99, 103, 104 (Città Castellana). Good illustrations of the inscription on the porch of Ss. Giovanni e Paolo are to be found in Bartram, *Lettering in Architecture*, figs. 11–14. The revival of Roman and early Christian types and motifs in Rome in the late eleventh and the twelfth centuries is briefly discussed by Claussen, *Magistri Doctissimi Romani*, pp. 239–41), and at some length by R. Krautheimer, *Rome: Profile of a City, 312–1308* (Princeton, 1980), pp. 161–202.

[66] A vivid reference to the mute utterances of imaged Prophets is given by the late ninth-century patriarch of Constantinople, Photius, in his description of the church of the Virgin of the Pharos, in the Imperial Palace at Constantinople. It is most likely that the texts he records were written on scrolls held up by the figures on the walls of the church: 'A choir of apostles and martyrs, yea of prophets, too, and patriarchs fill and beautify the whole church with their images. Of these, one (King David), though silent, cries out his sayings of yore, "How amiable are they tabernacles, O Lord of hosts! My soul longeth, yea, even fainteth in the courts of the Lord"; another (Jacob), "How wonderful is this place; this is none other but the house of God" ' (*The Homilies of Photius*, ed. Mango, p. 188; *idem*, *The Art of the Byzantine Empire*, p. 186).

wide selection of differing supports, some of which would have been quite novel to a contemporary observer. The effect of this would have been to arouse curiosity and interest and to focus attention sharply on the written word.

The one thing that is missing in this manifold production of script is the scriptorium and the manuscripts written by the monks. It is most unfortunate that not a single eighth- or ninth-century manuscript can be assigned with absolute certainty to San Vincenzo.[67] The community at this time was a large one, and it is very likely that there was an active scriptorium at the monastery.[68] Indeed, what we know of the life and work of one of its most distinguished members, Ambrose Autpert, presupposes the availability, and probably also the production, of books. Autpert, who acted as abbot for a brief spell in the late 770s, was a renowned theologian who had composed a commentary on the Apocalypse and mariological homilies, as well as an account of the foundation of the monastery and of the lives of the three founders.[69] From his own testimony we know that he had spent his adult life at San Vincenzo and had been educated there.[70]

One early book has been associated with San Vincenzo. This is a copy of the Gospels, in the British Library (Add. 5463), known as the Codex Beneventanus.[71] The connection with San Vincenzo is based on two things: on the name 'patris Atoni', who is recorded in the colophon as having commissioned the manuscript, and who has been identified with the Ato who was abbot of San Vincenzo in the mid-eighth century (739–60); and on the demonstrable presence of the book, in the tenth century, in a house subject to San Vincenzo, the convent of San Pietro in Benevento. The

---

[67] It is not until the eleventh century that there is fairly conclusive evidence for book production at the monastery. The Chronicle records that Abbot Ylarius (1011–45) had books made for the newly restored church of San Vincenzo (*Chron. Vult.*, III, pp. 77–8); and there is a late eleventh-century manuscript, containing liturgical offices and prayers, now in the Vatican Library, cod. Chig. D.V.77, which was made for use at San Vincenzo (L. Duval-Arnould, 'Les Manuscrits de San Vincenzo al Volturno', in *Una grande abbazia altomedievale*, ed. Avagliano, pp. 362–5); but compare McKitterick, below, p. 316.

[68] For the size of the community at San Vincenzo in the late eighth and the ninth centuries, see n. 1, above.

[69] J. Winandy, *Ambroise Autpert moine et théologien* (Paris, 1953); C. Leonardi, 'Spiritualità di Ambrogio Autperto', *Studi medievali* 3rd series 9 (1968), 1–131.

[70] Winandy, *Ambroise Autpert*, pp. 14–16. For the significance of the Apocalypse in relation to the display of script, see McKitterick, below, pp. 314–18.

[71] E.A. Lowe, *Scriptura Beneventana*, 2 vols. (Oxford, 1929), I, no. iv; C. Nordenfalk, *Vier Kanonestafeln eines spätantiken Evangelienbuches* (Göteborg, 1937), *passim*; *idem, Die spätantiken Kanontafeln* (Göteborg, 1938), pp. 177–8, pls. 52–7; *CLA* II, 162; D.H. Wright, 'The canon tables of the Codex Beneventanus and related decoration', *DOP* 33 (1979), pp. 133–55; Duval-Arnould, 'Les Manuscrits de San Vincenzo al Volturno', pp. 354–60.

manuscript is elegantly produced, with text in an expert uncial, colophons in alternating lines of red and black capitals, and canon tables which are either a reused sixth-century set, or else exact copies of a sixth-century exemplar.[72] If the association with San Vincenzo is correct, the Codex Beneventanus would provide clear evidence of a high level of scribal practice at the monastery as early as the middle of the eighth century.

However, the scripts found in the manuscript, the uncial of the main text and the capitals of the incipits and explicits have almost nothing in common with the scripts used in the first half of the ninth century for painted, carved, incised and cast metal inscriptions at the monastery.[73] One explanation for this could be that the scribes working in the scriptorium were trained in completely different traditions from those followed by the painters, masons, tilers and metalsmiths; another could be that a new type of capital script was introduced in the late eighth century.[74] A third possibility, of course, is that the Ato named in the colophon is not the same man as the Abbot Ato, and that the Codex Beneventanus was not written at San Vincenzo.

The context for the display of script at San Vincenzo al Volturno in the last decades of the eighth and the first half of the ninth centuries is to be found in the great increase in the practice and use of writing, and the enhanced status it attained, in western Europe, during this period. Beginning in the last quarter of the eighth century, manuscripts were produced in considerably greater numbers than had been the case in the preceding 200 years. A new 'lower case' script, caroline minuscule, was devised, and quickly adopted by nearly all the major scriptoria of Continental northern Europe; ancient scripts – Roman square capitals and rustic capitals – were revived, redesigned and used in new contexts and new combinations; and the old book-hands, uncials and half-uncials, were adapted to conform to

---

[72] According to current scholarly opinion, the canon tables, with their elegant marbled columns, carefully depicted capitals and rich vocabulary of late antique ornament in the arches, are not mediaeval but are a reused sixth-century set: H. Belting, 'Probleme der Kunstgeschichte Italiens im Frühmittelalter', *Frühmittelalterliche Studien* 1 (1967), 104; Wright, 'The canon tables of the Codex Beneventanus', *passim*. See Duval-Arnould, 'Les Manuscrits de San Vincenzo al Volturno', pp. 358–9. However, the last word on this matter has probably not yet been said.

[73] Reproductions of script from the Codex Beneventanus have been published by Wright, 'The canon tables of the Codex Beneventanus', ills. 1–5, 9, 10, 12–15.

[74] This explanation does not find support in the one example of eighth-century script that has been found in the recent excavations at San Vincenzo, a tombstone with the epitaph of a monk, Ermecausus. The bowed members of the letters of this inscription have the peculiar exaggerated swellings which are occasionally found in ornamental display capitals in manuscripts from both Italy and north of the Alps in the second half of the eighth century. There is no trace of anything resembling this script in the Codex Beneventanus. Ermecausus' epitaph will be described and illustrated in the forthcoming Final Report on the excavations.

new concepts of harmonious design. Scribes and illuminators tried out new ways of laying out their texts, and experimented tirelessly with display scripts and with the ornamented initial letter, a phenomenon which had its origins in Roman scribal practice, but which had been developed in new directions in the British Isles, and simultaneously also in scriptoria in Merovingian Francia.[75]

It was the Carolingians who exploited script and the written word most fully. Charlemagne was particularly concerned to promote correct usage in speech and writing, and wanted schools to be established in monasteries and episcopal seats throughout his realm, for the purpose of teaching the basic skills of literacy, grammar, the study of literature, the rudiments of music and *computus*.[76] Writing was employed by the Carolingians for eminently practical purposes. Under Charlemagne it came to be used in many areas of the day-to-day administration of the realm,[77] and the emperor made full use of the church, with its educated and literate clergy and its network of communications, in the governing, administration and defence of his far-flung territories. In the monastic scriptoria the skills of reading and writing were developed to facilitate the study and editing of scripture and the copying and dissemination of texts. But writing also had strong symbolic associations. First, the written word was closely identified with the Christian faith. Christianity was preeminently the religion of the Word of the Book, and Charlemagne was a devout Christian, concerned to strengthen the church within his Empire. Second, literacy and the widespread use of writing in all spheres of life had been among the most salient characteristics of ancient Roman civilization. Carolingian scribes employed late antique scripts and artists looked for example to late antique traditions of ornamenting books, at the same time that scholars read ancient texts with attention and writers imitated the Roman poets and historians, and while

---

[75] For a discussion of the varieties of display script employed in Carolingian scriptoria, see the chapter by McKitterick in this volume, below, pp. 301–4; and for the early development of the decorated initial letter: C. Nordenfalk, *Die spätantiken Zierbuchstaben*, 2 vols. (Stockholm, 1970); J.J.G. Alexander, *The Decorated Letter* (London, 1978), pp. 8–11; O. Pächt, *Book Illumination of the Middle Ages* (London and Oxford, 1986), pp. 45–54, 63–76.

[76] See, in particular, the circular letter, *De Litteris Colendis:* H.R. Loyn and J. Percival, *The Reign of Charlemagne: Documents on Carolingian Government and Administration* (London, 1975), pp. 63–4; P.D. King, *Charlemagne: Translated Sources* (Kendal, 1987), pp. 232–3; and paragraph 72 of the capitulary of 789, known as the *Admonitio Generalis*: King, *Charlemagne*, p. 217, ed. *MGH Cap.* I, nos. 29 and 22, pp. 78–9 and 52–64, at pp. 59–60.

[77] F.L. Ganshof, 'Charlemagne et l'usage de l'écrit en matière administrative', *Le Moyen Age* 57 (1951), 1–25, reprinted in translation in his *The Carolingians and the Frankish Monarchy* (London, 1971), pp. 125–42. Compare Nelson, below, pp. 258–96, and McKitterick, *Carolingians*, pp. 23–75.

their ruler assumed the Roman imperial title and established a fixed residence at Aachen in the manner of a Roman emperor. Third, literacy and the use of writing were restricted to an elite, largely, but not exclusively, made up of monks and clerics.[78] Script, with its connotations of communication and administrative control, of access to religious truth and ancient wisdom, of education and literary achievement, was an extremely potent and visible symbol of political and cultural dominance. Anyone with pretensions to power in the ninth century made sure he had the allegiance and the service of subjects who practised the skills of literacy.

The revival of interest in literacy, the uses of writing and the study of literature was not confined to northern Europe in this period. To a more limited degree, a similar revival had taken place in the Lombard kingdom in northern Italy, in the first half of the eighth century, and subsequently in the duchy of Benevento in the south.[79] Significant developments in script were also taking place in southern Italy during this period. It was in the second half of the century, perhaps in the scriptorium at Montecassino, that the characteristic and distinctive Beneventan script, the *littera beneventana*, first made its appearance.[80]

Similarly, the prodigal display of painted imagery and decoration at San Vincenzo in the late eighth and ninth centuries has to be understood in the context of the rapidly increasing production and exploitation of visual imagery in the Carolingian Empire during this period. The experiments and inventions in Carolingian painting between the 790s and the middle of the following century are among the most astounding developments in the history of western art. Frankish artists, with only the most rudimentary native tradition to draw on, established norms of naturalistic figurative representation and canons of ornamentation, which determined some of the broad paths painting and sculpture in northern Europe were to follow for the following 400 years. The most successful inventions came out of ateliers associated with the royal court, or located in the great monasteries which enjoyed royal patronage and were controlled by abbots or bishops who kept

---

[78] This assertion should now be modified considerably in light of the evidence presented by McKitterick, *Carolingians*, especially pp. 77–134, 211–70.

[79] M. L. W. Laistner, *Thought and Letters in Western Europe A.D. 500 to 900* (new edn, Ithaca, New York, 1966), pp. 268–71; G. Cavallo, 'La trasmissione dei testi nell'area benevento-cassinese', *Settimane* 12 (Spoleto, 1975), 360–8; *idem*, 'Aspetti della produzione libraria nell'Italia meridionale longobarda', in *Libri e lettori nel medioevo: guida storica e critica*, ed. *idem* (Bari, 1983), pp. 101–12; *idem*, 'Libri e continuità della cultura antica in età barbarica', in *Magistra Barbaritas: I barbari in Italia*, ed. G.P. Carratelli (Milan, 1984), pp. 603–62, at pp. 635–51.

[80] For the earliest phases of the Beneventan script, see E.A. Lowe. *The Beneventan Script*, second edition revised and enlarged by V. Brown, Sussidi Eruditi 33, 2 vols. (Rome, 1980), I, pp. 40, 93–121; and Belting, *Studien*, p. 4.

close ties with the emperor: the Court School,[81] and the small group of contemporary artists who produced the Coronation Gospels of Charlemagne now in Vienna,[82] the scriptorium which flourished for twenty years at Hautvillers under the episcopate of Ebbo of Rheims,[83] the scriptorium at Tours under the Abbots Adalhard and Vivian,[84] and that at Metz under Bishop Drogo,[85] to name the most prominent centres. The production of illuminated manuscripts increased enormously in this period, and to judge both from documentary evidence and from the meagre and fragmentary remains that survive, churches, palaces and other public buildings received more extensive and magnificent schemes of painted decoration than had been the case in the preceding centuries.[86]

There was a revival of pictorial decoration also in Italy during the later eighth and the first half of the ninth centuries. This occurred in various parts of the country: in Rome, where, after a caesura of 200 years, churches were once again sumptuously adorned with mosaics and paintings;[87] in the old Lombard north, where there is considerable evidence of wall-paintings of the highest quality, best preserved in Santa Maria in Valle at Cividale[88] and in San Salvatore at Brescia;[89] and in the south, at Benevento, in the palace church of Santa Sophia.[90]

The reference to Roman imperial precedent so clearly expressed in the monumental inscription in gilded metal letters on the façade of the main

---

[81] W. Koehler, *Die karolingischen Miniaturen*, 5 vols. (Berlin, 1930–82), II: *Die Hofschule Karls des Grossen*.

[82] Koehler, *Die karolingischen Miniaturen*, III: *Erster Teil: Die Gruppe des Wiener Krönungs-Evangeliar. Zweiter Teil: Metzer Handschriften*.

[83] J. Hubert, J. Porcher and W.F. Volbach, *Carolingian Art* (London, 1970), pp. 92–123; C.R. Dodwell, *Painting in Europe, 800 to 1200* (Harmondsworth, 1971), pp. 30–3.

[84] Koehler, *Die karolingischen Miniaturen, I: Die Schule von Tours*.

[85] Koehler, *Die karolingischen Miniaturen*, III.

[86] See my article, 'Excavated wall-paintings in Germany, England and Italy: a preliminary survey', in *Early Medieval Wall-Painting and Painted Sculpture in the British Isles*, ed. S. Cather, D. Park and P. Williamson, BAR, British Series (Oxford, forthcoming).

[87] Krautheimer, *Rome: Profile of a City*, pp. 109–42.

[88] H. L'Orange and H. Torp, 'Il Tempietto longobardo di Cividale', in *Acta ad archaeologiam et historiam artium pertinentia*, Institutum Romanum Norvegiae 7, 3 vols. (Rome, 1977).

[89] G. Panazza, 'Gli scavi, l'architettura e gli affreschi della chiesa di S. Salvatore in Brescia', *Atti dell'ottavo congresso di studi sull'arte dell'alto medioevo*, 2 (1962); B.B. Anderson, 'The frescoes of San Salvatore in Brescia', unpublished PhD dissertation, University of California, Berkeley (Ann Arbor microfilms, 1976); A. Peroni, 'Problemi della decorazione pittorica del S.Salvatore di Brescia', in *Seminario internazionale sulla decorazione pittorica del San Salvatore di Brescia, Brescia 19–20 giugno 1981* (Pavia, 1983), pp. 17–46.

[90] Belting, *Studien*, pp. 44–53.

church of San Vincenzo, and also apparent in some aspects of the pictorial decoration of the monastery,[91] is also in line with the cultural preoccupations of the age. Scribes and artists both north of the Alps and in Italy drew extensively on Roman imperial and late antique early Christian models for patterns and ideas. In part this phenomenon of cultural retrospection stemmed from a politically and ideologically grounded concern with antique, particularly early Christian, precedent, which was shared by the Carolingian emperor, the pope and by other contemporary rulers, in their different ways.[92] However, perhaps equally important was the continuing existence, in the eighth and ninth centuries, of great numbers of ancient monuments and artefacts, which, with their powerful associations with a great imperial civilization of the past, would have provided early mediaeval artists with a spectacular and enormously various exemplary range of naturalistic imagery and ornament.

San Vincenzo was open to influence both from Lombard Benevento to the south and from the Franks to the north, and in the later eighth century there were strong Lombard and Frankish factions in the community.[93] The monastery stood in Lombard territory, quite close to the border between the Beneventan principality and the southern frontier of the Carolingian Empire, which after 774 extended down to a point well south of Rome. Throughout the first two centuries of its existence, San Vincenzo had close connections with the Lombard court in Benevento, and with the Lombard aristocracy of the region.[94] It had been founded in the first decade of the eighth century, by three Beneventan nobles; the majority of its abbots and a considerable proportion of its monks were of Lombard origin, and throughout the eighth and ninth centuries it continued to enjoy the support and benevolence of the rulers of Benevento and of local Lombard landowners.[95] The monastery came to possess extensive property in Beneventan

---

[91] The most prominent antique motif in the painted decoration is a pattern of overlapping parti-coloured tiles used on some of the benches running round the walls of the assembly room, which were constructed and decorated in the years around 800. This design had been common and widespread in antiquity, but it appears to have been almost unknown in the early middle ages. The only other instance of its use in early mediaeval Italy is to be found at Farfa, in the crypt at the western end of the first abbey church, and probably dates to the 830s, when Sicardus was abbot. See Mitchell, 'The painted decoration', pp. 143–4.

[92] P.E. Schramm, *Kaiser, Rom und Renovatio* (4th edn, Darmstadt, 1984), pp. 9–43; Krautheimer, *Rome: Profile of a City*, pp. 109–42.

[93] For the Lombard faction in the monastery, see M. del Treppo, 'Longobardi Franci e papato in due secoli di storia vulturnese', *Archivio storico per le provincie napoletane* NS 24 (1955), 50ff.

[94] Belting, *Studien*, pp. 226–7.

[95] *Chron. Vult., passim.*

territory and in the city of Benevento itself, and Arichis II (758–87) had placed two of his most prestigious foundations, San Salvatore in Alife, and San Pietro, outside the walls of Benevento, both female houses, under the jurisdiction of San Vincenzo.[96]

However, the new Carolingian rulers of Italy also took an interest in San Vincenzo. Charlemagne, in a diploma of 787, issued at the request of the Abbot Paul, confirmed the possessions of the monastery, allowed it the privilege of electing its own abbot, and granted it immunity from lay interference.[97] There was one occasion on which he intervened directly in the affairs of the monastery. In 783 the abbot, Poto, a Lombard, was accused by one of the Frankish faction of refusing to join the community in chanting the customary psalm, *Deus in nomine tuo salvum me fac*, for the safety and health of the Frankish king. When report of this was brought to Charlemagne, he ordered that Poto be suspended, summoned to Rome, and tried before a papal court of enquiry, to find out the truth of the allegation. In the event, Poto was acquitted of the charge, but was required to take an oath of allegiance to the king, and ten monks, drawn from both factions of the community, were commanded to attest under oath to his innocence. The monks requested leave from the pope to go to Charlemagne himself. Whether they took the oaths, and what the outcome of the matter was, is not recorded. However, this affair shows on the one hand, that Charlemagne was concerned to preserve his name and honour at San Vincenzo, and, on the other, that both Frankish and Lombard interests were strongly represented in the monastery, and that relations between the two factions were by no means always harmonious.[98]

The monk John, who composed the Chronicle of San Vincenzo in the second quarter of the twelfth century, makes a lot of this Carolingian connection and has much to say about the interest of Charlemagne and his successors in the monastery and the love which they bore it. He tells how Iosue (792–817), the abbot responsible for the reconstruction of the main abbey church of San Vincenzo, was of royal blood, and had been educated at the royal (Carolingian) court, and goes on to claim that Iosue's sister was the first wife of Charlemagne's son and successor as emperor, Louis.[99]

---

[96] *Ibid.*, I, pp. 135, 348–9, 170. See Belting, *Studien*, p. 227.

[97] *Chron. Vult.*, I, pp. 212–15.

[98] The evidence for the affair of Poto is contained in two letters from Pope Hadrian to Charlemagne, preserved in the *Codex Carolinus: MGH Epp. merov. et karol.* I (=*MGH Epp.* III). 66 and 67, pp. 593–7. See del Treppo, 'Longobardi Franci e papato', 50–4; O. Bertolini, 'Carlomagno e Benevento', in *Karl der Grosse, I: Persönlichkeit und Geschichte* ed. H. Beumann (Düsseldorf, 1965), pp. 625–31; Belting, *Studien*, pp. 226–7.

[99] *Chron. Vult.*, I, p. 219.

According to the chronicler, Louis, as Augustus and successor to Charlemagne as emperor, together with his wife, visited San Vincenzo twice, on the second occasion for the dedication of Iosue's church, which is recorded as having taken place in 808. The imperial couple are said to have presented the monastery with many gifts, and at the request of the abbot and the monks consigned to it an ancient temple in Capua with its great columns, to provide a source of building-material for the new church.[100] The chronicler's chronology is seriously awry. None of these claims can be substantiated today, many seem unlikely, and some are demonstrably untrue. One has to be extremely sceptical of everything the chronicler says concerning Charlemagne's and Louis' involvement with San Vincenzo, since it has been demonstrated that John forged a number of the diplomas confirming possessions and granting privileges to the monastery, which purport to have been issued by the two rulers.[101] Nevertheless, the chronicler's fabrications contain a nucleus of truth, and they may well have been fanciful and disingenuous elaborations on a tradition, current among the monks, of substantial Carolingian intervention in the affairs of the monastery in the decades following Charlemagne's annexation of Lombard northern Italy in 774.

During the period in question, it was the Carolingians, above all others, who exploited painting and script as two potent and visible symbols of their authority, their power and their presence. The excavations at the monastery of San Vincenzo al Volturno have provided a rare opportunity of observing how a large and enterprising religious community, situated in a highly sensitive location, in the border marches between Carolingian and Beneventan territory, deployed these cultural symbols to its own advantage. Painted decoration and prominent inscriptions not only gave the monastery an air of splendour and superiority, but they also doubtless served to attract the interest of benefactors from the region, whose support was vital to the continued prosperity and success of the community. The paintings, which were to be seen in almost every room at San Vincenzo, and the prodigal

---

[100] *Ibid.*, pp. 220–1.

[101] Charlemagne did not die, and Louis did not succeed him as emperor, until 814. Federici, in his edition of the Chronicle, draws attention to the difficulty of reconciling the chronicler's account of Louis' visits to San Vincenzo with what is known of his itinerary and of events at the monastery during the relevant years (*ibid.*, p. 220 n. 2, and p. 221 n. 1, 225 n. 1). Of the four diplomas in the Chronicle ostensibly issued by Charlemagne in favour of San Vincenzo, Federici judges three to be later falsifications (see *ibid.*, pp. 140 n. 1, 183 n. 3, 186–7 n. 3, 211 n. 3, 212–13 n. 3), and of the four issued by Louis, one is a forgery (*ibid.*, pp. 223–4 n. 2, 233–4 n. 1, 289 n. 49, 309 n. 1). The interest allegedly shown by the Carolingian rulers for San Vincenzo is a theme which recurs throughout the Chronicle, for instance in the account of the eighth-century abbot and theologian, Ambrose Autpert (*ibid.*, pp. 177–92).

display of writing, in inscriptions of every kind in all parts of the complex, reveal the abbot and the monks as masters of an apparatus of cultural control, which was being developed and deployed by the most aggressive and successful powers in the contemporary world.[102]

Postscript

After this article was consigned to the editor, Professor Paolo Delogu drew my attention to the dedicatory inscription from the façade of Arechis II's palace-chapel at Salerno, S. Pietro a Corte.[103] This inscription, part of which came to light during excavation in 1987, consisted of gilded bronze letters, about 16 cm tall, which are very closely related, both in their design and in the manner of their fixing, to the characters of Abbot Iosue's great gilded metal inscriptions at San Vincenzo. Arechis' inscription must antedate those at San Vincenzo by at least a quarter of a century. There can be little doubt that it was either this inscription at Salerno, or a similar one on a contemporary structure elsewhere in the Lombard principality of Benevento, which served both as the inspiration and as the direct model for Iosue's gilded metal *tituli*. The origins and the cultural context of the display of script at San Vincenzo al Volturno in the early ninth century will have to be reconsidered in the light of this recent find at Salerno.

---

[102] For information, comment and help of various kinds, I should like to thank David Abulafia, Julian Brown, Guglielmo Cavallo, Cathy Coutts, Paolo Delogu, Eric Fernie, Andrew Hanasz, Sandy Helsop, Richard Hodges, Ernst Kitzinger, Michael Lapidge, Stephen Mitchell, Victoria Mitchell, James Mosley, Christopher Norton, Barry Singleton, David Thomson, Paul Williamson and, of course, Rosamond McKitterick.

[103] M.P. and P. Peduto, 'Chiesa di San Pietro a Corte', *Passaggiate Salernitane*, 3 (Salerno, 1988), 20–6, at 25–6; *idem.*, 'Un accesso alla storia di Salerno: stratigrafie e materiali dell'area palaziale longobarda. 1. La costituzione del documento archeologico e la sua interpretazione stratigrafica', *Rassegna Storica Salernitana*, 10 (1968), 9–28, at 13, fig. 1; M. Galante, 'Le epigrafi', *ibid.*, 44–5, at 42–5; P. Peduto, 'Nel mondo dei 'Longobardi', *Archeo*, 57 (November, 1989), 116–19, at 119.

9

Royal government and the written word in late Anglo-Saxon England

Simon Keynes

> Whatever is transacted by men of this world to endure for ever ought to be fortified securely with ranks of letters, because the frail memory of men in dying forgets what the writing of letters preserves and retains.[1]

Such statements extolling the advantages of the written record are quite commonly found in the proems of Anglo-Saxon charters, from the seventh century to the eleventh;[2] nor should the fact occasion any surprise, for it is only to be expected that those responsible for drafting and writing the charters themselves would wish to advertize the benefits of their own labours. It is a different matter, however, whether this appreciation of the value of the written word extended into any of the other routine procedures of Anglo-Saxon royal government: one might ask, for example, whether written documents had a part to play in the formulation and publication of royal law, and more generally in the operation of legal processes; or whether kings came to depend to some extent on written documents for conveying messages and instructions to others, including their officials in the localities; or whether information was transmitted from one official to another, or from any official back to the king, by the same means; or whether use was made of the written word in such matters as the assessment and collection of taxes, the performance of military services and the administration of royal estates. In addressing some of these questions it might be useful to glance initially across the Channel, before proceeding to survey the evidence which

A version of this paper was read at a symposium on Literacy and Society in Early North-Western Europe 400–1200, held under the auspices of the University of Copenhagen in May 1987.

[1] From a charter of King Æthelred the Unready, dated 995: Sawyer no. 883 (=*EHD* no. 118).

[2] Several examples happen to be included in *EHD*: Sawyer no. 1164 (=*EHD* no. 55); Sawyer no. 88 (=*EHD* no. 66); Sawyer no. 1257 (=*EHD* no. 77); Sawyer no. 362 (=*EHD* no. 100); Sawyer no. 773 (=*EHD* no. 113); Sawyer no. 832 (= *EHD* no. 115); and Sawyer no. 951 (=*EHD* no. 131). Many others could be cited.

bears more directly on the use made of the written word in late Anglo-Saxon royal government.

In his study of 'The use of the written word in Charlemagne's administration', Ganshof provided a most effective demonstration of the extent to which Charlemagne and his agents had recourse to written documents in conducting the affairs of the Frankish realm.[3] He made a basic distinction between those documents which originated in the palace, and those which were issued by the king's agents: among the former, a further distinction is made between those drawn up for the king's own purposes and those issued to the king's agents for their purposes (whether handed directly to them or despatched from the palace to the localities); among the latter, Ganshof distinguished between those used by the agents themselves for their own purposes and those which took the form of reports or returns addressed by them to the king. Ganshof illustrates the distinctions by copious reference to the corpus of Charlemagne's capitularies, adducing examples of written agenda for deliberations at general assemblies, minutes of these deliberations, instructions arising from the deliberations for the guidance or direction of the king's agents, reports or returns sent to the king by his agents in the localities, and so on. He also remarks on Charlemagne's attempts to codify and supplement the laws of the various peoples under his sway, and on the king's or emperor's insistence that 'iudices are to judge justly in accordance with the written law, not at their discretion'.[4] Ganshof was careful to emphasize that the use of the written word in Charlemagne's administration was not without its imperfections and failings, and that the practices of the late eighth and ninth centuries were not maintained thereafter; but while it would be plainly mistaken to think in terms of a government articulated by all the paraphernalia of a modern bureaucracy, we are left with a striking picture of what might be attempted and of what could be achieved by royal government in the early middle ages.[5]

So how far does Anglo-Saxon royal government match up in this respect

---

[3] F.L. Ganshof, 'The use of the written word in Charlemagne's administration', in his *The Carolingians and the Frankish Monarchy* (London, 1971), pp. 125–42.

[4] *Capitulare missorum generale* (802), ch. 26, in *MGH Cap.* I, no. 33, p. 96, trans. P.D. King, *Charlemagne: Translated Sources* (Kendal, 1987), pp. 233–42, at p. 239, and H.R. Loyn and J. Percival, *The Reign of Charlemagne: Documents on Carolingian Government and Administration* (London, 1975), no. 16, p. 76. Compare *Annales Laureshamenses*, s.a. 802 (trans. King, *Charlemagne*, p. 145).

[5] For more recent studies of this subject, see Rosamond McKitterick, 'Some Carolingian law-books and their function', *Authority and Power: Studies on Medieval Law and Government Presented to Walter Ullmann on his Seventieth Birthday*, ed. Brian Tierney and Peter Linehan (Cambridge, 1980), pp. 13–27; R. McKitterick, *The Frankish Kingdoms under the Carolingians, 751–987* (London, 1983), pp. 98–103; and McKitterick, *Carolingians*, pp. 23–75. See also King, *Charlemagne*, pp. 33 and 35–6, and Nelson, below, pp. 258–96.

to Carolingian government? One might say that the organization of the coinage in tenth-century England establishes the credentials of Anglo-Saxon government as nothing if not capable of a high degree of administrative 'sophistication',[6] but does it live up to what might therefore be our expectations in the use of the written word? Pronouncements on this subject in the past ten years or so have tended to push in different directions. Thus Campbell has taken the line that the processes of late Anglo-Saxon government generated various kinds of written record, particularly in the vernacular, and in this connection he cites examples of hidage lists, estate surveys, records of services owed for specific purposes, and administrative letters.[7] Wormald, on the other hand, has preferred to play down such evidence for a degree of 'pragmatic literacy' in pre-Conquest England, and the level of lay literacy which it might seem to imply. In particular, he has addressed himself to the problem of later Anglo-Saxon legislation, with far-reaching results. He does not, of course, deny that Anglo-Saxon laws existed in written form, but he does question the status of the extant written texts in relation to the process of law-making, and their function in relation to the administration of justice. Thus, while King Alfred's code was drawn up in written form, it was exceptional in this respect, and represented more of an attempt to express the king's ideological aspirations than to provide his judges with a practical work of reference.[8] As regards tenth- and eleventh-century legislation, what counted was the king's oral pronouncement of the law, and many of the extant written texts were more in the nature of 'minutes of what was orally decreed, rather than statute law in their own right';[9] put another way, 'it may have been the *verbum regis* rather than the written text which gave it the force of law',[10] and 'even in later Anglo-Saxon

---

[6] For an authoritative survey of the tenth-century coinage, see C.E. Blunt, B.H.I.H. Stewart and C.S.S. Lyon, *Coinage in Tenth-Century England from Edward the Elder to Edgar's Reform* (Oxford, 1989).

[7] James Campbell, 'Observations on English government from the tenth to the twelfth century', in his *Essays in Anglo-Saxon History* (London, 1986), pp. 155–70, at pp. 157–8; *idem*, 'The significance of the Anglo-Norman state in the administrative history of western Europe', in *ibid.* pp. 171–89, at pp. 173–5 and 178; and *idem*, 'Some agents and agencies of the late Anglo-Saxon state', in *Domesday Studies*, ed. J.C. Holt (Woodbridge, 1987), pp. 201–18, at pp. 214–15.

[8] Patrick Wormald, '*Lex Scripta* and *Verbum Regis*: legislation and Germanic kingship, from Euric to Cnut', *Early Medieval Kingship*, ed. P.H. Sawyer and I.N. Wood (Leeds, 1977), pp. 105–38, at pp. 115–25, 132–3 and 135.

[9] Patrick Wormald, 'Æthelred the lawmaker', *Ethelred the Unready: Papers from the Millenary Conference*, ed. David Hill, British Archaeological Reports, British series 59 (Oxford, 1978), pp. 47–80, at p. 48.

[10] Patrick Wormald, 'The uses of literacy in Anglo-Saxon England and its neighbours', *TRHS* 5th series 27 (1977), 95–114, at 111.

England, formal royal law-making may have remained oral, and our texts may be more in the nature of ecclesiastical records of decisions taken than legislative acts in themselves'.[11] Thus (as I understand it), tenth- and eleventh-century legislation was not formally promulgated *by the king* in written form, and those who produced the texts were doing so on their own initiative and for their own purposes, and might have felt free (because there was no such thing as a 'definitive' written code) to vary their texts from what originally had been orally decreed. Clanchy has demonstrated how increasing use was made of written documents for various purposes in the twelfth and thirteenth centuries, represented by the notion of the 'take-off' of literacy after 1066;[12] but while he acknowledges that 'administrative documents were certainly used in late Anglo-Saxon England', he does question the extent of their use, and concludes that England seems unlikely to have been 'governed by a bureaucracy using documents in its routine procedures before 1066'.[13] The most recent pronouncements on the subject are those of Loyn: he recognizes the existence of a royal secretariat or writing-office capable of producing charters and writs in some significant quantity, but he also remarks that 'acts of government in the tenth century tended to be oral', instancing law-making as an activity in which 'nine times out of ten the actual recording in writing was left in a surprisingly casual way to ecclesiastics and to individual or local enterprise'.[14]

The contrast, in Clanchy's terms, between the tenth century and the thirteenth is certainly striking, and cannot simply be explained away as a function of the presumed loss of hypothetical documents in greater number from the earlier period; but aeroplanes must taxi before they take off, and it remains an open question when the taxi-run began. For the purposes of this paper I intend initially to consider the role of written documents in the publication and enforcement of royal law in the tenth and eleventh centuries; and thereafter I shall discuss the more general question of the level of 'pragmatic literacy' during the same period, so that the evidence of royal legislation may take its place in the wider context of the extent to

---

[11] *Ibid.*, 112. See aso Hanna Vollrath, 'Gesetzgebung und Schriftlichkeit: das Beispiel der angelsächsischen Gesetze', *Historisches Jahrbuch* 99 (1979), 28–54; like Wormald, Vollrath plays down any connection between the promulgation of law and the written word, not least because it presupposes some degree of lay literacy and the existence of a body of royal scribes capable of producing the requisite number of copies of the law-codes (neither of which she seems willing to accept).

[12] M. Clanchy, *From Memory to Written Record: England 1066–1307* (London, 1979).

[13] *Ibid.*, pp. 16–17. Dr Clanchy tells me that this statement will be modified in the second edition of *From Memory to Written Record*, which he has in hand.

[14] H.R. Loyn, *The Governance of Anglo-Saxon England 500–1087* (London, 1984), pp. 106–18.

which late Anglo-Saxon government and administration were dependent on the use of the written word.[15]

The most natural point of departure for such an exercise is the concluding chapter of Asser's *Life of King Alfred*, in which Asser gives some account of the king's personal intervention in the legal affairs of his realm.[16] Asser describes how the people frequently disputed the judgements given by ealdormen or reeves in their local assemblies, and how in such cases the matter might be referred to the king for adjudication. He also describes how the king was in the habit of investigating nearly all judgements made by others, and how, if Alfred considered them to be unfair, he would ask the judges (either directly, or through a trusted agent) to explain the reasons for their judgement. If the judges claimed that they had not known any better in the circumstances, the king would rebuke them for their dereliction of duty, and would threaten to deprive them of their office unless they applied themselves forthwith to the pursuit of wisdom. So it came about that 'nearly all the ealdormen and reeves and thegns (who were illiterate from child-hood) applied themselves in an amazing way to learning how to read, preferring rather to learn this unfamiliar discipline (no matter how laboriously) than to relinquish their offices of power'; and if any one of them was slow on the uptake, the king insisted that he find someone else to help him by reading out books in English 'by day and night, or whenever he had the opportunity'.[17] Asser's remarks may create the impression that the king was concerned that his officials should acquire divine wisdom in particular – in other words, that the literacy which Alfred required of his officials was intended to be more in their cultural than in his 'pragmatic' interests; as Wormald remarks, the king's conception of wisdom was 'something moral and religious, and had very little to do with administrative expertise'.[18] Knowledge of divine wisdom and the exercise of secular power were certainly inseparable in Alfred's eyes, whether in his own case as king or in the case of his officials; but if Asser focusses on the one aspect of the scheme

[15] Anglo-Saxon law-codes are cited from *Die Gesetze der Angelsachsen*, ed. F. Liebermann, 3 vols. (Halle, 1903–16); see also *The Laws of the Earliest English Kings*, ed. F.L. Attenborough (Cambridge, 1922), and *The Laws of the Kings of England from Edmund to Henry I*, ed. A.J. Robertson (Cambridge, 1925). The following abbreviations are used in references to chapters of particular codes: *Alf.* (Alfred), *Edw.* (Edward the Elder), *As.* (Æthelstan) and *Edg.* (Edgar).

[16] Asser, ch. 106: see *Asser's Life of King Alfred*, ed. William Henry Stevenson (Oxford, 1904), pp. 92–5 (text), and Simon Keynes and Michael Lapidge, *Alfred the Great: Asser's 'Life of King Alfred' and Other Contemporary Sources* (Harmondsworth, 1983), pp. 109–10 (translation).

[17] It is not entirely clear whether the idea was to help the person learn how to read for himself, or whether it was to provide him with a permanent service.

[18] Wormald, 'Uses of literacy', 107.

which would have been most dear to his own and to the king's heart, the king himself may have been conscious of other advantages as well.

Asser's remarks clearly indicate that King Alfred regarded an ability to read English as an essential requirement for all those of his subjects who were in positions of authority, so that they might be the better qualified to discharge the responsibilities of their respective offices, and the better able to pass informed and appropriate judgements in legal proceedings. The question remains: what were the vernacular texts which the ealdormen, reeves and thegns were expected to read? Alfred was, of course, instrumental in the translation from Latin into English of certain books which he considered 'the most necessary for all men to know', as part of his grand design for the revival of learning in England.[19] The translations seem to have been intended for use in the school which the king had established for training the youth of his kingdom in reading and writing, for in the letter to his bishops, which he circulated with copies of his translation of Pope Gregory's *Pastoral Care*, Alfred alluded to his provision of translations as if it were specifically a part of the process by which 'all the free-born young men now in England' would be educated until such time as they were able to read English writings properly.[20] Thus any practical benefits of King Alfred's educational programme would not be felt until the opening decades of the tenth century and thereafter, when the youth of his day had become the next generation of royal officials. One has to assume, however, that at least some of King Alfred's generation of officials would have studied the translations in the course of their own pursuit of wisdom, whether by reading them for themselves or hearing them read by others.

Another text which King Alfred's officials must have been expected to read was the king's law-code, and indeed it is this text, more than any other, which would have instilled in them the knowledge of that kind of wisdom necessary for the proper discharging of their duties.[21] One should emphasize that the code was conceived as a written text, for the king remarks in his preamble how he had 'ordered to be written' (*awritan het*) many of the laws which his forefathers observed, and how he had not presumed 'to set down in writing' (*on gewrit settan*) many of his own;[22] and while there can be little doubt that a degree of political ideology lies behind its production, it is difficult not to believe that it was intended to serve a

---

[19] See Keynes and Lapidge, *Alfred the Great*, pp. 28–36.

[20] *Ibid.*, p. 126; for the school itself, see Asser, ch. 75 (*Life of Alfred*, ed. Stevenson, pp. 57–9 (text), and Keynes and Lapidge, *Alfred the Great*, pp. 90–1 (translation)).

[21] For the text of Alfred's law-code, see *Gesetze*, ed. Liebermann, I, pp. 16–123; see also *Laws*, ed. Attenborough, pp. 36–93 (with translation).

[22] *Alf.* Intr. 49.9.

practical purpose as well. Alfred's 'judges' would certainly have had much to gain from a perusal of the long opening section of the code, which comprises extracts from the Book of Exodus (including the Ten Commandments), followed by material derived from the Acts of the Apostles, showing how the Mosaic Law was modified for application to Christian peoples; and whatever the code's shortcomings as a work of practical reference, one can but imagine that they would have found much in it to their general advantage.[23]

The crucial question is whether copies of King Alfred's law-code were multiplied by the king's scribes and then distributed to the 'judges' throughout his realm, in the same manner as copies of his translation of Pope Gregory's *Pastoral Care* were circulated to the bishops; and also, whether the 'judges' were expected to have recourse to Alfred's code when deciding upon their judgement in a given case. It is impossible for the Anglo-Saxonist to match the several examples of ninth-century Carolingian manuscripts which contain collections of laws and capitularies, and which appear actually to have belonged to royal officials responsible for the administration of justice in a particular locality;[24] but is this significant, or merely unfortunate? In the case of King Alfred's code, all one can say is that it survives (in whole or in part) in six manuscripts, representing at least four different routes of descent from a common archetype; and there is textual evidence for other copies now lost.[25] The earliest of the surviving manuscripts dates from the second quarter of the tenth century, and the rest date from the eleventh and twelfth centuries; and while none has the appearance of a working copy, all attest in their different ways to an interest in Alfred's legislation which was sustained over many years. Nevertheless, one should certainly not rule out the possibility that copies of Alfred's code were quite widely disseminated in the tenth century, and that the king's 'judges' were expected to be familiar with the wisdom and guidance which it contained. King Edward the Elder issued an injunction to his reeves to the effect 'that you pronounce such judgements as you know to be most just and in accordance with the law-books' (*ðæt ge deman swa rihte domas swa ge rihtoste cunnon, 7 hit on ðære dombec stande*).[26] One might be tempted to

---

[23] For general comments on Alfred's code, see H.G. Richardson and G.O. Sayles, *Law and Legislation from Æthelberht to Magna Carta* (Edinburgh, 1966), pp. 15–16; J.M. Wallace-Hadrill, *Early Germanic Kingship in England and on the Continent* (Oxford, 1971), pp. 148–9; and Allen J. Frantzen, *King Alfred* (Boston, Mass., 1986), pp. 11–21.

[24] See McKitterick, 'Some Carolingian law-books', and *idem, Carolingians*, pp. 23–75.

[25] See *Gesetze*, ed. Liebermann, III, pp. 30–2, and Keynes and Lapidge, *Alfred the Great*, pp. 303–4.

[26] *I Edw*. Prol.

regard this as merely an echo of Charlemagne's insistence that '*iudices* are to judge justly in accordance with the written law, not at their discretion', were it not for the occurrence of several other references to the *domboc* in tenth-century Anglo-Saxon legislation, in contexts which make it clear that the reference is indeed to the composite law-code of King Alfred (composite in the sense that it incorporates a copy of King Ine's legislation, as well as material culled from other sources). Thus Edward the Elder decreed that a man who breaks the oath and pledge which the whole nation has given 'is to pay such compensation as the law-book prescribes' (*bete swa domboc tæce*),[27] an apparent reference to *Alf.* 1, on the need for every man to keep his oath and pledge; and he also decreed that one who harbours a fugitive 'is to pay such compensation as the law-book says' (*bete swa seo domboc sæcge*),[28] with reference to *Ine* 30 or *Alf.* 4. King Æthelstan decreed that anyone found guilty of breaking into a church 'is to pay such compensation for it as the law-book says' (*bete be þam þe sio domboc secge*),[29] with reference to *Alf.* 6. And still later in the tenth century, King Edgar decreed that all churchscot shall be rendered by Martinmas 'under pain of the full fine which the law-book prescribes' (*be þam fullan wite þe seo domboc tæcð*),[30] with reference to *Ine* 4, and that Sunday shall be observed as a festival from noon on Saturday until dawn on Monday 'under pain of the fine which the law-book prescribes' (*be þam wite þe seo domboc tæcð*),[31] with reference to *Ine* 3. In short, we may not have the dog-eared copies of King Alfred's code which the judges actually used, but tenth-century kings certainly issued laws which presupposed that copies of the code were widely available and that their judges were able to refer to them.

King Alfred's law-code was not the only legal document produced during his reign. The treaty between Alfred and Guthrum is ostensibly a record of oral agreements made between the two parties and confirmed on a particular day by the swearing of oaths.[32] It is copied twice in a manuscript written *c.* 1100: one version occurs near the beginning of the manuscript and the other near the end, and while both represent fundamentally the same text, their separation, and the slight differences between them, imply that they were derived by the copyist from quite different exemplars.[33] The differences

---

[27] *II Edw.* 5.   [28] *Ibid.*, 5.2.   [29] *II As.* 5.   [30] *II Edg.* 3.   [31] *Ibid.*, 5.

[32] For the text of the treaty, see *Gesetze*, ed. Liebermann, I, pp. 126–9; see also *Laws*, ed. Attenborough, pp. 98–101, and Keynes and Lapidge, *Alfred the Great*, pp. 171–2 and 311–13.

[33] CCCC 383, pp. 6 and 83–4: see N.R. Ker, *Catalogue of Manuscripts Containing Anglo-Saxon* (Oxford, 1957), no. 65, and Mary P. Richards, 'The manuscript contexts of the Old English laws: tradition and innovation', *Studies in Earlier Old English Prose*, ed. Paul E. Szarmach (Albany, NY, 1986), pp. 171–92, at pp. 181–4. The compiler of the collection of law-codes now represented by CCCC 383 seems to have derived his copies of the treaty from

between the two surviving versions of the text should be capable of some explanation. The (slightly fuller) version near the end of the manuscript seems the more 'official' of the two, in the sense that it is closer to the issuing authority; note, for example, the use of the first person, as in the reference to 'our' boundaries and in the formula 'we all declared'.[34] The (slightly shorter) version near the beginning of the manuscript appears, on the other hand, to have been intended for or copied by a party other than those directly involved, if only to judge from the reference to 'their' boundaries and from the formula 'they all declared'. Moreover, in the 'official' version the boundary is said to go 'up the Thames', whereas in the other version it is said to go 'along the Thames', as if the latter version, while plainly derived from the 'official' text, was re-cast from the point of view of someone already on the Thames, perhaps in London.[35] Perhaps I press the evidence (such as it is) too far, but it would appear that the surviving versions of the treaty descend ultimately and independently from written texts presumably drawn up at the time the oaths were sworn, and that these texts had been made for the benefit of the various parties concerned. One should add in this connection that further treaties were concluded with Scandinavian settlers in the early tenth century, and that (though now lost) they were certainly available to interested parties in written form: when King Edward the Elder decreed that the compensation for harbouring a fugitive should be in accordance with the *domboc*, if the offence were committed in his own kingdom, he added that it should be in accordance with the 'written treaties' *friðgewritu*) if the offence were committed in the 'east' or in the 'north'.[36]

There is further evidence for the use of the written word in the routine processes of law during the reign of King Edward the Elder. The 'code' known as *I Edward* is of special interest insomuch as it is an injunction addressed by the king specifically to all his reeves, as opposed to a more general record of legal pronouncements emanating from deliberations of the

a source or sources other than the early eleventh-century collection which lies behind much of the material in CCCC 383 (and which also underlies the collection of law-codes in the twelfth-century *Textus Roffensis* (Maidstone, Kent County Records Office DRc/R1; Ker, *Catalogue*, no. 373)).

[34] *Alfred and Guthrum*, 1 and 5. One should add that it is the more 'official' version which is represented in the early twelfth-century compilation known as *Quadripartitus*, which comprises Latin translations of a large number of Anglo-Saxon law-codes (see *Leges Henrici Primi*, ed. L.J. Downer (Oxford, 1972), pp. 12–28).

[35] A 'London' copy of the treaty would not be out of place in CCCC 383, which seems to have come from St Paul's. For further discussion of the treaty itself, see D.N. Dumville, 'The Treaty of Alfred and Guthrum', in his *Wessex and England from Alfred to Edgar* (Woodbridge, forthcoming).

[36] *II Edw.* 5.2, probably referring to the peace established by King Edward with the East Angles and the Northumbrians, at Tiddingford in 906.

king and his councillors; besides instructing the reeves to make judgements in accordance with the 'law-books' (*dombec*), the king indicates in what other respects he wishes legal procedures to be properly observed. There is no internal evidence as to the form of its promulgation, and one might assume that the surviving texts depend on an 'unofficial' record of an oral pronouncement. But in the code known as *II Edward*, which is a record of the king's pronouncements to his councillors at Exeter, we find a reiteration of Edward's injunctions on the proper treatment of repeated breaches of another man's rights (as in *I Edw.* 2.1): a man who thus misbehaves 'is to pay compensation as has been previously written' (*bete swa hit beforan awriten is*),[37] with the clear implication that King Edward's injunction to his reeves had been issued to them in written form.

It is the corpus of legislation associated with the name of King Æthelstan which provides the most remarkable evidence for the role of the written word in the publication and enforcement of Anglo-Saxon law.[38] Wormald characterized this material as 'so heterogeneous in form, that the king appears in three codes in the first person, in two in the third person, and in one in the second',[39] and he suggested that 'each of the codes owes its survival in its extant form to the archives not of the king, but of Archbishop Wulfhelm at Canterbury, who was clearly closely involved in their promulgation, and may even have been responsible for their written composition'.[40] One has to say that the so-called 'codes' of King Æthelstan are only heterogeneous insofar as they vary from a norm which is itself spurious: modern editors, for the sake of convenience, have branded a group of legislative texts from Æthelstan's reign as (the *Ordinance on Charities* and) *I–VI Æthelstan*, implying that they constitute a sequence of royal codes, when in fact they are texts which differ substantially in origin, status and nature; moreover, two of the 'codes' (*II Æthelstan* and *VI Æthelstan*) are clearly composite in their received form, combining material derived from texts of different type, and adding further to the semblance of heterogeneity.

I Æthelstan and the so-called *Ordinance on Charities* are injunctions addressed by the king specifically to his reeves; both are cast in the first

---

[37] *Ibid.*, 1.3, assuming that this is not merely a local reference to *I Edward*, which was probably copied immediately before *II Edward* in the manuscripts behind those which survive (CCCC 383, the *Textus Roffensis*, and *Quadripartitus*).

[38] For Æthelstan's legislation, see *Gesetze*, ed. Liebermann, I, pp. 146–83, and *Laws*, ed. Attenborough, pp. 122–69. See also Richardson and Sayles, *Law and Legislation*, pp. 18–20, and H.R. Loyn, 'The hundred in England in the tenth and early eleventh centuries', in *British Government and Administration*, ed. H. Hearder and H.R. Loyn (Cardiff, 1974), pp. 1–15, at pp. 4–7.

[39] Wormald, '*Lex Scripta* and *Verbum Regis*', pp. 118–19.

[40] Wormald, 'Uses of literacy', 112.

person, and in each the king declares himself to be acting with the advice of Archbishop Wulfhelm and other bishops. In *I Æthelstan*, the king requires of his reeves that they render tithes from his own property, adding that the bishops, ealdormen and reeves should do likewise in respect of their property as well; the reeves are further instructed to ensure that church dues are properly paid, and not to render to the king any more than what is legally owed to him.[41] In the *Ordinance on Charities*, the king instructs each of his reeves, from two of the king's rents, to supply a destitute Englishman with provisions every month and with clothing every year, and to free one penal slave per year, on pain of a fine of 30 shillings (which would itself be shared among the poor on a given estate).[42] Both injunctions appear to emanate from meetings of the king and his bishops, and it is not clear in what form (oral or written) they were conveyed to the reeves themselves; but if Edward the Elder issued a specific injunction to his reeves in writing, there is no reason to doubt that King Æthelstan was capable of doing the same. Indeed, the composite *VI Æthelstan* incorporates what appears to be an injunction addressed by the king to the officials of the shire-courts, threatening the reeves in particular with loss of office (and a fine) if they failed to perform their appointed tasks 'as I have commanded and as it stands in our writings' (*swa ic beboden hæbbe, 7 on urum gewritum stent*).[43] One cannot produce from Anglo-Saxon England anything quite as explicit as the letter sent by Charlemagne's *missi* to the counts, admonishing them to re-read their capitularies and to bear in mind what they have been orally charged to do (*ut capitularia vestra relegatis et quaeque vobis per verba commendata sunt recolatis*), urging them to seek guidance from the *missi* should they not understand any of the instructions which Charlemagne had given them either in writing or orally (*quod vobis domni nostri aut scribendo aut dicendo commendatum est*), and telling them to read the letter often and to keep it safe (*ut istam epistolam et saepius legatis et bene salvam faciatis*), 'that you and we may use it as evidence to see whether you have or have not

---

[41] The vernacular text of *I Æthelstan* is preserved in CCCC 201 (Ker, *Catalogue*, no. 49B) and in BL Cotton Nero A. i (*ibid.* no. 164), both of which are associated with Wulfstan, archbishop of York; see Richards, 'Manuscript contexts', pp. 176–81. There is a Latin translation of the code in *Quadripartitus*.

[42] The *Ordinance on Charities* is preserved only in Latin translation, in *Quadripartitus*. There may, incidentally, be some connection between the issuing of this ordinance and specific terms in two of King Æthelstan's charters: on 24 December 932, at Amesbury (Wilts.), the king granted an estate to his thegn Alfred, conditional upon the daily feeding of 120 poor (Sawyer no. 418), and on 11 January (933), at Wilton (Wilts.), he granted an estate to his thegn Wulfgar, conditional upon the annual feeding of ten poor on 1 November (Sawyer no. 379, spurious in its received form, but evidently based on an authentic text).

[43] *VI As.* 11. If not a reference to such documents as *I Æthelstan* and the *Ordinance on Charities*, this would presumably be a reference to full codes such as *II Æthelstan*.

acted in accordance with what is written in it';[44] but the analogy suggests that letters sent by the king to his reeves should not stretch the limits of credibility.

II Æthelstan and *V Æthelstan* are the only texts in the corpus associated with King Æthelstan which appear to be records of legislation enacted at meetings of the king and his councillors, intended for general publication.[45] According to its epilogue, *II Æthelstan* was promulgated in the great meeting at Grately, in the presence of Archbishop Wulfhelm and all the councillors whom the king had been able to assemble.[46] It is an impressive piece of legislation (though not comparable in conception or scale with King Alfred's law-book), and leaves one in no doubt as to King Æthelstan's determination to confront the problems of maintaining social order: after ranging over a variety of offences and procedures, it concludes with a firm declaration to the effect that the king's reeves must implement what has been decreed, and with a statement of the escalating scale of penalties for repeated breaches of the law.[47] It seems, however, that the king had some difficulty in enforcing his will. For *V Æthelstan*, promulgated in a subsequent meeting at Exeter, was expressly framed in response to the perceived disregard of all that had been done at Grately, and again one senses the king's determination to bring the people (and not least his own reeves) to heel; this code ends with an order that God's servants in every minster shall sing fifty psalms every Friday 'for the king, and for all who desire what he desires'.[48] Both *II Æthelstan* and *V Æthelstan* are cast in the

---

[44] *Capitula a missis dominicis ad comites directa* (806), Prol., and chs. 4 and 7, in *MGH Cap.* I, no. 85, pp. 183–4, trans. King, *Charlemagne*, p. 259.

[45] The two codes occurred together in the (burnt) Cotton Otho B. xi (Ker, *Catalogue*, no. 180); see Richards, 'Manuscript contexts', pp.174–5. They may also have occurred together in the early eleventh-century collection of laws which lies behind CCCC 383 and the *Textus Roffensis*; the text of *II Æthelstan* in CCCC 383 breaks off in *II As.* 6, owing to loss of leaves, and one can only assume that a text of *V Æthelstan* followed. Latin translations of both codes occur in *Quadripartitus*.

[46] *II As.* Epil.; this epilogue occurs only in the Latin translation of the code in *Quadripartitus*.

[47] *II As.* 13–18 (which include Æthelstan's legislation on the coinage) seem to have been interpolated into the code as originally conceived; but the section occurs in all of the surviving versions, and was probably present in it as originally issued. *III As.* 8 appears to refer back to *II As.* 15. *II As.* 26 (on swearing a false oath) seems to have been added to the codes as an afterthought.

[48] There may, again, be some connection between the issuing of this order and specific terms in two of King Æthelstan's charters: on 24 December 932, at Amesbury (Wilts.), the king granted an estate to Shaftesbury Abbey, conditional upon daily prayers for the king (Sawyer no. 419), and on 26 January 933, at Chippenham (Wilts.), he granted an estate to Sherborne Abbey, conditional upon annual prayers for the king on 1 November (Sawyer no. 422; see also Sawyer no. 423). Compare above, n. 42. The appearance of such clauses requiring charitable acts (from lay beneficiaries) or prayers for the king (from religious houses)

first person, and are ostensibly records of oral pronouncements; we cannot hope to know by whom they were drafted, and in themselves they afford no clues as to the means of their dissemination. It should be said, however, that the references in tenth-century legislation to the 'law-book' (*domboc*) of King Alfred need not be taken to imply that later laws were not issued in written form; the distinction is between a code which deserved and enjoyed a special status as a compilation of exceptional scope and enduring value, and other texts which built on its foundation.[49]

Some light is thrown on the publication of texts such as *II Æthelstan* and *V Æthelstan* by the code known (somewhat misleadingly) as *III Æthelstan*.[50] This is not a royal code at all, but rather a report from the bishops and other councillors in Kent back to the king (who is addressed in the second person), thanking him for his guidance and informing him of the measures which they have taken for the maintenance of the peace.[51] They acknowledge the help 'of the councillors whom you have sent to us' (*sapientum eorum quos ad nos misisti*), and proceed to describe, in effect, how they are implementing and supplementing the king's decrees; there are references to the king's injunctions on tithes (presumably *I Æthelstan*), to the Grately decrees (*II Æthelstan*), which are said also to have been proclaimed at Faversham, and to what was declared in the west (presumably *V Æthelstan*, issued at Exeter). But the crucial point in the present connection is that the Grately decrees are referred to as a *scriptum*,[52] and that the Kentish report is itself described as a *scriptum*.[53] In other words, at

suggests that a special attempt was being made, in the winter of 932–3, to gain divine favour (compare *Capitulare episcoporum* (793), in *MGH Cap.* I, no. 21, p. 52, trans. King, *Charlemagne*, pp. 223–4); but it was perhaps no more than a manifestation of the king's normal frame of mind (compare Simon Keynes, 'King Athelstan's books', in *Learning and Literature in Anglo-Saxon England*, ed. Michael Lapidge and Helmut Gneuss (Cambridge, 1985), pp. 143–201), and besides, *V Æthelstan*, though emanating from a meeting at midwinter, could not have been issued during the winter of 932–3, since it is known to have been promulgated at Exeter (which would not fit in with the king's itinerary implied by the charters).

[49] In addition to *II* and *V Æthelstan*, other codes were doubtless issued from time to time during Æthelstan's reign: for example, before *II Æthelstan* (see *II As.* 11 and 23.2); and after *V Æthelstan*, at Faversham (see *III As.* 2–3; *IV As.* 1; *VI As.* 10), Thunderfield (see *IV Æthelstan*, and *VI As.* 10), and Whittlebury (see *VI As.* 12).

[50] Preserved only in Latin translation, in *Quadripartitus*.

[51] The report opens with the word *Karissime*, presumably reflecting an initial greeting such as *Leof* (as in Ealdorman Ordlaf's letter to Edward the Elder, concerning the Fonthill dispute (Sawyer no. 1445)).

[52] *III As.* 5. Vollrath, 'Gesetzgebung und Schriftlichkeit', 43, regards the production of a written text of *II Æthelstan* for the Kentish authorities as something which proceeded from special circumstances, and she is reluctant to infer that it represented the normal means of publication.

[53] *III As.* Epil.

least one of the king's ordinances – the Grately code – was available to the officials of the shire-court in written form, and it was by means of a written report that the officials then sent their assurances of good faith back to the king.

IV Æthelstan and *VI Æthelstan* seem also to have been drawn up independently of royal authority, but unlike *III Æthelstan* were not intended for the king's benefit.[54] *IV Æthelstan* is normally regarded as a royal code (representing legislation promulgated in a meeting at Thunderfield, in Surrey), and may be so, but it is arguable that it is in fact (a translation of) a 'private' record of royal decrees, drawn up by another party for special reasons and purposes; certainly, it differs from the two undoubtedly 'royal' codes (*II* and *V Æthelstan*) in being cast in the third person, and thus lacks their sense of proximity to the issuing authority.[55] Moreover, it should perhaps be distinguished from what might have been a set of genuinely 'royal' decrees promulgated on the same occasion: for a short text preserved only in the *Textus Roffensis* seems to be an extract from a slightly different record of the Thunderfield legislation,[56] which to judge from its use of the formula *we gecwædon* (as in *II* and *V Æthelstan*) and from the fact that it is appended to a copy of *V Æthelstan* may well have been a more 'official' version of the council's proceedings. *VI Æthelstan* is known not to be royal: it runs in the name of the bishops and reeves of the 'peace-guild' of London, and records for their own benefit how they were supplementing the (king's) decrees at Grately, Exeter and Thunderfield; the king is cast in the third person, as in *IV Æthelstan*; and interestingly enough, there is a reference to the code itself as something which exists in written form (*þe on urum gewritum stent*).[57]

Four clauses at the end of *VI Æthelstan* seem to have no association with the London document in its original form, and were presumably added at later stages in its transmission; nor do they seem to have any original association with each other, for each represents a very different kind of text. *VI As*. 9 is apparently a supplementary declaration by the London peace-guild, concerning the liberation of thieves.[58] *VI As*. 10 records how all the

---

[54] *IV Æthelstan* is preserved only in Latin translation, in *Quadripartitus*. *VI Æthelstan* is preserved in the *Textus Roffensis* (but not in CCCC 383), and there is a Latin translation of it in *Quadripartitus*.

[55] The apparently retrospective reference to the meeting at Thunderfield, in *IV As*. 6, suggests that the code may have been drawn up some time after the meeting itself.

[56] It is, in effect, a shorter version of *IV As*. (Lat.) 6.1–3, but with an additional clause (*IV As*. (OE) 6.2b) inserted. On the relationship between the Latin and Old English versions of *IV Æthelstan*, see *Gesetze*, ed. Liebermann, III, pp. 112–13, and *Laws*, ed. Attenborough, pp. 210–11.

[57] *VI As*. 8.5.   [58] Cf. *VI As*. 1.4 and 12.1.

councillors (*witan*) made a pledge to the archbishop at Thunderfield, 'when Ælfheah Stybb and Byrhtnoth, son of Odda, attended the meeting at the king's command' (*þa Ælfeah Stybb 7 Brihtoð Oddan sunu coman togeanes þam gemote þæs cinges worde*): every reeve was to exact a pledge from his own shire, that all would observe the peace as decreed by King Æthelstan and his councillors at Grately, Exeter, Faversham and Thunderfield. It is possible to read this as a reference to a local assembly attended by two of the king's representatives who were charged with supervising the implementation of the law; but it seems more likely to be a reference to a general meeting of the king's councillors, to which Ælfheah Stybb and Byrhtnoth, son of Odda, had been summoned as local representatives, perhaps (given the context of the text's preservation) as reeves of the borough of London – in which case *VI As*. 10 might derive from their report back to the peace-guild.[59] *VI As*. 11 is a record of an injunction addressed by the king 'to his bishops and his ealdormen and all his reeves', throughout his realm; in other words, it is a royal order directed to the officials of the shire-courts, and again, given the context of its preservation, one imagines that it is derived from a copy delivered to the borough of London. It obviously complements *VI As*. 10, for it is aimed particularly at the reeves, insisting that they exact the pledge from those under their authority, and generally exhorting them to do their appointed duty ('as I have commanded, and as it stands in our writings'). *VI As*. 12 seems to be a record of a declaration made by the king to at least some of his *witan* at Whittlebury, in mitigation of his earlier decrees at Grately:[60] henceforth, young people who admit to theft are not to be killed if under fifteen years old (formerly twelve), and any one who admits to theft is not to be killed if the stolen property is worth less than 12 pence (formerly 8). The record is not, as it stands, a royal pronouncement; it begins by saying that the king has sent word of his change of heart to the archbishop, by Bishop Theodred, and it may be that the record derives from what Theodred himself, as bishop of London, reported to his own peace-guild.

The corpus of legal texts associated with the reign of King Æthelstan thus includes two injunctions addressed by the king specifically to his reeves (*I Æthelstan* and the *Ordinance on Charities*), two decrees made by the king

---

[59] Attestations of a thegn or thegns called Ælfheah occur throughout Æthelstan's reign, and can probably be rationalized in terms of one prominent between 928 and 934 and another less prominent between 934 and 938; but it is impossible to tell which, if indeed either, is Ælfheah Stybb. Attestations of a thegn called Byrhtnoth occur between 934 and 937; Odda, father of the Byrhtnoth named in *VI As*. 10, is presumably the Odda who dominates the lists of thegns in charters throughout Æthelstan's reign (and thereafter until 943).

[60] Compare *II As*. 1.

and his councillors to a wider audience (*II Æthelstan* and *V Æthelstan*), a report of the Kentish shire-court back to the king (*III Æthelstan*) and two records apparently drawn up independently of royal authority for the benefit of other local bodies (*IV Æthelstan* and *VI Æthelstan*); moreover, one of the latter records incorporates texts which appear to be derived from an injunction addressed by the king to the officials of the shire-courts (*VI As.* 11), and from two reports to the peace-guild of London, one perhaps by the two men who had represented the peace-guild in a royal gathering at Thunderfield in Surrey (*VI As.* 10), and the other perhaps by the bishop of London himself, who had attended a gathering at Whittlebury in Northamptonshire (*VI As.* 12). One could hardly wish for a better view of the administration of justice during Æthelstan's reign, or for a better demonstration of the extent to which it depended on the use of the written word: the king sent written instructions to his reeves, who were responsible for the implementation of the law in the localities; written texts of royal decrees were sent to the shire-courts, where they were duly published; the officials of the shire-courts sent written reports back to the king, to assure him that they were fulfilling his instructions; and local bodies drew up their own written statements of their local practice, augmenting them with other relevant records. The variety of the evidence from Æthelstan's reign is thus a sign not of any casual attitude towards the publication or recording of the law, but quite the reverse: the king must have had scribes at court who could produce the necessary documents, and the first generation of royal officials who had had the benefit of an Alfredian education were clearly literate enough to cope, and to respond.

There is nothing equal to the diverse material from Æthelstan's reign in the corpus of later Anglo-Saxon legislation, and the possibility must therefore exist that the feverish activity which seems to have characterized that period was not maintained (or did not need to be maintained) in quite the same way thereafter. Yet while the law-codes known to modern scholarship as *I Edmund*, *II Edmund*, *III Edmund* and *II–III Edgar* contain no obvious indication of the means of their promulgation, they do bear comparison in general terms with codes such as *II* and *V Æthelstan*, and it would be surprising if their status as records of royal acts of legislation was significantly different. The code designated *I Edgar*, otherwise known as the *Hundred Ordinance*, differs from the norm only insofar as it does not run in the name of a particular king; but there can be no doubt that it proceeded from a gathering of the king's council, and one imagines that it too was promulgated more widely in written form. The remaining legislative act of the central decades of the tenth century is *IV Edgar*, which stands out from these other codes as an example of a legal text which was certainly

issued in written form: it begins 'Here it is made known in this document
. . .' (*Her is geswutelod on þisum gewrite* . . .),[61] and the penultimate clause
directs that 'many documents are to be written concerning this, and sent
both to Ealdorman Ælfhere and to Ealdorman Æthelwine, and they are to
send them in all directions, so that this measure may be known to both the
poor and the rich' (*7 write man manega gewrita be ðisum* . . .).[62] Other
things being equal, one could argue that this explicit statement of arrangements for the publication of a law-code stands out because it is exceptional;[63] but other things rarely are equal in Anglo-Saxon England, and in
my own judgement the incidental evidence which has been assembled above
from earlier tenth-century legislation should be allowed to speak with the
same voice.[64]

The legislation of King Æthelred the Unready has been examined in
some detail by Wormald. Wormald does allow that 'when Æthelred and his
council pronounced law, a text was written on the spot';[65] but in accordance
with his views on later Anglo-Saxon legislation in general, he would appear
to contend that the extant texts owe their existence more to initiatives taken
by others than to the king.[66] I would express only one reservation.
Wormald's exposition proceeds mainly from his analysis of legislation
drafted on King Æthelred's behalf by Wulfstan, archbishop of York, and

---

[61] *IV Edg*. Prol.

[62] *IV Edg*. 15.1; compare Charlemagne's *Capitulare missorum de exercitu promovendo* (808),
ch. 8, *MGH Cap*. I, no. 50, p. 138, trans. King, *Charlemagne*, p. 263, and Loyn and
Percival, *Reign of Charlemagne*, no. 22, p. 97, for arrangements for the multiplication of
copies of a capitulary. More attention needs to be given to the significance of the differences
between the Old English versions of *IV Edgar* (in BL Cotton Nero E.i (Ker, *Catalogue*, no.
166), and in CCCC 265 (*ibid*. no. 53)), on the one hand, and the Latin version (which
precedes the OE version in CCCC 265), on the other; for if the extant OE versions descend
from a text which seems to have been directed towards the Danelaw, the Latin version
appears to represent a text directed elsewhere. The specific reference to Ealdorman Ælfhere
(of Mercia) and Ealdorman Æthelwine (of East Anglia), to the apparent exclusion of any
other ealdormen, is most readily to be understood on the basis that the code was issued in the
early 970s (when these two dominated the scene: see Cyril Hart, 'Athelstan "Half-King"
and his family', *ASE* 2 (1973), 115–44, at 133 n. 6), and need not imply that the code's
distribution was restricted to those areas with which they are known to have been
connected. Curiously enough, *IV Edgar* is conspicuous by its absence from *Quadripartitus*.

[63] Thus Vollrath, 'Gesetzgebung und Schriftlichkeit', 43–7, is inclined to regard the provision
for the mutiplication of written copies of *IV Edgar* as something which proceeded from
special circumstances, namely that the ordinance in this form was intended for publication
in the Danelaw.

[64] An investigation of the extent to which the surviving tenth-century codes were indebted to
(what might have been written texts of) earlier codes would be one way forward; see
Wormald, 'Uses of literacy', 112.

[65] Wormald, 'Æthelred the lawmaker', p. 64.

[66] *Ibid*., pp. 56–7 and 64–5.

preserved in manuscripts associated with Wulfstan himself; and while one cannot dispute that this legislation affords 'a unique opportunity to examine Anglo-Saxon written law in the making',[67] one does wonder whether 'it is the most important indication of what Anglo-Saxon legislation was really like'.[68] That is to say, Wulfstan was for ever revising material of his own in the course of his long career as a royal law-maker, first for Æthelred and subsequently for Cnut; and while he might well have felt free to adapt for his own purposes the legislation which he had himself drafted, it need not follow that earlier law-codes had been made in the same way, or that what certainly applies to Wulfstan's codes is necessarily applicable to the rest.[69]

Whatever the status of the extant codes as records of royal decrees, Wormald must, however, be right to insist that it was the king's (spoken) *word* which counted, for it was in the king that the authority ultimately lay. As Ælfric remarks, in one of the homilies in his First Series (written *c.* 990): 'One thing is the ordinance (*seo gesetnys*) which the king commands (*bytt*) through his ealdormen and reeves; quite another is his own decree (*his agen gebann*) in his own presence'.[70] But if King Alfred has used the written word to project his ideological aspirations, both he and his successors in the tenth century were no less conscious of the advantages it could bring in the more practical world of the publication and administration of royal law. That is not to say, however, that they were trying to bring the people under the rule of written law. The difficulty (as Wormald has observed) is to find a connection between the world of the Anglo-Saxon law-codes, and the real world of Anglo-Saxon crime and punishment.[71] It is perfectly true that there is no recorded instance of a royal law-code cited by chapter and verse, but should we necessarily expect there to be so? What counted, indeed, was the king's oral decree; and it was the function of the tenth-century law-codes to assist in the process of bringing knowledge of the king's decrees into the localities, not to provide a permanent frame of reference. One might add

---

[67] *Ibid.*, p. 49.   [68] *Ibid.*, p. 58.

[69] It should be noted that a fundamental distinction is to be made between the contexts in which the 'pre-Wulfstan' codes (*I–IV Æthelred*) are preserved (variously the *Textus Roffensis*, CCCC 383, and *Quadripartitus*), and the contexts in which the 'Wulfstan' codes are preserved (CCCC 201, BL Cotton Nero A.i, and BL Cotton Claudius A.iii, all associated in some way with Wulfstan himself; only *VII Æthelred* occurs also in *Quadripartitus*). The manuscript of *IX Æthelred* was lost in the Cotton fire (Ker, *Catalogue*, no. 170); the fragment designated *X Æthelred* was entered on a blank leaf of a service-book (*ibid.* no. 392), and it would be of great interest to know precisely when, where and under what circumstances.

[70] Benjamin Thorpe, *The Homilies of Ælfric*, 2 vols. (London, 1843–6), I, p. 358; see also *EHD* no. 239c. Malcolm Godden advises me that the image is likely to be Ælfric's own.

[71] Wormald, 'Uses of literacy', 112–13; *idem*, '*Lex Scripta* and *Verbum Regis*', p. 122; and *idem*, 'Æthelred the lawmaker', p. 48.

that it was one thing to have the laws circulated in writing to the shire-courts, and to expect reeves to be able to refer to texts of King Alfred's code; but it would be another to imagine that the reeves themselves approximated in any way to the modern conception of the professional lawyer. For the 'judges' of the tenth and eleventh centuries were certainly not men in bowler hats with brief-cases and rolled-up umbrellas, and with access to shelves of written law; rather, they were men like Æthelric, bishop of Selsey, 'a man of great age and very wise in the law of the land, who, by the command of the king [William I], was brought to the trial in a wagon in order that he might expound the ancient practice of the laws'.[72] Perhaps a better analogy would be with the sheriffs who kept the peace on the American western frontier in the nineteenth century: they were expected to be able to enforce laws which were written, but copies of the published codes were scarce, badly drawn up, full of misleading misprints, out of date and as often as not written in language which the sheriffs could not understand; much would always have depended on the sheriff's sense of natural justice, and on his susceptibility to bribery and corruption.[73]

The evidence for the extensive use of written documents in the dissemination of law is complemented by indications that the written word permeated other aspects of royal government and administration; but there remains no mistaking that written documents never threatened to supplant purely oral forms of conducting the affairs of the realm. We may consider, for example, the agency of communication between the king at the centre and those who exercised authority in the localities. In his translation of St Augustine's *Soliloquies*, King Alfred refers to a lord's 'written message and his seal' (*ærendgewrit and hys insegel*), as if it were commonplace in his reign for the king (and perhaps any other lord) to make known his will by means of a written document associated with the impression of a seal;[74] but we also know from Asser that the king had communicated with his 'judges' through his 'trusted men' (*suos fideles*).[75] Both King Edward the Elder and King Æthelstan sent written injunctions to their reeves; but Æthelstan (for

---

[72] From the report of the trial held on Pinnenden Heath (Kent) in the 1070s, trans. *English Historical Documents 1042–1189*, ed. David C. Douglas and George W. Greenaway (2nd edn, London, 1981), no. 50. Compare the reference in the poem *The Gifts of Men* to the one who 'knows the laws, where men deliberate' (*Sum domas con, þær dryhtguman ræd eahtiað*); see *The Exeter Book*, ed. George Philip Krapp and Elliott van Kirk Dobbie, Anglo-Saxon Poetic Records 3 (Columbia, 1936), p. 139, and *EHD* no. 213.

[73] See, for example, Philip D. Jordan, *Frontier Law and Order* (Lincoln, Nebraska, 1970), pp. 155–74.

[74] See Keynes and Lapidge, *Alfred the Great*, pp. 141 and 300.

[75] Asser, ch. 106: see *Life of Alfred*, ed. Stevenson, p. 93 (text), and Keynes and Lapidge, *Alfred the Great*, pp. 109–10 (translation).

one) seems also to have operated through personal representatives. For, as we have seen, the officials of the Kentish shire-court, in reporting to the king, acknowledged the help 'of the councillors whom you have sent to us',[76] and the king sent word of his change of heart at Whittlebury to the archbishop of Canterbury, by Theodred, bishop of London;[77] one might be inclined to regard Ælfheah Stybb and Byrhtnoth, son of Odda, who are named in *VI As*. 10 as attending an assembly at the king's command, as the king's representatives at a local assembly, but it was suggested above that they are more likely to have been local representatives summoned to a royal assembly. Unfortunately, one can but guess whether such personal representatives, like Charlemagne's *missi dominici*,[78] carried the king's instructions with them in the form of written documents; but in view of King Alfred's remarks in the *Soliloquies*, it seems likely that sometimes they did. After all, much was to be gained by the simple expedient of putting instructions down in writing: Bishop Wealdhere told a correspondent that he had been 'at pains to intimate this to you by letter (*per litteras*) so that it may not be divulged and known to many',[79] and Charlemagne complained to one of his *missi* that he had given him instructions by his own mouth, 'and you have not understood it at all'.[80]

In the later tenth and eleventh centuries, the nature of communication between the centre and the localities is somewhat clearer, and it remains apparent that kings depended as much on messages conveyed orally by their trusted representatives as on letters conveyed by their agents.[81] Two vernacular charters from the reign of King Æthelred the Unready reveal how royal government articulated with the shire-courts. Sometime between 990 and 992 a dispute arose between a certain Wynflæd and a certain Leofwine, over the possession of two estates in Berkshire.[82] Wynflæd had

---

[76] *III As*. 1.   [77] *VI As*. 12.1.

[78] See, for example, McKitterick, *Frankish Kingdoms*, pp. 93–7; compare Helen M. Cam, *Local Government in Francia and England* (London, 1912), p. 53.

[79] *EHD* no. 164 (dated *c*. 705); see Pierre Chaplais, 'The letter from Bishop Wealdhere of London to Archbishop Brihtwold of Canterbury: the earliest original "letter close" extant in the west', in his *Essays in Medieval Diplomacy and Administration* (London, 1981), no. XIV. On the greater security afforded by a written letter, see also *The Exeter Book*, ed. Krapp and Dobbie, p. 225 (Riddle 60).

[80] *Responsa misso cuidam data* (802×813), ch. 6, in *MGH Cap*. I, no. 58, p. 145, trans. King, *Charlemagne*, p. 268.

[81] Of course there may not always have been any such distinction. One should bear in mind that news of King Æthelstan's achievements in 927 was transmitted back to court by a certain Peter, and by means of an extraordinary (written) poem; see Michael Lapidge, 'Some Latin poems as evidence for the reign of Athelstan', *ASE* 9 (1981), 61–98, at 83–93.

[82] Sawyer no. 1454: *Anglo-Saxon Charters*, ed. A.J. Robertson (2nd edn, Cambridge, 1956), no. 66.

produced witnesses in the king's presence who swore that she had been given the estates by one Ælfric (probably Leofwine's father), whereupon the king sent word of this to Leofwine, who insisted that the matter be referred to the shire-court; so 'the king sent his seal to the meeting at Cuckamsley by Abbot Ælfhere [of Bath], and greeted all the councillors who were assembled there' (*sende se cyning be Æluere abbude his insegel to þam gemote æt Cwicelmeshlæwe 7 gretle ealle þa witan þe þær gesomnode wæron*), commanding them to settle the case. It is possible that this was a message conveyed orally by the abbot on the king's behalf, supported by an impression of the king's seal, but it is also possible that *insegel* in this instance refers to a sealed writ.[83] The second charter concerns a dispute between Godwine, bishop of Rochester, and a certain Leofwine, about the possession of Snodland in Kent.[84] On becoming bishop, Godwine found some documents (*swutelunga*) in the church archives, and with them laid claim to the estate; the suit came to the king's attention, and 'he sent a letter and his seal to Archbishop Ælfric' (*sende he gewrit 7 his insegl to þam arcebisceope Ælfrice*), commanding that it should be settled in the Kentish shire-court. We may wonder in this instance whether the seal was physically attached to the king's letter, or whether it was separate; but whatever the case, it is as clear an example of a reference to an administrative communication in writing as one could reasonably hope to get.[85]

It should be noted that laymen, and in particular the king's thegns, were among those employed by the king for conveying messages to the shire-courts: we have not only the example of the 'councillors' sent by King Æthelstan to the Kentish shire-court, but also that of Tofi the Proud, a thegn of Cnut's who came to a meeting of the Herefordshire shire-court 'on the king's business' (*on þæs cinges ærende*).[86] Indeed, it is perhaps in this context that we should bear in mind the three surviving seal-matrices which depict men brandishing swords, and which are inscribed, respectively,

---

[83] Compare F.E. Harmer, *Anglo-Saxon Writs* (Manchester, 1952), p. 545 (no. 21), where the phrase *sigillum regis E.* is used in reference to a sealed writ of Edward the Confessor.

[84] Sawyer no. 1456: *Charters*, ed. Robertson, no. 69.

[85] See Pierre Chaplais, 'The Anglo-Saxon chancery: from the diploma to the writ', in *Prisca Munimenta*, ed. Felicity Ranger (London, 1973), pp. 43–62, at 56; and Simon Keynes, *The Diplomas of King Æthelred 'the Unready' 978–1016: A Study in their Use as Historical Evidence* (Cambridge, 1980), pp. 137–8. Perhaps the king's seal was employed on its own when the message was conveyed orally to the shire-court by one such as a trusted abbot; and perhaps a letter and seal were employed when the message was directed to an individual, and carried by a king's messenger.

[86] Sawyer no. 1462: *Charters*, ed. Robertson, no. 78, and *EHD* no. 135. The same phrase, *on þæs cinges ærende*, is used in the *Anglo-Saxon Chronicle* in connection with Bishop Aldred's expeditions to Rome (*Anglo-Saxon Chronicle* MS. C, s.a. 1049) and to Cologne (MS. D, s.a. 1054).

'SIGILLUM GODWINI MINISTRI', SIGILLUM ÆLFRICI' and 'SIGILLUM WULFRICI'.[87] The obvious similarities between them suggest that they should be considered as a group, and furthermore that they might have been issued to the thegns in question in connection with their performance of 'official' duties on behalf of the king: the matrices were presumably used in some way to establish their holder's credentials, whether in support of an oral message or a written document.[88]

Nor should it be forgotten that it was apparently commonplace in the late tenth century (and quite possibly long before that) for the king to convey messages to his thegns by means of written documents. It is Ælfric, again, who envisages the following situation: 'if the king sends his writ to any one of his thegns, and he despises it so greatly that he will not hear it, nor look at [any] of it, the king will not be very gracious to him when he learns how he has scorned him'.[89] The implication seems to be that the thegn was not expected to be able to read the writ himself; but Ælfric was trying to alarm those who might refuse to *listen* to God's instruction, so it is possible that he might have tailored his analogy to suit its purpose. Administrative letters of the kind which Ælfric probably had in mind might have served various purposes, for example an order to a king's reeve telling him to make ready for a visit to a royal estate, or a summons to a meeting of the *witan*, or an instruction to the local official that a certain man should be brought to justice or that a dispute should be settled; but unfortunately such documents, being of merely passing interest to the parties concerned, would effectively have had no chance of survival or preservation.

---

[87] See Keynes, *Diplomas*, pp. 138–40, and references; see also T.A. Heslop, 'English seals from the mid-ninth century to 1100', *Journal of the British Archaeological Association* 133 (1980), 1–16 and *idem*, 'A walrus ivory seal matrix from Lincoln', *Antiquaries Journal* 66 (1986), 371–2 and 396–7.

[88] That thegns had a role in King Æthelstan's administration might be suggested by *VI As*. 11, which imposes a fine on those thegns who neglect to follow the king's guidance; see also *IV As*. 7. For King Æthelred's use of thegns on a diplomatic mission to Normandy, see *EHD* no. 230. A thegn's duties in the king's service are implicit in *Geþyncðo* 3 (*Gesetze*, ed. Liebermann, I, p. 456, trans. *EHD* no. 51). A particularly interesting allusion to the role of thegns in 'official' (though in this instance not actually royal) business occurs in Sawyer no. 1462: the Herefordshire shire-court appointed three thegns to go to the mother of a certain Edwin, to establish her position with respect to land which Edwin was claiming against her; whereupon she made an oral declaration of her bequest of all her property to her kinswoman Leofflæd, and said to the thegns 'Act well like thegns, and announce my message to the meeting before all good men, and inform them to whom I have granted my land and all my possessions' ('doð) þegnlice 7 wel · abeodað mine ærende to ðam gemote beforan eallon þam godan mannum 7 cyðaþ heom hwæm ic mines landes geunnen hæbbe'). For further discussion of the role of thegns as the king's messengers, see Campbell, 'Some agents', pp. 210–13.

[89] *Homilies of Ælfric: A Supplementary Collection*, ed. J.C. Pope, 2 vols., Early English Text Society OS 259–60 (London, 1967–8), II, p. 659; see Keynes, *Diplomas*, pp. 136–7.

The writs which do survive date from the reigns of Cnut and Edward the Confessor, and owe their preservation to the care of certain religious houses which valued them as evidence of title to land or privileges; there is a danger, therefore, that writs will be regarded as a feature only of the last phase of Anglo-Saxon royal government, and as having most to do with the affairs of particular churches. Yet it is striking that even the surviving examples attest to the great variety of purposes which a writ could be made to serve, announcing to the suitors of the shire-court not only transfers of land or grants of privileges, but also appointments to high office and much else besides. Indeed, there seems no reason to dissent from Harmer's belief that the surviving writs are but the rump of a long tradition of administrative letters stretching back at least as far as the reign of King Alfred the Great, and that people other than the king were also accustomed to convey messages in written form.[90]

I turn finally to a consideration of the place of written documents in late Anglo-Saxon society, and in particular to the evidence provided by the corpus of vernacular charters and wills. Besides affording some reassurance that the world of the royal law-codes was not far removed from reality, these sources certainly have to be understood in the context of a society in which considerable respect was accorded to the written word. It must be emphasized again that this does not represent a change from what can be observed in the earlier Anglo-Saxon period, when disputes often turned on the possession of written evidence of title to an estate (usually in the form of a royal diploma, which would not necessarily have been in favour of any of the disputing parties). For several of the later accounts of legal proceedings attest in much the same way to the value attached to written evidence; while the greater quantity of surviving wills adds new precision to our appreciation of the penetration of the written word into at least the upper levels of lay society.[91]

A graphic illustration of the part played by the written word in routine legal processes is afforded by one of the best-known cases in Anglo-Saxon law. A single sheet of parchment preserved in the archives of Christ

[90] See Harmer, *Writs*, pp. 10–24 and 57–61 (and Chaplais, 'Anglo-Saxon chancery', pp. 50–61); see further Simon Keynes, 'Regenbald the Chancellor (*sic*)', *Anglo-Norman Studies*, 10, ed. R. Allen Brown (Woodbridge, 1988), pp. 185–222, at pp. 214–17.

[91] For the value attached to written documents, see Keynes, *Diplomas*, p. 34, and A.G. Kennedy, 'Disputes about *bocland*: the forum for their adjudication', *Anglo-Saxon England* 14 (1985), 175–95; see also Patrick Wormald, 'Charters, law and the settlement of disputes in Anglo-Saxon England', in *Settlement of Disputes*, pp. 149–68, and *idem*, 'A handlist of Anglo-Saxon lawsuits', *ASE* 17 (1988), 247–82. The charters, wills and other documents which survive in their original form, on single sheets of parchment, have much to reveal about the use of the written word; all such charters, etc., are listed, with general discussion, in Simon Keynes, *A Handlist of Anglo-Saxon Charters: Archives and single sheets* (forthcoming).

Church, Canterbury, is inscribed with an account of the history of an estate at Fonthill in Wiltshire, written by Ealdorman Ordlaf and addressed to King Edward the Elder.[92] The account recalls a sequence of events which seems to have extended from the last year of Alfred's reign (898–9) into the first year of Edward's (899–900), the purpose of which was to explain how the estate in question had ended up in the hands of the bishop of Winchester. The document is of some interest in showing how at one stage a former owner of the estate had established his right to the land by producing a relevant document, which was duly read and found to be in order. Its chief interest, however, is as an example of a written document submitted by a layman to the king in connection with a legal dispute, in support of the defendant's title to the disputed estate; it would be wishful thinking to suppose that the document was actually written by Ealdorman Ordlaf himself (since he might not have had the benefit of an Alfredian education), but the script is certainly compatible with a date in Edward the Elder's reign, and a note on the dorse, to the effect that the claimant abandoned his suit when the king was at Warminster, is added by a different scribe, which tends to confirm the document's status as an original. Incidentally, Ordlaf's submission was committed to writing not because he was unable to attend the hearing, for he is named in the dorse as one of the witnesses present at Warminster; one is reminded, therefore, of the provision in Charlemagne's general capitulary for the *missi* (802), that 'if there be anything which they themselves, together with the counts of the provinces, cannot correct or bring to a just settlement, they should refer it without hesitation to the emperor's judgement along with their written reports' (*cum brebitariis suis*).[93]

Several of the disputes which took place in the later tenth century seem similarly to have turned on the possession of diplomas or other forms of written evidence of title to the disputed estate. Some of the records of such disputes were (like the Fonthill letter) apparently prepared by one of the parties involved for submission as evidence in the dispute itself, and others seem to have been drawn up by or on behalf of the successful party as a permanent record of a dispute's outcome; but one should not forget that the evidence of the written word took its place beside other forms of establishing or maintaining one's rights, whether by witnesses or oaths, and that Anglo-Saxon legal procedure was never so cut and dried as to exclude the more informal role of coercion, compromise and corruption. Thus the

---

[92] Sawyer no. 1445: *Select English Historical Documents of the Ninth and Tenth Centuries*, ed. F.E. Harmer (Cambridge, 1914), no. 18, and *EHD* no. 102.

[93] *Capitulare missorum generale* (802), ch. 1, in *MGH Cap.* I, no. 33, p. 92, trans. King, *Charlemagne*, p. 234, and Loyn and Percival, *Reign of Charlemagne*, no. 16, p. 74.

dispute between Wynflæd and Leofwine (which was cited above in another context) began at a meeting in the king's presence when Wynflæd produced witnesses in support of her own claim to have received the land from Ælfric; when contested by Leofwine, the matter was referred to the shire-court, and two of Wynflæd's original witnesses (Archbishop Sigeric and Ordbriht, bishop of Selsey) each sent a 'declaration' (*swutelunge*) to the meeting, which in this context seems to mean a written statement in support of Wynflæd's case; Wynflæd then produced the requisite number of supporters, but in the event a compromise was reached, and the settlement of the dispute was committed to writing.[94] Similarly, in the dispute over Snodland in Kent (also cited above) the bishop of Rochester produced his evidence (*swutelunge*, presumably in the form of the written documents which he had recently found in his church) at a meeting of the shire-court, and a compromise was agreed whereby the other party gave up his own-*swutelunga* relating to the land and in return received it on lease for the duration of his life; again, a record of the settlement itself (incorporating the names of all the witnesses) was duly committed to writing.[95]

Two other splendid examples of disputes which turned on the possession of written evidence in the form of charters are provided by the *Libellus Æthelwoldi episcopi*, an early twelfth-century Latin account of the refoundation and endowment of Ely Abbey in the early 970s, based on a (lost) vernacular record of the same process (which seems itself to have been drawn up in the aftermath of the anti-monastic reaction precipitated by King Edgar's death in 975).[96] In the first, a dispute over land which had been appropriated from Ely Abbey was decided in part on the principle that 'the person who had the charter was nearer [to the oath] that he should have the land, than the one who did not have it'.[97] In the second, we are told how

---

[94] Sawyer no. 1454: *Charters*, ed. Robertson, no. 66. One wonders how many (besides Dr Chaplais, to whom I am grateful for the explanation) would have appreciated the cleverness of the scribe who produced the chirograph: instead of separating the parts with the normal word CYROGRAPHUM, he devised the legend CPILREOTGURMAEFSUTM, which produces (when the letters are read alternately) the words CIROGRAFUM PLETUM EST.

[95] Sawyer no. 1456: *Charters*, ed. Robertson, no. 69. See also Wormald, 'Settlement of disputes', pp. 157–61.

[96] The material in the *Libellus* is well known by virtue of its incorporation in the *Liber Eliensis* (see *Liber Eliensis*, ed. E.O. Blake, Camden 3rd series 92 (London, 1962), between p. 73 and p. 117, and pp. 395–9). For an edition of the *Libellus* itself (with translation and commentary), see Simon Keynes and Alan Kennedy, *Anglo-Saxon Ely: Records of Ely Abbey and its Benefactors in the Tenth and Eleventh Centuries* (Woodbridge, forthcoming).

[97] *Libellus*, ch. 35: *Liber Eliensis*, ed. Blake, pp. 98–9. The Fonthill letter (Sawyer no. 1445) affords another example of the same principle in operation: on one occasion, Helmstan produced written evidence in support of his title to the land, and (in Ealdorman Ordlaf's

Bishop Æthelwold and the abbot of Ely had failed (through no fault of their own) to get hold of the charters relating to a newly acquired property, and, since the charters had fallen into the hands of the brother and kinsmen of a previous owner, how they feared 'that claims and trickeries could arise at some time'; they turned first to Ealdorman Æthelwine, promising him some land elsewhere if he would intervene on their behalf to obtain the charters, but the ealdorman did nothing, and kept the land; so in desperation they turned to Ealdorman Byrhtnoth, asking him to buy the charters for the abbey, which he duly did; and as their payment for the charters, they gave 30 mancuses and another charter which they knew the brother wanted.[98] Needless to say, it may be doubted whether all the laymen who struggled over the possession of royal diplomas in the late tenth century would have been able to comprehend the Latin text of the documents they so earnestly desired, though the vernacular endorsement and boundary-clause would have told them all they needed to know.[99]

The corpus of surviving wills attests in a similar way to the recognition, in at least some quarters of Anglo-Saxon society, of the value of the written word. It seems to have been normal practice in the tenth and eleventh centuries, as before, for any individual to determine the disposition of his property after his death by means of a declaration made orally in the presence of witnesses; the oral declaration generally sufficed, and it was not a necessary part of the process to have the will recorded in writing.[100] A written record of the declaration was, however, sometimes made, and in such cases one might ask whether the record was intended to serve a particular purpose, and who was responsible for its production. The existence of a written text of a will would obviously have been to the advantage of a prospective beneficiary, as the record of an act which might have involved provisions of some complexity, and which might not have been expected to come into effect for some time. There may also have been circumstances in which it was desirable from the testator's own point of

---

words) 'then it seemed to all of us who were at that arbitration that Helmstan was nearer to the oath on that account'.

[98] *Libellus*, ch. 38: *Liber Eliensis*, ed. Blake, pp. 100–1.

[99] For the distinction between comprehension of Latin and the vernacular, see Kelly, above, p. 52. In the school established by King Alfred, 'books in both languages – that is to say, in Latin and English – were carefully read' (Asser, ch. 75: see *Life of Alfred*, ed. Stevenson, p. 58 (text), and Keynes and Lapidge, *Alfred the Great*, p. 40 (translation)); for attempts to maintain this practice, see D.A. Bullough, 'The educational tradition in England from Alfred to Ælfric: teaching *utriusque linguae*', *Settimane* 19 (Spoleto, 1972), 453–94.

[100] See H.D. Hazeltine, 'Comments on the writings known as Anglo-Saxon wills', in *Anglo-Saxon Wills*, ed. Dorothy Whitelock (Cambridge, 1930), pp. vii–xl; see also Michael M. Sheehan, *The Will in Medieval England* (Toronto, 1963), pp. 5–106.

view to have a written record made of his oral declaration, so that an accurate account of his intentions could be conveyed to another party: for example, the testator may have needed to convey his intentions to the king or to a local official (perhaps in order to secure formal approval), or to some other interested party, and chose to do so in writing because he was unable to achieve his purpose more directly. A written record of a will might thus have been made by an 'interested' ecclesiastic, acting in his capacity as a prospective beneficiary;[101] or the testator might have solicited the services of a 'local' priest or scribe, acting disinterestedly on the testator's behalf;[102] and one should perhaps not rule out the possibility that in one or two cases the will might have been written by the testator himself.

The wills themselves rarely afford much indication of the specific circumstances of their production in written form. It is apparent, however, that whereas the oral declaration might constitute the operative act of making a will, a written record was sometimes produced as a necessary part of the no less important process of its formal 'publication'. Thus in the 830s the Kentish reeve Abba declared his wishes as to the disposal of his property, and at the same time commanded that they be set down in writing;[103] the text of his will, including Abba's own attestation, was written by a scribe known to have belonged to the community of Christ Church, Canterbury,[104] but the names of the other witnesses were added by a different hand (presumably that of another Christ Church scribe), suggest-

---

[101] The case of Badanoth Beotting is particularly instructive; see Sawyer no. 296 and Sawyer no. 1510 (*Charters*, ed. Robertson, no. 6). Soon after purchasing an estate in Canterbury from King Æthelwulf in 845, Badanoth bequeathed it to the community of Christ Church, subject to the life interest of his wife and children. The documents recording these acts were written by a scribe known to have belonged to the Christ Church community: Nicholas Brooks, *The Early History of the Church of Canterbury* (Leicester, 1984), p. 361 (scribe 5). It was thus in effect the beneficiary who (at Badanoth's command) drew up the will, and it is apparent that this process extended to the formulation of the detailed terms of Badanoth's (ostensibly oral) declaration: see A. Campbell, 'An Old English will', *Journal of English and Germanic Philology* 27 (1938), 133–52, at 134–5.

[102] The will of Wulfgar (Sawyer no. 1533: *Charters*, ed. Robertson, no. 26), drawn up in the 930s during the reign of King Æthelstan, is a case in point. It was written by a scribe who has been identified elsewhere among additions to a manuscript apparently kept at the royal estate of Bedwyn (see M.B. Parkes, 'A fragment of an early-tenth-century Anglo-Saxon manuscript and its significance', *ASE* 12 (1983), 129–40, at 137 n. 51), in the vicinity of Wulfgar's own property. Note, incidentally, that Wulfgar states at one point that he would bequeath one of his estates verbally (*on wordum*), 'to such of my young kinsmen as obey me best', as if sometime in the future he expected to make an oral declaration supplementing his written will.

[103] Sawyer no. 1482: *Select English Historical Documents*, ed. Harmer, no. 2.

[104] Brooks, *Church of Canterbury*, p. 360 (scribe 3).

ing that in this case it was the written document which had been read out and witnessed by the assembled company. The will of King Æthelwulf of Wessex is known to have existed in written form, for at the beginning of Alfred's reign it was brought to an assembly at *Langandene* and was there 'read before all the councillors of the West Saxons';[105] its contents were also known to Asser, and are summarized by him in his *Life of King Alfred*.[106] Alfred himself made a written will at some stage during his reign, and entrusted copies of it to many different people; but at a later stage he felt the need to revise its detailed provisions, and accordingly had to recover and destroy as many of the copies of the earlier will as he could find, to clear the ground for the revised version.[107] It was also during Alfred's reign that Ealdorman Alfred (of Surrey) had his will drawn up in writing expressly for the purposes of giving notice of his intentions to the king and his councillors, and to his kinsmen and friends; the text itself was written by one scribe on the face of a sheet of parchment, and the names of the witnesses (presumably to a formal reading aloud of the written text) were added on the dorse by a different scribe.[108]

Several of the later tenth- and eleventh-century wills were committed to writing out of more than a basic respect for the written word, in the sense that the purpose which the document was intended to serve was seemingly to enable a record of the testator's intentions to be conveyed to parties other than those who were present when the oral declaration had been made. The will of Ealdorman Æthelmær, for example, is cast in the form of a written document (*gewrit*), by means of which the ealdorman informed the king and others 'what his will was on his last day', where the implication could be that the testator was on his death-bed, and accordingly unable to make his declaration in the presence of suitable witnesses.[109] The will of Wulfgeat of Donington, on the other hand, looks like the record of an oral declaration made while the testator still had expectation of life; but the record contains a concluding request to a certain Æthelsige that he make the will known 'to my lord and to all my friends', as if for some reason Wulfgeat was unable to do so himself, and perhaps explaining why in this case the will was produced

---

[105] See Keynes and Lapidge, *Alfred the Great*, p. 175 (from King Alfred's will).

[106] Asser, ch. 16: see *Life of Alfred*, ed. Stevenson, pp. 14–16 (text), and Keynes and Lapidge, *Alfred the Great*, pp. 72–3 (translation).

[107] Sawyer no. 1507: *Select English Historical Documents*, ed. Harmer, no. 11, and *EHD* no. 96; see also Keynes and Lapidge, *Alfred the Great*, pp. 173–8.

[108] Sawyer no. 1508: *Select English Historical Documents*, ed. Harmer, no. 10, and *EHD* no. 97.

[109] Sawyer no. 1498: *Wills*, ed. Whitelock, no. 10.

in more than one copy (in the form of a chirograph).[110] The will of the
ætheling Æthelstan, eldest son of King Æthelred the Unready, is especially
revealing. It would appear to have been drawn up in written form on the day
that the ætheling received word from his father (via Ælfgar, son of Æffa)
that he might make his will, and it seems that the ætheling died later that
same day (25 June 1014); it must have been obvious, in other words, that
the ætheling would be unable to make his declaration in what might have
been the proper way for one of his station, and indeed the ætheling begs the
councillors 'who may hear my will read' (*þe minne cwyde gehyron rædan*) to
help ensure that it be allowed to stand.[111] The confirmation of wills must
indeed have been part of the routine business of government, and it is easier
to understand how things worked in practice if it is assumed that the
'publication' of a testator's oral declaration to the appropriate authority was
often accomplished by means of a written record which could be read to an
assembled company, in much the same way as the king's oral pronouncements on matters of legal import were committed to writing in order that
they might be conveyed to and published by his officials in the localities.

One should not overlook the detailed account of the making of a will
which occurs in the *Libellus Æthelwoldi Episcopi*. A layman called Siferth,
who was afflicted by gout, came on one occasion to Ely and made an oral
declaration of his bequest of two hides at Downham (in Cambridgeshire) to
the abbey; he came back to Ely on a subsequent occasion and repeated his
declaration, and on his return home made the declaration yet again, 'in the
presence of the leading men of his region beyond Upware in the place which
is called *Hyravicstouue*'. But when the crunch finally came, recourse was
made to the written word:

Then when this same man Siferth of Downham felt that his sickness was overpower-
ing him and the hour of his death approached, and as he lay at Linden without hope
of recovering his health, he sent for Abbot Byrhtnoth [of Ely] and for the brothers of
the church. And present there were Ælfric of Witcham, Ealdstan and his son Wine,
Leofric, Byrhthelm, Ælfhelm of *Redeuuinclen* and Eadric, one of the leading men of
Ealdorman Æthelwine, and the priest Oswald, and Sexferth with his son. Then
Abbot Byrhtnoth arranged for the will of Siferth to be written down in a tripartite
chirograph, in the presence of his wife and his daughter and all the people mentioned
above, and had it read out before them all. When it was read, he had it cut, and
Siferth kept one part of the chirograph, giving the second part to the abbot. The
third part he sent at once by the aforesaid Byrhthelm to Ealdorman Æthelwine, who

[110] Sawyer no. 1534: *Wills*, ed. Whitelock, no. 19. Similarly, perhaps, a certain Eadric the
Long sent a chirograph of his will to King Edgar: *Libellus*, ch. 38, *Liber Eliensis*, ed. Blake,
p. 100; see also Sawyer no. 1520, *ibid.* pp. 157–8, which is (a Latin translation of) an
(originally tripartite) chirographic will, cast in the form of a letter from the testator (a
daughter of Ealdorman Byrhtnoth) to King Cnut and his queen.

[111] Sawyer no. 1503: *Wills*, ed. Whitelock, no. 20, and *EHD* no. 129.

at that time was dwelling at Ely, and asked him to allow his will to stand, just as the abbot had written it and set it down at Linden in the witness of the aforementioned men. And when Ealdorman Æthelwine heard this and saw the chirograph, he sent Wulfnoth of Stowe back there to him with Byrhthelm and asked him what it was he wanted concerning his will. He [Siferth] soon reported back to him [Æthelwine] through them [Wulfnoth and Byrhthelm] just that he wanted his will to stand free from challenge or alteration, just as the aforesaid abbot had set it down in the chirograph. When Ealdorman Æthelwine heard this, he granted that it should stand in its entirety, just as Siferth had made it.[112]

This will, therefore, was evidently written on Siferth's behalf by (an agent of) the abbot of Ely, and while the story conveys an impression of a somewhat cumbersome procedure (not helped by the fact that Ealdorman Æthelwine was apparently rather slow on the uptake), there can be no mistaking the importance which was attached to the document, and its place in the context of public administration.[113]

It would seem reasonable to conclude that royal government in the tenth and eleventh centuries depended to a very considerable extent on the use of the written word, and that late Anglo-Saxon society was well accustomed to such manifestations of 'pragmatic literacy'.[114] It is, of course, difficult to be sure whether this can be regarded as a direct outcome of King Alfred's provisions for teaching the youth of his day how to read and write; but one might well suppose that the effects of his programme on succeeding generations would have been roughly equivalent to the effects which current programmes for making children 'computer-literate' are likely to have in our own years to come. But in thus maintaining that the taxi-run for the 'take-off' of literacy began many years before 1066, one should be careful not to imply that the extensive use of written documents in royal government was necessarily a guarantee of effective government, or that late Anglo-Saxon government was exclusively bureaucratic. Among the various types of written document which would have been generated by kings in conducting the affairs of their realm, I have dealt in particular with documents connected with the publication of law and the administration of

---

[112] *Libellus*, ch. 12, *Liber Eliensis*, ed. Blake, pp. 86–7.

[113] For a similar account of a will drawn up in multiple copies by an interested ecclesiastic on behalf of an ailing testator, see Sawyer no. 1458 (*Charters*, ed. Robertson, no. 41).

[114] The boundary-clauses incorporated in royal diplomas represent another aspect of pragmatic literacy, and should not be overlooked. The surveys must have been made in the localities, and submitted in written form to the agency responsible for producing the diploma; in some cases a survey in an older title-deed for the same estate may have served the purpose, but in other cases the survey presumably existed on a separate sheet of parchment; see Sawyer nos. 255 and 1547; compare Sawyer no. 1862. The 'unattached' boundary-clauses which are copied in certain cartularies (e.g. BL Cotton Claudius C.ix, from Abingdon) may reflect such procedures in some way.

justice, and with administrative communications of different kinds. One thinks otherwise of a king's general correspondence, such as the letters (*indiculi*) which King Alfred sent to Asser,[115] or the letters which two couriers took to Rome on Alfred's behalf in 889,[116] or of the two letters which King Cnut sent to his people in England from abroad.[117] One thinks of the written provisions which kings and other members of the royal family made for the disposal of their property; of documents emanating from meetings of the king and his councillors, such as that which must have been produced to record Wulfbald's come-uppance (subsequently used for the account of Wulfbald's crimes incorporated in a royal diploma);[118] of administrative documents such as the Burghal Hidage, and of records generated in connection with the performance of services due from the holders of land, or in connection with the assessment and collection of different kinds of tax (including *heregeld*, and tribute from Welsh rulers).[119] One thinks of treaties, whether with trading partners or with Viking armies; and one might even think of royal diplomas.[120] There most certainly was extensive use of the written word in the routine procedures of late Anglo-Saxon royal government; but whether it all worked smoothly is another matter, and that it should have precluded a role for oral processes of communication is out of the question.

Needless to say (perhaps), such a degree of dependence on the written word presupposes the existence of a body of scribes in the king's service; for while kings might on occasion have relied on others to produce the written records of government,[121] it is simply inconceivable that they could have done so as a matter of normal course. Little is known of the actual

---

[115] Asser, ch. 79: see *Life of Alfred*, ed. Stevenson, pp. 63–6 (text), and Keynes and Lapidge, *Alfred the Great*, pp. 93–4 (translation). Asser replied in writing.

[116] *twegen hleaperas Ælfred cyning sende mid gewritum*: Anglo-Saxon Chronicle, s.a. 889.

[117] *Gesetze*, ed. Liebermann, I, pp. 273–5 and 276–7 (=*EHD* nos. 48 and 53); see Simon Keynes, 'The additions in Old English', *The York Gospels*, ed. Nicholas Barker (Roxburghe Club, 1986), pp. 81–99, at 95–6.

[118] Sawyer no. 877: *Charters*, ed. Robertson, no. 63, and *EHD* no. 120. See also Simon Keynes, 'Crime and Punishment in the Reign of King Æthelred the Unready', in *People and Places in Northern Europe 500–1600*, ed. I.N. Wood and N. Lund (Woodbridge, forthcoming).

[119] See Campbell, 'Observations on English government', pp. 157–8, and 'The significance of the Anglo-Norman state', pp. 173–5.

[120] For the production of diplomas in the tenth and early eleventh centuries, see Keynes, *Diplomas*, pp. 14–153, and *idem*, 'Regenbald', pp. 185–7.

[121] Thus the document recording King Æthelred's confirmation of the will of Æthelric of Bocking (Sawyer no. 939: *Wills*, ed. Whitelock, no. 16.2, and *EHD* no. 121) was written and read during the course of a meeting of the royal council; and to judge from its tone it was drafted by a member of the community of Christ Church, Canterbury.

organization of the royal secretariat in the tenth and eleventh centuries, beyond the likelihood that it was a permanent office attached to the king's household, staffed by some laymen as well as by priests of the royal chapel, who accompanied the king on his peregrinations around the kingdom.[122] But one royal scribe who is known to us by name is the thegn Ælfwine, a *scriptor* of King Æthelred's who received a grant of land in Oxfordshire in 984;[123] and two others are Swithgar and Ælfgeat, who are associated with Regenbald the king's chancellor in charters of King Edward the Confessor.[124] There would have been plenty of work to keep such men fully occupied.[125]

---

[122] See Keynes, *Diplomas*, pp. 134–53, and *idem*, 'Regenbald', pp. 187–95; but compare Pierre Chaplais, 'The royal Anglo-Saxon "chancery" of the tenth century revisited', in *Studies in Medieval History Presented to R.H.C. Davis*, ed. Henry Mayr-Harting and R.I. Moore (London, 1985), pp. 41–51.

[123] Sawyer no. 853: *Charters of Burton Abbey*, ed. P.H. Sawyer, Anglo-Saxon Charters 2 (London, 1979), no. 24.

[124] See Keynes, 'Regenbald', pp. 208–10.

[125] Compare Chaplais, 'The royal Anglo-Saxon "chancery" ', pp. 43–4.

IO

Literacy in Carolingian government

Janet L. Nelson

I THE CONTEXT OF LITERACY

Nearly forty years ago, Ganshof published 'The use of the written word in Charlemagne's administration'.[1] That paper, in only eighteen pages, provided a comprehensive survey, and a lucid classification, of the documentary evidence, especially the capitularies, of Charlemagne's reign. Ganshof's study remains fundamental. The limited aim of the present paper is partly to supplement it, partly to set the material in a different context. Literacy can be examined, not just in quantitative terms of measurable 'uses', but in qualitative terms, as a form of ideology through which power is constructed.[2] The adjective 'written' refers to things, 'literate' to persons. Hence in dealing with *literacy* rather than with Ganshof's 'written word', I hope to consider aspects of social practice with which Ganshof was not concerned.

Ganshof's definition of 'administration' rested on a sharp distinction between 'written records' used 'to furnish proof of individual rights' and 'documents which formed part of an administrative routine'.[3] Implicit here

---

[1] Originally published as 'Charlemagne et l'usage de l'écrit en matière administrative', *Le Moyen Age* 57 (1951), 1–25, trans. J. Sondheimer as 'The use of the written word in Charlemagne's administration', in F.L. Ganshof, *The Carolingians and the Frankish Monarchy* (London, 1971), pp. 125–42.

[2] Social scientists have written much on literacy. I have found especially helpful: B.V. Street, *Literacy in Theory and Practice*, Cambridge Studies in Oral and Literate Culture 9 (Cambridge, 1984); also J. Goody, *The Logic of Writing and the Organisation of Society* (Cambridge, 1986). Both these give extensive references. Among mediaeval historians, the pathbreaker has been M. Clanchy, *From Memory to Written Record: England 1066–1307* (London, 1979). This exemplary study shows what can be done with the evidence from twelfth- and thirteenth-century England. B. Stock, *The Implications of Literacy: Written Language and Models of Interpretation in the Eleventh and Twelfth Centuries* (Princeton, 1983), and D. Cressy, *Literacy and the Social Order* (Cambridge, 1982), are full of insights on, respectively, the eleventh/twelfth and sixteenth/seventeenth centuries. See also H.J. Graff, *The Legacies of Literacy: Continuities and Contradictions in Western Culture and Society* (Bloomington and Indianapolis, 1987).

[3] Ganshof, 'The use of the written word', p. 125.

is a further distinction between the private and public domains. Only the latter came within Ganshof's purview: for him, administration was the sphere of the state. But what in the Carolingian period was the public domain? Was there a Carolingian state at all? Such questions – and they are important ones in the history of political ideas – have generated much debate precisely because the categories they employ are hard to pin down to early mediaeval realities.[4] The term 'government' directs attention to such realities, and, specifically, to the operations of legitimate power. Here the useful distinction to be made is not between private and public, but, instead, between two levels: local and central. Basic types of governmental activity – peacekeeping, the mobilizing of military force, the imposition of generalized economic exactions – operated at one or the other level, or involved interaction between the two. For Marculf, compiling a collection of legal form-documents *c. 700*, *praeceptiones regales* (royal precepts) and *cartae pagenses* (local charters) were complementary instruments.[5]

As far as peacekeeping was concerned, the Franks, as often happens, recognized the workings of power more clearly abroad than at home. Among the Saxons, disputes could be settled by *pagenses infra patriam* ('locals within their native region', that is, in this case, Saxony itself) *cum propriis vicinantibus, more solito . . . iuxta consuetudinem* ('with their own neighbourhood-dwellers, in the traditional way . . . according to custom'); or in the same local courts in the presence of royal commissioners (*missi*); or in the palace in the presence of the king.[6] In those parts of the Empire that had once been Roman and where counties were ancient territorial units, the local courts were presided over by the count or his deputies, but with the co-operation, still, of *pagenses*.[7]

To wield force, the ruler maintained a military household, whose members had retinues of their own. Some individuals of both sorts of group resided not with the ruler at the palace but on estates in the countryside,

---

[4] See especially J. Fried, 'Der karolingische Herrschaftsverband im 9.Jh.', *Historische Zeitschrift* 235 (1982), 1–43; and, not least for a fine survey of the mainly German historiography, H.-W. Goetz, '*Regnum*: Zum politischen Denken der Karolingerzeit', *Zeitschrift der Savigny-Stiftung für Rechtsgeschichte*, 117, germanistische Abteilung, 104 (1987), 110–89. English-speaking students will find some relevant comments in J.L. Nelson, 'Kingship and empire', in *The Cambridge History of Medieval Political Thought* ed. J.H. Burns (Cambridge, 1988), pp. 211–51, at pp. 224–9.

[5] *Marculfi Formularum Libri Duo*, ed. A. Uddholm (Uppsala 1962), p. 18.

[6] *MGH Cap.* I, no. 27, c. 4, p. 71.

[7] See J.L. Nelson, 'Dispute settlement in Carolingian West Francia', and W. Davies, 'People and places in dispute in ninth-century Brittany', in *Settlement of Disputes*, pp. 61–2, 73, 273. In taking *pagenses* to mean 'local men with legal competence', I do not share the view of E. Magnou-Nortier, 'Les *pagenses*, notables et fermiers du fisc durant le haut moyen âge', *Revue Belge de Philologie et d'Histoire* 65 (1987), 237–56.

where their mobilization was the job of the local count, who himself had his own retinue. If a region were attacked, all its inhabitants could be called out to fight. Military obligation was multi-layered, and in each layer at once 'public' and 'private'. Some *pagenses* were more equal than others: the less equal preferred to deal directly with the ruler, or with his immediate agents (*missi*, royal vassals) rather than via the count.[8] Like the maintenance of internal order, Carolingian military organization involved complex interactions and trade-offs between central and local power.

Some modern scholars have credited the Carolingian state with a realm-wide tax system inherited from the later Roman Empire. But it seems likelier that the only generalized land-tax imposed by ninth-century rulers was a new imposition to pay off Danish intruders, not an ancient survival. The texts that allegedly prove the persistence of a Roman tax-system seem rather to show Carolingian rulers imposing exactions, like other landlords, on the tenants of their own estates, and backing up similar exactions on the estates of churches whose resources were in part at the rulers' disposal.[9] But some generalized economic demands *were* made by Carolingian rulers: if greater use of the written word accounts for the vast increase in the evidence for economic activity in the Carolingian as compared with the Merovingian period, increased economic activity may be partly responsible for the increase in the extant records. Rulers who want to control and exploit coinage and markets, and to protect merchants while taking a cut of their profits, have obvious uses for written documents. The Carolingians, especially in the ninth century, resumed these aspects of Roman imperial practice for a mixture of motives, including fiscal ones.[10] The issuing of letters of protection for merchants, the maintenance of toll-stations, the licensing of mints and markets, imposed considerable governmental

---

[8] *MGH Cap.* I, no. 73, p. 165; cf. no. 50, pp. 137–8. On Carolingian military organization, essential now are T. Reuter, 'Plunder and tribute in the Carolingian Empire', *TRHS* 35 (1985), 75–94, and the same author's paper in *Charlemagne's Heir: New Perspectives on the Reign of Louis the Pious*, ed. Roger Collins and Peter Godman (Oxford 1990).

[9] Indispensable on the ninth-century evidence are recent papers by J.-P. Devroey, especially 'Polyptyques et fiscalité à l'époque carolingienne: une nouvelle approche?', *Revue Belge de Philologie et d'Histoire* 63 (1985), 783–94; 'Les Premiers Polyptyques rémois, VIIe–IXe siècles', in *Le Grand Domaine aux époques mérovingienne et carolingienne* (Ghent, 1985), pp. 78–97; and 'Réflexions sur l'économie des premiers temps carolingiens (768–877)', *Francia* 13 (1986), 475–88.

[10] See F.L. Ganshof, 'The institutional framework of the Frankish monarchy', in Ganshof, *The Carolingians and the Frankish Monarchy*, pp. 86–110, at pp. 99–100; and especially now the fine discussion of P. Johanek, 'Der fränkische Handel der Karolingerzeit im Spiegel der Schriftquellen', *Untersuchungen zu Handel und Verkehr der vor- und frühgeschichtlichen Zeit in Mittel- und Nordeuropa*, Part IV: 'Der Handel der Karolinger- und Wikingerzeit', Abhandlungen der Akademie der Wissenschaften in Göttingen, Philologisch-Historische Klasse, 3rd series, 156 (Göttingen 1987), pp. 7–68, at pp. 20–32.

requirements, and an 'administrative routine' of sorts to link centres and localities.

How did that routine impinge on 'individual rights' in early mediaeval practice? Landlords, lay as well as ecclesiastical, wielded jurisdictional and fiscal powers on their own estates as holders of immunities. Originally, the immunity consisted of powers granted by the ruler, hence not 'private', but 'public', in the sense that they remained in principle the ruler's monopoly, but could be delegated and exercised on his behalf. In some parts of Gaul, until the seventh century, landlords when they acquired or transferred property through gift or purchase, used a registry staffed by royal agents to validate and lodge their titles.[11] Over time, bundles of land and power would be acquired in a variety of ways, and inherited as 'individual rights', yet they retained an association with the ruler's unique authority. Further, while such powers were exercised locally, the centre could intrude, through summons to judicial assemblies, or to war.

In the last few decades of the Merovingian period, up to *c.* 750, such intrusions of central power became rare: not only had the links dwindled between the two levels of government, but the higher level had all but ceased to function. This is why Ganshof saw a decline of the written word in administration immediately before the Carolingians' advent.[12] There were no late Merovingian capitularies, nor after *c.* 700 any more Merovingian royal judgements, and very few royal charters. There were, however, plenty of non-royal charters and much activity in non-royal courts. In short, there was government, but it was government in non-royal places, at the level of the *patria*.

What the Carolingians did was to take up again the threads that linked *patria* and palace. Ninth-century land-surveys are inconceivable without a continuous sub-Roman tradition of record-using landlordship. Carolingian *notitiae* of judgements in county courts are inconceivable without a similarly continuous tradition of the use of documents in legal proceedings all over the so-called 'barbarian' west. Continuities with the Merovingian period are offset, on the other hand, by a huge increase in the coverage and volume of the Carolingian evidence, especially from the reign of Charlemagne onwards. The Carolingians operated on a different scale from their predecessors. Of the capitularies printed in the standard *MGH* edition, only some 25 pages relate to the Merovingian period, over 700 pages to the Carolingian.[13] The *Leges*, and the *formulae*, survive virtually

---

[11] See I. Wood, 'Disputes in late fifth- and sixth-century Gaul: some problems', in *Settlement of Disputes*, pp. 7–22, at p. 13.

[12] Ganshof, 'The use of the written word', p. 125, and compare Wood above, pp. 63–8.

[13] These figures are intended to be no more than impressionistic.

exclusively in manuscripts of the Carolingian period, even if their contents may be earlier; and charters, and notices of judgements in courts, survive from many parts of the Carolingian Empire in vastly greater numbers for the later eighth and ninth centuries than from the preceding period.[14] There was, it seems, an explosion in the volume of written documentation in Carolingian government.

Why and how did this come about? Most historians, following Ganshof, have tended to examine the phenomenon primarily in terms of the motives of Charlemagne. Ganshof wrote of 'use', and in the singular. He, and others in his wake, assumed that Charlemagne's utilitarian, even bureaucratic, aim was greater efficiency in communicating orders and information to his agents, in ensuring those agents' accountability and in securing compliance with their directives. This is what Ganshof meant by the term administration, and it was by criteria of administrative efficiency that he judged Charlemagne's programme a failure.[15] Werner, still using Ganshof's criteria, but with his chronological scope extended to cover the ninth century, has recently come to the opposite conclusion: namely that Carolingian government was surprisingly efficient.[16] Later in this paper, I shall have to join the game of assessing an early mediaeval regime's performance in terms of its use of written documents.

I want first to move the goalposts: to consider what was written, not only as the outcome of a ruler's aims but as the product of collaboration on the part of some (at least) of the ruled; and not only as an object or means of action in a pragmatic sense, but as a determinant of action in a sociological sense. Literacy is a kind of technology: literacy is also a frame of mind, and a framer of minds. For instance, no 'individual right' was more valued than legal freedom: precisely here, the production and presentation of a written *carta* of manumission continued throughout the period from the fifth to the ninth centuries to be required by law courts as symbol, test and proof of liberation. So crucial was the link between document and status that freedmen were called *cartularii*: 'charter-men'.[17] Further, the property of a freedman who died without leaving a will was taken over by the royal fisc as

---

[14] Nelson, 'Dispute settlement', pp. 45–6.

[15] Ganshof, 'The use of the written word', pp. 133–5; compare also in Ganshof, *Carolingians and the Frankish Monarchy*, chs. XII, 'The last period of Charlemagne's reign: a study in decomposition', and XIII, 'Charlemagne's failure'.

[16] K.F. Werner, '*Missus-marchio-comes:* entre l'administration centrale et l'administration locale de l'Empire carolingien', in *Historie comparée de l'administration*, ed. W. Paravicini and K.F. Werner, Beiheft der *Francia* 9 (Munich, 1980), pp. 191–239.

[17] See H. Mordek, 'Unbekannte Texte zur karolingischen Gesetzgebung. Ludwig der Fromme, Einhard und die Capitula adhuc conferanda', *DA* 42 (1986), 446–70, at 458–9, with further references.

heir.[18] The free, whether landlords or tenants, were thus legally identified as issuers, holders, users of documents. Rulers too found a symbolic identity through their commitment to written rules: *lex scripta* was the hallmark of both the biblical leader of Israel and the Christian Roman emperor. But at the same time it became the collective possession of the new Israel, the Christian people: the faithful Franks.[19] Whatever the Carolingians did in promoting the written word, they did not act alone, nor were the collective goals wholly utilitarian.

If literacy in government has to be understood in the context of its other uses and effects, complex interactions need to be looked at over time. Where Ganshof concentrated heavily on Charlemagne's reign, I shall follow Werner in looking also at the reigns of his successors. The ninth-century practice of literacy in government at central and local levels will show a variety of uses, for the written word was not equally important for government east and west of the Rhine, nor, within each composite kingdom, in each region, while traditions in Italy were in some respects distinctive.[20] The ideological impact of literacy also varied and some rulers showed themselves more aware of its potential than others: here the evidence from the reigns of Louis the Pious (814–40) and Charles the Bald (840–77) deserves special attention.

A crucial feature of the cultural context of Carolingian literacy was the church's commitment to the practice of the written word. Latin was the unique medium of orthodoxy in the early mediaeval west. Carolingian reformers did not choose to make it so: they received it as such from Christian late antiquity. But though the medium had remained the same, its function had changed.[21] In the fourth and fifth centuries, despite some

---

[18] *Formulae imperiales* no. 38, ed. K. Zeumer, *MGH Formulae*, pp. 315–16.

[19] For early mediaeval law in general, see P. Wormald, '*Lex scripta* and *verbum regis*: legislation and germanic kingship, from Euric to Cnut', in *Early Medieval Kingship*, ed. P.H. Sawyer and I.N. Wood (Leeds, 1977), pp. 105–38; and for the Carolingian period, J.L. Nelson, 'Legislation and consensus in the reign of Charles the Bald', in *Ideal and Reality in Frankish and Anglo-Saxon Society*, ed. P. Wormald (Oxford, 1983), pp. 202–27 (reprinted in J.L. Nelson, *Politics and Ritual in Early Medieval Europe* (London, 1986).

[20] C.J. Wickham, *Early Medieval Italy: Central Power and Local Society 400–1000* (London, 1981), pp. 60–2; and *idem*, 'Land disputes and their social framework in Lombard-Carolingian Italy, 700–900', in *Settlement of Disputes*, pp. 105–24, at pp. 112, 122–4.

[21] See McKitterick, *Carolingians*, pp. 7–22. On the aims of Carolingian reformers, and the constraints they worked under, I have also found the following helpful (though my own conclusions sometimes differ from theirs): A. Guerreau-Jalabert, 'La "renaissance carolingienne": modèles culturels, usages linguistiques et structures sociales', *Bibliothèque de l'Ecole des Chartes* 139 (1981), 5–35; M. Richter, 'Die Sprachenpolitik Karls des Grossen', *Sprachwissenschaft* 7 (1982), 412–37; R. Wright, *Late Latin and Early Romance in Spain and Carolingian France* (Liverpool, 1982); M. van Uytfanghe, 'Histoire

diversity of literary forms and styles, the discourse of Latin Christendom was democratized: those who could not read Cicero could read the Vulgate Bible or Orosius, while those who could not read at all, but who spoke even fairly basic Latin, could understand scripture or the liturgy when it was read out. Between that world and the Carolingian world lay three centuries of linguistic evolution and a notable expansion of Christendom itself: spoken Latin had diverged from written Latin, while much of Christian Europe was inhabited by speakers of non-Romance languages. Carolingian reformers wanted to reassert uniformity of belief and practice, and to impose uniform standards on lay people. By insisting on latinity, they privileged Romance- over germanic-speakers; but by insisting on correct latinity, they highlighted the gap between the written language and the evolving vernaculars.

How far were these outcomes intended? The reformers were not only interested in accessibility. Operating in an extremely inegalitarian world, they assumed and exploited differentials in access to power. Latinity's potential for restrictiveness was thus a recommendation. Within the church hierarchy itself, full control of Latin was not for the lower clergy: it was enough that they be able to read, or use as aids to memory, a small number of basic texts. A full command of Latin, active as well as passive, was expected of the higher clergy, themselves *potentes*, members of the magnate class. It took special pleading and a lot of *utilitas*, that is, political and perhaps military capacity, to make up for a certain lack of *eruditio* in an episcopal candidate.[22] Yet the phenomenal level of latinity acquired by some aspirants to and holders of high ecclesiastical office was itself a significant source and symbol of their authority, to be paraded in synodal decrees and in letters and poems that also constituted a public discourse.[23] The conditions under which these churchmen wielded their power imposed a particular kind of widened access to latinity: namely, that lay magnates too should be enlisted among the ranks of the actively literate – writers, and connoisseurs of style, as well as readers. Handbooks of spirituality and private prayers produced by ecclesiastical *potentes* for lay *potentes* signalled an entente: the two wings of the Carolingian elite were to be united in

du latin, protohistoire des langues romanes et histoire de la communication', *Francia* 11 (1983), 579–613; M. Banniard, 'Théorie et pratique de la langue et du style chez Alcuin', *Francia* 13 (1985), 579–601.

[22] Lupus of Ferrières, *Correspondance*, ed. L. Levillain, 2 vols. (Paris 1927–35), II, no. 74, p. 16.

[23] Letters: see G. Constable, *Letters and Letter Collections*, Typologie des sources du moyen âge occidental 17 (Turnhout 1976), pp. 11–16. Poetry: see P. Godman, *Poetry of the Carolingian Renaissance* (London, 1985), and *idem, Poets and Emperors* (Oxford, 1986).

their capacity to handle Latin as a written medium in private and in public.[24]

For Carolingian churchmen, the written mode always coexisted with the oral mode. The Word was both medium and message. Whatever emphasis the church put on writing, it always stressed, at the same time, that Truth was revealed through speech. Preaching meant the oral explication of Holy Writ. Hincmar (c. 805–82) preferred to argue and prescribe *et verbo et scripto*. For Regino of Prüm (d. 910), things worth recording were to be learned *in chronicorum libris* or *ex relatione patrum*.[25] If access to literacy meant different things at different levels of the church's own hierarchy, so with the laity, while the church's mission was universal, and all Christians knew what holy books looked like from the outside, direct knowledge of what was inside was hightly restricted. It was no part of the Carolingian programme to provide, as it were, access courses for *pauperes*, even if some *pauperes* might well benefit from having their names inscribed on a church's list of registered poor, or (along with nobles) in a Memorial Book.[26] Churches were decorated with *tituli*, dedicatory inscriptions, so that the faithful, physically separated from the liturgical books beyond the chancel rail, saw writing incised or painted on the walls above and about them. These texts were explicated in sermons and pictures – so that, as Bede put it, pictures could 'offer those unable to read, a sort of live reading (*viva lectio*) of the Lord's story'.[27] But 'without an accompanying text (*inscriptio*), how could you know if a picture of a woman with a child on her knees was the Virgin and Child or Venus with Aeneas?'.[28] A minimal amount of text was required as authentication. Only for the elite few was writing a medium of private spirituality aimed at self-control. For the rest, the written word was a public medium of control imposed externally. It was in

---

[24] Compare my comments in 'Public *Histories* and private history in the work of Nithard', *Speculum* 60 (1985), 251–93, reprinted in *idem, Politics and Ritual*, pp. 195–237, at pp. 201–4.

[25] For Hincmar, see my 'Kingship, law and liturgy', *EHR* 92 (1977), 241–79, reprinted in *idem, Politics and Ritual*, pp. 133–71, at p. 145; Regino, *Chronicon*, ed. F. Kurze, *MGH SS i.u.s.* L, p. 73.

[26] G. Constable, 'The *Liber Memorialis* of Remiremont', *Speculum* 47 (1971), 261–77.

[27] *Bedae Venerabilis Opera Pars III Opera Homiletica Pars IV/Opera Rhythmica, Homiliarum Evangeli Libri Due*, I.13, ed. J. Fraipont, CCSL 122 (Turnhout, 1955), p. 93. Walafrid, *De exordiis et incrementis*, c. 8, ed. V. Krause, *MGH Cap.* II, p. 482, and *De exordiis et incrementis quarundam in observationibus ecclesiasticis rerum*, ed. A. Knoepfler (Munich, 1980), p. 24.

[28] *Libri Carolini*, IV, c. 16, ed. H. Bastgen, *MGH Conc.* II, Suppl., p. 204, and see McKitterick, below, p. 309, for further comment.

the preface to a collection of *tituli* that the Frankish scholar Hrabanus (d. 856) set out the range of the church's uses of the written word:

> Since the benign Law of God rules the wide world in mastery,
> how holy it is to write out the Law of God!...
> No work arises which age, full of years, does not destroy, nor wicked
>   time overturn:
> Only things written escape this fate, repel death,
> Only things written in books renew what has been.
> The finger of God carved things written on rock well fitted for them
> When he gave the Law to his people.
> These things written show in their record
> Everything that is, has been, or is to come . . .[29]

In its own law-making, and in its institutional organization, the church practised what it preached: documents were used, and appealed to as authoritative. On this depended its bid to control a part of the lives of laypeople. Uniformity of correct belief and practice was an overriding imperative: Latin was its medium.

A Latin text could be read individually, privately. It could be reconverted into speech, and read out to a public, collective, audience. Correct writing, as Charlemagne knew, was indispensable to such correct reading; and the deployment of a new script, Caroline minuscule, played its part in creating a 'grammar of legibility' which could then be applied to other than religious texts.[30] But all that was only for those who understood correct Latin, spoken if not written. In the eighth and ninth centuries, correct Latin, the written *lingua franca* of the Frankish Empire, was no one's mother tongue. Those who read and wrote it had to learn a language that was more or less new. Regrettably, we know virtually nothing about how it was taught. But the proof that it *was* taught lies in both the vast output surviving from ecclesiastical scriptoria and, as significantly, the few remnants of labours in aristocratic ones.

Early mediaeval technology and Frankish tradition alike imposed a consensual face-to-face style on political relationships within the aristocracy of warriors and landholders. The key institution where decision-making took place was the assembly, whether realm-wide or local. There the medium was the spoken word: magnates and lesser men participated in deliberations *viva voce*, and heard, literally, the 'word of the king' (*verbum regis*) or his representative. Decisions might be set down under lists of headings (*capitula*), but they were conveyed in *adnuntiationes*, oral

---

[29] The text of Hrabanus' prefatory poem is now conveniently accessible, with English translation, in Godman, *Poetry*, pp. 248–9. My own translation here is less elegant, but more literal, than Godman's.

[30] See D. Ganz, 'The preconditions for caroline minuscule', *Viator* 18 (1987), 23–44.

statements to faithful men. Thus the written word, even when extensively used, always coexisted with the spoken word.[31] At no point during the Carolingian period is it helpful to oppose 'writtenness' to orality – to regard the one as excluding the other. Thus, for instance, the father of Odo of Cluny, a Neustrian noble celebrated in the mid-ninth century (so Odo's biographer tells us) for his abilities as a judge, knew Justinian's laws *memoriter* ('by heart'), presumably in Latin.[32] Additions to codified laws of peoples (*leges gentium*) were spoken and heard: in Italy, *c.* 806, faithful men claimed not to be bound by the additions made to *Lex Salica* by Charlemagne in 803 'in his council', on the grounds that they had not been personally present to hear them announced by the ruler. Charlemagne, reminding his son King Pippin of Italy 'of when and how we spoke with you about these *capitula*', told him to 'make the additional laws known' to those in his Italian realm and to order obedience to them.[33] The argument of the faithful men was not challenged in principle: Charlemagne did not assert that written instructions from Aachen could validly be substituted for decisions made and heard at Pavia.

Seldom do capitularies or other texts mention translation into spoken vernaculars. Hincmar in the *De Ordine Palatii*, for instance, in the most detailed extant account of assembly proceedings, says nothing about translating capitularies before they were discussed by magnates or presented to the faithful men at large.[34] There are a few references in Charlemagne's capitularies to translation into the *lingua teutisca*, and it has been suggested that the word *intellegere* in a number of capitularies means 'understand in translation'. The absence of reference to translation into the *lingua romana* has been taken to mean that the *lingua romana* was in fact still Latin during Charlemagne's reign.[35] Within a generation of Charlemagne's death, we have Nithard's rendering of the Strasbourg oaths in 842 to show that the *lingua romana*, when written down, looked quite far removed from Latin.[36] In 876, a germanic vernacular text of the oath by which Louis the German's sons swore the division of the East Frankish realm was widely posted.[37] There may well have been others of whose

---

[31] Compare Nelson, 'Legislation and consensus', *passim*.

[32] John of Salerno, *Vita Odonis*, c. 5, *PL* 133, col. 46.

[33] *MGH Cap.* I, no. 103, p. 212; compare *ibid.*, no. 39, p. 113.

[34] Nelson, 'Legislation and consensus', pp. 103–9.

[35] Richter, 'Sprachpolitik'.

[36] Nithard, *Histoire des fils de Louis le Pieux*, III. 5, ed. P. Lauer (Paris 1926), pp. 102–8. See Wright, *Late Latin*, pp. 122–6.

[37] *Annales Fuldenses*, s.a. 876, ed. F. Kurze, *MGH SS i.u.s.* VIII, p. 89.

existence no record survives. Nevertheless, the extant number of capitularies in germanic vernacular is extremely small.[38] Otherwise, the written language of government was Latin, and the fact that there is much more ninth-century evidence of it, at both royal and local levels, in the West Frankish and Italian kingdoms than in the East Frankish one must be at least partly explicable in terms of Latin's more ready accessibility to Romance-speakers than to German-speakers.[39] Yet similarity is not the same thing as identity. Not least of the advantages offered by Latin, whether spoken or written, to Charlemagne's regime was that it transcended the linguistic divide at the Empire's heart, between East and West Franks. Not Frankish, therefore, but Latin could serve both to unite the Franks and to mark them out as a ruling *gens*, the chosen people of God – who of course had also chosen Latin as His medium.

Both dualities, of mode and of language, are evident in a procedure fundamental to the whole structure of political authority in the ninth century, namely oath-swearing. In Francia, in 792, rebels had claimed not to be bound to fidelity *quod fidelitatem non jurassent* ('because they had not sworn [an oath of] fidelity')![40] Oath-swearing was the fundamental act of obligation, and oaths were sworn by the spoken word, and in the vernaculars. But the record thereof was kept, almost invariably, in Latin alone. Churchmen, whose own organization rested on written authorities and procedures, did not attempt to oust the oral mode on this territory. Just as Charlemagne generalized and regularized the swearing of fidelity to himself, so, repeatedly, did Charles the Bald: his capitularies were drafted by bishops who themselves swore fidelity orally while repeatedly invoking the written texts of oaths as the basis of political relations.[41] There is little mileage left in the debate as to whether the oral or the literate mode was 'constitutive' in Carolingian legislation. The idea of alternative modes is belied by the frequency of cross-referencing from one to the other. Some of the detailed evidence to be discussed below shows that things written often lacked formal precision or completeness precisely because they assumed the complement of things spoken and remembered: some capitularies are very obviously aids to memory or agendas for discussion.[42]

---

[38] Werner, '*Missus-marchio-comes*', p. 199 and n. 27, lists four instances.

[39] The importance of this distinction is pointed out by McKitterick, *Carolingians*, pp. 21–2.

[40] *MGH Cap.* I, no. 25, p. 66.

[41] Compare Nelson, 'Kingship, law and liturgy'.

[42] See H. Mordek, 'Karolingische Kapitularien', in *Überlieferung und Geltung normativer Texte des frühen und hohen Mittelalters*, ed. *idem*, Quellen und Forschungen zum Recht im Mittelalter 4 (Sigmaringen, 1986), pp. 25–50, and below, pp. 280–2.

Measuring the extent of lay literacy in the Carolingian world in any strictly quantifiable sense is, of course, impossible. But that need not deter efforts at more impressionistic assessments. Two kinds of distinction are helpful here. First, we need to differentiate between, on the one hand, members of the ruling elite, that is, the high aristocracy, occupying high secular or ecclesiastical office, and, on the other hand, the broader class of *mediocres* and even some *pauperes*, free persons of lesser status and dependent on the political power of *potentes*. The former group may be termed the actively literate, those fully in command of Latin, able to wield public power by conveying their will through their own written words; the latter group were those familiar with procedures involving documents, able to find notaries to draw up documents when needed, and experienced in witnessing the transactions of their fellows – in short, such 'knowledgeable neighbours' as were referred to in a capitulary of 816: persons whose literacy may be termed passive or pragmatic.[43]

Only a few members of the high aristocracy certainly wrote, as well as read and used, written texts. Some offspring of landholders of 'mediocre' status may have acquired basic capacity to read and write, and the survey of the tenants of St Victor, Marseilles, lists some half-dozen boys 'at school', presumably in training for holy orders.[44] But not all schoolchildren were destined for an ecclesiastical career: one set of episcopal statutes even suggests that girls as well as boys received some instruction from parish priests, possibly to prepare them for future godparental duties, for these were taken very seriously by the Carolingian church.[45] The mass of free (or freedmen) landholders, however, whether owners or tenants, were passive participants in literacy: they were regular users of documents of specific legal types in specific legal contexts, and though they could certainly not themselves have written the documents, and probably could not even read them in full, they could recognize standard *formulae*, and display remarkable expertise on matters of formal correctness. In 857, for instance, at a court held near Tours, in a case that turned on the validity of a title of sale, 'nearly all the *coloni* [free peasants] gave witness that they had not seen [the document] being corroborated, nor were the names written down there

[43] *MGH Cap.* I, no. 134, c. 1, p. 268.

[44] Polyptych of St Victor, Marseilles, ed. B. Guérard, *Cartulaire de l'abbaye de St. Victor de Marseille*, 2 vols. (Paris, 1857), II, pp. 637, 639, 642, 647, 648. I am grateful to J.-P. Devroey for drawing these references to my attention.

[45] Girls at school: *Statuta* of Bishop Riculf of Soissons, c. 16, *PL* 131, col. 21, forbid girls' acceptance; godparental duties: see J. Lynch, *Godparents and Kinship in Early Medieval Europe* (Princeton 1986), pp. 305–32.

those of *coloni* of that *villa* of which the disputed property formed part, but they were from another *villa* which was not of the *coloni* whose names were recorded'.[46]

The second kind of distinction to be made is between Romance-speakers and others. The bulk of our evidence for active lay literacy comes from regions of Romance-speakers. But the survival of the two vast charter-dossiers of St Gall and Redon, both sited in non-Romance-speaking regions, shows that Romance-speaking was not a necessary condition for widespread pragmatic lay literacy.[47] Other variables were crucial: whether or not the region had once been part of, or strongly influenced by, the Roman Empire, and whether or not the Christian church had been implanted in the region long enough before the Carolingian period for the habit of Latin documentation to have become established. Where those conditions were absent, as for instance in Saxony, little evidence survives for either passive or active lay literacy; but where those conditions were fulfilled, whatever the local spoken language, the charters and court records indicate that most of the free population, and some of the unfree too, were passively, pragmatically, literate: that is, landholders and tenants habitually used documents, and were even connoisseurs (as in the Tours case) of their formal traits. This must mean (and the researches of McKitterick and Davies have recently demonstrated for Alemannia, Rhaetia and Brittany) that notaries were very widely available in many parts of the Carolingian world. Though in regions north of the Alps these notaries seem, for the most part, to have been clergy or monks, they could produce records for transactions in which no church interest was involved. This must have been, like moneylending, a significant (and, in a small way, lucrative) service performed by clerics for local lay communities.[48] Only in Italy does it seem certain that a lay notariat persisted.[49]

The two ways of participating in literacy can be associated with two different classes of persons. For a count or *missus* who conveyed his will in his own written words and used documents to wield, and be seen to wield, public power, writing was a regularly used form of both self-expression (which could obviously be used in other contexts too) and official action; for the man who got a notary to draw up a legal document, the written word was

---

[46] See Nelson, 'Dispute settlement', pp. 56–9.

[47] See below, p. 276.

[48] W. Davies, 'The role of the priest in the local community in 'east Brittany in the ninth century', *Etudes Celtiques* 20 (1983), 177–96, at 191–2, and McKitterick, *Carolingians*, pp. 115–26.

[49] Wickham, 'Land disputes', pp. 107, 112; *idem*, *The Mountains and the City: The Tuscan Apennines in the Early Middle Ages* (Oxford, 1988), pp. 11–12, 18 and n. 5.

something less personal, less frequently used, associated with affirmation of status rather than office. While the actively literate were not just involved in government but were themselves governors and the direct agents of the ruler, the passively literate, like Aristotle's citizens, participated in ruling only in a much looser sense, for instance, through serving on panels of assessors or witnessing settlements of disputes.[50]

Latin literacy, like all literacy, entailed grades of exclusiveness: to read Latin as distinct from merely speaking it was one thing, while to write it required a further skill. Most rarefied, most technically difficult of all, was the capacity to understand Latin poetry: yet as early as the 790s, this was a preferred medium of public communication and display at the Carolingian court, and even in these early days of the renewal of learning, some laymen as well as ecclesiastics were able to master it, even to the extent of writing it themselves.[51] This kind of Latin was very evidently the badge of an elite, distinguished also by its possession of wisdom (*sapientia*). All judges were to understand that 'the wise (*sapientes*) framed the law for the people, so that it should not stray from the path of truth'.[52] *Lex* (law) was often used to denote rights embodied in written documents such as polyptychs, or a written code.[53] *Legislator* could still mean 'giver of judgement', 'speaker of law', but the model of legislation was increasingly that of written Roman law.[54] In the generation after Charlemagne, more members of the lay elite absorbed the values of their ecclesiastical colleagues. The noblewoman Dhuoda advised her son that 'God is learned about through books.'[55] Bishop Jonas of Orleans pointed a moral for Count Matfrid: 'if men make such efforts, with the conduct of legal disputes in view, to learn so greedily and to understand so precisely the prescriptions of secular laws which have been issued by mortals, how much the more should they strive to learn

---

[50] Aristotle, *Politics* III.1, trans. T.A. Sinclair, *Aristotle, The Politics* (Harmondsworth, 1962), pp. 102–3. Nevertheless, says Aristotle, 'it would be ridiculous to deny their participation in authority'.

[51] Godman, *Poetry*, pp. 22–4, 49–53, 196–207, 262–5, 274–7, gives examples. An acrostic poem was dedicated to William the Constable, count of Blois, ed. Ernst Dümmler: *MGH Poet.* I, pp. 620–2.

[52] *Admonitio generalis*, c. 63, *MGH Cap.* I, no. 22, p. 58.

[53] Compare Nelson, 'Dispute settlement', pp. 49–50, 247; *idem*, 'Kingship and empire', p. 225; and below, pp. 273–9.

[54] See J. Devisse, *Hincmar et la loi* (Dakar 1962) and J. L. Nelson, 'Translating images of authority: the Christian Roman Emperor in the Carolingian World', in *Images of Authority*, ed. M. M. McKenzie and C. Roueché (Cambridge, 1989), pp. 194–205, which differs from my earlier paper. 'On the limits of the Carolingian Renaissance', *Studies in Church History* 14 (1977), pp. 51–67, reprinted in *idem, Politics and Ritual*, pp. 49–67, at pp. 53–6.

[55] Dhuoda, *Manuel pour mon fils*, ed. P. Riché, Sources Chrétiennes 225 (Paris, 1975), I.7, p. 114.

heavenly laws'.[56] Odo of Cluny's father, the wise judge, had Justinian's laws at his fingertips.[57] Only two wills of prominent laymen survive from the ninth-century Carolingian world: both Eberhard and Eccard had law books, including Roman law books, among the most valued personal possessions which they bequeathed to their closest kin and friends.[58]

The specific location of the written word in the Carolingian world is the key to its function in the construction as well as in the deployment of power. It was not just the means whereby a ruler issued commands or standardized the conduct of legal business. It defined membership of the realm: the free, the faithful men in the widest sense, were those capable of receiving and using written documents in public courts. It also defined a ruling cadre: those lay as well as ecclesiastical persons with direct command of Latin. The routinization of government presupposed the legitimation of its agents. Through active participation in literacy, that is, a capacity to write and read as well as simply use documents, the elite of the Carolingian world declared itself. Women shared its distinguishing trait: thus Eberhard left a law book to his daughter, while his wife, in a charter she herself issued, declared the value of written documents in 'making [a property division] binding, according to law'.[59] Though gender prevented them from exercising public office,[60] it did not deny them privilege: women as noble holders, or transmitters, of property rights, claimed through literacy membership of the governing class.

II   CAROLINGIAN GOVERNMENT

The foundation of power, whether that of ruler, lay aristocrat or great church, was efficient landlordship. Since power had to be devolved to the localities where the estates were, much turned on control of local agents: an extremely difficult business, even for kings. The first qualification of a 'good

---

[56] Jonas, *De Institutione laicali* I.20, *PL* 106, col. 161.

[57] See above, p. 267.

[58] P. Riché, 'Les Bibliothèques de trois aristocrates laïcs carolingiens', *Le Moyen Age* 69 (1963), 87–104, reprinted in *idem, Instruction et vie religieuse dans le Haut Moyen Age* (London, 1981), at pp. 99–100, 103.

[59] *Cartulaire de Cysoing*, ed. I.de Coussemaker (Lille, 1883), no. 1, p. 3, no. 3, p. 7.

[60] For the exceptional case of a Breton *tirannissa*, see W. Davies, *Small Worlds* (Duckworth, London, 1988), p. 78. I am grateful to Professor Davies for letting me see part of her book in page-proof. She rightly points out that the extensive powers over property which many women exercised are a different matter from formal public powers or a role in public decision-making. The same goes for queens in this period, though the case of the empress Engelberga constitutes a partial exception: see P. Stafford, *Queens, Concubines and Dowagers* (London, 1983), pp. 134–6, 138–9.

bailiff' was that he should 'know how to render account to our *missus*'.[61] That this meant 'written accounts', and hence included literacy as well as numeracy, is confirmed by the main prescriptive text dealing with royal estate-management, the *Capitulare de Villis*.[62] The essential regular contact between ruler and bailiffs was here envisaged as maintained through a whole series of annual reports: first, a statement of yields was to accompany the payment to the palace, on Palm Sunday, of cash raised from sales (c. 29); secondly, apparently at the beginning of Lent, when that two-thirds of the total of available Lenten foodstuffs earmarked for the court's consumption was sent to the palace, it had to be accompanied by a list of the final one third remaining at the estate 'in a written document (*per brevem*), and [bailiffs] are not to omit this, as they have hitherto been doing' (c. 44); thirdly, three separate lists had to be sent in (*per brevem*) of renders already paid, renders still owing and produce remaining (c. 55); fourthly, every Christmas, a complete annual report had to be submitted, of total yields from parts of the estate in demesne and from dependent tenements, and of all revenues and resources, from mills to mines (c. 66). Another capitulary clause seems to envisage regular (?annual) assemblies of tenants on each royal estate at which accounts were settled. 'Each one is to make his own return unless he is ill, or ignorant of [how to render] accounts' (*rationes nescius*), in which case the bailiff or some other reliable person was to make the return on that tenant's behalf.[63] This presupposes a fairly widespread basic numeracy, if not literacy, among the peasant population. If bailiffs themselves were not literate, they must have been expected to have access to a notary.[64]

None of this precluded oral instructions and face-to-face contact. It was the arrival of the ruler himself, or one of his great men, or the threat of being haled to the palace, which backed the barrage of written requirements. C. 47 of the *Capitulare de Villis* offers a nice example of a dual mode of communication: when royal huntsmen, falconers or other *ministeriales* serving in the palace were sent to royal estates, they were to be given every assistance 'according to what we or the queen have ordered in written instructions, or according to what the seneschal or butler have told them

---

[61] *MGH Cap*. I, no. 77, c. 19, p. 172.

[62] *MGH Cap*. I, no. 32, pp. 82–91. For comment and bibliography, see J. Martindale, 'The kingdom of Aquitaine and the "Dissolution of the Carolingian fisc" ', *Francia* 11 (1984), 131–91, at 160–1 with n. 152.

[63] *MGH Cap*. I, no. 33, c. 9, p. 93.

[64] *MGH Cap*. I, no. 32, c. 12, p. 84, shows that some hostages were kept on royal estates. Bailiffs could have been responsible for keeping lists of those – though the list in *MGH Cap*. I, no. 115, pp. 233–4, was probably drawn up at the palace or by a commander in the field: Ganshof, 'The use of the written word', p. 132.

following our oral instructions'.[65] The king and queen employed the written mode in their own immediate communication with local agents, but apparently used the oral mode when going through household officers. Interestingly, the same duality, but also the same indication that even quite low-level local agents were literate (or had access to literate persons) appears in the correspondence of another great landlord, the archbishop of Rheims. When Hincmar wanted to communicate with his bailiffs (whom he termed 'plebeian persons'), he sent instructions *et verbo et scripto* ('through word and through writing').[66]

Charlemagne expected his *missi* to know how to draw up surveys: he sent them models to imitate: *et sic cetera breviare debes* ('and this is how you must write up your survey of the rest').[67] How far were such instructions carried out in the case of royal estates? Though Ganshof himself was sceptical in 1951, now, thanks to his own and others' subsequent work, the patchy evidence for the making of inventories of Carolingian royal estates, if not in Charlemagne's reign, then later in the ninth century, has become cumulatively impressive.[68] The production of such surveys makes historical sense, too, in light of successive partitions of the royal lands between Carolingian heirs, and, in the early 840s, fraternal conflicts that necessarily involved hand-outs of royal lands to win noble support. That was why Charles the Bald's bishops advised him in 845 to send *missi* to 'make surveys recording everything that had been in the royal service or held by royal vassals under your father and grandfather, and what now remains', so that the extent of recent losses could be gauged.[69] The contemporary author Nithard, himself a lay magnate, explains that in October 842, the three-way division of the *imperium* between the sons of Louis the Pious had to be postponed for lack of a complete (or up-to-date?) *noticia*, and that while Lothar tried to push through a division, nonetheless, his brothers' envoys insisted that a thorough survey must be made first.[70] Contemporary annalists confirm that during the following nine months, the realm was

---

[65] *MGH Cap.* I, no. 32, c. 16, p. 84.

[66] Flodoard, *Historia Remensis Ecclesiae* III, c. 28, ed. I. Heller and G. Waitz, *MGH SS* XIII, p. 553.

[67] *MGH Cap.* I, no. 128, c. 16, p. 253.

[68] See in addition to the articles of Devroey cited above, n. 9, R.H.C. Davis, 'Domesday Book: Continental parallels', in *Domesday Studies*, ed. J.C. Holt (Woodbridge, 1987), pp. 15–39.

[69] *MGH Cap.* II, no. 292, c. 20, p. 403 =*MGH Conc.* III, no. 11 p. 95. The Council of Soissons (853), *MGH Cap.* II, no. 259 c. 6, p. 268, shows Charles giving similar attention to church property.

[70] Nithard, *Histoire*, IV. 5, ed. Lauer, p. 136.

'described', that is, detailed surveys were made of all royal assets. The same sources agree that those who made the survey were, or included, laymen.[71] Nithard himself was evidently a connoisseur of such data. Subsequent divisions, less directly documented, probably gave the spur to some surviving surveys of ecclesiastical estates, which were, of course, given the Carolingians' control of the church's material resources, also among major royal assets.[72]

Each count in his county had a watching brief over royal estates. A charter of 871 shows that persons receiving lands from the fisc were expected to produce documentary evidence of the original grant: otherwise they risked seeing their lands resumed into the fisc.[73] If, on the other hand, a lay *potens* could produce such documentary evidence, he might successfully resist in a public court the counterclaims of even a very powerful ecclesiastical party.[74] Records of peasant services and renders were accepted in royal courts as proofs of landlords' rights. The case studies we have relate, unsurprisingly, to ecclesiastical landlords, like the monastery of Cormery which in 828 before a royal tribunal successfully rebutted the counterclaims of a group of peasant tenants by producing 'a survey to be read out, wherein was detailed how in the time of Alcuin's abbacy the *coloni* of that estate . . . had declared on oath what they owed'.[75] In 864, the Edict of Pîtres enforced peasants' obligations to perform services of cartage and labouring *sicut in polipticis continentur* ('as it says in the estate-surveys').[76] It seems likely that lay landlords too availed themselves of such documents, for use both by stewards on their estates to impose demands on peasants, and in courts to back up those impositions. Walafrid seems to have more than his own stamping ground of Alemannia in mind when, listing the servants which any *potens* would have, he puts the couriers (*veredarii*) first, and the

---

[71] *Annales Bertiniani*, s.a. 842, ed. F. Grat, J. Vielliard and S. Clémencet (Paris 1964), p. 43: 'missi strenui . . . deligerentur, quorum industria diligentior discriptio fieret'; *Annales Fuldenses*, s.a. 843, ed. Kurze, p. 34: 'descripto regno a primoribus'.

[72] Compare J.L. Nelson, 'Charles the Bald and the church in town and countryside', *Studies in Church History* 16 (1979), 103–18, reprinted in *idem*, *Politics and Ritual*, pp. 75–90.

[73] G. Tessier, *Recueil des Actes de Charles II le Chauve*, 3 vols. (Paris, 1943–55), II, no. 347, pp. 272–4. This case involved powerful noblemen. Martindale, 'The kingdom of Aquitaine', 153–4, points out that benefices were often granted orally (*verbo regis*), and cites evidence from the earlier Carolingian period; but she also observes that Tessier, *Recueil*, II, no. 411, shows Charles the Bald creating a benefice by charter in 876. For further cases see following note.

[74] The case of Perrecy, disputed between Count Eccard of Mâcon and Archbishop Wulfad of Bourges, shows two charters and a notice of judgement all concerning a benefice: Nelson, 'Dispute settlement', pp. 53–5. Eccard won the case.

[75] Nelson, 'Dispute settlement', pp. 48–51.

[76] *MGH Cap.* II, no. 273, c. 29, p. 323.

notaries (*commentarienses*) second.[77] The former could carry written as well as oral orders, while the latter could produce, and keep copies of, the documents required.

Coincidentally, Alemannia is the region where, thanks to the archive of St Gall, we can see lay landholders using documents in a variety of transactions and over the whole period from the mid-eighth to the late ninth centuries.[78] Most of the documents preserved by the abbey naturally record grants made to it; but in a few cases, records of transactions between laypersons survive, presumably when the lands involved subsequently came into St Gall's possession. For instance, the settlement of a property dispute between two brothers and two other men was recorded by a priest, Prihectus.[79] It would be interesting to know where this document was kept before it entered the St Gall archive. Some laypersons who used the services of a local priest as notary may have used their local church as a repository for their documents. Persons powerful enough to have their own notaries presumably had their own archives too. In 760, for instance, a noble grantor of land to the abbey of St Gall specified that should some future abbot try to grant this land away as a benefice, the *pagenses* should collectively enforce its restitution to the abbey. In 817, another grantor provided that in such circumstances, his grant should be recovered by his kinsman and transferred to another royal monastery.[80] Though the only copies of these two documents to have survived are the abbey's own, their terms would make most sense in the long run if the benefactors, and their descendants, also kept copies themselves. When Count Eccard of Mâcon left lands to Fleury in his will, he also bequeathed the records that established his rights to them. Before 876, these documents presumably reposed in Eccard's personal archive.[81]

If record keeping had long since been a normal part of Dark Age landlordly activity, there were some potential advantages here for kings. The payment of tributes, or hire-fees, to Vikings, often viewed by modern historians (and by some ninth-century critics) as a dereliction of royal duty, had strikingly positive consequences from the standpoint of royal government. Charles the Bald, to raise the payments required, notably in the 860s,

[77] Walafrid, *De exordiis*, c. 32, ed. Krause, p. 516; *De exordiis*, ed. Knoepfler, p. 102.

[78] See McKitterick, *Carolingians*, pp. 77–134.

[79] Michael Borgolte, 'Kommentar zu Austellungsdaten, Actum- und Guterorten der älteren St Galler Urkunden (Wartmann I and II mit Nachtragen in III und IV)', in *Subsidia Sangallensia*, I: *Materialien und Untersuchungen zu den Verbrüderungsbüchern und zu den älteren Urkunden des Stiftsarchivs St Gallen*, ed. Michael Borgolte, Dieter Geuenich and Karl Schmid (St Gall, 1986), Kommentar no. 254, p. 388.

[80] *Ibid.*, Kommentar no. 36 (760), p. 338; no. 228 (817), p. 371.

[81] Nelson, 'Dispute settlement', p. 54.

tapped the resources of his realm more systematically than any of his predecessors had had to. There was a snowball effect: only if the king and his advisers had had some idea of how many free and unfree manses existed could they have calculated the flat rates required to raise four thousand pounds of silver in 866: 6 *denarii* per free manse, 3 *denarii* per unfree.[82] But, at the same time, a stimulus was given to the production of new surveys to allow maximum assessments of liability.[83] Charles the Bald exploited landlords' expertise for a further purpose when in 869 he ordered surveys (*breves*) to be compiled and brought to the early summer assembly by bishops, abbots, abbesses, counts and royal vassals, so that, on the basis of this information, men and materials could be requisitioned to complete the fortification at Pîtres, whereby the key valleys of Seine and Oise were to be rendered immune to Viking penetration.[84]

The production of surveys by landlords can be linked in these instances with royal demands. But surveying was of direct benefit to landlords themselves. It has recently been argued that many extant ninth-century estate-surveys were products of 'private' rather than 'public' initiative.[85] The difficulty of applying such categories becomes obvious when we consider that the allegedly 'private' survey of the lands of the church of Rheims in 845 was made precisely because of the intersection of royal with episcopal interests in these estates.[86] A crucial consequence of the incorporation of the church into the Carolingian state was that kings could demand the military services of men who held church lands as benefices. The importance of benefice-holders to Charlemagne's military capacity is suggested in a capitulary, probably of 807, which instructs *missi* and, in their localities, *vicarii*, the subordinates of counts, to make surveys of 'all benefices held by our men and by others' men', and to bring these lists to the king. The maintenance of benefices was then to be compared with that of allods, in order to prevent benefices from being 'destroyed' or assimilated to allods, since only benefices kept 'correctly' were in a state to enable their holders to perform military service at the king's command.[87] Was Charlemagne demanding access to the service of *all* benefice-holders, in

---

[82] *Annales Bertiniani*, s.a. 866, ed. Grat, Vielliard and Clémencet, pp. 125–6. For full explication of the meaning of this passage, I am indebted to S. Coupland, 'Charles the Bald and the defence of the West Frankish kingdom against the Viking invasions', unpublished PhD thesis, University of Cambridge, 1987, ch. 7, pp. 148–51.

[83] The production of the Polyptych of St Bertin may belong in this context. See also following note.

[84] *Annales Bertiniani*, s.a. 869, ed. Grat, Vielliard and Clémencet, pp. 152–3.

[85] Davis, 'Domesday Book: Continental parallels', pp. 20–1.

[86] Nelson, Charles the Bald and the church', in *idem, Politics and Ritual*, p. 78.

[87] *MGH Cap.* I, no. 49, c. 4, p. 136; compare *ibid.*, no. 48, c. 1, p. 134.

effect asking his *missi* to compile a Domesday Book? This capitulary should be interpreted in the light of another clearly derivative from it, which mentions only benefices of 'bishops, abbots, abbesses, counts and royal vassals', thus excluding benefices created on the allods of lay landlords.[88] Those were exactly the limits of the demands of Charles the Bald in 869. The comparison with Domesday in fact highlights the limits of 'normal' royal government in the middle ages, that is, government in any kingdom not recently acquired by a conquest that involved the wholesale displacement of an indigenous elite. Under 'normal' circumstances, the resources of lay landlords were not easy for rulers to tap directly. What is remarkable is that a series of powerful Carolingian rulers *were* sometimes able to confiscate the allodial lands of rebels or traitors: and it is significant that in such cases Charles the Bald ordered surveys of the confiscated lands.[89] A survey, in short, was a most effective sign, as well as instrument, of royal power, even though that power intruded only fitfully into lay landlordship.

This combination of the symbolic and the political suggests how literacy oiled the wheels of the Carolingian war-machine. Written orders played only a limited part in maintaining a chain of command, with rapid communications between ruler and local warlords. Here again, *missi* and counts were the key agents, responsible for ensuring the appearance of *fideles capitanei* with their men and equipment at a specified hosting-point. But the *memoratorium* recording such arrangements in 807 assumed prior orally-transmitted instructions (the captains were to come 'to the said [summer] *placitum*', the place evidently having been announced at the winter assembly) and specifically provided for *missi* to send oral instructions to royal vassals further down the chain.[90] It is hard to see how the use of written orders in itself could have hastened mobilization, as Ganshof suggested in explaining the speed with which Louis the Pious was able to crush the revolt of Bernard of Italy.[91] If Charlemagne sent letters to abbots of royal monasteries listing the equipment their men were to bring with them when presenting themselves for army service, there is no evidence that he sent similar letters to individual laymen.[92] Only from ninth-century Italy

---

[88] *MGH Cap.* I, no. 80, cc. 5–7, p. 177.

[89] *MGH Cap.* II, no. 274, c. 5, p. 330. Compare also *ibid.*, cc. 6 and 7, p. 330. This capitulary relates to Burgundy.

[90] *MGH Cap.* I, no. 48, c. 3, p. 135.

[91] Ganshof, 'The use of the written word', p. 267. Compare Werner, '*Missus-marchio-comes*', p. 198, noting that Charlemagne too achieved rapid mobilization when necessary. Surviving written orders, of course, allow us to see some of the pressures brought to bear by Louis.

[92] *MGH Cap.* I, no. 75, p. 168, a summons to Abbot Fulrad of St Quentin, survives in a single, late, manuscript.

are such generalized orders implied in Louis II's requirement of 866 that all those called up for service should bring precisely the personnel and equipment specified in their written summons to the host.[93] So much for what Ganshof termed 'efforts to infuse more regularity, more efficiency and even, if I may use the word, something more rational' into Carolingian military organization: efforts which in Ganshof's view, of course, 'proved vain'.[94]

Other concerns than efficiency and rationality are implied in Carolingian applications of the written word to military requirements. In 822, Louis the Pious had royal monasteries listed under three categories: those owing host service and gifts as well as prayers; those owing gifts and prayers; those owing prayers.[95] Correct liturgical texts were indispensable to this particular type of military service performed by the church for the Carolingians.[96] Alongside such religious concerns were political ones. In 829, Louis ordered counts to produce written lists of those liable for service in their counties.[97] These orders were repeated by Charles the Bald in 864; and in 865, Charles demanded written reports from *missi* in Burgundy as to how energetically 'counts and royal vassals *and other faithful men*' had complied with mobilization orders.[98] Such documentation could provide a basis both for the distribution of royal grace and for its withholding.

Parallel to check-lists of this sort went the use of the written word in the recording of those who owed fidelity to the king. The first appearance of royal instructions for the compilation of lists is Charlemagne's call for *missi* to present him with lists of faithful men or oath-swearers.[99] Similar instructions in 802 said nothing about lists, but stressed, instead, the public circumstances of the oath-swearing: it was this publicity which was to bring home to the swearers the magnitude of their commitment.[100] But clearly the public act and its recording could complement each other: in June 854 at

---

[93] *MGH Cap.* II, no. 218, c. 6, p. 96.

[94] F.L. Ganshof 'Louis the Pious reconsidered', *History* 42 (1957), 171–80, reprinted in Ganshof, *Carolingians and the Frankish Monarchy*, pp. 261–72, at p. 267.

[95] E. Lesne, 'Les Ordonnances monastiques de Louis le Pieux et la *Notitia de servitio monasteriorum*', *Revue de l'Histoire de l'Eglise de la France* 6 (1920), 449–93.

[96] Compare *Epistola de litteris colendis, MGH Cap.* I, no. 29, pp. 78–9. See M. McCormick, 'The liturgy of war in the early Middle Ages', *Viator* 15 (1984), 1–23, and *idem, Eternal Victory* (Cambridge, 1987), pp. 347–62.

[97] *MGH Cap.* II, no. 188, c. 5, p. 10.

[98] *MGH Cap.* II, no. 273, c. 27, p. 321; *ibid.*, no. 274, c. 13, p. 331.

[99] *MGH Cap.* I, no. 25, c. 4, p. 67: 'omnes iurent. Et nomina vel numerum de ipsis qui iuraverunt ipsi missi in brebem secum adportent.'

[100] *MGH Cap.* I, no. 33, c. 2, p. 92.

Attigny, Charles the Bald gave orders that all *Franci* in his realm who had
not yet done so should swear fidelity: though this capitulary says nothing
about recording the names of oath-swearers, it is in fact an aid to memory (it
is headed *memorialia capitula*) whose 'hidden agenda' evidently included
the compilation of such lists.[101] One list actually survives, dated 3 July 854
'in the public court at Rheims'. It contains seventeen names of men 'who
had sworn in the past', and a further forty-seven names of new oath-
swearers.[102] In this case, Hincmar was clearly at work. He had been named
as a *missus* for the Remois in November 853.[103]

Missi were the crucial links between the ruler and his faithful men
throughout the realm; they participated in the assemblies at which the
decisions embodied in capitularies were reached. They were told to take
with them copies of the capitularies and make known the contents in the
areas for which they were appointed (*missatica*).[104] They also had to 'do
justice', that is, preside in court over the settlement of disputes and the
punishment of malefactors. The expression *annuntiare iustitiam* suggests
judgements given orally, but, as noted above, written documents were also
integral to legal procedure.[105] How was the task of publicizing assembly
decisions carried out? The capitularies themselves do not specify, but one
copy gives a revealing glimpse of a *missus* in action:

The *capitula* were made and consigned to Count Stephen, so that he might make
these manifest in the city of Paris in the public assembly, and so that he might read
them out before the *scabini*. And this he did. And all consented together, saying that
they were willing to observe it at all times and forever. Further, all the *scabini*,
bishops, abbots and counts confirmed these *capitula* by writing beneath in their own
hands.[106]

This was no ordinary capitulary, as the exceptionally high number of its
manuscript witnesses shows: it was a set of additions to *Lex Salica*, hence a
text with special connotations of collective 'gentile' solidarity.[107] But a
similar procedure is hinted at in another, humbler case where the record of
Charlemagne's settlement of a dispute between peasants and lords over
services is ordered to be 'publicly announced', that is, read out, by the count

---

[101] *MGH Cap.* II, no. 261, c. 13, p. 278.

[102] *MGH Cap.* II, no. 261, p. 278. Compare Hincmar's letter to Count Bertram of Tardenois
'pro sacramento regi agendo', ed. E. Perels, *MGH Epp. merov. et karol.* VI, no. 68, p. 36.

[103] *MGH Cap.* II, no. 260, c. 1, p. 275.

[104] See Werner, *'Missus-marchio-comes'*, pp. 196–205.

[105] *MGH Cap.* I, no. 33, c. 31, p. 97; compare *ibid.*, no. 34, c. 16, p. 101.

[106] *MGH Cap.* I, no. 39, pp. 111–12; compare *ibid.*, no. 40, c. 19, p. 116.

[107] See below, p. 291.

of the palace to those concerned.[108] Record and announcement represented more than belt and braces. Faithful men wished to hear read out what had been decided at the previous assembly before they appended their written 'consent', just as they wished to shout their assent to royal successions, as well as subscribing a document to the same effect. In other words, what determined the medium was not only the concern of rulers and *missi* for compliance, but also the preference of the receivers. The result was, not a duplication, but recourse to distinct yet complementary media. The embodiment of the legislators' word in a text confirmed its authenticity, solemnized it, gave it permanence. The reading-out of the text was a further guarantee of its correctness, which at the same time enabled those who could not read it to 'receive' it and consent. The *scabini* who heard Count Stephen presumably did not see themselves as mere passive objects of others' power but as active participants in the final stage of a process of decision-making. They expressed this through hearing of the spoken word; but they also put their hands to a written text.

Missi were ordered to use documents for a variety of purposes, including the maintenance of communication both ways between centre and localities. So that all *missi* might publicize them at local assemblies, those with capitularies had to send copies on to those without them, *ut nulla excusatio de ignorantia fiat* ('that no excuse be made on grounds of ignorance').[109] *Missi* also had to bring written reports back to Charlemagne concerning the implementation of the written instructions they had taken from his oral pronouncements.[110] They were told to bring him lists of names: of all the *scabini*, advocates and notaries whom they had appointed;[111] of all strangers who had immigrated into their *missatica*, of their county of origin and of who their lords were; and of all 'bishops, abbots or others of our *homines* who failed to attend the assembly' summoned by the *missus*.[112] Reports were to be sent in about all who were unable to pay the army-fine for non-appearance at the host.[113] If the *missi* together with the local counts could not succeed in righting wrongs or bringing malefactors to justice, they were to refer cases, with dossiers (*cum brebitariis suis*) to Charlemagne himself.[114] What was done with these documents when – if – they reached the centre? There is no evidence of their preservation in a central archive. Having been 'brought' to court and served as aids to memory in oral exchanges between ruler and agent, the lists and records were perhaps then

[108] *MGH Cap.* I, no. 31, pp. 81–2.

[109] *MGH Cap.* I, no. 67, c. 6, p. 157.

[110] *MGH Cap.* I, no. 40, c. 25, p. 116.

[111] *MGH Cap.* I, no. 40, c. 3, p. 115.

[112] *MGH Cap.* I, no. 58, c. 2, p. 145.

[113] *MGH Cap.* I, no. 64, c. 12, p. 153.

[114] *MGH Cap.* I, no. 33, c. 1, p. 92.

taken back to the archive of the *missus* who could have further use for them. The list of oath-takers in the public court at Rheims in 854 seems to have been kept in Hincmar's archive.[115]

Despite the proliferation of written instructions, it is doubtful if standardization was ever aimed at: the written word so often cross-referred to spoken words addressed to particular individuals. Charlemagne was displeased when face-to-face telling had apparently failed to convey to a *missus* the message that tolls could be taken wherever 'ancient custom' allowed: was a written answer more likely to sink in? Charlemagne's response was one of eight given to a list of queries sent in by a *missus*. But in fact though all were on points of law, all were more or less obviously fraught with political implications. Charlemagne's written word might prove helpful to a beleaguered *missus* out in the provinces. What could be done, for instance, about *potentes*, including bishops, who refused to attend when the *missus* summoned an assembly? Charlemagne's reply threatened them with his ban, 'and if they then disdain to attend, you must make a list of their names and lay it before us at our general assembly'.[116] To be blacklisted thus before the king was surely a greater threat to *potentes* than anything a *missus* alone might threaten. So this testy document probably reveals more about the local political problems one *missus* had run into than about the poor understanding of both written and oral instructions on the part of *missi* in general.

Evidently not all counts were in fact literate in Charlemagne's time. The *missi* quoted above hoped the counts would read the written orders they were sent, but foreseeing that they might not be able to, ordered that any count in doubt over his orders, whether written or oral instructions, should send a deputy 'who understands well' for refresher instructions. 'Read your capitularies and you will recall what you were ordered to do through the spoken word.'[117] Each count was also told to 'make a list of any persons who are rebellious or disobedient towards you', and either to send the list immediately to the *missus*, or read it out to him when he came round on circuit.[118] Constant interchange was envisaged by these *missi*: counts must have needed their couriers. Some of Charlemagne's successors seem to have expected more literacy of their counts. Both Louis the Pious and Charles the Bald bombarded their counts with capitularies. Louis asked them, like the *missi*, to produce lists of those liable for military service;[119] Charles issued his counts with the same instructions, and also told them to produce

---

[115] Above, p. 280.

[116] *MGH Cap.* I, no. 58, c. 5, p. 145.

[117] *MGH Cap.* I, no. 85, preface and c. 4, p. 184.

[118] *MGH Cap.* I, c. 3, p. 184.

[119] *MGH Cap.* II, no. 188, c. 5, p. 10.

lists of markets operating in their counties so that unauthorized ones could be suppressed.[120] Hincmar of Rheims sent to Count Theodoric a list of the names of the men of the church of Rheims who were 'hastening on the king's service'; he also sent the same count some capitulary-texts to supply models for a projected division of the realm.[121] Nearly all the evidence of literacy at this level is indirect. A dozen counts received letters from Hincmar, while Lupus wrote to two others. A few counts are known to have owned books, patronized writers and had books or poems dedicated to them. One remarkable manuscript of gentile *leges*, and also containing the 819/20 capitulary of addenda to *Lex Salica*, was written out by 'Autramnus the unworthy lay advocate [of St Amand]' sometime in the second half of the ninth century.[122] Otherwise it seems impossible to say whether any particular manuscript of capitularies belonged to a lay *missus* as distinct from an ecclesiastical one.[123] BN lat. 4995 may represent the collection of a lay *missus*: it includes a copy of capitulary no. 39 whose exemplar certainly was once in the hands of Count Stephen of Paris.[124] BN lat. 4626 seems to reflect the interests of a Burgundian *missus*: interestingly it partly overlaps in content with BN lat. 4995.[125] The yield is small for so large a body of material. But many capitularies survive in tenth-century, or later, collections.[126]

It has often been observed that no capitularies survive as 'originals'. But Mordek has recently addressed the key question: what would an 'original' have looked like? Mordek points to two significant survivals. First, there is a manuscript roll preserved in Colmar which contains the names of partici-

---

[120] *MGH Cap.* II, no. 273, c. 27, pp. 321–2, c. 19, pp. 317–18.

[121] Flodoard, *Historia Remensis Ecclesiae* III, c. 26, ed. Heller and Waitz, p. 545.

[122] BN lat. 4632: see Mordek, 'Karolingische Kapitularien', p. 41 no. 88.

[123] The arguments of R. McKitterick, 'Some Carolingian law-books and their function', in *Authority and Power: Studies on Medieval Law and Government Presented to Walter Ullmann on his Seventieth Birthday*, ed. B. Tierney and P. Linehan (Cambridge, 1980), pp. 13–27, are attractive, but I am not, in the end, convinced.

[124] This is a tenth-century manuscript. Mordek, 'Karolingische Kapitularien', pp. 39–40, raises the question of whether such collections were made for clerical or lay office holders, but seems to incline to the former.

[125] BN lat. 4626, formerly at Mâcon, is a small collection made in the late tenth or early eleventh centuries. It contains capitularies: nos. 20, 39, 40, 57, 138, 139, 140, 141, 260, 266, 267, 274. *MGH Cap.* II, no. 267, c. 8, p. 292: 'that every priest make a list of all malefactors in his parish', points to an ecclesiastical *missus* as the transmitter of the original form of this capitulary – an *allocutio*. BN lat. 4995 shares with 4626 the following: nos. 39, 40, 139, 140, of which 39 and 139 are addenda to gentile *Leges*.

[126] As observed by R. McKitterick, *The Frankish Church and the Carolingian Reforms, 789–895* Royal Historical Society Studies in History 2 (London, 1977), pp. 1–44, the best introduction in English to the capitularies' form and function.

pants at the Aachen Reform Synod of 816: a list which must have been drawn up by one of the participants himself, and, as Mordek graphically says, 'carried home in his travelling-bag'.[127] Then there is a comparable roll containing extracts from the decrees of one of Charlemagne's last great synods of 813.[128] Both these were written up at or immediately after the assemblies that gave them birth, by individual participants, in provincial hands rather than in chancery script: they were personal productions, made without courtesy of any standardized central office, for local use in spreading information orally as well as through the text itself. Content, not form, was what mattered to these enterprising record makers. Rather than wait for an 'official', approved text (if such ever appeared), they wrote up their own, based on their memory of discussions that had been carried on in a language often quite different from that of the written texts. Hence those texts' 'stupendous variety of forms'[129] – which did nothing to vitiate their content, provided that that was associated with the royal name, and gained wide currency as such. It would follow from Mordek's analysis, therefore, that what gave a capitulary authority was not just its origin, but its reception: in both, the written word played a crucial role – but a role symbolic rather than strictly functional. 'Writtenness' lent credibility in the eyes of people predisposed to believe; and the same frame of mind ensured the acceptance of both genuine and forged capitularies.

A recent discovery by Mordek illustrates the interplay between written and spoken in Carolingian government. A manuscript leaf dating from the second quarter of the ninth century has a list of eighteen questions on points ranging from legal procedure to the conduct of royal agents. The list is headed 'capitula still to be deliberated on' (*adhuc conferenda*); and c. 9 carries the further note: 'to be deliberated on before it is written up'.[130] What we have here is not then simply a matter of law being first orally promulgated in an *adnuntiatio*, then consigned to a document; nor are these questions being put by a *missus* to the ruler. Rather, the list is in the nature of an agenda for discussion at an assembly, and it clearly emanates from the agenda-setters, that is, from the court. In a fine piece of detective work, Mordek shows that the author of the original list was probably Einhard, and the date 819: conclusions which underline the small number of personnel concerned, and the episodic timing of the capitularies' production in short bursts of activity.[131] Finally, the manuscript itself – a provincial

---

[127] Mordek, 'Karolingische Kapitularien', p. 32.

[128] *Ibid.*, p. 33, with nn. 42, 43.   [129] *Ibid.*, p. 35.

[130] Mordek, 'Unbekannte Texte', 469. An English version of this paper is forthcoming in *Charlemagne's Heir*, ed. Godman and Collins.

[131] Mordek, 'Unbekannte Texte', 462–4.

copy – points towards places other than the court as crucial in the proliferation of capitulary texts. Like legal *notitiae* of dispute settlement, capitularies show that Carolingian government, revealed in the play of power through the application of law, was also local government.

Documents sent up to the court from the provinces are similarly rare. One example is a report sent to Charlemagne from the *missus*, Vernarius, sent to hear claims lodged in favour of the abbey of St Victor, Marseilles. Ganshof called this document 'muddled' and 'incomprehensible'.[132] But Vernarius' findings are clear enough. He reported holding a local inquest in which the written word was used alongside oral testimony: *pagenses* reported what they knew, and also inspected a *carta* and pronounced it acceptable. From the ninth century, a number of other records of court hearings presided over by *missi* or counts illustrate the importance of written as well as oral proofs, and their accounts are often no less 'confused' than that of Vernarius.[133]

Of the literacy of officers below comital level, we know next to nothing. If viscounts were involved with the production of coinage,[134] some use of written material may well have been involved. Though the 'law' which *vicarii* were supposed to 'know' need not have meant written law,[135] they were told to make reports of the state of all benefices in their official areas and to bring these documents to Charlemagne.[136] They probably came from the social echelon where more than passive literacy might be expected. A *formula* survives for written instructions from count to *vicarius* on 'the basic rules for the exercise of their office'. Ganshof commented: 'it is hard to believe counts often made use of it'.[137] But it is harder still to doubt that counts and *vicarii* often communicated with each other in writing. Even *centenarii*, otherwise poorly documented, were told in 854 to supply *missi dominici* with written lists of names of all *Franci homines* in their official areas.[138]

---

[132] Ganshof, 'The use of the written word', pp. 130, 135.

[133] Vernarius' report, ed. J.H. Albanes and U. Chevalier, *Gallia Christiana Novissima*, II (Marseilles and Valence 1899), no. 41, cols. 33–4. Compare *ibid.*, no. 42, cols. 34–5. For a comparable text, see Nelson, 'Dispute settlement', p. 53.

[134] *MGH Cap.* II, no. 273, c. 14, p. 315: an early reference to these officers.

[135] *MGH Cap.* I, no. 57, c. 4., p. 144. Compare the story of Viscount Genesius told by Adrevald of Fleury, *Ex Miraculis Sancti Benedicti*, c. 25, ed. O. Holder-Egger, *MGH SS* XV.1, p. 490.

[136] *MGH Cap.* I, no. 49, c. 4, p. 136.

[137] Ganshof, 'The use of the written word', p. 129.

[138] *MGH Cap.* II, no. 260, p. 274. The *Franci homines* were free men whose special military roles attracted special royal protection: Werner, '*Missus-marchio-comes*', pp. 212–13 and n. 86. For *centenarii*, see Nelson, 'Dispute settlement', p. 55.

Charlemagne expected notaries to be widely available: plaintiffs seeking his justice were to come to the palace armed with *litterae*, following 'ancient custom'.[139] Oath-helpers when needed at the palace had to present themselves with documents and seals.[140] When gifts of horses were sent to Charlemagne, each one had to arrive with a written note of its name.[141] The volume of local written documentation in the form of charters and legal *notitiae* suggest that notaries were not hard to find.[142] Charlemagne ordered that each bishop, abbot and count was to have 'his own notary'; he also told *missi* to send him lists of the names of notaries they had 'chosen throughout the particular places'.[143] Whether this means that these were permanent 'county notaries' is another matter, however. The only region where there is good evidence for those is Italy.[144] Elsewhere, part-timers could be recruited as necessary. Any *potens*, whether *missus*, count, bishop or abbot, was likely to have at least one notary in his household. When a group of peasants from Mitry sought judgement from Charles the Bald in 861, they brought a notary with them.[145]

Carolingian rulers ordered *missi* and counts to refer to capitularies. To find how many capitulary texts were envisaged, it might seem sensible to ask how many counts and *missi* were active at any one time in any Carolingian realm: but we do not know the answer to that second question. 'More than 200 counsellors' of three kings were present at an assembly in 862;[146] forty-three *missi* for Francia and Burgundy (but not Aquitaine) attended an assembly of Charles the Bald's in 853.[147] Could anything like such a number of copies of capitularies have been produced? Not, surely, by the royal notaries, of whom there were never more than three or four active at any one time, even in the best-run chanceries.[148] Facilities for reproducing documents centrally seem to have been severely limited throughout the Carolingian period. Charlemagne ordered *tres breves* to be made of one *capitulum* dealing with Tassilo of Bavaria: 'one to be kept in the palace, one

---

[139] *MGH Cap.* I, no. 44, c. 8, p. 124.

[140] *MGH Cap.* I, no. 61, c. 14, p. 149.

[141] *MGH Cap.* I, no. 57, c. 5, p. 144.

[142] See above, p. 270.

[143] *MGH Cap.* I, no. 43, c. 4, p. 121, with note 'e' for the significant expansion of the heading 'De notariis' in Wolfenbüttel, Herzog August Bibliothek Blankenburg 130, from northern Italy (Mordek, 'Karolingische Kapitularien', p. 42 and nn. 100, 101); *MGH Cap.* I, no. 40, c. 3, p. 115, where the 'singula loca' may be places where local court assemblies were regularly held.

[144] *MGH Cap.* I, no. 158, cc. 12, 15, p. 319.

[145] Tessier, *Recueil*, II, no. 228. See Nelson, 'Dispute settlement', p. 52.

[146] *MGH Cap.* II, no. 243, p. 165 n.*.

[147] *MGH Cap.* II, no. 260, pp. 275–6.

[148] Tessier, *Recueil*, III, pp. 46–93, especially p. 91; *Die Urkunden Lothars I und Lothars II*, ed. T. Schieffer, *MGH Diplomata Karolinorum* III, pp. 14–40.

for Tassilo to have with him in his monastery, a third to be kept in the chapel of the sacred palace'.[149] About the same period, Charlemagne ordered copies of Paul the Deacon's Sermon Collection to be sent to *religiosi lectores* throughout his realm.[150] In 808, four copies of a capitulary about military mobilization were demanded: one for the ordinary *missi*, the second for the local count, the third for the special officers organizing the mobilization, the fourth to be kept by 'our chancellor'.[151] According to Ganshof, Louis the Pious tried to ensure a 'wider and more regular circulation for the capitularies', in one case ordering the chancellor 'to have as many as . . . thirty-four copies made, a great number for the time'.[152] But the actual figure is supplied, not by Louis, but by Ganshof, calculating from his assessment of the number of archiepiscopal sees in the *regnum Francorum*: what the capitulary actually says is that every archbishop, along with every count based in the archiepiscopal city, is to receive a copy. Did Louis, or his draftsman, tot up the numbers involved? Just one manuscript of this particular capitulary survives.[153] It is true that a great many manuscripts survive, by contrast, of the Aachen Rule for canons and canonesses, of which Louis likewise ordered multiple copies; but the manuscripts, mostly considerably later than Louis' reign, reveal not so much the ultimate implementation of 'central government policy', as its conditioning under the pressure of local vested interests, in this case, cathedral chapters. For similar reasons, and over a similarly lengthy timespan, many manuscripts of Paul the Deacon's Sermon Collection were eventually copied.[154]

Louis showed more general concern than his father over the reproducing and preserving of capitulary texts, especially early in his reign. He ordered 'archbishops and their counts [!] . . . to collect copies of capitularies from our chancellor, and to have these copied for the bishops, abbots, counts and other faithful men throughout their dioceses, and to read them out in their counties before everyone, so that our orders and our wishes can be made known to all'. Assembly decisions were to be carefully recorded in capitularies and preserved 'in the public archive', to be used by 'our successors'.[155] A manuscript including a collection of capitularies issued

---

[149] *MGH Cap.* I, no. 28, c. 3, p. 74.   [150] *MGH Cap.* I, no. 30, pp. 80–1.

[151] *MGH Cap.* I, no. 50, c. 8, p. 138.

[152] Ganshof, 'Louis the Pious reconsidered', 266.

[153] *MGH Cap.* I, no. 150, c. 26, p. 307. For the manuscript, see above, n. 143. Compare the will of King Alfred of Wessex, who after making various bequests, including '100 mancuses to each of my ealdormen', admitted: 'I do not know for certain whether there is so much money, but I think so': S. Keynes and M. Lapidge, *Alfred the Great* (Harmondsworth 1983), p. 177.

[154] Compare Mordek, 'Karolingische Kapitularien', pp. 42–3.

[155] *MGH Cap.* I, no. 150, c. 26, p. 307; *ibid.*, no. 137, p. 275.

between 817 and 821 survives. But it is unique.[156] The one attempt at a more comprehensive collection made during Louis' reign, that of Abbot Ansegis of St Wandrille, was a piece of 'private enterprise' conceived as an act of piety. It was very far from complete.[157]

But Ansegis' collection was used extensively by the drafter(s) of Charles the Bald's capitularies from 853 through to 873. Ansegis is cited by book and chapter repeatedly and correctly.[158] The capitularies he 'received' in effect set the agenda for Charles and his counsellors, imbuing them with, among other things, a continuing concern with the reproduction of capitulary texts certified as 'correct' because copied from the palace exemplar. A note attached to one copy of the capitulary of Servais (853) suggests that chancery staff, now as in Louis the Pious's reign, found difficulty in having capitularies copied on the scale required. First, Servais, c. 11, says that *missi* are to collect copies of the capitularies of Charlemagne and Louis from the chancery – apparently copies of Ansegis' collection are meant; but the additional note shifts the responsibility for copying on to the *missi* themselves: 'Send your *missus*, with a scribe and parchment, to the palace, and there he can get a copy from our archive [literally: cupboard] and take a copy.'[159] In 861, Charles issued an edict about the currency which he ordered to be 'read out in our palace, and in cities and in public assemblies and courts'.[160] Of the Edict of Pîtres (864), Charles stated his will 'that these decisions be made known to you [faithful men] in writing, so that you can hear them more fully, and also by constant reference back to the written text may more firmly keep in mind what we have ordered to be given and read out and kept in every county'.[161] 'Kept' could even imply a comital archive. But the next sentence indicates, yet again, that churchmen are the vital intermediaries: 'It is our will that [copies of] these decisions should be transmitted in open speech by bishops and by their subordinates in every county of their sees, so that those decisions may be understood by everyone.'[162] We have an example of this 'system' in practice: Hincmar

---

[156] BN lat. 2718: see Mordek, 'Karolingische Kapitularien', p. 38. This collection contains only nine capitularies. For two comparable collections, see Nelson, 'Legislation and consensus', Appendix 1, pp. 112–14.

[157] Mordek, 'Karolingische Kapitularien', p. 37, points out that Ansegis managed to find only twenty-six out of the hundred capitularies we know to have been produced under Charlemagne and Louis the Pious, but compare McKitterick, *Carolingians*, p. 35, on Ansegis.

[158] See Nelson, 'Legislation and consensus', pp. 95, 98 and n. 36, 99.

[159] *MGH Cap.* II, no. 260, cc. 11, 13, n.*, p. 274. The additional note is in BN lat. 4626. Compare above, n. 125.

[160] *MGH Cap.* II, no. 271, p. 302.   [161] *MGH Cap.* II, no. 273, *adnuntiatio*, c. 3, p. 311.

[162] *Ibid.*, where *aperto sermone* seems to have the double connotation of the directness of oral communication *per se*, and of using straightforward language.

received from Charles in Italy a copy of the capitulary of Pavia, which he copied and sent on to his suffragan the bishop of Châlons with a request that he have a further copy made for himself, and then send the text on to the bishops of Toul and Verdun.[163]

Overenthusiastic use of Occam's razor has led some scholars to credit Archbishop Hincmar of Rheims with virtually sole responsibility for writing and collecting capitulary texts in the kingdom of Charles the Bald.[164] But the continuing lack of formal standardization (as with capitularies of earlier reigns) implies some diversity of locale, and of interest, in their preservation. The 853 capitulary of Servais, for instance, survives in four distinct forms, three of them pointing to different local origins.[165] The sizeable manuscript family of the great Edict of Pîtres similarly suggests preservation in multiple forms.[166] The unique question-and-answer format of the capitulary of Quierzy of 877 suggests the activity not of Hincmar, but perhaps of Abbot Gauzlin of St Germain.[167] Nor was Charles the Bald's the only Carolingian successor-kingdom in the ninth century to produce capitularies.[168]

Ganshof in his *Recherches sur les Capitulaires* paid scant attention to the

---

[163] Flodoard, *Historia Remensis Ecclesiae* III, c. 23, ed. Heller and Waitz, p. 532, referring to *MGH Cap.* II, no. 221, pp. 101–4.

[164] See J. Devisse, 'Essai sur l'histoire d'une expression qui a fait fortune: *consilium et auxilium*', *Le Moyen Age* 74 (1968), 179–205; and Nelson, 'Legislation and consensus'. I would now wish to revise my suggestion that MS Yale Beinecke 413 should be closely associated with Hincmar: its capitulary texts, including that of the Edict of Pîtres, contain a number of errors and odd variants which tell against that view. Mordek, 'Karolingische Kapitularien', p. 38 n. 68, rightly questions whether the contents of every manuscript in a Rheims hand should be assigned a Rheims origin, let alone assigned to Hincmar's authorship.

[165] *MGH Cap.* II, no. 260, pp. 270–6. Of Boretius' eleven manuscripts, two (nos. 1 and 2) can be linked with Rheims, three (nos. 3–5) seem to derive from an exemplar in the Sens area, while another (no. 6) has Burgundian connections (see above, n. 125).

[166] *MGH Cap.* II, no. 272, pp. 310–28.

[167] *MGH Cap.* II, no. 281, pp. 355–61. The connection with Gauzlin has been inferred from the preface to excerpts from this capitulary in no. 282, pp. 361–3, from a now-lost manuscript used by Sirmond: 'Et tunc iussit Gauzlenum cancellarium, ut haec sequentia capitula in populum recitaret.' See further K.F. Werner, 'Gauzlin von Saint-Denis', *DA* 35 (1979), 395–462, at 410–12; and R. Kemper, 'Das *Ludwigslied* im Kontext zeitgenössischer Rechtsvorgänge', *Deutsche Vierteljahrsschrift* 56 (1982), 161–73, at 172–3. I owe this last reference to the kindness of David Yeandle.

[168] An impressive run of Italian capitularies is printed in *MGH Cap.* II, nos. 201–25. For a collection of letters and *acta* relating to the divorce project of Lothar II, made by Bishop Adventius of Metz, see N. Staubach, *Das Herrscherbild Karls des Kahlen: Formen und Funktionen monarchischer Repräsentation im früheren Mittelalter* (Münster, 1982), pp. 153–214. The liveliness of the tradition of church legislation in the East Frankish kingdom too has been demonstrated by W. Hartmann, 'Vetera et nova', *Annuarium Historiae Conciliorum* 15 (1983), 79–95 (with references at 80 nn. 7 and 8 to the same author's other related studies).

capitularies of Charlemagne's successors. His few comments centred on the
increased number of references in these texts to the consensus of the
aristocracy: symptoms, according to Ganshof, of the ever-growing weakness of royal power during the ninth century.[169] But an alternative, and no
less plausible, diagnosis is of strengthened rulership. The number and
variety of extant capitularies certainly diminishes after Charlemagne's
reign. For instance, some twenty sets of instructions from Charlemagne to
his *missi* survive, whereas we have only about half that number from Louis
the Pious' reign; yet while many of Charlemagne's instructions are in
summary form and clearly memory-aids to accompanying oral messages,
Louis' instructions are much fuller and references to oral messages are
rarer. The distribution of capitularies through Louis' reign is very uneven,
with the last years virtually bare. Subsequent reigns show a very varied
picture. Since the East Frankish kingdom of Louis the German has left
many fewer, and much less impressive, texts than Charles the Bald's, there
is clearly no direct ratio between fewer capitularies and dwindling royal
power. But Mordek proposes a subtler correlation: observing that concern
for the production of 'correct official exemplars', and greater elaboration of
the capitularies' form, were characteristic of the reigns of Louis the Pious
and Charles the Bald, Mordek suggests, perhaps a little paradoxically, that
'the stronger the ruler was, the more formless were the capitularies';
conversely the weaker the regime, 'the more necessary it must have been to
coerce the capitularies within the corset of a formally-ensured writtenness'.[170] But the argument here surely rests on a prior assumption that Louis
and Charles were weak rulers? Efforts to ensure the diffusion of official texts
hardly look like *prima facie* evidence for royal incapacity. It is from Louis'
reign that we have precious evidence proving that at least some capitularies
were being put into effect soon after they were issued: Adrevald describes a
dispute involving two monasteries in which rules prescribed a decade before
were actually applied.[171] A mandate of Charles' shows him responding to a
case of clerical usury by applying current law via capitularies.[172]

But the capitularies' *raison d'être* was frequently not the immediate

---

[169] F.L. Ganshof, *Recherches sur les Capitulaires* (Paris, 1958), pp. 34–7, 88–9. For a
different view, see Nelson, 'Legislation and consensus'. See further G. Schmitz, 'Zur
Kapitulariengesetzgebung Ludwigs des Frommen', *DA* 42 (1986), 471–516, at 474–5.

[170] Mordek, 'Karolingische Kapitularien', p. 36.

[171] F.L. Ganshof, 'Contribution à l'étude de l'application du droit romain et des capitulaires
dans la monarchie franque sous les Carolingiens', in *Studi in onore di Eduardo Volterra*,
III, Pubblicazioni della Facoltà di Giurisprudenza dell'Università di Roma 42 (Milan
1971), pp. 585–603, is the fundamental study. See also Mordek, 'Karolingische
Kapitularien', pp. 44–5; Nelson, 'Dispute settlement', pp. 47, 63.

[172] G. Schmitz, 'Wucher in Laon', *DA* 37 (1981), 520–58, at 554.

implementation sought by modern legislators. Two particular types of capitulary show especially clearly the symbolic and normative, as well as the more obviously practical, purposes to which these texts were put. First, there are the gentile *Leges* and the *Addenda* thereto. Though case-law evidence shows virtually no reference to these in regions north of the Alps, they survive from those regions in strikingly large numbers of manuscripts. Mordek's recently discovered capitulary offers a clue to the *Leges'* function, for the very points against which is noted 'to be deliberated on' (*conferendum est*) relate to substantive problems arising from *Lex Ribuaria*.[173] The *Leges*, then, were the collective possession of those who *par excellence* used and applied them: the wise conferred on and interpreted, then received, the written results. Their status as law-users and law-finders was publicly and repeatedly declared in this series of acts. No wonder Counts Eberhard and Eccard were so careful to enumerate their bequests of books of *Leges*.

Secondly, there are capitularies prescribing relations between Carolingian rulers: these could take the form of succession plans, or (increasingly often after 843) records of arrangements made at meetings of two or more fellow rulers and their faithful men. The 806 *Divisio* project may or may not have been 'the first Carolingian arrangement for the succession ever recorded in writing' but it was not a novelty for the Franks: already in 587, the Treaty of Andelot spelled out the nature of fraternal concord in terms of mutual behaviour as well as boundaries.[174] Such documents, evoked by particular occasions, had relatively poor chances of survival: but for Gregory of Tours we should have no text of Andelot, while the 806 *Divisio* has survived only by the skin of its teeth. But Ganshof rightly noted the solemnity of the 806 document. It was couched in quasi-liturgical form, and a copy sent to the pope for his subscription.[175] Such formal traits indicate substantial ones: these were not administrative documents, but they were of prime governmental importance as statements of the ideology that underpinned the regime: brotherly love and solidarity between rulers, and promises not to poach each other's faithful men, remained, in the ninth century as in the sixth, fundamental norms, needing especially solemn affirmation precisely because they were so often more honoured in the breach than in the observance. No less significant were

---

[173] Mordek, 'Unbekannte Texte', 453–7. See also R. Kottje, 'Die *Lex Baiuvariorum* – das Recht der Baiern', in *Überlieferung und Geltung*, ed. Mordek, pp. 9–23.

[174] Ganshof's comment on the 806 *Divisio* is in 'The use of the written word', p. 126. The text of Andelot is reproduced from Gregory of Tours' *Libri Historiarum* IX.20, in *MGH Cap*. I, no. 6, pp. 12–14.

[175] *MGH Cap*. I, no. 45, pp. 126–30.

those capitularies in which the mutual obligations of Charles the Bald and his faithful men were recorded.[176]

But capitularies of the most formal normative or legislative type were not for every day: there might be no direct ratio between their volume or survival-rate and other forms of documentation commonly used in central or local government. From twelfth-century England, the constitutions of Henry II are poorly preserved, and in 'unofficial copies', yet what survive in large numbers are 'administrative documents', notably pipe rolls, relating more or less directly to royal resources, and a wide variety of legal records.[177] From the Carolingian world, too, the survival of diverse sorts of written text, produced locally as well as centrally, shows the wide extent of participation in governmental literacy, despite the relatively limited amount of material that could be termed legislative. The less formal types of documentation have suffered immense losses in subsequent centuries. The scale of this loss seems especially clear in the case of the Carolingians' interventions in economic affairs. For instance, the *Praeceptum negotiatorum* surviving in the imperial *formulae* of Louis the Pious' reign must surely have engendered numerous particular applications, but none is extant.[178] The toll-list from Raffelstett opens a unique window on the spread of the use of such documents by the late ninth century.[179] Written toll exemptions, written grants of market and mint rights, look like the tip of an iceberg. Royal agents were authorized to requisition supplies and post-horses through the presentation of special documents (*tractoria*) which presumably were recognizable to local suppliers.[180] The most telling sign of a system working effectively is the standardized minting of coins, and, most significantly, an across-the-board revaluation of the coinage of Charles the Bald's kingdom in 864.[181] If that could be done – and the surviving coins themselves show that it *was* done – then why doubt the feasibility of the production by counts of lists of markets, or royal written authorization of

---

[176] See Nelson, 'Kingship and empire', pp. 225–9.

[177] Clanchy, *From Memory to Written Record*, pp. 41–8, and compare pp. 212–13.

[178] *Formulae imperiales*, no. 37, ed. Zeumer, *MGH Formulae*, pp. 314–15. Compare also model privileges for Jewish merchants, *ibid.*, nos. 30, 31, 52, pp. 309–11, 325. See Johanek, 'Der fränkische Handel', pp. 55–7.

[179] *MGH Cap.* II, no. 253, pp. 249–52. See P. Johanek, 'Die Raffelstetter Zollordnung und das Urkundenwesen der Karolingerzeit', in *Festschrift für B. Schwineköper*, ed. H. Maurer and H. Patze (Sigmaringen, 1982), pp. 87–103.

[180] *Formulae imperiales*, no. 7, ed. Zeumer, *MGH Formulae*, p. 292. See Ganshof, 'The use of the written word', pp. 127 and n. 20.

[181] Edict of Pîtres, *MGH Cap.* II, no. 273, cc. 8–24, pp. 314–18. See P. Grierson and M. Blackburn, *Medieval European Coinage*, I: *The Early Middle Ages (5th–10th Centuries)* (Cambridge, 1986), pp. 230–3 and plates 38–41 (with further references).

market-rights?[182] Underlying such royal requirements, uniquely documented at Pîtres (864) was a firm political will: markets meant profits and Charles the Bald was intent on denying these to local lords unless they had (and presumably paid for) his approval.

Icebergs, in the nature of things, remain largely submerged. But some clues to this one's scale can be observed, finally, in miscellaneous evidence from Charles' kingdom. There are several examples of what would later (in Capetian times) be classified as mandates: royal instructions directly addressed to individuals, or groups, in the second person. Some of these documents were in the nature of manifestos, designed to form the basis of an entente with political opponents: the precise wording of those sent to 'Franks and Aquitainians' in 856 shows a revealing responsiveness to the nuances of the spoken language.[183] Others ordered specific action in particular cases: in instructions sent with royal officers responsible for investigating the affairs of the Aquitainian monastery of Charroux, Charles informed 'all bishops, abbots, counts, *missi* on circuit and their deputies, *vicarii* and *centenarii*, and all our faithful men', of the appointment of these officers, and told them to give whatever help might be required.[184] Thanks to Hincmar's carefulness (and, more recently, the sharp eyes of Schmitz), we have a mandate from Charles to the archbishop, ordering him to collect *capitulatim* authoritative texts on the matter of usury, so that action could be taken in the case of clerical moneylenders at Laon.[185] The use of letters to convey information to royal agents about governmental arrangements is also well attested in Charles' reign. A 'letter close' survives in the original, written in an ordinary, non-chancery minuscule: Charles in 876 addresses his 'special people, the Barcelonans', sending them thanks and 'a suitable reward' for their fidelity reported to him by 'our faithful man, the Jew Judas', together with orders to continue in their loyalty. A postscript (in which Calmette wanted to see Charles' own hand!) adds that the same messenger is bringing ten pounds of silver from the king to the bishop of Barcelona, to repair his church.[186] It is fairly obvious that such communica-

---

[182] See T. Endemann, *Markturkunde und Markt in Frankenreich und Burgund vom 9. bis 11.Jhdt.* (Konstanz and Stuttgart, 1964), pp. 27–34, 40–8, 98–9, 210–11; Johanek, 'Der fränkische Handel', pp. 24–5.

[183] *MGH Cap.* II, nos. 263–5, pp. 282–5.

[184] Tessier, *Recueil*, II, no. 375.

[185] See Schmitz, 'Wucher in Laon'.

[186] Tessier, *Recueil*, II, no. 417, with Tessier's comments at III, p. 37, apparently dissociating himself from the view of J. Calmette, 'Une lettre close originale de Charles le Chauve', *Ecole française de Rome. Mélanges d'Archéologie et d'Histoire 22 (1902)*, 135–6. Compare also Tessier, *Recueil*, I, no. 224, and II, no. 329. An earlier example of the same genre is *MGH Cap.* I. no. 111, p. 225 (Mordek, 'Karolingische Kapitularien', p. 32).

tions depended on the personal services of a relatively small number of royal clerks and couriers, some of whom were part-timers, or shared with other lords. Charles arraigned one of his former notaries, Ragamfrid, a monk of St Denis and client of Hincmar's, before the Council of Soissons in 853 and accused him of having forged royal diplomas.[187] A decade later, Hincmar told Pope Nicholas of a mishap to some correspondence, when a courier entrusted by Louis the German with letters for the pope was stopped *en route* and accused before King Charles of theft of some church property, whereupon he fled, and, added Hincmar, 'I never heard where he went with the letters!'[188] But the communications system survived such occasional breakdowns. Hincmar's correspondence preserves an example of the amount of documentation that could arise from a single case. Hincmar wrote to the abbot of Corvey over a property lease, and later wrote to acknowledge receipt of the survey he had asked for. He then wrote to the East Frankish king to inform him of these developments; to a Thuringian magnate 'to restrain him from disturbing those lands'; and finally to the peasants residing on the estate in question 'to tell them to be obedient henceforth to the abbot of Corvey'.[189] It seems safe to assume that royal business would have generated similar dossiers, though none has survived.

How long did such practices persist? Any attempt even to sketch an answer to that question must distinguish between different regions of the Carolingian world. Ottonian government, as Leyser has said, functioned with 'a modest array of institutions', and made relatively little use of the written word.[190] But then Saxony itself in the ninth century yields little evidence for lay participation (whether active or passive) in literacy: Hincmar's assumptions about the literacy of Saxon peasants may have been on the optimistic side, based as they probably were on conditions in his home-diocese of Rheims. The picture is one of regional variation. In the valleys of the Loire and Saône/Rhône, for instance, where continuities in the functioning of court-assemblies have been seen as lasting through to *c.* 1000, the number of charters and legal *notitiae* increases in the tenth century.[191] But the situation is often reminiscent of that in the late seventh

---

[187] *MGH Cap.* II, no. 258, p. 265. Tessier, *Recueil*, III, p. 58 and n. 2, apparently hesitated to make this identification.

[188] *MGH Epp. merov. et karol.* VI, no. 169, pp. 158–9. (J. Devisse, *Hincmar, archévêque de Reims*, 3 vols. (Geneva, 1975–6), II, p. 598 n. 201, mistranslates somewhat.)

[189] Flodoard, *Historia Remensis Ecclesiae* III, c. 24, ed. Heller and Waitz, p. 535.

[190] Karl Leyser, *Rule and Conflict in an Early Medieval Society: Ottonian Saxony* (London 1979), p. 102. See further *idem*, 'Ottonian government', *EHR* 96 (1981), 721–53, reprinted in *idem*, *Medieval Germany and its Neighbours* (London, 1982), pp. 69–101.

[191] This is true for most regions of Carolingian Europe north of the Alps. In France, the pioneering work of G. Duby, *La Société aux XIe et XIIe siècles dans la région mâconnaise* (2nd edn, Paris, 1971), exploited the increasing riches of the Cluny cartulary through the

and early eighth centuries, namely, the 'top layer' of royal activity dwindles, while government, and the use of the written word, continues lively at local level. Even this contrast misleads; for the continuing interest of ecclesiastical communities in the written word ensured that capitularies were copied and kept, and that new synodal and canonical material was produced, in places like Mainz, Trier and Metz. If in many parts of the tenth-century Latin west (including some, like England, that had never belonged to the Carolingian Empire), churchmen knew their capitularies and kept records of property transactions, laymen did not forget what it meant to participate in literacy.[192] In their legal procedures, they continued to preach, and sometimes to practise, the message of Charlemagne.[193] In that sense, the post-Carolingian nobility maintained something of the substance of Carolingian government.[194]

Charlemagne's Empire has been called the first Europe. One thing that gave it unity was the use of the written word, sufficiently generalized to extend 'vertically' through the free population, and 'horizontally' transcending regional boundaries: the same capitularies could circulate north and south of the Alps, for instance. I have argued that the elite of the Carolingian world actively participated in literacy as a means of group-identification, for their own benefit: hence that the 'effectiveness' of literacy in government should be appreciated as much for its symbolic as for its pragmatic function. For Charlemagne, capitularies and decrees were intimately linked to the precepts of God: all of them were to be observed by all men as the condition of 'having our grace'.[195] In this sense the reception of the written word was the litmus test of political loyalty. We should not be surprised that the *Admonitio generalis* or the *Addenda* to *Lex Salica* were relatively frequently copied, while what appear to us more 'practical'

---

period. The charter-collections of St Gall and Redon are exceptional in being much fuller for the ninth century than for the tenth.

[192] Much of the northern Continental as well as the English evidence is assessed by P. Wormald, 'Æthelwold and his continental counterparts', in *Bishop Æthelwold: His Career and Influence*, ed. B. Yorke (Woodbridge, 1988), pp. 13–42. See also Wormald, 'Charters, law and the settlement of disputes in Anglo-Saxon England', in *Settlement of Disputes*, pp. 149–68.

[193] This seems to me a plausible reading of the *conventum* between Count William of Aquitaine and the Chiliarch Hugh, ed. J. Martindale, '*Conventum inter Guillelmum Aquitanorum comes et Hugonem Chiliarchum*', *EHR* 84 (1969), 528–48. As has often been remarked, the world of the *conventum* was also that of Bishop Fulbert of Chartres, whose advice to Count William was based in part on his reading of Carolingian capitularies.

[194] This view has been put forward in a number of papers by K.F. Werner, notably 'Kingdom and principality in twelfth-century France', in *The Medieval Nobility*, ed. T. Reuter (Amsterdam 1978), pp. 243–90.

[195] See Mordek, 'Karolingische Kapitularien', p. 49 n. 140, quoting a recently discovered capitulary of Charlemagne, ed. Mordek 'Unbekante Texte'.

capitularies have often survived only in a single manuscript.[196] The significance of the written word, in a world in which texts proliferated, can be gauged by attempts to distinguish between forbidden and prescribed texts, and between authorized and forbidden uses of texts. No one was to dare to use a psalter or gospel-book for divination.[197] Charms and spells were prohibited; *pseudografia* were denounced; 'a most false letter' alleged to have dropped from heaven was 'not to be read but burned, lest through such written things (*scripta*) the people be put into error'.[198] Nuns were not to write out love-songs (*winileodas*) and circulate them outside their convents.[199] False charters of manumission were to be exposed and rejected.[200] Errors in written texts were dangerous (even if errors in the interpretation of texts were still more so).[201]

'Bad' writing was opposed by good writing, a prime function of which was to identify the legitimate, the righteous. The naming and listing that were fundamental uses of the written word in Carolingian government recall the name-lists used for religious purposes in liturgical commemoration: Memorial Books, also called Books of Life, contained the names of the saved. God read them.[202] The ruler too wanted name-lists, signifying his power over those named, and their claims to his concern. Such lists were inspired by the Old Testament. The Book of Numbers set out the work-methods of Israel; the Books of Kings showed these methods in practice.[203] In enjoining that surveys be made, that lists be drawn up and kept, Carolingian rulers followed the path of Moses and Solomon. At the same time, their agents, and those they ruled, inscribed themselves as their collaborators: a new Israel.[204]

---

[196] For instance, the *Capitulare missorum* of 802, MGH Cap. I, no. 33, pp. 91–9; the *Capitulare missorum de exercitu promovendo* of 808, *ibid.*, no. 50, pp. 136–8; the *Capitulare de Villis*, above, p. 273.

[197] MGH Cap. I, no. 23, c. 20, p. 64; compare also c. 34: 'nec cartas per perticas appendant propter grandinem'. For antecedents of such prohibitions, see R. Markus, 'From Caesarius of Arles to Boniface: Christianity and paganism in Gaul', in *The Seventh Century: Change and Continuity*, ed. J. Trapp, Proceedings of the Colloquium at the Warburg Institute, 8–9 July 1988 (forthcoming).

[198] MGH Cap. I, no. 22 (*Admonitio generalis*), c. 78, p. 60.

[199] MGH Cap. I, no. 23, c. 19, p. 63.

[200] MGH Cap. I, no. 58, c. 7, p. 145; *ibid.*, no. 104, c. 7, p. 215.

[201] MGH Cap. I, no. 29, p. 79.

[202] Compare above, n. 26. See Memoria. *Der geschichtliche Zeugnis Wert des liturgischen Gedenkens im Mittelalter*, ed. K. Schmid and J. Wollasch, Münstersche Mittelalter-Schriften 48 (Munich, 1984).

[203] Amid numerous references in the Old Testament to enumerating and surveying, see Num. 1–4; 33.1–2 xxxiii; 1–2 II Reg. 24.9; I Par 28.11–19; II Par. 35.4.

[204] My thanks are due to Rosamond McKitterick for her editorial skill and patience, and also for her kindness in allowing me to read parts of her book, *Carolingians*, in advance of publication.

Text and image
in the Carolingian world

Rosamond McKitterick

The functions of writing and painting in early mediaeval western Europe
must be set in the context of the uses, levels and distribution of literacy in
the societies of the barbarian west, many of which have been discussed in
the preceding papers in this volume. It is clear from Nelson's paper in
particular that there is a growing consensus concerning the wider possession
of, and resort to, literacy by the Franks at a number of different levels,
especially as far as Carolingian government is concerned, and it is on the
Franks in the eighth and ninth centuries that I concentrate in this paper.
The Franks (and others under Carolingian rule) increased their resort to
literate modes of legal, governmental and administrative transactions from
the end of the eighth century. Carolingian civilization, indeed, was one
largely dependent on the written word for its religion, its law, its government, its learning and its recording of the past. Its members, lay and cleric,
attained widely divergent levels of both pragmatic and learned literacy that
in a few telling cases we can document with some precision.[1]

But it is not on this broader context I wish to dwell; I want rather to look
at some of the manifestations and consequences of the uses of the written
word, and to examine in particular the relationship between image and text
in Carolingian book painting; this relationship is both a visible manifestation of the use of the written word and a consequence of literacy.

A starting point is to consider whether the Carolingians say anything
about the relative value of writing and pictures. One view is expressed by
Hraban Maur, a widely respected scholar and teacher, abbot of Fulda and
archbishop of Mainz, in a poetic epistle to Bonosus, dated *c.* 835.

Even if painting is dearer to you than all art, I ask you not to scorn the thankless
labour of writing, the effort of singing and the fervour and ardour of reading. For
writing is worth more than the vain shape of an image [or picture] and gives the soul
more beauty than the false painting which shows the form of things in an unfitting

[1] I have discussed these matters fully in my *Carolingians*.

manner . . . Writing reveals the truth by its countenance [appearance], its words and its meaning. The picture sates the sight while it is still new but it palls once it is old, quickly loses its truth, and does not arouse faith.[2]

Hraban Maur was undoubtedly influenced by the prevailing attitudes towards pictures and images in the Frankish kingdoms in the aftermath of the Iconoclasm dispute. Yet, in his attitude to letters and writing, and his perception of their power, he was also drawing on his intellectual training. He may, for example, have been impressed by Isidore of Seville's *Etymologiae*, and, in particular, Isidore's discussion of the significance and power of certain letters. Isidore was certainly available at Fulda's library in Hraban's time.[3] Although no discussion of letters as such is incorporated into Hraban's own encyclopaedia, *De rerum naturis*, his treatment of 'grammar' in the *De institutione clericorum* shows a preoccupation with words and their meaning, and grammar's importance for understanding texts. His odd little tract, *De inventione linguarum*, moreover, is concerned exclusively with different alphabets and letter forms.[4]

I shall return to the significance of Hraban Maur's phrase that writing reveals the truth by its appearance, words and meaning. For the moment, however, let us compare Hraban's suspicion of the potential moral shortcomings, not to say snares, of pictures. The assembled prelates and lay magnates at the Reform Council of Tours in 813, for example, advised the clergy to abstain from all that is temptation for the eyes and ears, that is, painting and music, for when the eyes and ears are bewitched, numerous faults penetrate.[5] Two decades earlier Theodulf of Orleans in his *Libri Carolini* (*c.* 791) was more specific:

Pictures shaped by the art of artists always lead those who glorify them into error . . . it is certain that they are the invention of artists and not the truth . . . A picture is painted in order to convey to the onlookers the true memory of historical events and to advance their minds from falseness to the fostering of truth. But sometimes – quite the contrary – it inclines the mind to think falseness instead of truth.[6]

---

[2] Hraban Maur, ed. Ernst Dümmler, Carmina No. 38, *MGH Poet.* II, lines 1–19, p. 196.

[3] Isidore of Seville, *Etymologiarum sive originum libri xx*, ed. W.M. Lindsay (Oxford, 1911), I.iii and iv, and compare Hraban Maur, *De institutione clericorum* III.18, *PL* 107, cols 395–6. For modern discussions, see Maria Rissel, *Rezeption antiker und patristischer Wissenschaft bei Hrabanus Maurus: Studien zur karolingischen Geistesgeschichte* (Frankfurt, 1976), pp. 270–4, and Elisabeth Heyse, *Hrabanus Maurus' Enzyklopädie 'de rerum naturis'*, Münchener Beiträge zur Mediävistik und Renaissance Forschung 4 (Munich, 1969), p. 44.

[4] Hraban Maur, *De institutione clericorum* III.18, *PL* 107, cols. 395–6, and compare his discussion of language 16.1–3, *PL* 111, cols. 435–51, and *De inventione linguarum*, *PL* 112, cols. 1579–83. See the definition of pictures in *De rerum naturis XXI.* 9, *PL* 111, col. 563.

[5] *MGH Conc.* II.1, no. 38, c. 7, p. 287.

[6] Theodulf of Orleans, *Libri Carolini*, I, c. 2, ed. H. Bastgen, *MGH Conc.* II, Suppl. pp. 12–14 and especially p. 13.

While it was acknowledged by many Carolingian scholars that a picture was a kind of literature for the uneducated man (*pictura est quaedam litteratura illiterato*), taking up Gregory the Great's famous dictum to that effect, only rarely is there some understanding that beauty in the form of an image or picture could enhance rather than distract the faith.[7]

This estimation of words above images is in direct contrast to some ninth-century Byzantine writers, who esteemed images above words. The Patriarch Photios in his seventeenth homily, for example, and speaking of the image in the main apse of Hagia Sophia in Constantinople, dedicated in his presence in 867, declared:

For even if the one introduces the other, yet the comparison that comes about through sight is shown in every fact to be far superior to the learning that penetrates through the ears. Has a man lent his ear to a story? Has his intelligence visualized and drawn to itself what he has heard? Then, after judging it with sober attention, he deposits it in his memory. No less – indeed much greater – is the power of sight. For, surely, having somehow through the outpouring and effluence of the optical rays touched and encompassed the object, it too sends the essence of the thing seen on to the mind, letting it be conveyed from there to the memory for the concentration of unfailing knowledge. Has the mind seen? Has it grasped? Has it visualized? Then it has effortlessly transmitted the forms to the memory.[8]

The early ninth-century Byzantine patriarch, Nicephorus, also thought pictures were superior to words, because sight is more persuasive and convincing than hearing. He declared that pictures brought deeds vividly before one, without the intervention of words, transforming the auditor of the text into an eye-witness of the deed.[9] Both Photios and Nicephorus, however, thought with reference to the spoken rather than the written word. In that written texts were read aloud, however, their distinction is indeed between word and image. Morrison has interpreted the perception of pictures implied by these writers as 'calculated, stylized misunderstanding of the visual'. He stresses that 'one characteristic of that way of understanding [or misunderstanding] was the assumption that signs could

---

[7] For Gregory the Great, see his *Epistola ad Serenum, MGH Epp.* II, 270.13 and 271.1, p. 195, though the Latin phrase cited is taken from Walafrid Strabo, *De rebus ecclesiasticis*, c. 8, *De imaginibus et picturis*, *PL* 114, col. 929, and also ed. A. Knoepfler, *De exordiis et incrementis quarundam in observationibus ecclesiasticis rerum* (Munich, 1890), p. 24. Compare, however, the aesthetic ideas and philosophical interpretations of John Scotus Eriugena, elucidated in Rosario Assunto, *Die Theorie des Schönen im Mittelalter* (Cologne, 1963), particularly in his translation of Dionysius the Areopagite's *De divinis nominibus*.

[8] *The Homilies of Photius, Patriarch of Constantinople*, English Translation, Introduction and Commentary, ed. Cyril Mango, DOS 3 (Washington DC, 1958), p. 294.

[9] Nicephorus, *Antirheticus III Adversus Constantinum Copronymum* 3 and 5, *PG* 100, cols. 380D and 381D, cited by W.C. Loerke, 'The monumental miniature', in *The Place of Book Illumination in Byzantine Art*, ed. K. Weitzmann (Princeton, 1975), pp. 61–97, at p. 96. I am grateful to John Mitchell for telling me about these statements and directing me to these references.

actually mediate to an interpreter the thing signified, and not merely communicate knowledge about it'.[10]

It is within the wary acceptance of the didactic value of pictures and the conviction that writing was more reliable, more truthful and unambiguous, that Carolingian book painting has to be seen. Yet it is not so much with the Carolingians' attitude to pictures and painting, nor, following Camille's example, the degree to which Carolingian illuminations could or did become text substitutes for the illiterate, that I wish to explore.[11] These are more purely visual perspectives. I wish to focus on the reasons for, and possible consequences of, Hraban Maur's conviction of the superiority of writing to pictures, a conviction he shared with many others. Nowhere is it more clearly expressed, for example, than by Theodulf of Orleans in his *Libri Carolini*:

> Painters are thus able to commit events to the memory [that is, in pictorial form] but things which are perceptible only to the mind and expressible only in words cannot be grasped and shown by painters, but by writers . . . O glorifier of images, gaze then at your pictures and let us devote our attention to the Holy Scripture. Be the venerator of artificial colours and let us venerate and penetrate secret thought. Enjoy your painted pictures and let us enjoy the word of God.[12]

Theodulf provides, in short, a clear statement of Christianity's emphasis on the revelation of Christ recorded in the written text of the Gospels. There is not space here to explore the diverse implications of Theodulf's statement, particularly the idea that some things can only be expressed in words, so I draw out only one or two. At one level it can be read as a simple and pragmatic conviction of a literate scholar of the intrinsic superiority and clarity of writing as opposed to pictures. But in the context of the Carolingian reception and promotion of the Christian faith, a religion of the book, as well as that of their resort to writing in every aspect of their administration, drawing thereby on their Roman inheritance, the Carolingian attitude towards texts and pictures is a crucial clue to the impact of the written word on a warrior society and the response it evoked.[13] It does much to explain, moreover, the types of image we find in Carolingian book painting. Quite apart from the close relationship between pictures and the text they illustrate to be observed in Carolingian books,

[10] Karl Morrison, *I Am You* (Princeton, 1988), ch. 9 and especially ch. 10 on the 'participatory bonding through painting: the iconoclast dispute 726–843'. I am very grateful to Karl Morrison for permitting me to read these chapters in advance of publication.

[11] Michael Camille, 'Seeing and reading: some visual implications of medieval literacy and illiteracy', *Art History* 8 (1985), 26–49.

[12] Theodulf of Orleans, *Libri Carolini* III, c. 23 and II, c. 30, ed. Bastgen, *MGH Conc.* II, Suppl., pp. 153 and 98 respectively.

[13] For a fuller exposition of the impact of the written word on Frankish society in the eighth, ninth and tenth centuries see McKitterick, *Carolingians*.

there is an extraordinary devotion to the decorated letter, and to the elaboration of a hierarchy of scripts. This type of book painting, unparalleled anywhere else in western Europe, is surely what Hraban Maur had in mind in his statement that writing 'reveals the truth in its appearance, words and meaning'. We can go further. Paintings were tolerated, even encouraged, when they were of letters or were visual translations of a text.

The Frankish conviction of the importance of the written word is in fact elaborated in art. We can see this first in the hierarchy of scripts in Carolingian books, and secondly in the role of the text itself as image.

HIERARCHY OF SCRIPTS

Scribes in Roman Gaul, as elsewhere in the western Roman Empire, had employed the main script types of the Roman script system. Under Frankish rule books and documents in Gaul continued to be written in these script types, though we find the square capitals (*capitalis quadrata*) and rustic capitals (*capitalis rustica*) used in due course for titles rather than for whole texts,[14] save in a handful of exceptions whose use of rustic capitals for the text script appears to have been deliberate antiquarianism.[15]

Books in early Frankish Gaul, to the end of the seventh century, were written either in uncial or half-uncial, and very occasionally in late Roman cursive (as in the Paris Avitus papyrus codex).[16] For the most part cursive hands were reserved for documents and non-literary texts, or used as an annotating hand in books. The Frankish kings and their notaries evolved their own distinctive charter cursive.[17]

Choices of types of scripts for particular purposes had of course been made in the Roman period as well. Surviving evidence, for example, suggests a preference for capitals, whether square or rustic, for non-Christian texts, and uncial for Christian writings in the fourth century, just as the codex appears to have been the Christians' preferred format for the book.[18] The lawyers and notaries, moreover, also wrote in tironian notes, a form of shorthand, and we find these still being used by scribes in the

---

[14] See Rosamond McKitterick, 'The scriptoria of Merovingian Gaul: a survey of the evidence' in *Columbanus and Merovingian Monasticism*, ed. Howard B. Clarke and Mary Brennan, BAR, International Series 113 (Oxford, 1981), pp. 173–207.

[15] For example, in the Utrecht Psalter in the ninth century: see below p. 311 and n. 55.

[16] BN lat. 8913+8914 (*CLA* V, 573).

[17] See, for example, the facsimiles of Merovingian royal diplomata in Philippe Lauer and Charles Samaran, *Les Diplômes originaux des Mérovingiens* (Paris, 1908).

[18] The case for the codex is argued by C.H. Roberts and T.C. Skeat, *The Birth of the Codex* (London and Oxford, 1983), and see my review in *The Library* (1985), 360–3. The new perspective and context for the adoption of the codex form for the book by the Jews is proposed by Stefan Reif, above, pp. 145–7.

writing offices of the Frankish kings as late as the second half of the ninth century.[19] Different letter forms, therefore, were recognized as suitable or appropriate for different purposes in the late Roman world. Such recognition is still evident in the documents and codices of Carolingian Europe. Uncial script is used for the grander liturgical books, and the new caroline minuscule which emerged in the mid-eighth century after a long process of evolution was the standard book-hand.[20] The Glazier Sacramentary, now in New York, but written at St Amand *c.* 860, is a fine and elegant example of caroline minuscule in its perfected form. It was given by Charles the Bald's first wife to the monastery for women at Chelles. Roman rustic capitals provide an effective division of the text, and the first word of each prayer is given an enlarged square capital letter. Rustic and square capitals, in other words, are of higher rank than the minuscule: a hierarchy of scripts is acknowledged. Such full acknowledgement is to be observed in all the grander codices from the Carolingian period.[21]

The use of a hierarchy of scripts was a well-established scribal technique by the beginning of the eighth century in the Frankish kingdoms. Earlier instances of a hierarchy of scripts can be observed in some manuscripts of the first half of the seventh century, such as Lyons Bibliothèque de la Ville 602 or 604, written in half-uncial but with uncial employed for the chapter headings, and capitals for the colophons.[22] In Luxeuil books of the late seventh and early eighth centuries, the scribes used their peculiarly distinctive calligraphic cursive minuscule, and drew on a hierarchy of scripts for display purposes, just as Tours and many other Carolingian centres were to

---

[19] Still the best guide is E. Chatelain, *Introduction à la lecture des notes tironiennes* (Paris, 1900). On the use of tironian notes in the Carolingian chancery, see M. Jusselin, 'La Chancellerie de Charles le Chauve d'après les notes tironiennes', *Le Moyen Age* 33 (1922), 1–89, and for their significance in the Merovingian period, see David Ganz, 'Bureaucratic shorthand and Merovingian learning', in *Ideal and Reality in Frankish and Anglo-Saxon Society*, ed. Patrick Wormald (Oxford, 1983), pp. 58–75.

[20] See the masterly exposition by Bernhard Bischoff, *Paläographie* (Berlin, 1979), pp. 143–51, transl. David Ganz and Daíbhí Ó Croinín, *Latin Palaeography: Antiquity and the Middle Ages* (Cambridge, 1990). On scripts differentiated by function, the two apparent grades of runes are significant: the 'normal' or 'Danish' runes primarily used epigraphically for inscriptions on stones and the 'short branch' or 'Swedish–Norwegian' runes used particularly for everyday correspondence. The latter were quicker to write and so possibly also the ones used by traders. See Else Roesdahl, *Viking Age Denmark* (London, 1982), pp. 20–1.

[21] New York Pierpont Morgan Library, G57. Compare, for example, the layout of such books as the Moutier-Grandval Bible, BL Add. 10546, and the magnificent products of the Lothar Court School: see Wilhelm Koehler, *Die karolingischen Miniaturen*, 5 vols. (Berlin, 1930–82), I: *Die Schule von Tours*, and IV: *Die Hofschule Kaiser Lothars. Einzelhandschriften aus Lothringen*.

[22] *CLA* VI, 782a and 782b, and 783.

do from the late eighth century onwards.[23] A hierarchy of scripts was not simply decorative in function. Both because it served to mark out important parts of the text as a form of punctuation, and because the status of the script used enhanced and reflected the status of particular sections of the text, the elaboration of different grades of script according to degrees of formality or rank was a significant development in western book illumination. In the austere mid-ninth century Paris Sacramentary from St Amand, the large capital V and T signal the beginnings of the two central prayers of the canon of the mass – *Vere dignum* and *Te igitur*. Uncial is used for the two opening lines and for the opening words of the *sanctus*. The letters of the words in the abbreviated forms in the latter case $\overline{scs}$ constitute a symbolic invocation.[24] Alternatively, capitals or uncials could be reserved for title pages, or the letters could be elaborated to form very large fancy capitals and enlarged initials as in the eighth-century Chelles copy of Augustine's *De Trinitate* (Oxford Laud misc. 126) where a whole page is made up of lines of fancy display script, smaller capitals, uncial and half-uncial.[25]

Attitudes towards the written word, or particular texts, could be expressed in the rank of the script used. The Anglo-Saxons south of the Humber, for example, wrote their charters in uncial, a high-ranking book-hand also used for the Word of God in gospel-books. This was to make a statement about the power and associations of the written word itself.[26] Use of book-hand in Carolingian private charters is a reflection of a similar kind of thinking. In the triumph of caroline minuscule – essentially an evolved, disciplined, harmonious and orderly script – over the older Merovingian book-hands, we may be observing an assertion of the appropriateness of one kind of script as against another in the Carolingian world. But it is difficult for us to interpret this assertion precisely, with our minds fogged as they are by aesthetic considerations, response to the similarity between caroline minuscule and modern Roman type faces to which we are accustomed, and our own appreciation of its legibility.[27] Of assistance is the emergence in the

---

[23] On Luxeuil and the identification of its books by means of its display scripts, see E.A. Lowe, 'The "script of Luxeuil": a title vindicated', in his *Palaeographical Papers 1907–1965*, ed. Ludwig Bieler, 2 vols. (Oxford, 1972), II, pp. 389–98. On Tours, see E.K. Rand, *A Survey of the Manuscripts of Tours* (Cambridge, Mass., 1929), though many of his judgements on Tours scripts and practice are now ripe for revision.

[24] BN lat. 2291, fol. 21v.

[25] *CLA* II, 252.

[26] Compare Kelly, above, pp. 39–44.

[27] For discussions of the significance of particular types of script see M.B. Parkes, *The Scriptoria of Wearmouth-Jarrow* (Jarrow Lecture, 1982), and David Ganz, 'The preconditions for caroline minuscule', *Viator* 18 (1987), 23–44. Some interesting Byzantine parallels are commented on by Judith Herrin, *The Formation of Christendom* (Oxford, 1987),

course of the ninth century of 'house styles' of script, that is of styles of writing a deliberately designed, calligraphic script based on the standard type produced in a particular atelier or scriptorium, and confined to grander books, side by side with local or regional styles used for the commoner library books and administrative texts needed in the Carolingian world.[28] In other words, even within the category of caroline minuscule itself there is a hierarchy of grades of formality according to function. It is primarily to the usefulness and functional nature of caroline minuscule and how in its time it lent itself to the efficient reproduction of texts in an orderly and disciplined manner that its phenomenal success and influence as a script type can be attributed.

TEXT AS IMAGE

As well as the understanding derived from reading the words on pages such as these, the letters have visual impact. Letters themselves can be images. Letters rarely have a meaning apart from the words they construct, but the obvious exceptions are the Greek letters alpha and omega (never, incidentally, transliterated into A and Z in the west) which acquired a symbolic value, signifying Christ as the beginning and the end. The famous eighth-century Gelasian Sacramentary, now Vat. reg. lat. 316, fol. 3v, uses the alpha and omega letters as the central motif in its frontispiece.[29] It is also used for the frontispiece to Augustine's *Quaestiones* on the Heptateuch, now BN lat. 12168.[30] Indeed, a great many Frankish manuscripts, particularly those from the north of the Seine in the eighth century, make these two letters the centre-piece of their illumination and the only portion of the decoration with a meaning and significance in addition to the celebratory and aesthetic. Yet once letters acquired meaning when grouped to form words they did not lose their symbolic value. When one thinks of the Drogo Sacramentary, for example, made at Metz for its archbishop in about 830 (BN lat. 9428), this is manifest. The illustration for the mass for Easter Sunday is appropriately illustrated with an historiated initial D containing

---

pp. 404–7. But all make comparative assumptions about legibility, ease and discipline of writing a particular kind of script which are open to question.

[28] I address some of these problems in R. McKitterick, 'Manuscripts and scriptoria in the reign of Charles the Bald, 840–877', in *Giovanni Scoto nel suo tempo: l'organizzazione del sapere in età carolingia'*, ed. C. Leonardi and E. Menesto (Perugia, 1989), pp. 271–302.

[29] Illustrated in Jean Hubert, Jean Porcher and W.F. Volbach, *Europe in the Dark Ages* (London, 1969), pl. 175, p. 164, and see the facing page in the manuscript, fol. 4r, *ibid.*, pl. 189, p. 180.

[30] Illustrated in *ibid.*, pl. 188, p. 179.

three events from Easter morning.[31] The dominant effect, however, is of the letters $\overline{DS}$, the standard abbreviation for *DEUS*. The letters are the picture, and the symbol. It enhances the understanding and rams home by sheer visual impact the overwhelming import of the empty tomb and Christ's Resurrection: *Iesus est Christus Filius Dei* (John 20.30).

Because of the inevitable discrepancy between graphic representation and the sound of words, even in the apparently most phonetically transcribed of languages, letters can be defined, in part, as mnemonic devices. They form a written code, similar in function, as far as the reader is concerned, to musical notation, for they record and preserve oral delivery.[32] However decoratively writing may have been deployed by Carolingian artists, and whatever the tensions between the opposed requirements of legibility and regularity for letters, and the variation and ambiguity of decoration, letters never lost their value as symbols, and the meaning is thus not obscured. Alexander has described the decorated letter as 'an illogical combination of opposed requirements' but it is this apparent illogicality which gives Carolingian painting its strength, and in which the potentially different functions of writing and painting were combined.[33] Meaning is enhanced, for a number of different levels of understanding are appealed to simultaneously.

In many cases, pictures are added to texts to spell out the meaning and associations. Pictures are literally bound into the text. In the pages containing Jerome's preface to the Pentateuch in Charles the Bald's First Bible, for example, square capitals on purple parchment are used for opening words, and thereafter gold uncials on purple. The large initial letter D contains eleven signs of the zodiac around the edge of the letter. Personifications of Sol and Luna drive their chariots in the bowl of the letter. Some reference to the creation of the sun, moon and stars in Genesis 1.6 is therewith intended.[34] Further decorated initials from the Bible are also assisted by pictures to reinforce their meaning. The initial at the beginning of the text of Judith, for example, contains the head of Holofernes, the Q at the beginning of St Luke's Gospel has within it the

---

[31] Illustrated in Jean Hubert, Jean Porcher and W.F. Volbach, *Carolingian Art* (London, 1970), pl. 147, p. 160, and in colour in Florentine Mütherich and Joachim Gaehde, *Carolingian Painting* (London, 1977), pl. 29, p. 91.

[32] See the pertinent observations of Susan Rankin on the function of early musical notation: 'From memory to record: musical notations in manuscripts from Exeter', *ASE* 13 (1984), 97–112.

[33] J.J.G. Alexander, *The Decorated Letter* (London, 1978), p. 8.

[34] BN lat. 1, fol. 8r, illustrated *ibid.*, pl. 7, p. 53.

evangelist's symbol.[35] Similarly in the Drogo Sacramentary, the central prayer of the canon of the mass, beginning *Te igitur*, is enhanced by pictures of the high priest Melchisedech offering up sacrifices, and sacrificial animals, from the Old Testament, with the obvious associations with the offering up of bread and wine and the sacrifice of Christ. The T itself assumes the form of the cross of the crucified Christ.[36] We find this iconography adopted in many Carolingian mass books, from the Sacramentary of Gellone, written at Meaux in the early eighth century, onwards; and it is a striking instance of the use to which Isidore's statement of the significance of the letter T, pointing to precisely this image, was put by the Carolingian book painters.[37]

In many Carolingian manuscripts, however, letters form pictures or images on their own, without any assistance from illustrations; meaning and sense are conveyed by the words they form. They are potent symbols of the power of the written word. Examples may be invoked at random among the many possible. The *explicit* of the Bible of Theodulf with its address to the reader, is the most marvellous image in the clarity of its design.[38] The *Quoniam Quidem* page from the beginning of St Luke's Gospel in the Morgan Gospels, produced at Tours between 857 and 862, has a wonderfully clever positioning of the letters *quoniam* and *quidem*, there is a delicate imitation of the tail of the Q in the word *ordinare*, and a notable elegance and balance in the composition as a whole.[39] The Rheims school of painting can be invoked for examples too. The Douce Psalter (Oxford Douce 59) was produced at Hautvillers under the patronage of Ebbo, archbishop of

---

[35] See the illustrations in *La Neustrie: les pays au nord de la Loire, de Dagobert à Charles le Chauve viie–ixe siècle*, ed. Patrick Perin and Laure-Charlotte Feffer, exhibition catalogue, Musées et Monuments départementaux de Seine-Maritime (Rouen, 1985), pl. 109 (BN lat. 1, fols. 301, 347), p. 240.

[36] BN lat. 9428, illustrated in Mütherich and Gaehde, *Carolingian Painting*, pl. 28, p. 90. Compare the 'T' in the Sacramentary of Gellone, BN lat. 12048, fol. 143, illustrated in Hubert, Porcher and Volbach, *Carolingian Art*, pl. 203, p. 193, and the discussion by B. Teyssedre, *Le Sacrementaire de Gellone et la figure humaine dans les manuscrits francs du viiie siècle* (Toulouse, 1959). BN lat. 1141, fol. 6v, painted by the palace school of Charles the Bald, is illustrated in Mütherich and Gaehde, *Carolingian Painting*, pl. 34, p. 100.

[37] Isidore, *Etymologiae* I.iii.9: *Tertia T figuram demonstrans Dominicae crucis unde et Hebraice signum interpretatur*. On the *Te igitur* initials generally, see Rudolf Suntrup, '*Te igitur* Initialen und Kanonbilder in mittelalterlichen Sakramentarschriften', in *Text und Bild: Aspekte des Zusammenwirkens Zweier Kunste in Mittelalter und früher Neuzeit*, ed. C. Meier and U. Ruberg (Wiesbaden, 1980), pp. 278–382.

[38] BN lat. 9380, fol. 347. Illustrated in *La Neustrie*, ed. Perin and Feffer, and see the comments by Florentine Mütherich, *ibid.*, pp. 257–9, at p. 258.

[39] New York Pierpont Morgan Library, Morgan 860, fol. 96r, illustrated in Alexander, *Decorated Letter*, pl. 8, p. 55. For a different treatment compare BN lat. 261 (Gospels du Mans) fol. 76, illustrated in *La Neustrie*, ed. Perin and Feffer, p. 231.

Rheims, for an unknown but wealthy, and possibly royal, client. The initial words of Psalm 101 (2) *Domine exaudi orationem meam*, or those of Psalm 26 (27): *Dominus illuminatio mea et salus mea quem timebo*, achieve their effect not simply by delicate decoration and the gold letters on purple parchment, but also by the sensitive deployment of capital and minuscule letters. The words of the Lord were directed by the scribe to illuminate the heart and mind of the reader.[40] In the Rheims manuscripts the impact of the written word is enhanced by the lavish use of gold and pigments. At St Amand in the ninth century, a monastery under the patronage of the west Frankish king Charles the Bald, on the other hand, the letter in such manuscripts as Laon 199 is an image embellished with delicate and restrained abstract and zoomorphic ornament.[41] In the Laon Origen we have a fine example of St Amand work, with a particularly effective layout of initial, uncial and minuscule. Similarly in the Second Bible of Charles the Bald, another St Amand product, meaning and letter are combined in the design for the beginning of Genesis; a superb instance of the scribe's sense of pattern and harmony is the *incipit* page from the book of Joshua on fol. 80 in the same manuscript.[42]

All these examples are of letters which can be understood as images because of their visual appeal to the senses. But there are a number of Carolingian manuscripts which actually use letters to make pictures. These are the copies of *carmina figurata*, poems, in other words, like the story of the mouse's tale in *Alice through the Looking Glass* or George Herbert's *Wings*, or acrostic poems such as those of the late antique author Optatianus Porphyrius which were very popular as models for the verse experiments of the Carolingian poets.[43] Hraban Maur's *De laudibus sanctae crucis*, for example, is such an imitation. Sets of letters are enclosed by the contours of patterns or figures to form separate phrases or verses in addition to the main text. The representation is of the emperor Louis the Pious, and the dedication poem reinforces the image of him as the Christian warrior. Within the halo or nimbus the letters form the inscription *Tu Hludouuicum christe corona* (You Christ crown Louis) and on the cross staff is proclaimed

---

[40] Oxford, Bodleian Library, Douce 59, fols. 101r and 25v. See also the Ebbo Gospels, Epernay, Bibliothèque Municipale 1, especially fol. 19r illustrated in Mütherich and Gaehde, *Carolingian Painting*, pl. 15, p. 61.

[41] Laon, Bibliothèque Municipale 199 (Origen) especially fol. 4r, the initial 'P'.

[42] BN lat. 2 (Second Bible of Charles the Bald), fols. 11r and 80r, illustrated in Mütherich and Gahde, *Carolingian Painting*, pl. 48, p. 126, and Alexander, *Decorated Letter*, pl. 9, p. 57, respectively.

[43] See Berne Burgerbibliothek 212, associated with the royal court: Bernhard Bischoff, 'Die Hofbibliothek Karls des Grossen' in *idem, Mittelalterliche Studien*, III (Stuttgart, 1981), pp. 149–69, at p. 155.

'The true victory and salvation of the king are all rightly in your cross, O Christ'.[44] Another example from this same Vatican manuscript depicts Christ himself with, again, different verses within the pictorial elements. In Christ's nimbus, for example, are the words *Rex regum et dominus dominorum* (King of kings and Lord of lords) and *Alpha et Omega*.[45]

A similar conceit but an entirely different context is provided by the Harley Aratus.[46] The text is the *Phaenomena* of Aratus, a non-mathematical exposition of the chief features of the celestial globe, in the translation made by Cicero. It was copied in an atelier in Lotharingia between 820 and 850, and produced for a patron with some connections with the royal palace of Lothar. The text is the section in caroline minuscule under the picture whereas the pictures of each constellation are made up of the text of the *scholia* from Hyginus' *De Astronomia* which dealt with the myths of the stars and provided a catalogue of stars in each constellation. It is an intriguing layout for a commentary on a text. The letters form the image which is the subject of the commentary the letters form, and are further differentiated from the main Aratus text by the use of rustic capitals. Typical of the layout in this manuscript are Centaurus and Eridanus, with the rustic capitals in red, and only the head, hands and feet painted in. Note, too, the estimate of the number of stars in the constellation, *sunt stella XLII*, and the positioning of the stars in the case of Centaurus to build the framework of the picture formed by the letters.[47]

At a much more basic level of relationship between text and picture there are captions explaining particular images. The Sacramentary of Marmoutier, for example, provides an illustration for the clerical grades. The meaning, however, would not be clear without the labels accorded each

[44] Vat. reg. lat. 124, fol. 4v, illustrated in Mütherich and Gaehde, *Carolingian Painting*, pl. 12, p. 54. See also the Vienna copy of this work, Österreichische Nationalbibliothek 652, of the first half of the ninth century. For a lucid exposition of the significance of these pictures see Elizabeth Sears' contribution to *Charlemagne's Heir: New Perspectives on the Reign of Louis the Pious*, ed. Roger Collins and Peter Godman (Oxford, 1990), and P. Bloch, 'Zum Dedikationsbild im Lob des Kreuzes des Rabanus Maurus' in *Das erste Jahrtausend*, ed. Viktor Elbern, 3 vols. (Düsseldorf, 1962), I, pp. 471–94.

[45] Vat. reg. lat. 124, fol. 8v.

[46] BL Harley 647, illustrated in G. Cavallo, 'Libri e continuità della cultura antica in età barbarica', in *Magistra Barbaritas: I barbari in Italia*, ed. Giovanni Pugliese Carratelli (Milan, 1984), pp. 603–62, at pl. 528 and pl. 529, pp. 616–17, and see the discussion by Patrick McGurk, 'Carolingian astrological manuscripts', in *Charles the Bald: Court and Kingdom*, ed. Margaret Gibson and Janet Nelson, British Archaeological Reports International Series 101 (Oxford, 1981), pp. 317–32.

[47] BL Harley 647, fol. 12r (Centaurus), illustrated in Cavallo, 'Libri e continuità', pl. 529 (with Eridanus from fol. 10v in pl. 528).

figure.[48] A notorious instance of the caption alone supplying a picture with its identity is the story related in the *Libri Carolini* by Theodulf of Orleans about the man who venerated pictures and who was shown two pictures of beautiful women without any captions. 'The painter supplied', he wrote, 'one picture with the caption "Virgin Mary", and the other with the caption "Venus". The picture with the caption "Mother of God" was elevated, venerated and kissed, and the other, because it had the caption "Venus", was maligned, scorned and cursed, although both were equal in shape and colour, and made of identical material, and differed only in caption.'[49] Theodulf was making a point about the images, but we can note that it is the written word which gives the picture in this case its identity, and its power.

In a portrayal of the evangelist St John in the Gospels of Francis II (BN lat. 257, fol. 147v), on the other hand, the essential identification of this figure on this page is not provided by an evangelist symbol. Instead the first words of his Gospel: *In principio erat verbum* are supplied in the picture. That is, words provide a telling substitute for an image.[50]

Wholesale conversions of an image into words are provided in a great many Carolingian poems and prose extracts. The recently identified

---

[48] Sacramentary of Marmoutier, Autun, Bibliothèque Municipale 19 bis, fol. 1, though assistance is rendered the illiterate by the addition of symbolic objects denoting office; thus the *ostiarius* or gatekeeper holds two keys, the subdeacon brandishes a chalice and ewer, the lector holds a jewelled book and so forth. But the manuscript is provided with instructive captions throughout. Fol. 1 is illustrated (with the wrong modern caption) in *La Neustrie*, ed. Perin and Feffer, pl. 19, p. 86. Compare St Gall, 64 fol. 12 (illustrated in Hubert, Porcher and Volbach, *Carolingian Art*, pl. 161, p. 175), where, in the picture of Paul being reviled by the Jews from the Epistles of Paul, the figures are labelled in order to identify them ('Paulus', 'Judei et gentes') with the Terence plays in BN lat. 7899, where all the characters are neatly identified with labels (an example is *ibid.*, pl. 172, p. 187). One can think too of the many dedication pictures (Hraban Maur in Vat. reg. lat. 124, fol. 2, or Vienna 652, fol. 2v, Boethius and Symmachus in the *De Arithmetica* from Tours which belonged to Charles the Bald, now Bamberg Staatsbibliothek HJ.IV.12, fol. 2v (illustrated in Cavallo, 'Libri e continuità', pl. 534, p. 620), or the copy of Isidore of Seville's *De fide catholica contra Iudaeos* in BN lat. 13396 (illustrated in *La Neustrie*, ed. Perin and Feffer, pl. 113, p. 278) depicting Isidore presenting his tract to his sister Florentina. In all these books it is only the captions which identify the figures or explain what is happening in the picture.

[49] Theodulf of Orleans, *Librie Carolini* IV, c. 16, ed. Bastgen, *MGH Conc.* II, Suppl., p. 204.

[50] There are many other Carolingian manuscripts about which the same point could be made, but in this case, BN lat. 257, fols. 147v and 148r, the point is somewhat vitiated by the fact that the opposite page has the evangelist symbol. But in terms of the reader's apprehension of the picture on the left hand page (fol. 147v) it is still the words which provide identification and context that it is the Gospel of John. The symbol on fol. 148r itself bears a scroll with what appear to be intended to represent tironian notes, and it is surrounded by a roundel bearing the inscription evoking the power of John's words and the potent symbolic meaning of the eagle. The visual image, in other words, is reinforced and strengthened by the inscription – each complements the other. For further comments on inscriptions compare Mitchell, above, pp. 193–4.

description of the basilica of St Denis has to be read for the image to be invoked.[51] Theodulf describes with admiring clarity the beautiful cup he was offered as a bribe.[52] Ermold the Black describes the wall paintings at Louis the Pious' palace and church at Ingelheim.[53] John Scotus Eriugena describes the glories of Charles the Bald's new palace chapel at Compiègne.[54] In all such descriptions the meaning of the words provides the pictures for the imagination's eye.

From the few examples I have cited it can be seen how many different uses of writing there are in Carolingian painting. At the very least, decorated letters or carefully arranged letters and words arrest and direct the attention to particular texts. But generally, more is demanded of the reader than his understanding of the words on the page: religious sensibility, faith and knowledge, the understanding of language, the emotions, aesthetic sense, material appraisal and appreciation of the media and skills employed are all involved.

A further dimension of the relationship between image and text needs to be considered. Because most of our extant Carolingian painting is in the form of book illumination, it follows that the illustrations, as distinct from the ornament, therein will be dependent on, or at least related to, the text. That, indeed, is a fundamental principle of book painting. Yet the degree of dependence can vary considerably; Carolingian illustrations often supply an independent comment on the text, though this comment itself springs from a textual source. The relationship between image and text may best be demonstrated by looking briefly at the Stuttgart and Utrecht Psalters.

Most of the extant Carolingian psalter illustrations, for example, are either simply decorative, as in the Corbie Psalter (though there are many exceptions even in this manuscript) or literal illustrations of the text, as in

---

[51] *Descriptio Basilicae Sancti Dionysii*, ed. Alain Stoclet, 'La Descriptio basilicae sancti Dionysii: premiers commentaires', *Journal des Savants* (1980), 103–17, and compare Bernhard Bischoff, 'Eine Beschreibung der Basilika von Saint-Denis aus dem Jahre 799', *Kunstchronik* 34 (1981), 97–103, and Werner Jacobsen, 'Saint-Denis in neuem Licht: Konsequenzen der neuentdeckten Baubeschreibung aus dem Jahre 799', *Kunstchronik* 36 (1983), 301–8.

[52] Theodulf of Orleans, 'Versus contra iudices', lines 163–204, ed. Ernst Dümmler, *MGH Poet.* I, pp. 493–517, at pp. 506–7, trans. Peter Godman, *Poetry of the Carolingian Renaissance* (London, 1985), pp. 162–4.

[53] Ermold the Black, *In honorem Hludowici*, ed. and trans. Edmond Faral, *Ermold le Noir: Poème sur Louis le Pieux et épîtres au roi Pépin* (Paris, 1964), pp. 156–64.

[54] John Scotus Eriugena, CCCC 223, pp. 342–4. See M. Foussard, 'Aulae sidereae, vers de Jean Scot au roi Charles', *Cahiers Archéologiques* 21 (1971), 78–89; M. Viellard-Troiekouroff, 'La Chapelle du palais de Charles le Chauve', *ibid.*, 69–109; and Yves Christe, 'Saint-Marie de Compiègne et le temple d'Hezechiel', in *Jean Scot Erigène et l'histoire de la philosophie* (Paris, 1977), pp. 477–81.

the Utrecht Psalter. In the Utrecht Psalter it is not one simple image suggested by the text that is chosen. Instead there is a masterly amalgamation of a set of literal visual translations of particular verses in a Psalm to form convincingly coherent composite pictures.[55] In the illustration to Psalm 23, for example, the individual elements are suggested by each phrase in the Psalm. There are the green pastures in which are the still waters by which the Psalmist is led. Herds of sheep and cows graze. 'Thy rod and thy staff they comfort me' is illustrated with the Psalmist, a little to the right of a table, holding a rod, the other end of which is held by an angel. The table itself, and the little group of aggressive archers in the bottom right hand corner of the picture, together illustrate the verse 'Thou preparest a table before me in the presence of mine enemies'. The angel pours oil on the Psalmist's head and the Psalmist holds a chalice according to the verse 'Thou anointest my head with oil; my cup runneth over'. To complete the picture is the little church to portray 'And I will dwell in the house of the Lord for ever'.[56]

From a practical point of view we have in this picture a series of unrelated representations put together to form a composition dependent for its unity and coherence as a picture on the juxtaposition of images and its aesthetic. It is a composite picture and it has, as it were, a semantic structure of its own. One can read it, but only if one knows the words of the Psalm. It is the text which gives the illustration its meaning. The separate elements of the picture are a mnemonic device for recalling the verses of the Psalm.

The book itself, produced at Hautvillers near Rheims in the 820s, under the patronage of Archbishop Ebbo of Rheims, may have been given by Ebbo to his patroness Judith, wife of the emperor Louis the Pious. It was certainly available to her son Charles the Bald by the early 860s, or at least, to artists working for him, for the ivory carvings of the book covers of Charles the Bald's Psalter, BN lat. 1152, illustrating Psalms 50 and 51, appear to have been modelled on the Utrecht Psalter drawings for the same Psalms.[57] The psalter text was the one best known by Carolingian

---

[55] Utrecht Psalter, Utrecht Bibliothek der Rijksuniversiteit, script. eccl. 484, facs. ed. K. van der Horst and Jacobus H.A. Engelbregt, *Utrecht-Psalter*, Codices Selecti phototypice impressi 75, 2 vols. (Graz, 1982 and 1984), and also the older E.T. de Wald, *The Illustrations of the Utrecht Psalter* (Princeton, 1932). Useful studies are Francis Wormald, *The Utrecht Psalter* (Utrecht, 1953), and Suzy Dufrenne, *Les Illustrations du Psautier d'Utrecht: sources et apport carolingien* (Paris, 1978), and her references.

[56] Utrecht Psalter, fol. 13r. illustrated in de Wald, *Illustrations*, pl. XX.

[57] Danielle Gaborit-Chopin, *Ivoires du Moyen Age* (Fribourg, 1978), pp. 188–9, and pls. 74–6, pp. 62–3. See also A. Goldschmidt, *Die Elfenbeinskulpturen aus der Zeit der karolingischen und sächsischen Kaiser*, 4 vols. (Berlin 1914–26), I, no. 40; H. Fillitz, 'Elfenbeinreliefs vom Hofe Kaiser Karls des Kahlens', in *Beiträge zur Kunst des Mittelalters: Festschrift für H. Wentzel zum 60. Geburtstag*, ed. R. Becksmann, U.-D. Korn

Christians, and formed an essential part of the early education of both
Carolingian clerics and aristocratic laymen and women. Judith was
acclaimed for her learning. If she did own this extraordinary book she
would have fully appreciated and been able to understand what phrases
these illustrations expressed, and she would also have known and been able
to read the text.[58]

Yet even in the Utrecht Psalter there are instances of illustrations which
provide a commentary on portions of the text. The illustration to Psalm 11
(12) is one such. To illustrate the phrase *in circuitu impii ambulant* (the
ungodly walk in a circle) there is a banal literal rendering, with the impious
shown walking round a circular object. To their left, however, is a group of
seven men pushing a wheel or turnstile. The explanation for this picture
was suggested by Panofsky. She thought that this odd little scene could be a
pictorial reference to St Augustine's comment on this verse: 'the ungodly
walk in a circle, that is, in the desire of temporal things as a cycle of seven
days, which revolves as a wheel'.[59]

More straightforward are the prophetic illustrations. Many Psalms were
interpreted by patristic and early mediaeval commentators as foretelling
the coming of Christ or as events in his Life and Passion. The illustration
to the third verse of Psalm 115 (116), for example: 'The snares of death
compassed me round about . . . I shall find trouble and heaviness and will
call upon the name of the Lord' is a representation of the Crucifixion of
Christ.[60] Generally, however, the artist of the Utrecht Psalter preferred
illustrations which were in direct rather than symbolic relation to his
text, and visual transliteration rather than the juxtaposition of associated
images.

The artist of the Stuttgart Psalter, on the other hand, working at St
Germain-des-Prés in Paris for an unknown patron, provided learned visual
commentary rather than literal illustration for many of the Psalms in his

and J. Zahlten (Berlin, 1975), pp. 41–51; and Peter Lasko, *Ars Sacra 800–1200* (Harmondsworth, 1972), pp. 35–7. The covers are illustrated in Hubert, Porcher and Volbach,
Carolingian Art, pls. 230–2, pp. 251–3.

[58] On Judith, see Elizabeth Ward, 'The Empress Judith', in *Charlemagne's Heir*, ed. Collins
and Godman, and on the education of women generally, see McKitterick, *Carolingians*, pp.
223–7.

[59] Utrecht Psalter, fol. 6v, illustrated in Hubert, Porcher and Volbach, *Carolingian Art*, pl.
85, p. 200, and see the discussion by Dora Panofsky, 'The textual basis of the Utrecht
Psalter illustrations', *The Art Bulletin* 25 (1943), 50–8. Compare D. Tselos, *The Sources of
the Utrecht Psalter Miniatures* (2nd edn, Minneapolis, 1960).

[60] Utrecht Psalter, fol. 67r, illustrated in de Wald, *Illustrations*, pl. CV.

book.[61] It is not possible here to do justice to the richness of the imaginative and intellectual response to the text revealed in the pictures in this marvellous book.[62] A few examples must suffice. The text of Psalm 18 (19) includes the verses: 'In them hath he set a tabernacle for the sun, which cometh forth as a bridegroom out of his chamber and rejoiceth as a giant to run his course. It goeth forth from the uttermost part of heaven and runneth about unto the end of it again, and there is nothing hidden from the heat thereof.' This is a perplexing set of images to illustrate. Eusebius, Athanasius and pseudo-Jerome, however, all interpreted these verses as a reference to the Ascension of Christ, and this is what the artist portrays in the upper right-hand corner of fol. 23r. Another example is provided by Psalm 37 (38), vv. 12 and 14. The verses illustrated are:

My kinsmen stood afar off
As for me, I was like a deaf man and heard not.

The first of these verses, 'My kinsmen stood afar off', was associated with Christ's trial before Pilate by Jerome and Rufinus. Although the exegetical association with Christ's trial is preserved by the artist, he does not illustrate the text of John: 19, v. 10 Jerome had in mind when writing his commentary, where Christ is brought before Pilate, but the account in Matthew: 26, v. 62. On fol. 49r Christ is depicted before the High Priest and two bodyguards (though the latter may have been intended to represent, more tellingly, the two false witnesses). The second verse illustrated, 'As for me, I was like a deaf man and heard not', was interpreted as an allusion to Peter's denial of Christ by both Jerome and Augustine. Again the artist was sensitive to differences between the Gospel texts. Peter is portrayed warming himself beside a brazier of coals as in John: 18, v. 18 and Luke: 23, v. 56, where he is beside a fire, whereas in Matthew: 27, v. 69, Peter is simply sitting 'without the palace'. It appears to be Luke's account the artist is following here. It is these interpretations which form the subject of the artist's picture. He added clues for the reader in the form of captions. The young woman in the depiction of Peter's denial has the caption *ancilla*.

---

[61] Stuttgart Psalter, Stuttgart, Württemburgische Landesbibliothek Biblia fol. 23, ed. in facsimile, *Der Stuttgarter Bilderpsalter Bibl. fol. 23 Württembergische Landesbibliothek Stuttgart*, 2 vols. (Stuttgart, 1965), and see the discussion of the scriptorium of Saint Germain-des-Prés by Bernhard Bischoff, 'Die Handschrift, Paläographische Untersuchung', in *ibid.*, II, pp. 15–30.

[62] See the commentary by Jakob Eschweiler, Bonifatius Fischer, Hermann Josef Frede and Florentine Mütherich, 'Der Inhalt der Bilder', in *ibid.*, II, pp. 55–150, and compare the older but still valuable page by page commentary by E.T. de Wald, *The Stuttgart Psalter. Biblia folio 23 Württembergische Landesbibliothek Stuttgart* (Princeton, 1930), with half-tone facsimile.

Round Peter's head are the words of Christ's warning from St Luke's
Gospel 23, v. 61: *non cantabit hodie gallus donec ter me negabis* ('the cock
shall not crow this day, before thou shalt thrice deny that thou knowest
me'). A literate reader of the Psalm is assumed therefore. Without a
knowledge of the text, of patristic commentary on it, and of the Gospel texts
invoked by the exegetes, the picture is meaningless.

A caption is also felt necessary to explain a want of inspiration on the
artist's part in the illustration to Psalm 42 (43), vv. 4–5: 'Why are thou so
cast down O my soul, and why art thou so disquieted within me?' The image
on fol. 55r is simply that of the Psalmist addressing a glum man sitting upon
a hilltop who is helpfully labelled *Anima*.

An evocative image is provided, on the other hand, by one of the pictures
for Psalm 90 (91) on fo. 107r, with a set of personifications of the words in
verses 5–6: 'His faithfulness and truth shall be thy shield and buckler. Thou
shalt not be afraid for any terror by night, nor for the arrow that flieth by
day; for the pestilence that walketh in darkness; nor for the sickness that
destroyeth in the noon day.' Here Christ is portrayed as man's 'shield and
buckler', placed in the middle of a shield and attacked by six serpents.

The artist of the Stuttgart Psalter was clearly familiar with the commentaries and interpretations of the Psalms, or parts of them, by Augustine,
Jerome, Rufinus, Bede, Cassiodorus and Isidore of Seville. On the basis of
his knowledge he painted a commentary on the text to expound it to the
reader and remind him by visual means of the additional hidden purport of
the words. It is possible that this artist was not the first to do this. It is
certain that he was not the only one, but it is nevertheless remarkable to find
so many patristic associations and extrapolations, possibly well known to
those who had received instruction in the school, translated into painted
images.[63] The pictures are eloquent witnesses of the words they illustrate;
text and picture are interdependent for their meaning, but it is the
underlying exegetical texts, not the actual text of the Psalms, which provide
this meaning. Still other illustrations in the Stuttgart Psalter are visual
translations of the metaphors in the text. Again, without the text, the
pictures are incomprehensible.[64]

Only rarely do we find instances of an artist providing an independent
iconographic commentary on a particular text which goes further than any
known exposition. Such an instance is provided by a group of apocalyptic

[63] Florentine Mütherich, 'Die Stellung der Bilder in der frühmittelalterlichen Psalter Illustration', *Stuttgarter Bilderpsalter*, II, pp. 151–222.

[64] Heinz Meyer, 'Die Metaphern des Psaltertextes in den Illustrationen des Stuttgarter
Bilderpsalters, in *Text und Bild*, ed. Meier and Ruberg, pp. 175–208.

illustrations. Consideration of these serves to demonstrate an assertion of image over text, but in terms which reinforce the written word, and the book, as a symbol of power and the key to all mysteries, and the gift of writing bestowed by the Christian faith and the law of God.

The crucial verses of the Book of Revelation are those at the beginning of chapters 5 and 10: 'And I saw in the right hand of him that sat on the throne a book written within and on the back side, and sealed with seven seals' (5 v. 1); 'And he had in his hand a little book, open (*libellum apertum*)' (10 v. 2). The association of the Lamb on the throne with Christ was made by the earliest patristic commentators. Christ in Majesty, holding a book, often with the four beasts – calf, lion, eagle and man – representing the four evangelists, and the twenty-four elders grouped in adoration round Him, moreover, was portrayed many times in both eastern and western art in the early middle ages.[65] Some Carolingian examples are the famous Christ in Majesty page from the Lorsch Gospels, the ceiling mosaic in the royal palace at Aachen, the Christ in Majesty in the Metz Sacramentary (BN lat. 1141) written to mark Charles the Bald's coronation as king of Lotharingia in 869, and the Lamb adored by the twenty-four elders in the Codex Aureus in Munich (Clm 14000), also written for Charles the Bald.[66] The Lamb in this last named picture holds a roll rather than a codex. Significantly, the page facing the Codex Aureus Lamb is the famous portrait of King Charles the Bald himself, joining the twenty-four elders in their adoration of the Lamb and the Book. It was painted in about 870, and provides a record for the brief period when Charles the Bald seemed likely to repossess Aachen, sit on his grandfather's throne and so contemplate the significance of the magnificent apocalyptic mosaic above him.[67]

---

[65] See the survey by F. van der Meer, *Apocalypse: Visions from the Book of Revelation in Western Art* (London, 1978), and *idem, Maiestas domini. théophanie de l'apocalypse dans l'art chrétien*, Studi di antichità cristiana 13 (Vatican, 1938) and the still useful Henri Omont, 'Manuscrits illustrés de l'apocalypse aux ixe et xe siècles', *Bulletin de la Société française de réproduction de manuscrits à peintures* 6 (1922), 62–95.

[66] Lorsch Gospels, Vat. pal. lat. 50+Bucharest Alba Julia library s.n., fol. 18v, facs. ed. Wolfgang Braunfels, *The Lorsch Gospels* (New York, 1967) and the fol. 18v also illustrated in E.G. Grimme, *Die Geschichte der abendländischen Buchmalerei* (Cologne, 1980), pl. 14, p. 41. The Aachen mosaic is illustrated in Hubert, Porcher and Volbach, *Carolingian Art*, pls. 35 and 36, pp. 40–1. BN lat. 1141, fol. 2v, illustrated *ibid.*, pl. 140, p. 152, and Clm 14000 (Codex Aureus), fols. 5v and 6r, illustrated in Mütherich and Gaehde, *Carolingian Painting*, pls. 37 and 38, pp. 106–7.

[67] Felix Kreusch, 'Kirche, Atrium und Porticus der Aachener Pfalz', in *Karl der Grosse, Lebenswerk und Nachleben*, ed. Wolfgang Braunfels, 4 vols. (Düsseldorf, 1965), III: *Die Kunst*, pp. 463–533, and the discussion by H. Schnitzler, 'Das Kuppelmosaik der Aachener Pfalzkapelle', *Aachener Kunstblätter* 29 (1964), 17–44, responded to by H. Schrade, 'Zum Kuppelmosaik der Pfalzkapelle und zum Theoderich-Denkmal in Aachen', *ibid.* 30 (1965), 25–37.

The Carolingians were, of course, not alone in their appreciation of the meaning of the visions of St John the Divine.[68] But they do seem to have elevated the Book of the Apocalypse as a potent symbol of the power of the written word and of the Christian faith. Carolingian exegetes were clear that the phrases *librum scriptum intus et foris* and *libellum apertum* were references to the Old and New Testaments. Haimo of Auxerre, for example, writing in the mid-ninth century, stated that the book with the seven seals signified the Old and New Testaments, though in his commentary on chapter 10.2 he asserted that the book with the seven seals was the Old Testament and the little open book (*libellum apertum*) was the New Testament.[69] In their association of the Lamb's Book with the seven seals with the Old and/or New Testaments the Carolingians were following the allegorical tradition of western apocalyptic commentary from Victorinus of Pettau (in Jerome's revision), Tyconius, Primasius, Bede and Ambrose Autpert.[70] The latter in particular, a verbose eighth-century Italian writer, was drawn on most heavily by Haimo of Auxerre in spelling out the sign of Redemption symbolized by the little open book.[71] It is significant, moreover, that the manuscript tradition of Ambrose Autpert's commentary, with early ninth-century copies associated with the leading centres of Corbie and St Denis, indicates that his work was known in the Frankish kingdoms.[72]

Not only do the exegetes stress the crucial significance of the apocalyptic book; illustrations of the Apocalypse of which we have the first extant

---

[68] See, for example, Gerald Bonner, *Saint Bede in the Tradition of Western Apocalypse Commentary* (Jarrow Lecture, 1966).

[69] Haimo of Auxerre (attributed to Haimo of Halberstadt), *Enarratio in Apocalypsin, PL* 117, cols. 1013–14 and 1062.

[70] The commentary to ch. 5 in Tyconius does not survive and that on ch. 10 is laconic: see Tyconius, ed. F. Loe Bue and G.G. Willis, *The Turin Fragments of Tyconius' Commentary on Revelation*, Texts and Studies NS 7 (Cambridge, 1963). See also Primasius, *Commentaria in Apocalypsim, PL* 68, cols. 820–1 and 863; Bede, *Explanatio Apocalypsis, PL* 93, cols. 145 and 160.

[71] Ambrose Autpert, *Expositionis in apocalypsin libri I–V*, ed. Robert Weber, *Ambrosii Autperti Opera*, CCSL Continuatio Medievalis 27 (Turnhout, 1975), pp. 230 and 390. Compare to Beatus of Liebana, *In Apocalipsin libri duodecim* III.4 and V.10, ed. H.A. Sanders, *Beatus of Liebana, In Apocalipsin libri duodecim*, Papers and Monographs of the American Academy in Rome 7 (Rome, 1930), pp. 305–6 and 438.

[72] On the manuscript tradition of Ambrose Autpert see *Ambrosii Autperti Opera*, ed. Weber, p. xiii, discussing BN lat. 12287–8 (Corbie) and Vat. reg. lat. 96 (St Denis *c.* 850) and Oxford, Bodleian Library Laud misc. 464 (767), *CLA* II, 253 (written in early caroline minuscule probably in Central Italy but at a very early date at St Denis). It is tempting to see in this last named manuscript the surviving remnant of the scriptorium of San Vincenzo, Ambrose Autpert's own monastery, of which otherwise we have little extant evidence; see Mitchell, above, pp. 217–19.

examples in western book painting in the ninth century make this apprehension of the divine gift of the written word, the law of God and the means of Redemption in the book with the seven seals the central symbol in their picture cycles. The earliest of them, the Trier Apocalypse, for example, stresses visually on almost every page, and especially in the illustration for chapter 10 verse 2, the gift of the book.[73] It also insists on the importance of writing. On page after page there is the image of John writing. On fol. 4v in particular John is told *scribe ergo quae vidisti* ('write what you have seen'), and the artist provides the eloquent image of the scribe John. It expresses succinctly the Carolingian understanding of the relation between the visual image and the text. The whole manuscript is an attempt to present what John saw and what he wrote down. The text is thus as potent an image of John's vision as the pictures which accompany it. The picture cycle itself is transformed from a text translated into a set of images into a triumphant visual confirmation of the gift of the written word through Christ.

In three related Bible manuscripts this was expressed in a different way in the remarkable and original frontispieces to the Book of Revelation. In the Moutier Grandval Bible and the Vivian Bible from Tours (BL Add. 10546 and BN lat. 1), the Lamb on the throne and the book with the seven seals form the upper half of the picture.[74] The bottom half of the page contains the figure of an old man holding on to a scarf, or veil, held also by the four evangelist symbols. An inscription explains the top picture of the Lamb, and follows standard Carolingian interpretations: 'The innocent lamb wonderfully opens his father's law sealed with seven seals; a new law out of the womb of the old, behold, is made clear for enlightened hearts, bringing light to a multitude of nations.' Only in the third manuscript in this group, the Bible of San Paolo fuori le Mura, or Third Bible of Charles the Bald, is there a partial explanation of the curious iconography of the bottom half of the frontispiece in each of the three Bibles. It reads as follows: 'The innocent Lamb, slain for our sake but triumphantly risen, has torn away the veil from the law. He is worthy to loose the seven seals of that book.' Christ the Lamb and the Four Gospels thus represent the New Law which unveils

---

[73] Trier Stadtbibliothek 31, facs. ed. Richard Laufner and Peter K. Klein, *Trier Apokalypse* (Graz, 1975), fol. 32r, and compare fol. 29r.

[74] BN lat. 1, fol. 415 v; BL Add. 10546, fol. 449 r, illustrated in Hubert, Porcher and Volbach, *Carolingian Art*, pl. 125, p. 136, and Herbert L. Kessler, *The Illustrated Bibles from Tours*, Studies in Manuscript Illumination 7 (Princeton, 1977), no. 107 (BL Add. 10546), and *ibid.*, no. 108 (BN lat. 1). See also the discussion by van der Meer, *Apocalypse*, pp. 77–80, and Kessler, *Bibles*, pp. 69–83, and compare the stimulating exposition by Yves Christe, 'Trois images carolingiennes en forme de commentaires sur l'Apocalypse', *Cahiers Archéologiques* 25 (1976), 77–92, and J. Croquison, 'Une vision eschatologique carolingienne', *Cahiers Archéologiques* 4 (1949), 105–29.

the Old Law, personified as the ancient Moses, and inaugurates the new church.[75] Did Ingobertus, the scribe of the San Paolo Bible, and the artists of the other two Bibles, wish to identify the newly reformed and expanding Frankish church with this new church? It would seem, indeed, that armed with the gift of the New Law and in the possession and use of writing, the means to faith, knowledge and power, the Carolingians were confident that they were living at the dawn of a new era. The power bestowed by the written law and its relevance for the exercise of royal government is expressed in other illustrations in the Vivian Bible, presented to Charles the Bald in about 846. In the presentation portrait of the king, the monks of Tours are depicted giving their magnificent Bible to Charles. It symbolizes the belief that the written word, the Christian faith and the law were the means to effective rule. It is no accident that in this same manuscript Moses was depicted teaching the word and law of God to a king and his nobles.[76]

These paintings have, above all, one clear message. It is the same as that expressed in the opinions on the relative values and function of writing and painting I cited at the beginning of this chapter in the elaboration of the hierarchy of scripts, the role of letter as image and the close relationship between illustrations and their texts in Carolingian illuminated manuscripts. It is, quite simply, the paramount importance of the written word in the Carolingian world.

[75] Bible of San Paolo fuori le Mura, fol. 331v, illustrated in Kessler, *Bibles*, no. 109. For discussion see Joachim Gaehde, 'The Turonian sources of the San Paolo Bible', *Frühmittelalterliche Studien* 5 (1971), 359–400, at 392–4. A facsimile edition of this manuscript is being prepared by Florentine Mütherich and Girolamo Arnaldi.

[76] BN lat. 1, fols. 423r (Charles the Bald enthroned) and 27v (Exodus frontispiece). Very similar to it is BL Add. 10546, fol. 25v, and the frontispiece to Leviticus in the San Paolo Bible, fol. 31v: see Kessler, *Bibles*, nos. 88, 87 and 89 respectively.

Conclusion

Rosamond McKitterick

It will be clear from the essays in this book that there were many uses of literacy in the early middle ages. There are, of course, more questions that need to be raised, arising in part out of the topics addressed in this book, as well as relating to the obvious areas left unexplored which we outlined in the introduction. We have tried to demonstrate how literacy, because it covers both the content of the written tradition and the levels of individual or collective achievement in it, must be discussed in terms of its diverse historical contexts if it is to be understood. It is, moreover, only on a selection of possible historical contexts that we have concentrated. Whether any general conclusions may be drawn from our particular examples has still to be considered. It may be useful here, therefore, to pull together some of the various threads unravelled in the course of our investigations in the foregoing chapters.

Two common themes have emerged, and these are relevant for any understanding of literacy in society generally. First, there is the intertwining of the symbolic function and practical uses of writing. Consideration of this theme underlines the importance of the second, namely, the possibilities of a complex interrelationship between writing and other elements of social and cultural practice.

Some papers, notably those of Kelly, Keynes, Nelson and Noble, focussed largely on the practical uses of writing. Others, particularly those of McKitterick, Mitchell and Mullett, placed greater emphasis on the various manifestations of the symbolic function of writing. The papers by Stevenson, Reif, Wood and Collins, in the context of particular Irish, Jewish, Frankish, Visigothic and Islamic communities in the early middle ages, set out primarily to heighten our perceptions of the broader social and cultural practices within which the uses of literacy are to be understood. It proved impossible, however, to focus exclusively on one theme or element of literacy at the expense of another in any of the essays in this book. Each study, implicitly or explicitly, has stressed the complexities and interdependence of the issues involved and the need for further debate; a great

319

variety of assumptions and convictions about the written word in early mediaeval Europe has been exposed.

How does one define literacy on the basis of the studies in this book? Our common conviction, expressed in the introduction and reiterated here, is that literacy is not just a matter of who could read or write but one of how reading and writing skills functioned, of the adjustments – mental, emotional, intellectual, physical and technological – necessary to accommodate them, and the degree to which special skills and knowledge were involved. Clearly, whether one considers Byzantium, Anglo-Saxon England or Carolingian Francia, or any of the other regions we have discussed, it is necessary to distinguish between literary or intellectual and functional literacy, with, on the one hand, authoritative texts in the religious and secular spheres, literature of all kinds, learned treatises and expositions, and, on the other, institutional and personal administration, management and record keeping, and official and private communication. Literacy, therefore, could involve the composition of literature and the spread of a written tradition amongst a substantial proportion of the population. For the most part, the studies in this book have concentrated on functional literacy rather than intellectual or learned literacy, but we nevertheless saw, in the diversity of both the Christian and the Jewish societies examined in the foregoing chapters, how crucial a role authoritative texts, especially legal and religious ones, could play in shaping the lives and ideals of a community. To the extent that societies developed the kinds and range of literacy they needed, literacy can be approached from an entirely functionalist standpoint, and one could see this well illustrated with the papacy's exploitation of literacy in the early middle ages. But literacy in the early middle ages was not only a quantitative matter of who could read and write, and a kind of technology. It was also a mentality, a form of ideology through which power could be constructed and influence exerted, a frame of mind and a framer of minds; it was both the consequence of, and had as a consequence, particular kinds of social practice.

Orality, with literacy, nevertheless retained its centrality in early mediaeval societies. This was most manifest in the many discussions of charters. At whatever other levels they need to be appreciated, one essential function of the charter was to serve as a written record of an oral transaction. The social role of a document is also clear; one need only recall Nelson's emphasis, with reference to a charter of manumission, on the crucial link between document and social status. When methods of reading and writing, and the technical skills necessary for literacy, were examined, it was striking how often oral forms of instruction and teaching, especially perhaps in Jewish education, but also just as evident in Merovingian Gaul, Ireland and elsewhere, were maintained. In the societies in which the roles of writing, pictures and speech were considered, moreover, especially in Byzantium and in Carolingian Francia, it can be seen that each had its place. In other words, literacy is not a social or cultural phenomenon that can be isolated from other media; it interacts with and complements other forms of human discourse, expression and communication.

A common preoccupation of our essays was the interpretation of particular kinds of evidence, and the exploitation, furthermore, of categories of extant material that had not hitherto received much exposure in relation to literacy. In questions about lay literacy, for example, book-ownership and donations of books to individuals or institutions loomed large. What is one to make of the ownership of books by Jews in Egypt, Arabs and Christians in Umayyad Spain or counts in Carolingian Francia, or the lavish gifts of books to monasteries such as those supplied by Mummadona to the monastery she founded at Guimaraes? They may not necessarily provide incontrovertible evidence of the possession of reading skills on the part of the owner, but they are highly significant for what they reveal of attitudes to the written word and the book, of the knowledge of how to acquire them, and what texts to acquire, of the recognition of the necessity of particular texts to carry out religious devotion and observance, and of the appropriateness of a gift of books, and thus of the written word, in particular contexts.[1]

Letters, too, proved to be fruitful indicators of literacy, and especially lay literacy, in both the functionalist and symbolic senses, for as Mullett explained, the writing and receiving of letters was both a means of communication and a 'multi-media experience' – oral, material and visual – and had its own rituals. Not only did a remarkable proportion of representations of literacy in Byzantium involve people reading, presenting, writing and receiving letters, but individual members of the Cairo Jewish community, of the Merovingian and Carolingian aristocracy, of the upper and educated classes in Al-Andalus and the Christian kingdoms of northern Spain, also exchanged friendship letters.

Pictures have also been shown to be central to considerations of literacy, especially in the Byzantine and Carolingian contexts discussed by Mullett and McKitterick, for they are linked with the symbolic, as opposed to the practical, functions of writing. Both the Byzantines and Carolingians commented on the relative value of pictures and writing, and came to opposite conclusions, but the examination of the relations between words and pictures in a number of key manuscripts from both the west and the east, with the role of text as image discussed by McKitterick, the remarkable display of literacy at San Vincenzo described by Mitchell and the

---

[1] I have discussed the implications of the ownership and possession of books in the Carolingian world in McKitterick, *Carolingians*, pp. 135–64, 244–66.

representation of literacy expounded by Mullett, revealed societies where
books, the written word and communication in writing were not only taken
for granted but accorded a supreme position in political and ideological
terms.

The very survival of evidence enabling one to assess literate practices in
the early middle ages, however, was a common preoccupation for all the
contributors. All commented how in the very early period mere shreds of
evidence survive in contrast to the greater volume of material from later
centuries. This presents special problems of interpretation in determining
how typical or representative one tiny morsel of information might be. Even
when charters were being considered, many that might have revealed much
in the original document in terms of the handwriting, or the names of
witnesses recorded, survive only in later copies which lack such essential
and helpful information. We also exposed areas where enough work has
simply not been done to uncover possible caches of evidence; this is
particularly the case with the Jews but also for many other local, and
sometimes quite isolated, communities, such as the different regions in
northern Italy or Graubünden in the Alps (old Roman Rhaetia) in western
Europe. In the examination of the technology of writing itself the cultural
and technical implications of the coincidental change from uncial to
minuscule scripts in both Carolingian Europe and Byzantium still needs a
convincing interpreter.

The uses of literacy in the early middle ages were most clearly manifest in
the context of government and administration. We saw the workings of the
papal bureaucracy, and the support provided by regional deacons and
subdeacons, notaries and *defensors* in posts designed to serve the papal
administration. The popes kept archives. That and the great wealth and
range of documents produced, with a Register of papal letters, indicate the
papacy's commitment to the use of writing, the degree to which knowledge
of the written word was assumed and depended upon in papal transactions
at every level, and also the extent to which the papal officials were direct
continuators of Roman administrative practices. Literacy was necessary for
the proper functioning of the papal system. Both the form of the papal
letters and the structure and arrangement of the Register itself follow
Roman methods. The financial administration of the papacy probably gave
rise, as Noble suggests, to the devising of many different kinds of record.
Noble also notes a shift, certainly within the papal administration, in the
nature and use of documents and in the accessibility of the archive, which
involved a change in the probative value from the public document in the
archives to the private copy in the hands of the recipient. That is, there is a
privatization of the modes of documentary proof which to some extent is

also mirrored in the other successor states of western Europe and which deserves fuller scrutiny.

In the continuity of forms and purposes of administration, then, there is manifest a clear instance of the strength of the Roman Empire's heritage for the papacy at least; but such following of administrative forms, and their gradual adaptation to particular circumstances, is to be observed in the barbarian successor states as a whole. The different scales and degrees of adaptation, and the other influences at work in each context, account for the lack of homogeneity in the societies considered in this book. The Visigoths, for example, certainly preserved several of the administrative practices of Roman Spain in all of which writing played a key role. Even in the later Christian kingdoms of northern Spain, as Collins observed, such practices, in an etiolated form, are still recognizable, and in Islamic Spain it is arguable that existing practices at the time of the Arab takeover in 711/12 may have provided some kind of model for administrative routines established thereafter. Byzantine government and bureaucracy also certainly needed literacy, though there is remarkably little surviving evidence to document the precise ways in which it was exploited.

Anglo-Saxon government exploited the written word for the formulation and publication of royal law, in the operation of legal processes, in communication, in assessment, in the administration of estates and in military matters. The evidence provided by Marculf's Formulary, the laws, and instructions emanating from the royal courts, discussed by Wood, suggests that Merovingian royal government should also be considered as tied firmly to the written word. The Christian kingdoms of northern Spain used the written word for their day-to-day administration, too, and for a time at least, under Ramiro III of León, there was a royal chancery in that the episcopal scriptorium of León appears to have served the purposes of a royal chancery, a situation which should be compared with that prevailing in Anglo-Saxon England at the same time; only from the tenth century is there clear enough evidence to posit the existence of an Anglo-Saxon royal chancery. Written documents played a vital role in publishing and enforcing royal law in both Francia and in Anglo-Saxon England. It was the function of the late Anglo-Saxon king's law-codes, for example, to assist in bringing knowledge of the king's decrees into the localities, rather than to provide a permanent frame of reference. In other words, the written word played an essentially active role in administration, and was not just a system of recording past decisions and actions for symbolic effect.

The Carolingian evidence for the use of literacy in government and administration represents a huge explosion in the volume of written documentation and was the outcome of collaboration between the ruler and the ruled. Effective exploitation of literate modes, was, as is abundantly clear in the case of the Carolingians, a means of exercising power. Rulers like the Frankish kings, who wanted to control and exploit coinage and markets, to protect merchants while taking a cut of their profits, to keep track of their landed possessions, to keep in touch with their local agents, to lay down guidelines for particular courses of action and to provide a frame of reference for future action, as well as to promote their prestige in relation to the present and to posterity, had obvious uses for written documents, providing their potential for such purposes was known. With the Franks, the Roman heritage, and the example provided by the Christian church, were again of the utmost importance. Literacy was perceived as a practical and useful tool and as a potent instrument of power. The use of the written word gave the Carolingian Empire unity: the elite of the Carolingian world actively participated in literacy as a means of group identification, for their own benefit; hence, as Nelson pointed out, the 'effectiveness' of literacy in government should be appreciated as much for its symbolic as for its pragmatic function. A government that depended to a considerable extent on the written word was in any case not necessarily an effective government, nor a bureaucratic one, but its assumption of the value of literacy and exploitation of literate modes has much to tell us of the literate mentalities of that society as a whole.

Side by side with the exploitation of literate modes in government are royal initiatives for the promotion of literacy. Alfred of Wessex, for example, attempted to enlarge the scope of books available in English in order to promote learning and philosophy and to improve the calibre of the nobility. In Merovingian Gaul, the royal court had a role to play in the education of the nobility; it acted as a clearing house for the placing of the sons of officials and magnates in appropriate households for their upbringing, and as a focus of talent. The court also transcended, to some extent, the tendency for culture in Merovingian Gaul to be of a regional character and modified the old distinction between Romanized southern Gaul and the barbarized north. Similarly, the learned and cultured court of the caliphs of Umayyad Al-Andalus served as a focus for the entire country – Arabs, Jews and Christians served there and there also existed a learned class from which the caliphal bureaucracy was drawn. In northern Spain, the royal court appears to have played a similar role to that in Merovingian Gaul, in that it acted as a place where training in basic pragmatic skills could be provided. Royal authors are not unknown – one need only think of the extensive writing and translating activity of King Alfred, or the Chronicle of Alphonso III, king of the Asturias. In Mitchell's view, indeed, the Carolingian rulers are the rulers who, above all others, made themselves 'masters of an apparatus of social control' and exploited both painting and script as two potent and visible symbols of their authority, their power and their presence.

It is clear when considering the use of literate modes in the various successor kingdoms of early mediaeval Europe that while writing may have been exploited for legal transactions between institutions, particularly ecclesiastical ones, and between individuals, appreciation of the value of the written word need not necessarily have extended into any of the other routine procedures of royal government. In other words, if we are to make a distinction between local and central levels of administration, and between private and official uses of literacy, as we must, do the various private and public uses of literacy have to be recognized, in theory at least, as potentially separate and self-contained phenomena? As Kelly, Keynes, Nelson and Wood have demonstrated, the private and the public domain interlocked and were certainly influential upon one another as far as the functional use of literacy was concerned. Many of the methods and forms of administration in the early mediaeval kingdoms, moreover, are inconceivable without a continuous sub-Roman tradition of record keeping, use of documents in legal proceedings and resort to written means to exert governmental control enduring from the Roman period.

In the exploitation of literacy for the purposes of government and administration, there appears to be a clear link between strong central government and an extensive use of literacy in most of the kingdoms considered in this book. But when faced with a lack of central government, there is not a concomitant decline in the use of the written word. With a weakening of central power there is still a local exercise of power to be reckoned with, in non-royal places, and there is much written documentation emanating from small local power bases and from individuals in local communities, above all in relation to legal transactions, which could, with justice, be regarded as the most telling witness to the role of literacy in early mediaeval societies. Nearly every chapter in this book discussed the workings of law and the degree to which written records were required and desired by those involved in the transactions, whether by a slave receiving his charter of manumission, a church insisting on a record of a rich gift or a family disputing the grant of a piece of property away from the family. It is the extensive private, or at least non-governmental, resort to the written word which is so remarkable a feature of early mediaeval societies, and does much to counter the old beliefs in restricted clerical literacy.

Formularies for charters provide an indication of the special importance attached to the written word and its correct application, though studies elsewhere have also suggested that those societies which displayed the greatest interest in the production of formal records were also those most suspicious of and best able to take steps to counter the existence of forged documents.[2] The greater emphasis there is on written records, then, the more determined could be the efforts to circumvent or manipulate their use. On this reading, which needs to be tested more widely, a society which can produce a 'forgery' – whether a charter, a text such as the Donation of Constantine,[3] a *tour de force* like the Le Mans forgeries,[4] the clever propagandistic fabrications of the Patrick dossier by the church of Armagh in the seventh and eighth centuries, analysed by Stevenson in this volume, or the many instances provided of blatant and subtle forgeries in a great variety of contexts in the studies produced for the anniversary celebrations of the Monumenta Germaniae Historica – is one essentially appreciative of literacy and the power of the written word.[5] Forgeries, indeed, are a remarkable treasure trove of evidence for the uses of literacy which is only beginning to be exploited, and it is a wonder that more has not been made of them in this context long since.

The role of the church and of Christianity, or, in the case of Islamic Al-Andalus and the Jewish communities of the eastern Mediterranean, of a religion of the book, as a mediator of literacy has figured in every chapter in this volume. The initiative in introducing the use of written documents was undoubtedly taken by the church in many instances. Certainly in Anglo-Saxon England the anxiety on the part of the church to hold written title-deeds to property, and the need of clerics to persuade lay Anglo-Saxons of the validity of written documents, appears to have been the principal factor in the introduction of literate modes for legal transactions. Thus the success of literacy is most fruitfully assessed by considering the extent to which the use of the written word superseded, or was accommodated within, the established procedures of society. As runic inscriptions show, the pagan Anglo-Saxons (like the pagan Irish) were not entirely ignorant of writing, but Latin and the Roman alphabet were introduced by foreign missionaries from the end of the sixth century onwards.

Yet in the case of Anglo-Saxon England, the introduction of the written word was effected by Christian missionaries from Ireland and from Rome. This must prompt one to reflect, first, on what had made the literate character of the Christian church quite as it was, and, secondly, the

---

[2] Roger Collins, 'The role of writing in the resolution and recording of disputes', in *Settlement of Disputes*, p. 211.

[3] See *Das Constitutum Constantini (Konstantinische Schenkung)*, ed. Horst Furhmann, *MGH Fontes* X.

[4] *Actus pontificum Cenomannis in urbe degentium*, ed. G. Busson and A. Ledru (Le Mans, 1901), and see Walter Goffart, *The Le Mans Forgeries: A Chapter from the History of Church Property in the Ninth Century* (Cambridge Mass., 1966).

[5] *Fälschungen im Mittelalter, MGH* Schriften 33, 5 vols. (Hanover, 1988).

response and strength of native and indigenous culture. In the case of Ireland, Stevenson showed that, while some seventh-century accounts make a link between Christianity, the arrival of St Patrick and literacy, Christianity gave impetus to the use of writing but did not introduce it, nor did it overwhelm native culture, whether oral or written, in the vernacular. In the case of Rome, and bearing in mind St Augustine of Canterbury's known connections with Pope Gregory, Noble has demonstrated the enormous extent to which the written word had an established function in administration and social intercourse, and how in its turn, that owed much to its Roman past. Consideration of the role of Christianity at least, in other words, also involved the Roman heritage: it is this pair of twins in the ancestry of the germanic successor states of western Europe considered in this book which are of such fundamental importance when assessing the subsequent, and consequent, uses of literacy. It was, for example, particularly evident in Wood's discussion of Merovingian Gaul as well as in Collins' on Visigothic Spain. Further, we know from the clear evidence in early Kentish sources of links between the Franks and the south-east Anglo-Saxons. The exact political relations are still disputed, with much to recommend the attractive, if extreme, position adopted by Wood that the Merovingians were the overlords of the early Kentish kings,[6] but there seems little doubt that in religious and ecclesiastical terms communication with Frankish Gaul, with its own distinctive Romano-Christian-Frankish literate culture, was a further contributory factor in the adoption of the written word in Anglo-Saxon society and its adaptation to Anglo-Saxon needs.

Cross-cultural interchange of this kind, with elements of the Roman past as mediated through different germanic and non-germanic cultural traditions, however elusive, as well as the influence exerted by the Christian church, was a recurrent theme in all the early mediaeval societies discussed above. The extent to which there was such exchange should not be underestimated, difficult though it might be to chart. Look how absorption into the Arab world opened up the Spanish Christians to new currents, not only from Arab culture, but also from Christian communities in the east, as well as the links forged between southern Arabic Spain and northern Christian Spain. Remember Collins' suggestion that the evident literacy of the Arabs in Umayyad Al-Andalus might have been influenced by the survival of an educated laity from the Visigothic period onwards. We saw, too, how Jewish communities under Islam emulated Islamic centralization of authority and standards in their own communal, religious and literary

[6] Ian Wood, *The Merovingian North Sea*, Occasional Papers on Mediaeval Topics 1 (Ålingsas, 1983).

requirements. In the technical spheres, who can tell what influences might have been operating? When we consider, for example, the Jewish religious tradition, with education based on the text of the Pentateuch in Hebrew expounded by a *rabbi*, and possessed of an almost cultic function, in strong contrast to the liturgical rituals of western Christian priests, how are we to account for the change in the medium of transmission among the Jews in the ninth century, with a sudden explosion of activity in the copying of scrolls on to codices, with oral traditions committed to manuscript and a wide dissemination of texts, so that we witness the creation of a corpus of written sources of instruction and inspiration, very similar to that we encounter in the Christian kingdoms of the Franks, Anglo-Saxons, Lombards, Visigoths and Greeks? Are we observing a fundamentally western and Christian model being adapted and exploited by eastern and non-Christian communities? Certainly the emphasis on philosophical study in early mediaeval Jewish communities appears to have been the result of observation of the practices within Christian and Muslim theological circles. Developments within the Christian or Islamic communities of Spain, Italy and the Frankish regions may even have had some impact on mediaeval western European Jewish literacy, though the foundations for these are seen, at present at least, as eastern. Whatever the different influences at work in later centuries, certainly Judaism has always been a fundamentally literate religion, with, from the earliest times in ancient Israel, textualization for the permanence of knowledge, guidance and edification of the faithful. The earliest Christian literate traditions were, after all, founded in part on this very same Jewish literate tradition, so it is hardly surprising if different streams of cultural practice seem occasionally to flow together before once more making a separate course. Such cultural interchange, and the changes effected by different environments and the contact with native cultures, were no doubt greatly enhanced by the social and political transformations of the early mediaeval world between the end of the fourth century and the end of the ninth.

The weakness of the divide between lay and cleric, and the overlapping of lay and ecclesiastical interests and practices were evident in a number of the chapters in this book. The overlapping structure of lay and ecclesiastical magnates in Merovingian Gaul, for example, suggests a remarkably literate aristocracy and the evidence for education certainly diminishes any assumptions of a divide between secular and ecclesiastical education. In relation to early Anglo-Saxon England, too, Kelly countered the traditional view of literacy as an ecclesiastical preserve and looked at the ways in which the lay Anglo-Saxons used the written word and the extent to which writing superseded speech and memory as the standard method of conveying and storing information. Unlike Ireland, for example, written documentation came to occupy an important place in secular Anglo-Saxon society and was used in ways which could imply a degree of literacy among certain sections of the laity. Although at first, in the seventh and early eighth centuries, the rituals associated with the written document were probably more important to laymen, in time the production of chirographs on a regular basis and the great range of different types of vernacular document covering aspects of land tenure and property ownership indicate that secular society took a strong interest in and placed great reliance on written documentation. Keynes shows how the initiatives regarding secular uses of literacy in the earlier Anglo-Saxon period were reinforced in the tenth and eleventh centuries: laymen, and in particular king's thegns, were among those employed by the king to convey messages to the shire-courts and to whom the king sent written messages, and people other than the king were accustomed to conveying messages in written form. The evidence of vernacular charters and wills, the routine confirmation of wills, and such famous issues as the Fonthill dispute, add a new precision to our general appreciation of the penetration of the written word into at least the upper levels of lay society throughout the Anglo-Saxon period.

In both Ireland and England, of course, the vernacular language was very different from that of the Christian church's literary language, and Latin had to be learnt as a foreign tongue. In both England and Ireland, therefore, one might expect, and we find, links between the vernacular literary tradition and lay literacy, with, above all, the production of laws in the non-Latinate vernacular. There is also in Ireland the existence of the learned class or *filid* and in England a clear sense that the written word had been securely accommodated within secular society for literature and legal transactions, as well as religious expression by the ninth century, together with the foundations laid for the outstanding literary activity of the later Anglo-Saxon period. Vernacular literacy in England was encouraged as a substitute for latinity. In this King Alfred played a key role, but he was able to build on the moves already made for translation from Latin, composition of literary texts in the vernacular and the strong tradition of vernacular documentation in the ninth century. There is thus far more to this than simply a weak command of Latin on the part of Christian clerics. Nevertheless, both Stevenson and Kelly stressed how important Latin literacy was to the church, and how in the sixth and seventh centuries there was a substantial technical and economic investment in the creation and storage of permanent written documents in Latin within the Christian centres of Ireland and England. Despite this substantial commitment to Latin literacy, in Ireland at least the church was unable to influence secular ways of transacting legal business, whereas in Anglo-Saxon England it was. In other words, the case of early Christian Ireland, perhaps because the Irish church lacked the substructure of Roman imperial administration to support it, counters the notion that literacy necessarily effects social change. It also reinforces the suggestion made earlier that there may have been more of a surviving substructure of the old Roman imperial administration surviving in Britain, or alternatively that the links between England and the Romanized and Christian Continent in the fifth and sixth centuries in the secular as well as the religious spheres were far closer and stronger than we can now detect precisely in the extant evidence.

Lay literacy in Merovingian Gaul was not confined to the highest stratum of society, even though most of the prominent people were members of a secular and ecclesiastical elite. Signatures on charters, for example, indicate that officials and other members of lay society and the royal court could write, and knowledge of law was common among those royal servants about whom we have information. The resort to written records on the part of members of Merovingian lay society, moreover, demonstrates the great extent to which Merovingian society needed and demanded documents; all sorts of transactions had to be set down in writing and registered in the local archives. It is to be noted that most of the literate figures of Merovingian Gaul attested to in surviving legal documents and letters were also administrators. Wood also demonstrated how a sense of style and awareness of Latin literary forms were preserved in Merovingian Gaul; there, at least, continuity in both language and cultural forms is preserved, and it is arguable that this linguistic continuity also prevailed far longer, that is, well into the Carolingian period, than is commonly maintained.[7] In other words, the emergence of lay and vernacular culture in the former Roman provinces of the Continent was expressed in the same language, namely Latin, as that of religion and the administration. Latin *was* the vernacular. Thus the issue of language, whether written or spoken, the status of the vernacular languages and the role of oral communication in relation to written texts present a different set of problems on the Continent from those we encounter in the British Isles. Latin undoubtedly played a distinct cultural role on the Continent, and promoted unity, in a very different way from that on the western side of the North Sea. The blend of social and governmental literacy in the administrative classes of sixth- and seventh-century Francia was a continuation of the traditions of their Gallo-Roman predecessors and was handed on to the Carolingians. The ample use the Carolingians made of

---

[7] I have reviewed the linguistic situation prevailing in Carolingian Francia, with reference to recent philological research, in McKitterick, *Carolingians*, pp. 7–22, and argued the case for Latin being the vernacular not only before *c*. 800 but for much of the ninth century as well, in the Romance regions of Gaul, while it was the accepted language of administration and the church as a second language in the germanic regions.

their Latin heritage was fully revealed by Nelson in her chapter, especially the degree to which Carolingian government assumed a functioning and literate class of administrators.[8] Latin also continued in use in the Christian communities of late Umayyad Spain, and is evident in the liturgy and inscriptions. This is not to say that there is not a divide between written Latin and spoken Latin/Romance, and that it may have been as large a divide as between rhetorical Greek and the common Greek of the eastern Empire; but this divide did not constitute such an obstacle to the attainment of literate skills as used to be thought.[9] Indeed, aristocratic and lay literacy is not a problem in Byzantium: it was widespread. What is a problem, however, is the level of clerical literacy, for there was, as Mullett pointed out, an element of the monastic tradition which regarded books as luxury objects (as indeed they were) and which scorned book-learning.

In the Islamic society of Umayyad Spain, a distinction between lay and ecclesiastical literacy makes little sense for no separate priestly class existed. There was a learned class, drawn on for the bureaucracies of the caliphate, and it comprised Christians and Jews as well as Arabs. There is evidence of book buying and book reading and the existence of a fairly substantial urban market for books as well as the considerable output of new works in a variety of genres in the tenth century. Collins suggests, however, that though there is a rough correlation between the adoption of Islam and an increasingly Arabized intellectual and material culture in Spain, the ground for these developments had already been prepared in the preceding Catholic and Visigothic period. Better evidence of lay literacy can be found in southern Spain in the Arab period rather than in the Visigothic period and comes from the activities of such men as Paul Alvar. Within the Christian Latin community in the Visigothic Christian kingdoms of northern Spain one can also find many instances of literate members of the upper ranks of society, with aristocratic and royal libraries and lay aristocrats exchanging letters. Inscriptions and a substantial body of charters from the north of Spain in the ninth and tenth centuries also witness to laymen employing written documents for their legal business, though there is no certain evidence of a lay notariat such as one can find, for example, in the diocese of Milan in the eighth and ninth centuries.[10] Despite the evidence for some lay literacy in northern Spain, it should be noted that Collins observed an ecclesiastical

[8] For a fuller treatment of other aspects of Carolingian lay literacy see McKitterick, *Carolingians*, pp. 211–70.

[9] For full discussion of the linguistic situation in Spain see Roger Wright, *Late Latin and Early Romance in Spain and Carolingian France* (Liverpool, 1982), pp. 145–207.

[10] See, for example, samples of their activity in *I placiti del 'Regnum Italiae'*, ed. C. Manaresi, 3 vols. (Rome, 1955–60), and the discussion by Chris Wickham, 'Land disputes and their

monopoly of the production of governmental and private documents which is not found to the same extent elsewhere in western Europe at the time, and especially not in the Carolingian world.[11] Collins suggested that such an ecclesiastical monopoly of the written word indicated a more limited dissemination, but not a lack, of literacy in the upper levels of secular society and that there is sufficient indication in the extant material that literacy was becoming increasingly necessary, especially for judges and the administration of the law.[12] In other words, manifestations of lay literacy in Christian Spain are essentially those of pragmatic literacy: Pamplona, León and the kingdom of the Asturias did not entirely lose sight of their Visigothic heritage.

In the Jewish context, the evidence is largely concerned with those we would call the laity, though again, the distinction between lay and cleric is hardly appropriate. Jews were 'a people of the book' and the huge variety of material in the Cairo Genizah with its practical emphasis and wealth of information about social and business communications witnesses to the thorough permeation of literate modes throughout Jewish society. Literacy in the communities studied by Reif is in any case closely allied with the language question, for it does not necessarily entail an acquaintance with literature but an ability to read and write a language or more than one language. Trilingualism – in Hebrew, Aramaic and Arabic – was quite normal, and it led to a variety of choice in the language written in particular contexts. Just as we observed above, to different extents, in relation to Ireland, England and Frankish Gaul, how language became a way to proclaim an adherence to a particular tradition, so among the Jews, veneration of older traditions could continue in one language while new ones went into the vernacular. This is a fascinating, and instructive, congruence of cultural response in relation to the reception of religious and legal traditions.

For all considerations of lay literacy, whether for the selection of societies considered in this book, or for the others that could have been included, education is of prime importance, and remains a subject meriting further investigation, building, of course, on the foundations laid down by Riché three decades ago.[13] Some educational provision has to be understood from

social framework in Lombard-Carolingian Italy, 700–900', in *Settlement of Disputes*, pp. 104–24, especially p. 112.

[11] See McKitterick, *Carolingians*, pp. 77–134, for a full discussion of the process of the production of charters and the personnel involved, especially in the private and local sphere.

[12] Compare Roger Collins, '*Sicut lex Gothorum continet*: law and charters in ninth- and tenth-century León and Catalonia', *EHR* 100 (1985), 489–512.

[13] Pierre Riché, *Education et culture dans l'occident barbare, vie–viiie siècles* (3rd edn, Paris,

indirect evidence, that is, by implication, whereas in Gaul there is more reference to school and schooling throughout the early mediaeval period. Generally, however, broader and more secular elements in education not specifically directed towards clerical training are still being guessed at, or, at best, merely sketched in; it may be that this unsatisfactory state of affairs will have to continue, given the lacunae in our evidence. Nevertheless, the wealth and variety of material unearthed and discussed in the chapters in this book suggests a much more widely based effort at education and training in at least pragmatic literacy than has hitherto been acknowledged.

As we stated in our introduction, we set out to provide some early mediaeval contexts in which to observe and consider the implications of the uses, levels and distribution of literacy in Europe. We have provided for each of the societies selected, whether Irish, Anglo-Saxon, Frankish, Visigothic, Greek, Italian or Jewish, a factual basis from which assessments of the significance of literacy in the early middle ages can be made by those reading the relevant chapters. We have ourselves offered some suggestions of what that significance might be.

In the diverse uses, both functional and symbolic, of literacy in the early middle ages, much of importance has been revealed about both practical ways of conducting business and administration, and observing religion, and about attitudes of mind, *mentalités*, of leading groups in the early middle ages. It would be idle to pretend that what we have uncovered necessarily permeated unchanged to the lowest levels of society in any one of the various communities we have studied, or even that it did so in similar ways. Nevertheless, we do maintain that no person in society remained unaffected by the activities of those groups able to make the most of the opportunities afforded them by acquisition of the technical skills of reading and writing associated with literacy and of knowledge of the written word and all that that implied. Early mediaeval society as a whole, in whatever historical context one chooses to see it, was one in which literacy mattered, and where literacy had repercussions right down the social scale, from the king issuing directives, and the nobleman endowing a monastery with books, to the freed slave clinging to his new social status by means of a written charter. Literacy's importance and relevance throughout the early middle ages is, on the evidence presented in our essays, as a major force in the most crucial and formative period in the development of European civilization.

1962), English trans. John J. Contreni, *Education and Culture in the Barbarian West, Sixth through Eighth Centuries* (Columbia, South Carolina, 1976), with updated bibliography, and Pierre Riché, *Ecoles et enseignement dans le haut moyen âge* (Paris, 1979).

Index

Manuscripts are listed under their modern locations